Mitch Abramson

BACK FROM THE OTHER SIDE

MITCH ABRAMSON PUBLISHING

Copyright 2009
By Mitch Abramson
All rights reserved. Printed in the USA
No part of this book may be reproduced
in any form without written permission.

For information, contact
Mitch Abramson Publishing
PO Box 165
Chaska MN 55318
www.trailopen.com

First Edition, First Printing
ISBN 978-0-578-04972-4

CONTENTS

Introduction	6
Chapter 1 – Created in the Image of…	14
Chapter 2 – Brazil to Brooklyn	20
Chapter 3 – Brooklyn, Punchball and the Catholics	27
Chapter 4 – The Racetrack	30
Chapter 5 – Coming of Age in Greenwich Village	59
Chapter 6 – LSD	64
Chapter 7 – Schizophrenic Processes	82
Chapter 8 – Mental Hospital Life	107
Chapter 9 – Hell Puts on a Smile – LA 1973	133
Chapter 10 – Best Use of Cocaine for Sex	156
Chapter 11 – Worst Use of Cocaine for Sex	165
Chapter 12 – Epiphany in Sperm – To Be or Not To Be	183
Chapter 13 – Yearning for Salvation: The Speaker Meeting	200
Chapter 14 – Miracle, Religion and the Plastic Light	206
Chapter 15 – A Born-Again Turkey is Still a Turkey	214
Chapter 16 – The Meditation Observation Exercise	236
Chapter 17 – Observation-Exercise-Reintegration	244
Chapter 18 – Pornographic Epiphany – Las Vegas	266
Chapter 19 – Use the Force, Luke! Miracles…	281
Chapter 20 – Ending of Schizophrenic Processes	306
Chapter 21 – Paltrownian Synchronicity – Britney's Dream	327
Chapter 22 – Jacob Angel	331
Chapter 23 – Sexual Showdown	338
Chapter 24 – Patience: Reintegration 101	388
Chapter 25 – The Tree of Knowledge	410

PREFACE

The wasp is the most formidable predator in the caterpillar's life. Sphecius *speciosus*, Family *Nyssonidae* occasionally spawns a Genus *horriblis*, which will, in a special horror, sting the caterpillar to simply immobilize it, not kill it. Now sufficiently helpless, our victim is dragged to the nest, where the mother wasp inserts its eggs *inside the caterpillar*, and the egg larvae grows, feeding on the still-living captive. The wasp slowly takes over more and more of what was once the *"other,"* and in destroying this helpless creation, has it eaten alive, crowning her victim's death with an extension of herself.

You will discover within these pages that this has happened to you as well. We have all been injected. We have all had *something* placed inside of us. Our reaction to the traumatizing parental authority insures it. Within our legendary 'fall,' *we have lost understanding of what we have lost.*

This account will reflect much of your own inner conflict. Be prepared to enter a world of degradation and sexuality never before explored from a perspective beyond the culturally approved mindset. Returning from a mental breakdown needing months of hospitalization in order to simply "function" again, one man makes the unmedicated journey through heretofore uncharted psychic territory to share with the reader a perception of inner life which holds a key to *self*-awareness that has until now remained hidden. Throughout this work the reader will find keys by which his or her own problems may be unlocked, and medications you were told were yours forever can fall by the wayside.

Brave souls, let me hold a light for your own journey.

The Prophet from Trailopen.com – November 2009

Introduction

Saved by Compulsion – Spring 1981

What's my wife gonna say? My wife... Real life! What did I do? What am I doing using up my family's rent money shooting coke and having sex with anonymous men? This is beneath contempt. This is inhuman. This is like the guy eating bugs in the early Dracula movies. I have to cut this shit out. I have to stop this. My wife is pregnant! What kind of sick man am I? Maybe I better kill myself. End it, end it, end it! Where? Where should I do it? Where should I shoot myself? In the car? I do have the gun.

I have to turn on the ignition in order to get the cigarette lighter working, and the act jars my nerves. Anxiously I scan the dark parking lot from behind the wheel, carefully lowering the driver's side window. *I have a gun, motherfuckers*! Now lit and smoking, I chase more Tequila with a mouthful of warm beer. I rationalize:

'*You can* **always** *kill yourself. You don't have to do it right* **now**. *Just stop. Stop using drugs. Then you won't have to kill yourself. Clean up. Work. Save. Own a house. A car. A boat. A dog. Don't kill yourself, get rid of the gun before you do.*'

OK, that's responsible. Yes, here's some hope. The best, most productive and positive thing is to get rid of the gun.

Can't just throw $175 away though, responsibility insists. *I could sell it to Big Eva! But Eva and I have already agreed it's a crappy weapon. A small, poorly made revolver, I could sell it to someone else. Complicated, that.*

A few more swigs of tequila with the beer chaser and this fresh cigarette is actually starting to taste good. I take my first deep breath in over an hour. A sudden sharp light sears the parking lot darkness. The back door opens, and I stiffen to see someone exit the bookstore on his way to his car. My eyes stare down at the dashboard for what seems an eternity, tracking him with peripheral vision. His car door opens and I shudder with relief as the sound of his ignition sweeps over me, immediately renewing the effects of the valium, tequila, cigarettes and beer. This somewhat impotent collection of palliatives do little to end the post-injection coke paranoia.

Maybe I should trade it back to Big Eva for some more coke. Then <u>never buy it back</u>! HA! *She'll be pissed at me, and I wouldn't be able to buy any more coke from her. Then I could be straight!* **What genius**! *Yes, the truly responsible thing to do is to end my relationship with Big Eva* and cocaine. I'll get rid of the gun and screw up my coke connection at the same time. This act will now put an end to this whole cocaine, perverted sex and suicide track.

Yes, it's time to get hold of my life and be responsible. I exhale an "at last" kind of sigh. It's the courageous thing to do – the responsible thing to do, and it's... it's just the right thing to do.

I congratulate myself on taking this giant step to give up cocaine and perversion. I gratuitously start to compare myself to everybody I know who's still using drugs but who has not yet taken this courageous step.

Those losers... I'm stopping. It's a done deal. But I reason there is still a little rain left to fall. Some work left to be done to complete this new sacrifice, for in order to screw up the coke connection I have to trade the gun for some more. It's a dirty job, even a dangerous one, given the current climate over there, but somebody's gotta' do it.

I can't just throw all that coke away. That would be just stupid... thankless. So the good life; puppies, lawns with flowers and children laughing, yes. It's starting now – officially – but I'll have to use up this last score first. Symbolic.

'At least a gram,' an eager bad-cop voice says in my head.

'I don't really care,' says good-cop. 'I'm above such considerations. I may just throw the shit away anyway.'

'Yeah, right, responds bad cop. I could shoot half a gram maybe. Holy shit... That would be in-fucking-credible. Hmm... get fucked in the ass while I'm rushing on half-a-gram? After all, it will be my last time...'

This dedication to my new clean life has me looking urgently at my watch in that early morning hour wondering... wondering if it's not too late... not too late to call Eva.

* * *

The couch in the psychiatrist's waiting room makes a *hissing* sound as you sit on the large leather cushion. I imagine a satanic snakelike image. I consider it might also sound like a final anguished "*Ooohh*" sound of a sighing man giving up or in. Beneath grammatical structure but clearly within the nuance of my observation, I imagine dialogue: '*Is the couch pillow hissing or groaning?" What does that mean to you? Something satanic is hissing like a snake at the same time there's this submission of the guy giving it up... What is he giving up? His life, no, his spirit, his life's spirit?... to who...? to death.. I don't know... or to* anonymous cock? Is that the same thing? What comes to mind? *A strong desire to escape this conversation – along with a desire for drugs.*'

What part of the cushion you displace with your weight appears to pop up again next to you. My cocaine addiction ended. I did, however, find gambling from an employee's perspective as a pari-mutual clerk at the racetrack too much of a temptation. Not too much time passed before I eschewed this good paying job for a little more suffering in its stead.

* * *

She slowly placed the newspaper down and looked up from the breakfast table. Her attractive brown eyes looked concerned. Janice did not miss two days of work a year, had never bounced a check in her life, and seemed perplexed that her husband of one year was not going to work. I suddenly felt terribly ashamed. These feelings were all new to me.

"*How much do you owe them?*" she asked.

I saw the narrowing circumstances closing in on me, forcing out my confession. I no longer had my job as a pari-mutual clerk, having just yesterday been escorted out of the money-room in handcuffs. The police had informed me I would be charged with embezzlement for theft of racetrack funds if I failed to come to an arrangement with the track. When I woke up in the morning, I had some difficulty believing it was all real.

I looked up half-panicked. It was as if I were coming out of some forest into this communal clearing; where people in this other world lived; awakening as one does from a dream, still unclear as to what really happened.

"*I'm not going to work today,*" was all I had told her. I'm jumping off a precipice of some kind. I am coming clean. I ignore the urge to make it sound like a joke. Something inside me is leaving. I am suddenly flooded with the realization that my good-paying job as a pari-mutual clerk was over and I was viscerally lessened somehow by this fact. I hadn't realized how the simple statement that I was a pari-mutual clerk had served me so well as a prestige factor in AA, NA – and especially GA. It had created a part of me in relation to others who also struggled to make a living with a family. I had – and again had no consciousness of it – acquired something vaguely referred to as "esteem," but apparently couldn't lose it fast enough. Repeatedly. I had failed now…again.

That job had *not been* un-cool, and $100 a day in the early 1980's was not bad for an ex-SSI mental patient with no marketable skills. So it was with a kind of sad surprise that I heard my own words coming out of me on their way to my wife. They brought a sadness I was unfamiliar with. It was as if I were a town crier learning of his own disaster as he spoke. Whatever sense of pride and self-satisfaction that even pretended to be in my voice disintegrated. I saw with embarrassment how foolish I had been to think I had been cool betting so crazily.

"*Twelve thousand dollars.*"

"*Twelve thousand dollars!*" she shrieked. "*Well, I'm not helpin' you. You're through.*"

I had lost it. I blinked as if awakening in a strange room. This new experience of lingering responsibility was something I had failed to consider. This is where the rubber meets the road in the world of parental responsibility. The words (*responsibility, family, father, children*) spoken by father and older males in the family along with meaningful looks and handshakes at the wedding had been heard, but they were words that drew in me only brief images of accomplishing god-like achievements. That's all. Sounds. I had married that good-looking girl I had enjoyed bedding and being around. But now there was a family to be considered. *My family.*

I could see the surprise and disappointment on her attractive young face, and it pained me in a way I had not experienced before. Not only had I failed terribly as a provider, but now I *was* that provider. That was my role in life, and somehow I had never been more acutely aware of it than now, as it had just been cracked open and humiliated. I suddenly ached in a new and desperate desire to have it all back: my job, my paycheck, my freedom from the gambling compulsion.

This sudden passion for normalcy surprised me – or that part of me yet to fully awaken – and the pain deepened as a growing ache in me reflected more awareness of what I had lost. *Maybe it didn't happen. It's dreamy. I really still had my job. I would wake up and laugh with relief.* Another part of my mental apparatus suggested that if this wasn't part of something unreal, I should quickly find a way to exist as though it were.

Real-life consequences were always met pharmaceutically. But that option was no longer viable, however, for I was no longer alone. My wife and baby reflected a reality I had simply run from ever since leaving the mental hospital. For the last twelve years, designer drugs and narcotics had been my stand-in for taking responsibility. Real-life consequences were never met without them.

A wave of realization swept over me with a new and dangerous electricity, alerting every part of me that no pill or injection could fix this. Nothing could fix this. The rest of me – pained and stupefied – stood still now with the full realization of my failure. As the disaster I had made became fully realized, I knew what I had to do. This was the final straw.

Not the most terrible straw. I had done worse. Much worse… before and after the mental hospital – but there was a final humiliation here that was simply too crushing. The defeat was suddenly too complete.

I retreated inside to embrace the only way out. I added conviction to ruminating desire. I will pursue this alien quest, and accelerate now into the tempting consideration of termination. I really wanted out.

There was nothing else *to* do. End it. For the first time in my life, I really wanted to. I would. Now. I could sense some kind of force rising up inside me, questioning my commitment, and I, assenting to it in self-consciousness sanctioned it, commissioned it consciously and let go of all that which keeps death's attraction in chains. Yes, I **want** to die. Take me, I thought; giving myself totally to this snarling, rushing energy swirling up from my loins, through my spinal column up through the neck, seizing my brain as it made my legs, arms and hands freeze. Not unlike some science-fiction self-destruct sequence, I was now set to terminate.

The blood! It chilled in a freezing vibration through every artery. The brain locked, denying further thought. I was on the quick path to the next world. I got up, genuinely sad and barely able to push one grieved limb in front of the other on my way to the bedroom for destruction. The complete conviction of what needed to be done – what would be done – became as impregnable as a glacier in my arctic mentality. Unmovable and unstoppable, its frozen climate raged only within the promise of dark relief.

As I got to the bedroom and closed the door, a small dart of thought flew across the frozen wasteland. It directed my attention towards the gun, and this sudden widening awareness gave rise to something totally unanticipated.

"*It's true*," I thought, and laughed. The dark spirit recoiled vigorously, palpably receding back from whence it came. *Was that snarling force cursing me?* The gun was no longer here. I had forgotten. I had given it to Big Eva as collateral for more cocaine at the end of my last binge! A spring of sunshine broke open my wild darkness.

I sat on the edge of the bed. Although I had never owned a bible, the proverb "*Laughter doth act as a medicine*" came to my mind. I laughed as my eyes grew moist. With warm blood coursing again through my body, I wiped my eyes and heard myself speaking aloud in a strange voice, "*How the hell did I get **here**?*"

Let's Talk 1

Dr. Harry Stack Sullivan used the term *"consensual validation"* to designate a process by which unhealthy interpersonal patterns are corrected. It is a cohesion by which reality is rather "pulled together."

To wit, *"A simple kind of consensual validation occurs in learning to talk. A two-year-old child, for example, achieves a consensus with his parents and siblings that the hairy, tail-wagging animal around the house is to be called a "dog." Everyone agrees on this consensus, and it is validated by many further experiences with dogs. In time the child learns that this vocal sound ""dog" is represented by letters d-o-g, and that this picture of d-o-g is both the same and different from the hairy animal running around the house. This general consensus is also validated by repeatedly reading in books, etc., describing many d-o-g-s in various situations. The child similarly learns that the particular dog in his house is by general agreement called Fritz, whereas various other dogs have other names."*[1]

"A three-year-old child playing in his backyard is accosted by a five-year-old from the neighboring house. The older child takes the ball from the younger boy and shoves him down when he tries to get it back.

Puzzled, fearful and angry, the three-year-old runs indoors and tells his mother about the incident. She replies that the five-year-old is a bully and telephones the mother of the five-year-old to get the ball back; complaining tactfully that the five-year-old pushed her child down. The ball is returned, and thereafter the five-year-old comes less frequently into their yard."

In this simple event the child and his mother reach a consensus that the five-year-old child is a bully; that consensus (and corresponding appropriate activity) is validated as the child watches and hears his mother telephone and get the ball back. The consensus is further validated when the child that evening hears his mother tell his father at the dinner table about the incident, and the father agrees with her opinions and actions.

If, however, the mother had become anxious over the idea of confronting the five year-old's parent, for example, she might say something like *"What did you say to annoy him? Why can't you share your things with other children? Why are you so selfish?"* In this case the child cannot correlate his feelings with the feelings and actions of his mother, and in this case no consensus is reached. The child knows that

---

[1] *Harry Stack Sullivan; The Man ands His Work;* AH Chapman (Putnam, 1975)

without provocation he was bullied, shoved down and robbed. He feels puzzled, fearful and angry. His mother confuses him and makes him anxious by blaming and criticizing him.

Worse still, he finds a painful interpersonal gap opening up between his mother and himself. Instead of consensual validation achieved by healthy communication, he feels anxiety, guilt and helpless anger at the injustice which is beyond his ability to understand or verbalize. He also feels isolated; he feels that, at least in this instance, his mother has no understanding of his problems and perhaps no interest in them. There is an injustice and consequent anger that the child is unable to express, but will by necessity repress – and resent.

If this instance is characteristic of his relationship with his mother throughout his childhood, there is a marked risk that an unhealthy interpersonal pattern, with much anxiety, will become ingrained in him, and that he will carry it into his later relationships with other people.

Now, the entrance of ourselves as children into this system of "life" birthed from Adam's fall needn't be all that traumatic to be "traumatic." Sullivan describes a very innocuous entrance into this world of personality protection which is common to all of us.

*"One of the truly remarkable characteristics of man is his development of speech, which is so extraordinarily suited to his purposes. When one observes a child, he sees a person who is interested in all that goes on about him, who is curious, who asks all manner of questions, and who uses speech as a wonderful means of getting acquainted with the world which opens out before him. Then comes the experience of anxiety in relationship with others – which is not to discount the influence of anxiety in the pre-verbal years- and the child discovers that certain magical qualities of speech may somehow save him from these painful decreases in his self-esteem. He learns that certain phrases such as "excuse me, I'm sorry," and other elaborations of words may win some semblance of approval. Thus a remarkable process occurs. At the very time a child is expanding his knowledge of the universe and the people in it, and is beginning to acquire skill with the marvelous tool of speech – which, when joined onto his lively curiosity, will hasten that expansion – he undergoes a change which is marked by withdrawal and constriction. **His curiosity is curbed**. His interest in people is dulled, **and he may become more concerned with the protection of his self-esteem**, and with the use of language for this purpose, than with much else.*

This process apparently occurs to some extent with all people in our culture–and any other of which I have any knowledge. Thus there appears to be almost a race between the circumstances which favor the use of language for the communication of ideas, and the circumstances favoring its use for their concealment and distortion.

Should the experience of anxiety be so intense that the concealment value of language is of primary importance; there is a considerable reduction in the person's curiosity and in the possibilities of him experiencing anything like a marked realization of his potentialities. Such are those that the psychiatrist sees as patients–and many others who never come his way. It is this remarkable intermingling of the communicative and defensive aspects of speech which characterizes every interview (a meeting with a patient).

I would maintain it is also these aspects of speech that characterize the beginnings of every relationship." [2]

---

[2] *"The Psychiatric Interview,"* Harry Stack Sullivan; Norton, (1954) pp xxi

CHAPTER ONE
Created in the Image of...

Something about the situation kept it hovering, waiting. The *Golden-Yellow Chalcid* sensed movement by the big leaf. This particular specimen of *Spiliochalcis mariae* was in reproductive mode and opportunity now existed in the sparse shrubbery under the portico of the new house. The wasp descended in an autopilot programmed before the beginning of time.

A *Lapdotera* froze as its slow senses realized – too late – what was over it, and now settling astride it. The caterpillar suddenly felt the wasp's dagger-like ovipositor plunging in painfully as the mother-wasp's funnel invaded the now-writhing body. Depositing her eggs into her paralyzed victim's back, the wasp's reproductive efforts would soon produce larvae, to feed and eat the still-living (but semi-paralyzed, narcotized and suddenly stupefied) host.

The mother wasp, reproducing in the same manner that its own parent had, would thus allow for an extended life of its own to take shape, and the caterpillar would succumb, forsaking a butterfly freedom to give its very life instead to the invading, growing tenant, completing the process with its own slow, inevitable destruction.

Unless...

Long Island, New York _ 1954

Having my own bedroom was a new experience. A large wooden placard of a cowboy character replete with chaps and spurs was on the wall, joined by a happy, smiling horse, and a cowboy hat so large it had its own separate peg on which to hang. I had graduated to my first pair of long pants myself, and it was safe to say I was every bit the cowpoke as I settled into my new five year-old world in the Long Island suburb.

The road across from our new house was more like a doorway into a wonderland than a wide strip of asphalt. Magical properties lay beyond it. As in all things in life, access to this new domain needed mom's approval, but this was not difficult to get. With permission obtained, opening the front door led immediately to a pathway which held only two minor obstacles: the occasional large flying insect, and a vague anxiety concerning some string with hanging white strips of cloth that ran alongside the walk leading from the front door to the road. Mom said the string and strips of cloth must be avoided because of something called 'grass seed,' and stepping in the wrong place would mean we would not have something else called a 'lawn,' but once past these unfriendly items, I was almost there.

Once it was clear no cars were coming, the street could easily be run across. Soon I became immersed in sights, sounds and smells that had never existed for me in that other place, which my parents called *Brooklyn*.

The pungent smell of heavy pollen amidst the tall weeds in the warm sun mingled with the towering cattails near the lake. The lake ran to the left, while a few acres of trees on the right held a magic all their own. The dark, cool mystery of the forest umbrella would occasionally allow a beam of sunlight to stream its way down into a small clearing. My older sister chopped away some branches in order to create a small haven within, and it was now complete with a place to sit and branches to climb.

It was magical, and produced something with real-life appeal as well. Mom had scolded us for getting green tree sap on her good cutlery in the making of our "fort" within the wooded area. Consequently, a sense of bonding with my older sister became part of my worldly landscape which included the lake, with its ducks and frogs; my dog running alongside, and of course the secluded, secret part of our small wooded area. Life was good. It was the last good memory I would have.

"You have holes in your pants… in the knees… leave them off tomorrow and I'll make them into shorts," mom said.

Something unpleasant overwhelmed my five year-old mind. I could only vaguely understand what holes-in-knees implied as emotion within me ran counter to having anything happen to my new long pants. It swept aside all consciousness. In my child-world, opposing anything mom said was consciously impossible, so to enter into a denial that it was happening occurred instantly, and one might even say *naturally*. *I can't accept what mom is saying, but I must always obey what mom is saying*. Consequently, I felt only vague dread. The wheels thus turning, any protest would have to live below consciousness. But silent-protest it was, for in the morning I dragged on my condemned pants and ran out to play. I would learn however, that insubordination comes with a price.

Out in the field, I heard her call my name. It would never sound the same again.

"We have to change these into shorts," she said, as I arrived huffing and puffing. I saw that she was pointing to the threadbare material over my kneecaps.

"No, Mom," I said, backing up, as all thought fled, too frightened to stay coherent while entering this new territory of independent – and contrary – opinion.

Her face appeared to work strangely; as if she were being watched. Onstage, following a direction only she was aware of, she appeared to be listening to some "other." She then explained a new reality to me in a tone of '*anybody-with-any-sense-knows-this-is-true.*' In a new voice full of tension, I was made the recipient of the irrefutable nature of her logic: "*What would the neighbors think of a boy with holes in his pants*? I stared uncomprehendingly. *"They have holes in them"* she reiterated, pinting to the knees. She had been working with the shrubs and had a pair of shears in her hand. She moved them towards me.

"No," I said.

Any thought to ask me what I found so important about these pants was banished; any attempt to see the benefit of purchasing new ones for me to wear before amputating these was not even considered. It was not about holes in the pants any longer. I was her first and only male child, and males listen to mother in our family. She grabbed me hard, and I had never been held in a hostile manner before. We were out in the street in front of the house, and my mother's sudden self-consciousness filled me in the same moment with my own, as I glanced around to see who she was listening to. *Where are these unseen judges who we must please? Who, where and what are these forces we need to obey*? There were no other people I could see, but the new houses, without trees in their front yards, peered out upon us through windowed eyes; curtain-less and silent.

"What would the neighbors think of a boy who had holes in his pants? We're cutting them into shorts right now," she said tersely, as the cold metal of the scissor entered the hole in my pants' knee.

I tried to pull away from the grotesque surgery only to find her holding me harder with one hand.

"*Hold still!*" came the command.

Unable to put my rage into words, the truth of what was loved more was being dealt face-up. My mother's worshipful urge to satisfy the demands of these unseen – yet somehow all-powerful – strangers at my expense birthed a realization of injustice, and consequent hate.

"I hate you!" came my response. *I wish you were dead*! I repressed. Her jaw slacked in disbelief.

She gasped and smacked me high on my left side, the first and last physical punishment I would ever receive from her. While tears ran down my cheeks, she prayed her demonic mantra aloud in a hypnotized, strangled voice. The curse was chanted over and over from the lips of my transfixed mother, setting in motion its larvic cycle, sealing its dynamism within me with its hypnotic suggestion:

"*What would the neighbor's think? What would the neighbor's think of a boy who walks around with holes in his pants?*

Centuries before the priests of Moloch demanded male firstborns be thrown into the fire to appease unseen spirits, and likewise this day would my manhood be made forfeit. Adding the emasculating amputation of my long pants to her quick abuse of me was her commitment, her gift, her offering to the alter of these unseen *other people*, *this... culture*. This surrender would not merely be to mother's power, however, but to a newer authority, for we always embrace that which corrupts us. In my hatred, I would embrace submission, humiliation and emasculation, along with a super-ego on steroids, for those that see psychological realities in that way. A self-conscious paranoia of "*what would the neighbors think?*" concerning my own thoughts and actions would readily indicate what was in store for me not knowing the correct answer.

If we can't love the (earthly) father we can see, we won't love the (heavenly) Father we can't see."

Roy Masters

I still held onto one hope. While hurt, hate and resentment simmered, there remained one possible avenue of redemption. Like the helpless drowning swimmer who can still see some light filtering down from the surface, I held out a desperate hand to that one who – from birth onwards – had, through some collective unconscious impression, been identified with faith, courage, wisdom and strength. Father would fix, father would right the wrong, father would make the world a bright place again. Justice would be administered by the chief administrator of such things.

In the re-telling of the day's tragic events to my dad, my five-year old spiritual intelligence was being reinforced by early success. I could discern immediately that he also thought nothing of a few holes in a boys pants and I began to experience genuine hope, or faith in some inexplicable rightness, in finding someone understanding the injustice of the day's earlier trauma. As the incident unveiled through my tearful recounting, however, his early empathy disappeared as he heard about the confrontation. *He turned to mother for guidance.* She directed him with a few pithy factoids.

He did not make a manly demand to know why she hadn't bought me a new pair of pants and gotten me into them first before assaulting me in front of the whole neighborhood. Any understanding over mother's psychotic over-reaction evaporated. I sought a heavenly bureaucrat. I got a demonic politician. The frozen crease at the mouth, the smiling eyes; the sudden *'lights-on, nobody's home'* mask of my father returned newly programmed to face me, now reflecting his paternal wisdom into my devastated brain.

"Ohh, *noo*," he cooed with a Halloween face in that make-believe insincere voice adults use when speaking (insincerely) to children. Mother had given her marching orders to this sudden imposter:

"You can't walk around..." The dull clown now had to search for words, partially forgetting what he was supposed to say, and, glancing up to his boss, got a look and another cue from mother.

"You can't have holes in your dungarees... oh, no... listen to your mother, mommy knows what's best," he stumbled to obey.

Glancing back to see if that met with her approval, more sounds were possibly uttered, but thankfully I couldn't hear what they were, for those who have drowned care little for such noise, and there was now a new and living replacement in my head that not only wasn't listening to father's words, but had a new voice all its own. I would call these thoughts mine for a long time. A new energy had taken up residence, replacing what was there before. I would not draw a sane breath again for fifty years.

Paranormal Taxi

Within a year of the emasculation, I was ready… apparently, to be finished off. Time to fully transform who was left into something that would bolt up in bed screaming out loud one night very soon. However, in some mysterious sway, I was led to 'believe' I was not entirely abandoned. Mercifully, I was given a sign.

I'm in the back seat of a taxi with my parents; on our way to the airport, destination Rio de Janeiro, Brazil. We are going for a foray into my father's import-export business. The taxi was one in which two extra seats in the roomy back seat folded out to face the normal bench seat of the traditional sedan. So sitting with my back to the driver, I asked where my toy dog was, which functioned pretty much as a teddy bear. I saw the look of panic on my mother's face, and after a few hurried words between mom and dad it was made clear we couldn't turn around to retrieve it, but the decision was made to have the dog sent to me via the efforts of my Aunt Sessa.

My aunt, a kindly eighty-year-old who spoke English haltingly and read the Yiddish daily paper, *The Forward*, was in actuality, my father's aunt. She seldom left the house.

Sitting in the taxi with my parents, I was suddenly no longer there at all, but in some kind of spirit/dream-world. Outside myself as if in dream but with no consciousness of myself at all, the scene consisted of a slightly confused Aunt Sessa appearing not completely confident as she approached some officious powers-that-be in a storefront with a package under her arm, which could only be my stuffed dog. An unspoken voice – – coming out of every atom of that scenery– made itself known to my mind: *"You'll never see that again."* The voice was not tormenting. It was clear and straightforward, and of course, one-hundred percent accurate.

Chapter Two _ Brazil to Brooklyn

I was now living in the stultifying confines of the Copacabana Hotel in Rio de Janeiro, Brazil. Bonded to my anxiety-filled, hungry-to-be-approved-of-mother, my days alone with her were a ready prescription for madness. I couldn't help but feel the weight of her apprehension. What to say and how to act were on the menu big and bold on a daily basis. When a noted actor staying at the hotel refused my older sister's entreaty for an autograph, the upset on the part of my mother was monumental. Apparently, with all this extra money being spent to pretend we were upper class, we still looked like wannabees from Brooklyn, left holding a piece of paper the important people wouldn't stoop to sign.

The beach was right across the street from the hotel. I was overwhelmed by the immensity of the ocean in the glaring sun. The mind momentarily freezes at the unfamiliar openness of the infinite horizon as the smell of the salt water overpowers the senses. The pounding of the huge waves combined to offer an unfamiliar warning in a continuous, muted crescendo.

"Go on in, honey," mom said. I'll be right here." My only previous encounter with swimming had been with the small lake on Long Island. A wave four times my height knocked me under the water and flipped me around with a power I had not imagined possible, and the undertow started dragging me out to sea.

I fought for my life while, seated on a blanket fifty feet from the water's edge, my mother sat posing to imaginary onlookers, cigarette holder held aloft, her nose in the air with lips pursed. Sitting in a cabana chair, one need only imagine the women at "*Ascot Opening Day*" in the Broadway show *My Fair Lady* to get "the look." She was a beautiful woman, and in the 1930s two teenagers in California had approached my mother tentatively looking for autographs while asking if she was in the movies. This was our family's version of winning an Oscar, and my mother unselfconsciously entertained a caricature of what a leading lady should look like.

While my father had accomplished a lot to get himself into a good position in the import-export business, most of his success was accomplished by skirting regulations and bribing customs agents. He imported people to accompany merchandise, each supposedly coming to Brazil as a new immigrant so as to allow that individual large amounts of duty-free items to enter the country with. The customs agents were in on it, and consequently saw nothing unusual when an African-American horse-trainer friend of my dad immigrated to Brazil with a 20' foot long commercial refrigeration unit fit for a large restaurant or hotel. My dad said the chief customs agents lived like millionaires. Then my dad's friends would return to wherever they came from with extra money in their pocket. African-American racetrack buddies from back in the States mingled with scam artists from France, Spain and Portugal, providing my childhood with a true multi-cultural experience.

My father however, had an unfortunate need to be sympathized with, and a good con man could ferret out that weakness and exploit it. Consequently, he could be manipulated by the right kind of hustler. In addition to – or because of – this flaw, he seemed to have a special relationship with that ethereal rule known as *Murphy's Law*, stating *"anything that can go wrong, will."*

His Brazilian partner, in whose name all the goods were ultimately registered, had a heart attack and died, leaving his widow with very little motivation to give anything back. I remember my father losing control and shouting after getting more bad news; like an apartment we owned – or, wait a minute, we were *supposed* to own (*what do you mean he never finished the paperwork?*) – rolled down a hill off its stilts, and the consequent realization of disaster had my dad becoming unglued.

We moved to less expensive digs, and while sitting up in bed getting ready to go to sleep in the new bedroom I shared with my sister, I noticed that the wide window I was sleeping alongside of could be accessed from the low roof that ran alongside it, and that seemed to attach to the next building, and the next, and so on, far out into the strange cityscape. The idea of invading bad guys so formed in my head that I became immediately aware of a severe itching in my throat, and it seemed reasonable to me at that time that in order to scratch it, I should start vibrating my vocal chords by starting to scream. And scream I did.

I returned to Brooklyn in time to enter the second grade.

We returned broke. What that meant to me was that I got to sleep on a couch in the living room of my father's aunt and uncle's house in Brooklyn. I got to stay up late watching TV with my uncle until 11 pm, an unprecedented perk for a second grader.

My father had been born in that house, and now we lived in the downstairs part of the attached old two-story dwelling owned by my father's aunt, the same one whose stuffed-dog visitation I had encountered on the way to the airport over a year before.

My real-live dog from Long Island had been placed in the care of my older cousin Phillip while I was away in Brazil. Phillip lived upstairs with his mother and father, my Aunt Edie and Uncle Floyd. She was my father's sister. Edie was literally certifiable, and took an unhealthy interest in my wellbeing, while at the same time despising that of her own son.

Years later she would be carted off to Bellevue Hospital having come at my cousin and uncle once too often with a butcher knife, which I had seen her do on occasion. She had also called the IRS to tell them my father *"claims he's broke but I know he made millions."* Dad got audited every year for 10 years, although the IRS would claim to have no knowledge of the communication when my father would attempt to tell them his sister had been committed to a mental hospital.

To make matters worse, Phillip had made the incredibly shortsighted decision of telling everyone that *Snap*, my dog, was *his* during the year I was away. My return, therefore, became an extra embarrassment for him as the more I walked my dog, the more the neighborhood learned that the pedigreed tri-color Collie was mine. Adding to this his mother's pathological adoration of me, and a cauldron of envy and frustration boiled deep within him, the brutal effects of which he made known to me on a consistent basis.

In addition, second grade in Brooklyn was an experience that was new in other respects. Swagger, bluster, crude and rude were the elements of the new atmosphere, and became a sudden and separate reality from the kind, postured "correct" setting of our bourgeoisie household. In a desperate attempt to get a line on how to cope, I turned for instruction in the art of living to the stronger parent– the dominating ruler of the family. My mother also happened to be a good-looking blonde with an hourglass figure.

"Smile with your eyes, Marty, and people will like you."

While my mother kept a convenient myopia as to why she would enjoy feminizing her son, she was unusually insightful, eager to please, and often kind and intelligent with her empathetic insights. This eagerness to be liked and approved of by first "being nice-to-the-other-person-as-a-way-to-avoid-their-disliking-you" genuinely charmed many an individual who was not often so disarmed. Many found themselves opening up to her.

On the philosophy of life, my father would quote his own father's limp credo of *"peace at any price."* Sometimes, the way of the coward is easily covered wearing the cloak of the amicable 'easy-going-guy;' an imaginary moral high ground that exists in the world of convenient rationalization. I did not realize until much later in life, however, how close my father was to his sister's psychotic state of mind.

* * *

I had cried out – in my mind at least – for help. The intimidating world of Brooklyn was something I could neither escape from nor cope with. I needed to capitulate. I had tried smiling with my eyes. I was being prepped. The stress of the trauma was demanding disorder. The vampire's chosen elect looking to get bitten, I responded when the call came.

"Pigtown is coming tonight." So the news was spoken of in serious tones by the older kids in the Brooklyn schoolyard circa 1956. The fact that this gang was to be invading "our turf" sounded both exciting and unreal to me. Something stirred in my nine-year old mind. Something deep and dark was growing hungry and surging to get out. I paid scant attention to the thought *"Why go out of the house?"* The sun now gone, a neighborhood kid said, *"they're around the corner."*

Why go to them? I finally bought a reason-ticket-to-ride: I was only nine-years old, I convinced myself. *I will have immunity from the gang style antics of the "big boys."* Energy overflowed to create movement and my body ambulated of its own accord down the dark side-street. Two strange boys peeled off from the larger group and quickly approached me, chilling the blood in my veins. Paralyzing fear froze my limbs, loins, and brain.

"C'mere, I wanna talk to you," said one, as he grabbed my arm, pulling me towards the dark alley. Without thinking I started to pull away, He hit me hard on my chest, as his friend came up on my other side. I had never been punched before.

"I said, c'mere," and he pulled me harder. It was enough reason to capitulate. *"Get on your knees."* I did so terrified... paralyzed. His friend stood close next to me.

The one who had grabbed me unzipped his fly and took out a thin penis. I froze at the unfamiliar sight. I had never seen another person's penis before, and from that angle it looked so totally foreign I had to think twice to be sure what it was.

"Open up your mouth. C'mon!"

"Holy shit," said his friend.

Losing any sense of consciousness while performing the act, I had my first taste of dick. After a few seconds he withdrew it, as his friend, emboldened by my compliance, eagerly stepped up to my face with his own tool.

"Here, take mine," he said. I did, and soon tasted something unlike anything I had ever tasted in my mouth before. The kid exclaimed,

"He did it! Oh man, he really did it!" allowing me an extra twist of humiliation. I was struck with the heretofore unconscious realization that I hadn't really had to be so compliant. Although I didn't realize at any conscious level that I could've yelled, run, screamed and fought, this extra flood of humiliation came with the acknowledging travail that I needn't

had been so compliant. It was as if another voice could now be heard that was drowned out by the emotion that had previously commandeered me: *"they wouldn't have really killed you."* I thought tentatively and imaginatively of myself refusing their demands. If the normal 'food' for this 'growth' was mere submission and humiliation reflecting mom's battery of three years before, being bluffed into sucking cock was even a more powerful nutrient than merely being physically compelled. For not only was I forced to endure the degrading position of my mouth on their sex organs, but my pride was twisted even further in being made the fool for doing it.

The reality of the current moment was added to the original traumatized psyche. The psychological seedling had been bloodied and had received dynamism. Crowned with real-life submission, humiliation and sperm, it would grow on its own. The post-traumatic stress disorder was alive and flourishing. At eight-years old, it was a growing part of me now. Nevertheless, it did not register in my waking life as something that had happened in any way, shape or form.

Larvae had found its home nutritious. Real-world reaction had bloomed into and out of the real-life womb of trauma's birth.

I was a pre-pubescent fourth grader looking for a clean pair of underwear one morning to go to school in. For some laundry-related reason there were no clean shorts for me. Consequently, my mother and sister conspired with barely concealed glee to get me into a pair of my sister's, which I did with less than fervent opposition. I sat in that fourth grade class feeling like I had a special secret throbbing like an alien in my strangely excited loins.

I liked to play "guns," and when alone, would make up a couple of pillows into a saddle on my bed. My air rifle in my hand, I could ride for long periods of time with *Ghost Riders in The Sky* playing on the Victrolla. In the neighborhood games of "guns" I found myself playing with a boy one day who pointed out his father's souvenir which lay uncared for – and apparently forgotten – in the back of a dusty and dirty garage: a WWII German helmet. I was drawn to it; fascinated by its allure. I put it on. Soon I was never without that helmet when we played guns. Once I tried wearing it around the neighborhood even when not playing guns. It drew stares ands taunts, so I took it off. I was not into arts and crafts in any way at that time, but I managed to buy a small bottle of paint to spruce up the helmet's insignia a bit.

We were Jewish, and my mother had good reason to object. A short time before this, she had been made aware by Jewish philanthropists bribing officials in the International Red Cross that her long lost Aunts and

Uncles from Austria might be alive in the USSR. My mom had come to the United States when she was four years old, and those relatives that stayed behind in Austria had been murdered in the camps. So it was assumed. Then word came that they might still be alive in Russia or somewhere like that, and my mother was frantic in her attempts to reach them, being very anxious to do everything possible. She contacted the local Congressmen. Then word arrived that they were dead; having been killed in the camps. Mom was very upset, very bitter.

"*Bastards*," she muttered, "*German bastards*." Everything from Germany went out into the garbage. Not even given away. *Out*!

I couldn't bring myself to care. I just didn't. At thirteen I had read "<u>The Rise and Fall of the Third Reich</u>," and saw pictures of concentration camp victims, but it made no connection with me at all. Instead, I started reading all the paperbacks I could find by WWII German and Japanese fighter aces, U-boat captains and tank commanders. I noticed I had an emotional attachment to the enemy cause. I agonized with the U-boat commander who had the British aircraft carrier sailing right across his bow but was out of torpedoes. I was furious with Hitler for not helping the Desert Fox beat the British – those strange people in their pan helmets and silly short pants. Somehow – and I couldn't understand how – my helmet disappeared.

It seemed like I had a life that was full of fantasy, nervous dread and misery. I had school which I hated (and often imagined blowing up), the other neighborhood kids I feared, and the bully-cousin who lived upstairs in our two-family house. He came home from his school about ten minutes after I got home from mine. In order to avoid his intimidating, bullying presence, I had to quickly change into jeans and run out to play at the after-school center and/or the schoolyard till dinnertime. Although I was comfortable at sports once the games started, the schoolyard held terrors nonetheless, and there were always predators to watch for, both real and imagined.

There was a bully here and there who would almost always make my life miserable. Hiding money in my sock was a normal activity. One day an older cousin by almost two years came to visit with my Aunt and Uncle. He and I were walking to a candy store when a local bully showed up and started pushing me around. Then he tried to push around my cousin. Jerry just stood there, and determinedly pushed the bully's arm back. He didn't make faces back at the bully, he just stood like a rock. The bully backed off!

I had never seen anything like that. The lineage I sprang from supported the paternal exhortation of "*peace at any price*," with the stronger inspiration (coming from my mother) always admonishing me on the imperative of being liked. I felt an uncomfortable annoyance and an unusual sense of embarrassment for being shown this different spirit, and that emotion had a life all its own – that would soon make itself known – both to me and to my cousin.

Beware the Committed Coward
    Within a year I was visiting this same cousin with my parents. It was his fourteenth birthday and he had received a single barreled shotgun. I was sitting downstairs almost in agony from what seemed like overwhelming tedium when things suddenly took on a different hue. Reality now held a sudden and different aspect within the air around me. Thick lines of energy seemed to permeate the room, and I felt a strange calmness or solemnity, as if I could suddenly rest from my anxious mental gymnastics. It seemed like a reflection of serenity. I stood and walked upstairs to Jerry's bedroom. I nodded to him, picked up his new shotgun, clicked open the breech, and, taking a shell from the box on his dresser, dropped it into the chamber with a soft *thunk*, and snapped the barrel back up. Lifting the stock to my shoulder, I clicked the hammer back, my finger curling inside the trigger guard, and brought the barrel up to his head. I could sense the leading that I had followed thus far encouraging me to simply do it, and everything would be all right. *Just do..that..you know what to do... just go ahead...* Jerry had sank wide eyed to his knees with his hands in the air, but still had enough courage and character to say my name in a reasonable voice with a little humor in it, voicing the words *"Marty, don't."*
    It snapped me out of it. I put the gun down and left the room. We never spoke of it.

Chapter 3 _ Brooklyn, Punchball and the Catholics

I had a close Jewish friend named Robbie, who lived next door in a structure identical to our own, and in the attachment to his house was the Sorvinos. An Italian family, they had a twenty year-old son named Antnee, who was studying to be a priest, and a younger son by two years named Peter, who was – by our standards – a neighborhood god.

Some people might think that the older ecumenical student was named Anthony, but in Brooklyn it was pronounced with just two-syllables. Ant-nee usually walked slowly with a stooped and serious – almost mournful – expression. Deep in thought, he seldom looked up. He wore high-waisted baggy pants and floppy short-sleeve shirts that hung down past his elbows, making his pale, long arms appear very thin.

His younger brother had the slicked back DA haircut, the tight white T-shirt with the Marlboro box rolled up in the short sleeve, the black leather Garrison belt – the buckle sharpened into a nasty weapon – worn hooked off the left hip slacked an inch or two, which was the tough-guy style that year. Pete had actual muscles hard with definition, had been in real street fights and was given a lot of respect.

"This is gonna' be *so boss*," crooned little Johnny McNulty, who normally was a diminutive type not given to such bold statements. But try as I might – for he was shorter, weaker and mentally much slower than me – I could find no fault in his statement. There were four older guys – high school kids – who needed us for a punchball game in the Sorvino's alley! In 1959 Flatbush, an activity of this magnitude signaled a new level of kid existence in my now twelve-year old life. Being chosen to play punchball with the big kids is not a casual affair.

Brooklyn alley punchball boiled down to a game based on a "batter," who stood at an identified "home plate" and depending on style, tossed the ball up a few inches with one hand, while swinging on it in a punching fashion with his other fist. Then the game pretty much resembled baseball. Rules and bases, though, were flexible based on the number of players actually playing the game and the layout of what was being used as a "field."

So the game is on and I am on Pete's team. Late in the game we're up two runs. They have men on base, and I make a jumping, stretching, reach-for-the-sky catch of a line-drive, holding it aloft, the pensie-pinkie roundness stuck hard between my index and middle finger. A potentially game-saving play, Pete smiles right at me and makes a "YEAH! with his fist aloft.

Life does not get any better than this. I am Duke Snider and Pee Wee Reese rolled into one and we have won the World Series for Brooklyn. I am outside myself in exhilaration and I cannot contain my smile. My brains feel like they're dribbling out of my ears and I know that I look like a fool with my face almost breaking in half, but for the moment I am past caring.

But what's this? Some interloper was now putting his voice into our game. It was Pete's older brother; the strange one, now somehow involving himself in our celestial activity, specifically singling out our local deity.

"*Pete, time for dinner,*" he called.

A pause, as all 11 of us hold our breath. It is two innings away from done, and it's 15-13.

Pete just swears under his breath, and with his hands on his bent knees, looks straight ahead like a shortstop. Antnee returns inside to the sound of the screen door closing behind him. Ballplayer chatter begins anew:

"*My man Pete!*"

"*Hooze up?*"

"*Hooze got daball? "*

"*Gimmeda fuckin' ball.*"

"*Up!*"

Two more plays go by. It's now two-out. A deciding moment in the game is approaching as the Sorvino screen door opens, and Antnee's call from the porch to Pete in the alley arrives with a stronger sense of impatience.

"*Pete! Momma and Poppa are sitting down!*"

"*Fuck... Mm...*"

A surreal freeze. All eyes, all voices, all attentions were cued as to whether or not sacrilege lines had been crossed. Those of us headed to study Wittgenstein and Kant in the halls of higher learning could already discern that the "F" word had been used in such proximity to the "M" sound that serious reflection was necessary to determine if acceptable cultural imperatives had been breeched. In the weeks to follow, future lawyers from this very group would spend countless hours attempting to consensually validate whether or not verbal impropriety had indeed transpired.

We were not left to wonder however, what had transpired in the mind of Pete's older brother. Anthony Sorvino, devout student-worshipper of the living Christ, was about to let us all know what he thought of Pete's response.

In the biblical account of David and Goliath, it is written, "then David *hastened* towards Goliath." I was about ten feet away from Pete, and, like everyone else, my jaw dropped and my feet froze. We were all caught up in a moment taking place outside ourselves, as the noise of traffic itself ceased to exist throughout all of Brooklyn.

Antnee had swung into a high gear of quiet rage as he strode down the path away from us to the gate where it opened into the alley not thirty feet from where our young, ready hero now stood with his fists clenching, Adams-apple bobbing and face working. Pete was not a poser. He was digging in.

As his older brother rounded the U-turn out of the walkway and into a confrontation line directly toward Pete, we all blinked and were forced to re-focus. Antnee's normally wan and mournful countenance could not be found. It had been replaced by something strangely alive and active with a resolve and purpose no one had imagined possible. No words were necessary to articulate further what that purpose was: "*You are going to be punished for that*" was clearly shining from every pore on his big-brother face.

In the countless summer hours to come dissecting every moment of the confrontation, it was generally agreed that Pete – although standing gamely with his fists raised – appeared to lack the appropriate mindset necessary to deflect his older brother's conviction.

The student-priest was converging on Pete with such speed that when he suddenly threw up his fists and feinted left we all flinched backwards with a collective gasp. Pete bit hard on the feint and we were all treated to that unique and unmistakable sound of a fist hitting someone's face with the full force of all knuckles. Blows continued to rain down on Pete with such relentless speed and power that it was difficult to know exactly how many had landed before he lay sprawled, face-down and limp in the alley dirt.

An eerie moment of silence descended upon the alley as Antnee stretched out his hand and helped him up. But while he was looking at Pete, he spoke not just to his brother, but to all of us; we, his sudden congregation.

"**Momma** and **Poppa** are waiting."

There wasn't a head that didn't bow just a little, and as we all gulped and blinked, he gently pointed his subdued younger brother in front of him, and the two walked the length of the alley to the gate entrance. As they walked up the center lane, it was as if they were leaving through a church aisle, leaving all eleven of us now parishioners; suddenly silent, reverent and wide eyed.

Take me, padre, oh somehow please take me too, for I am so lost…

Chapter 4 – The Racetrack

In the fourth grade I already had two "best friends." Robbie, who was eighteen months older and two grades up, lived two houses down from me. His mom and mine were tight, and we got along very well. His friends were older, but I seldom hung with him when they were around, and never had to eat too much shit just because I was younger. Rick, on the other hand, was my age, lived a block away, and was a constant companion. We slept over each other's house all the time.

Occasionally, a kid from my class would seek to enter my world as a friend, but never quite gelled enough (or was never really given the opportunity to), and hence would eventually get frozen out when we planned for weekend movie trips, etc. Such was the case with Phillip, a nice enough kid who I found myself hanging around with a couple of times after school. I saw his eyes grow large when I said I slept over Rick's house a lot. Phillip invited me to his house, with apparently an ulterior motive. He must have been talking to his mom about me, and over milk and cookies, she made her move:

"*We belong to a beach club at the Rockaways,*" she explained, and went on to tell me about all the fun things that were available with such a membership. I had a vague idea about the joys of shuffleboard, volleyball and oceanfront activities, but when she mentioned the terms, I saw it fade from possibility.

"We go every weekend through the Summer," she went on, "and we would like you to come, but we would have to get another membership ticket for you, so we would have to know that you would be coming, otherwise it would be, well, kind of a waste of a ticket…"

"Oh, the weekends?" I asked, suddenly serious. "On the weekends I go to the track… with my dad."

"What? What kind of track? she asked in a puzzled tone.

"The racetrack. Y'know, Aqueduct, Belmont… This weekend is the Memorial Handicap, and…"

"Oh, she said, That's something special. *This* would be *every* weekend. Of course you want to be able to do something special, like this weekend, you're going with your father…"

"No, I said, matter-of-factly. I go *every* weekend with my Dad."

"Huh?" she said, as the sincere shock of her reaction was made all the more obvious when she turned to her son with a look that said in words unspoken '*is this true?*' Phil looked back with a "*yes*" in his eyes also mirroring the middle-class notion how bizarre this all was.

In my head I immediately separated myself from these people. They lived in a, *well, smaller world? More constricted universe? Less wise to the larger things in life*, I suppose one could say. These were the *"normals,"* those not anointed with the magic my father and I were imbued with. My attitude had a lot in common with Ray Liotta's character in *"Goodfellas"* when he compares the 'wiseguy' lifestyle with the nine-to-fivers.

The Track

As a child of kindergarten age in Rio, I remember making my first bet, putting money in my wallet and noticing the strange smell of the Brazilian legal tender, the *Crucero*. Now back in Brooklyn, a typical weekend meant Friday night getting the Racing Form for my dad, and usually I went to the track Saturday, and sometimes Sunday as well. If I won on Saturday then certainly on Sunday.

It was religion. Trainers, owners and their ilk formed a kind of priesthood with groups like my father, touts and serious gamblers the faithful deacons. You cast your fate (money) into the hands of a foreign power (animals running in a circle). The intense rush is palpable as you experience the lack of control during the contest, the helplessness which possesses you as your fortune hangs on the performance of these high strung beasts pounding around into frenzied exhaustion. The unspoken "logic" of the gamble is tempered, of course, with the knowledge that you are different, specially imbued somehow to predict the outcome with almost supernatural insight, whereas other people (the ordinary patrons) cannot. There is nothing more frustrating to a track-fanatic than to see someone who doesn't "know" anything with a winning ticket, while you, the wise-guy horse expert, tear up your worthless investment. Your faith is in believing that voice in your head that whispers in countless ways *"you've got it,"* and the fact that you just lost can be excused with any number of reasons. Not the reasons that the unbelievers give: That these are dumb animals running around in a circle. No, the reasons I lost are too complex for the ordinary person to understand, but soon all would see the truth of my anointing as I would come home wealthy. I would chase that money that the house (the track) has taken from me, catch up with it, and get it back ten times over, riding home in glory, a champion astride my beast of transcendental prediction.

Remember the words of *Grandpa Joe* to *Charlie* in the original *Willie Wonka*? Speaking of winning the "Golden Ticket," he wisely intones,

"You deserve it more than anyone, Charlie, because you want it more than anyone."

We would go to the Clubhouse and there would be four or five groups of touts, trainers, assistant trainers, grooms and handlers who we would stay in contact with. Then there were my dad's friends who were just like him scattered around. Often my dad would send me to various groups to see who they liked in any particular race.

If it's Aqueduct, I first head over to Archie, a tout that hangs out about twenty feet from the ground floor grandstand entrance into the Clubhouse. I come out of the Clubhouse and spot him. Archie is a small, slightly hunched man in his late sixties. He always wears a trench coat. A perfect ringer for a male wicked witch in any Disney movie, he looks left, right, puts his hand over his mouth as he tucks his head down before speaking.

Many touts will do this using all kinds of different techniques. This behavior is necessary to maintain the appearance that he is such a valuable source of information that people are hanging around hoping to lip-synch his pick, thereby depriving him of the money that they should be paying him for his good information.

For example, if I'm a guy who doesn't know anything about picking horses but I come to the track once in a while, I might be willing to take a tip from a tout like Archie. After I bet it and if I win, it is expected that I should give him some money, or I will never be spoken to again. Sometimes a tout will ask the client to buy him a ticket on the tipped horse even before the race is run. Consequently, if I don't know much about the mysterious behind-the-backstretch goings on – but I believe that Archie does – then I make my offering to the priest.

What people don't generally know is that the question regarding all touts is this: *Is he always giving out the same horse*? Because the tout often has no insider info in every race, he's just picking horses himself. Also, it may be in his selfish interest to tell different people to bet on different horses, thereby increasing the chances for his own reward. If, for example, he knows so-and-so from the Turf Club is never gonna meet Gerry the bus driver in the Grandstand, and the tout is giving tips to both, he could tell each to bet a different horse. That way he doubles his chances of income while keeping more – but different - people winning.

Who can know what's in a man's heart? Archie was in Brazil with my dad when pop was scamming there, so he and my dad go way back and just share information. Archie covered his mouth when he asked me:

"Whose your dad like?

"All he's heard so far is a groom at Jacobs' barn says they love their horse, but I don't think Dad is all that impressed with it…" But I suddenly see (in my imagination) the horse winning and my dad asking Archie, didn't you have'em? I told Marty to tell ya," so I add quickly, but I could be wrong! Maybe the horse is *Man o'War*." Archie laughs, and responds to my raised and questioning eyebrow.

"Too early. Maybe I'll have somethin' later," he says.

I walk back into the Clubhouse, and approach Andy Orwell, the black trainer who also shared a couch in our living room in Brazil. He's a nice guy, who gave me a $25 bond on my Bar Mitzvah.

"*Chestuh sez dey lot bedder den dey looks on peypah.*" Translation: Chester Lewis, a trainer-friend of Andy's is more optimistic of his horse's chances than one would assume he'd be after studying the Racing Form (the "*peypah*").

I walk over to "Slots." He is from the neighborhood. My Dad says he's "connected." I think I know what this means, but am not completely sure. I arch my eyebrows. He motions me over.

"What'ya got?" he whispers.

"Chester says they're better than they look on paper and a groom at Jacobs' barn says they love their horse; but he's the chalk," I add with a shrug, demonstrating my level of interest in Jacobs' people backing their own lukewarm favorite. I raise my eyebrow, "Noo?"

"Eddie says he was watching the six-horse work out last week when he did 3 in 33 flat."

"Yeah, I saw that..." I had noticed the horse's quick three-furlong workout when I had studied the Racing Form the night before.

"The track was dead... horse was under tight wraps; couldn't blow out a candle afterwards..."

"Outa town horse," I mutter with growing interest, tantalized over the information that the horse had not appeared winded at all from a relatively quick workout (for this level) on a track which was in a sluggish condition. I re-open the Form to see if there's anything I've missed in my prior study of the animal's past performances.

"Opened at 20, now he's 12. Any more late money, I gotta' get on'm," Slots croons like a man falling in love.

I return to my father. As I start to give him the report, he looks into my eyes with a "just listen" look.

"I just got a tre*mend*ous push on the eight horse," my father says with a seriousness normally reserved for heart surgery. "*Brody* (the trainer) *says he's a lock*," my father says in a lowered voice, inhaling meaningfully through his nose while his eyes meet mine. His D-Day headlights hold me captive with the appropriate gravity, while we experience a moment of bonded lunacy. Not unlike a sergeant announcing to his squad that they're being tapped for a raid behind enemy lines, I was being swept up in the desire to wager heavily on this newly anointed beast. The penalty for failure could be painful: the chance that we might have to go home before the last race, leaving the track broken-out, disgraced and shamed before our allotted time.

He has taken me along to the track all my life because I am the only person in the world who will buy into all this serious drama with the appropriate delusionary abandon. The bottom line is we now have "information" on four different horses in the race. Whoever wins, therefore, will probably not be someone we bet on, but it very well could be one of the horses that somebody we knew liked, talked about and *did* bet on, and then we are like the religious person who thinks '*I know G-d was trying to speak to me but I missed the sign.*'

Variations on the following theme would be offered after a race: "Y'know," my father would say to me, '*I was standing with so-and-so,*' or '*I was on line and thought, I'm going to bet* (the eventual winner), *but so-and-so came up to me and said such-and-such. I knew I should have bet on that horse.*' Therefore, even in defeat, there is hope and rededication; as the mind simply plays and replays with itself that (in retrospect), *I knew I should have bet on the horse that won, but because I was misled by some horrible other person or terrible twist-of-fate (that seems especially reserved only for me), I missed what I knew I should have done; that is, bet on the winner. Thank G-d there's racing tomorrow and I will not make that same mistake again!*

Any normal person would point out the illogic of this 'woulda, shoulda, coulda' reasoning, but I was born into my father's perspective on this madness, and it was the only bond we shared.

Sometimes my dad would get into a very limited partnership on a cheap claiming horse. He would partner-up with one of the black trainers he was friendly with. Andy Orwell was one. Andy occasionally trained a horse called *Mondo Will*. We went back to the barns one morning before the races to talk with Andy and I got to see "*The Will*" up close. I was really excited, and *Mondo Will* became "my horse."

Months later at the track my Dad sent me over to ask Andy who he liked in the upcoming race. *Mondo Will* had been claimed some time before and was now owned and trained by someone else. He was running in this race. Andy (trainers often make side-money as touts) – also played the 'can't let people see who I like game' – drew me close, and thumbed his nail into a horse's number on his program indicating his choice. I nodded.

"Who you like, young man?" he asked me.

"*The Will*, of course! Eight to one? Heck of a price."

"Five horse whupped his ass last time out. Even the three-horse finished ahead of him the same race, and they be improvin'. Then afta' dat, next race up da track, and then again. No, can't bet emotion, Marty." Two black grooms from the backstretch who were standing with Andy - chimed in with the same sentiments.

I respond. "Says *'bumped at the start'* in the comments section for one race, and the other was heavy mud, and we know "*The Will*" has never been a great off-track horse. I throw those two races out and I'm only lookin' at one poor effort since he was on a level to run with these; well, close with these. And look at the price." I finish up with a glance at the tote board.

I had $28. It was my moment to show my thirteen-year-old balls. I bet it all on *Mondo Will* to win. He won easily, paying $18.80 for a $2 bet. I collected $263. In 1961 you could rent a nice two-bedroom apartment in Brooklyn for $75 a month. I was only a kid, and, on my way to the collection window, I passed Andy's group. When they looked up at me questioningly I shouted, "*got'm!*" flashing my blue ten-dollar win tickets giddily. It was then that I heard my first, long, drawn out "*mutha-fuckah!*"

But most times you lose. I remember my dad having to borrow money from a neighbor before going home. Why my dad brought me into the private conversations he needed to have with his friends in order to borrow money I do not know. Color us *no shame*. It was part of the religion, I guess. Watching dad kinda grovel for the loan was part of the apprenticeship. I guess.

My mother and father developed a strange ritual. If my dad won, or if he needed to bribe my mother in order to be allowed to go again the next day, he had to produce a "fufchick." A 'fufchik' was a bit of Yiddish meaning a fifty-dollar bill. My mother would start in a sing-song laughter – almost teasing – that she had better get a 'fufchick,' and would sally-up behind my father and put her hand into his pants' front pocket while he protested helplessly like a schoolgirl being felt up. In those days men's trousers had pockets you could put a lunch pail in, and who knows what was going on down there.

Fear and Loathing in the Schoolyard

I lived in a world of autopilot activities and imagination, seeking gratifications in my dreamworld. I would spend hours imagining I had won hundreds of thousands of dollars at the track, actually going over the race results of the previous day, giving interviews to the astonished sportswriters – and others I knew from my father's crowd at the track – on how I had not only picked nine winners in a row, but parlayed my bets. I even tried to make calculations on how my enormous imaginary bets would have reduced the pari-mutual payoffs. Between these types of activities – reading the Racing Form, calculating track variants and speed ratings –I developed quite well in math. Sometimes I would sit in my room and "stack" a deck of cards so I could put myself into a poker game and get dealt a straight flush to beat an opponent who had four nines.

My father had no patience to teach me how to throw a curve ball, although he was a very good semi-pro ballplayer and pitcher, nor did he feel obligated to teach me much about shooting pool, although he could run the table. My bonding with my mother might have had a lot to do with that, although it opens up a "chicken-or-the-egg" scenario about which came first. I guess we simply disliked each other. I often found myself joining my mother in subtly mocking him.

We all had our unnatural, unspoken and destructive roles. I assumed a mental superiority to him in every aspect of our lives except the racetrack. He pretended not to notice. Perhaps this was the reason he didn't care to teach me things he knew how to do well. The man was much closer in his "inner self" to his committed-to-insane-asylum sister than any one of us realized. She eventually committed suicide, but it was officially termed an accidental overdose.

When I was in the fifth grade a kid named Jeffrey told me *"you're dead after school. I'm going to kill you."* We wound up having some kind of tussle which was broken up by the after-school teacher but it was nonetheless very upsetting to me, as Jeffrey swore, upon us being separated, that now he was *really* gonna' kill me.

I took a chance and tried my father out for advice. He listened to me voice my apprehension and fear, and acted surprised and bewildered, as if it was beyond his comprehension that I would have any concern over this. I guess it was convenient for him to hide behind surprise and disappointment. Consequently I can't remember his words being of any help. A short time later while arguing with him he brought up the essence of the confidence I had shared with him by saying,

"Yeah, you're not scared of anything… except Jeffrey." I felt wounded even though I was probably being a snot at the time he swatted me with it. Needless to say, I didn't talk much to my father about anything meaningful after that. I tried to communicate with my mother about stuff like my concerns about sex. She reminded me that sex was a beautiful thing. I couldn't align my fantasies with anything beautiful, and dropped the subject. Mom and I went to a lot of Broadway shows together, and the

manner in which she treated my father – and the way he presented himself at social gatherings – was more than enough to reinforce my earlier impressions who had the power in the family.[3]

---

[3] *In our type of society, that sort of organization to which an analyst may refer to as the "Oedipus" complex is prone to develop. Instead of an attitude towards the father resembling adult awe or fear or respect or reverence, there grows an attitude of more or less concealed jealousy and hatred. "… even more destructive is the situation in which the woman is the "boss;" in such homes, any possible good which might derive from a benignant matriarchy is utterly swamped in the child's reaction to the woman's effort to be a man, yet conform to society, and the man's effort to protect his self-esteem.*
The matter of wretched adjustment of one to another parent, and of one or both to the conventional pattern to which they strive to conform, grows more and more important as we try to understand the coming of subsequent disaster to the offspring.
(Schizophrenia as a Human Process (Norton) pp 94)

Puberty

The sheer escapist revolution into breathless pleasure that taking myself in hand allowed me at the onset of puberty was alien to anything I had experienced in my life up until that point. It was like a parallel universe one visited when no longer in the tepid horror of everyday life, and by ministering to my aching hardness, I could compose my own passionate play in imaginative worlds of sexual theatre which left me literally gasping with unspeakable pleasure. Quickly flushing the unspeakable imaginings into forgetfulness via post orgasmic denial was as simple as the disposing of the guilty tissue. Life became an adventure into orgasmic dreaming, and then awakening from that dream. Dealing with the fantasy world I submerged into after-the-fact was as simple as disposing of the moist evidence. *Fuhgeddaboutit.*

While reading a Soldier-of-Fortune magazine, I came across a story of a street tough who, together with his gang, captured two of his rivals. He stripped them both naked and sent them running home through the streets. Upon reading this, I found myself unexpectedly in possession of a concrete-breaking erection, and came to revisit time and again that imagery and with it blind surrender to its sexual excitement.

Alone in my house one afternoon I stood naked with my bursting fourteen year-old staff inches from the window which overlooked the sidewalk. It was late afternoon and all the shades were down save this one. I could see a couple of high school girls approaching. I determined to spring full up to the window and wave my inspired manhood in their faces. At the last moment I retreated.

At thirteen I had received a BB gun. It turned out I was a pretty good shot. I would shoot birds and then feel bad picking up their lifeless (or worse, wriggling and dieing) bodies to take to the garbage. As puberty raged, I tried something else. On a warm summer evening with my parents out and we now occupying the upper floor of our Brooklyn home, I had managed to shoot and hit the garbage cans on the other side of the street. I then noticed Gary Conners, an older (sometimes) bully walking by.

In the schoolyard one evening weeks before, he and the older kids were drinking beer, and I overheard him talking about actually getting a blowjob from one of the local "bad girls." This from a female held in high esteem within the sexual imagination of all us aching young men; a super-fox who dressed in pants so tight you could see the outlines of her panties.

Alone in the upstairs of our house, I acted on impulse and shot the garbage can as he walked by. He stopped, walking over to the can to investigate. I shot him in the ass when he turned to walk away. I ducked down beneath the window sill. Some strange energy came over me. I was inundated with the most intense and overwhelming compulsion: *Stand up and callout to him*! *He can see you! He knows it's you and you better stand up and come clean*! *Now! Now! Now!*

I stood up from my crouch beneath the window and even though I could see the voice had lied to me because he wasn't even looking up at my window, a hypnotized zombie in motion tends to remain a hypnotized zombie in motion. I called out to him, waving for him to come up. As he came closer I compulsively did what I was sure I needed to do: *confess*.

I invited him in. He came upstairs, kind of tentative. Not angry. I told him what I had done. I offered to let him shoot me. He declined. He arrogantly walked to our refrigerator and swung the door open.

My heart skipped a beat as I was tempted to put into words what was bursting from beneath my chest, bursting to get out, but I couldn't admit the words to my own consciousness, let alone know what they might be should I allow them to come blurting out. I was breathing so hard I couldn't think. I knew not what I would blurt out were I to '*let go*,' as my nervous excitement simply kept on spiraling within my head until thought became impossible. I could plainly hear the pounding of my own heart. I was ready to explode out some words, some question from my unknown chest where it compressed into unconsciousness. It was "pull the trigger" time again, but just as I had been saved from killing my cousin I was equally delivered from the sexual and social consequences of asking this older boy more about what he had received from the neighborhood slut. *For who knows, maybe he'd like to tell me more about it in my bedroom*? I was saved from asking that question by his sudden departure, although it's possible he could have stayed for hours and I would not have asked it.

I was in the third grade when I noticed Rick around school. I knew I wanted to be friends with him. It was as if a part of me shot out from me to him, and it seemed as if it was made known to me the manner in which I would make a friendship with him my reality. It was almost as if a game plan of how to be pleasing, approving and agreeable was seen inside my own head. It would happen – I just knew it – and this was a totally unique experience. He told me his name was Richard, but everyone called him Rick. And it came to pass that we became best friends from grade school through high school.

I guess I was becoming like my mom. After all, she basted me continually in her ego-building "love" inasmuch as her words to me were concocted in such a way as to make me feel good about myself. That is, they were created in order to assuage my doubts and fears, to buck up "my" point of view by reinforcing whatever made me appear bright, strong, right, good, pure, smart, correct, unselfish, self-reliant, sensitive, insightful, loving, courageous and strong. In other words, mother would always try to convince me – in a myriad of ways – that I was something I wasn't. This was called "love." In one way or another I did that with Rick, and he did that with me.

We slept over each other's house all the time. We jerked off together. We had touched each other's equipment briefly. My sexual attitude was raging one fourteen year-old night. He was asleep, or more likely, pretending to be. My mind refused to take that greater possibility any further in its implication. He was on his back, with his pajama bottom fly open, the overly large head sloped off to the side, a sleeping plum to my hungry eye. The slumbering snake was exposed less than an inch behind the opening. With my heart beating so loud I thought I might see it explode in my mind's eye, I lowered my body into position while my trembling hand reached slowly over to him there, exploring the outer opening of his pajama. My index finger curled under the huge flopping head and moved it to a gentle rest outside its flannel cave. My consciousness composed of lightning flashes, I couldn't breath except for loud gulps of air. I think I might black out, and the notion of Rick suddenly jumping up yelling *"what the hell are you doing?"* also crosses my mind, but I reason in the same conflicted and bizarre *'this is not happening'* mindset that he is probably awake and knows what I'm doing. That is too scary to think about. Exciting and terrified, thought and denial battle for my consciousness as my head swoons dizzily.

There is something special about dick. Once you get past the offense of the piss slit and take the dumb-looking head into your mouth, it's an act unlike anything else in the physical world. It's the very epitome of the *"more than the sum of its parts"* definition of gestalt. The musky scent of his teenage crotch mingles with the rubber-like flesh shocking my taste buds, alarming neon explodes through my brain proclaiming *"you're really doing it!"* Immediately I realize the difference between the actual reality of my moment and the prior imagination of it. The curling of my tongue under and around it, the pleasure-giving ministrations as I suckle the head inside my mouth and attempt to take deeper the guest, all contribute in turning oral sex into an act that now becomes my entire new universe. A transformation of reality takes place, and suddenly there is nothing else. Worshipping its ugly attraction with the suckling ministrations beckons me into embracing some kind of energy deep inside and strangely specific to this act.

Somewhere in the tornado-like maelstrom that exists between my ears I intuit that the focus of it is somehow not as interested in Rick the person as it is in serving something else. The connection is made to something beyond – or beside – mere flesh.

As he starts to harden and grow, he turns away on his side. A couple of minutes later, he comes to lay on his back again and I have another go at it but he gets hard quickly and turns away again. We both lay in the dark breathing heavily. Silently, he reaches for some tissues and we both jerk off.

Neither of us ever mentioned what took place. I do not speak of it to him, and fail to confront it even in myself. It is even denied in fantasy, as it would be years before I could acknowledge my longings for Rick even in that realm.

Respecting the Rights of Others

Around this time, many of my junior high school associates were finding new uses for their male equipment. Group masturbation sessions occurred as panting cum-crazed youngsters tried to bond in circle-jerks. I came up with the idea of "stripping" the other guy in a hormone-crazed group one afternoon with the gang turning on the designated "it" as I would call out the boy's name. We would all rip the clothes off his struggling body, not without a few shirts being torn in the melee. Once stripped bare naked, all activity ceased, with heavy breathing all around, and a silently understood waiting period transpired for the recently denuded to get re-dressed so he could then rejoin the aggressive mob.

My name is soon called and they rush me. They circle warily, and I experience a slight fear mixing with a growing excitement, but the fear is not of being harmed. Allowing a strange new feeling to take over, I take a reason-to-ride on the "smart-wise-guy" persona and casually say,

"*I know I can't fight you'all. Why should I try? Go ahead,*" and I relax and start to sit as they charge, bowling me over on my back. I lay back, hands open-palmed in a surrender-kind of posture, having my clothes ripped from my body as I close my eyes to allow something new and dark the momentary freedom to grow up through my loins. My body pulsated pleasurably – not unlike the sensation in your stomach when a plunging elevator suddenly seems to rise to stop. But the sight, smell and feel of these howling adolescents ripping the clothes from my body, and the tingling excitement that ran through me signaled some new disposition in me, as if some new energy had found a home.

The Handball Game

It was not so much that I loved after-school sports as I was simply a daily refugee from the terrors of my own home. Motivated to flee the domicile as soon as I got home from school in order to avoid my bullying cousin, I had spent most of my Brooklyn after-school life from third to ninth grade in the schoolyard and/or the after-school center.

Consequently, I was fair-to-middling in stickball and softball, excellent in punchball and uneven in basketball. I did become good enough at hoops to get on the after-school team, however, but never started. I had an occasionally accurate turnaround jumper, was a fair rebounder but a poor ball handler and I fouled when defending. I was smoking a pack a day at fourteen and my ability to run up and down the court was hampered by increasing anxiety over my performance mixed with shrinking lungpower.

Rick, on the other hand, was the fastest runner in the neighborhood, and while only five-foot-something, could touch the rim on a straight-up jump. Although I whined that Rick got a first string basketball trophy and I only got the second string statue for my efforts, in reality it didn't matter.

My more lively – and all the more secret – basketball focus keyed on wearing those tight little satin-like basketball shorts, and patting Rick on his splendid behind after almost any play he made. Nights jerking off with the silky smooth texture wrapped around my ecstatic engorgement were more representative of my love of the game, and the real trophy for my season's efforts was the curiously constant stain which wouldn't wash out.

The game of handball, however, was a different story, and I had become a force to be reckoned with. I was a natural. I could beat older kids in the schoolyard who were far superior to me in basketball and other sports. While I didn't think about it at the time, my prowess at handball was all I had to show for years of after-school effort motivated by fear of my bully cousin at home.

For handball was much more than simply a game for me. Generally apprehensive and unsure of myself, when I strode on the handball court, a different Marty took over. My shoulders squared, my walk took on a jaunt and a touch of swagger, and when I looked at a new opponent, it was with a knowledge that his face was gonna look way different after he got a look at my stuff. I'd smack a "killer" from deep backcourt off the bottom few inches off the wall that rolled off un-returnable, and then look at my opponent with a *better get used to it* blank game-face as I sauntered up to serve. I had a fairly good left-hand which I came to supplement after hundreds of hours of practice with a surprisingly accurate backhand right. It was not that unusual for me to make a play that would elicit whooping exclamations from those on the sidelines waiting to play the winner. Not an easy accolade to get in a Brooklyn schoolyard.

It was therefore no exaggeration to say I was considerably conflicted regarding my game with Rick for the 9th grade championship of my Junior High School. Since the Junior High was 7th, 8th and 9th grade, this game was unofficially regarded as the championship of the whole school. What it boiled down to was the fact that while we were in each other's shadows as friends, I was jealous, tense, insecure and pretty dishonest with everyone and everything. In those personal difficult-to-define areas between friends, I was possibly more emotional with Rick than anyone.

The game spoke volumes. When a point was called in Rick's favor when it was close, I used my doubt and anger over that to argue ferociously about another point that was probably Rick's. His surprise and disapproval burned into my conscience. I won the bitterly contested game without much happiness and with more guilt than I thought possible. I think I made the referee (a distracted Gym teacher) believe the score was more in my favor than it was.

We were over Rick's house not long afterwards. We got into an argument over the game and I got very emotional. I was always giving in, and my *modus operandi* was to give in to another's demands to relieve the pressure on myself. My father's socially approved philosophy of *'peace at any price'* dovetailed nicely with this type of easy-going-guy, and the cowardice inherent in this type of behavior often had me agreeing with others' even when I believed I was probably right.

But this was the only time I had ever achieved something I had really wanted, and my handball prowess had been built on so many years of desperation that I was overwhelmed with guilt and conflicted with doubt. The sense that I had not won fair was both real *and* imagined, and I became furious in sticking up for myself concerning the game, as it's so much easier to believe you're right when you're angry. At this point in time, Rick chooses to "come out" to me.

"*C'mon Beckman* (we often called each other by our last names), *why don't you just jerk me off?*" Throughout all our mutual sex-play, neither of us had never spoken openly concerning a sexual act between us. I froze. Aware only of the personality pattern that appeared front and center in my mind, I interpreted his words as "*don't argue with me; just service me sexually when I tell you to.*" I saw myself a sexual supplicant with no rights to a point of view. That last analysis colored and overwhelmed my ashamed and confused consciousness, and after a second of frozen silence, I turned and ran from his house, followed by his tormenting laughter.

Had we then removed ourselves into a sexual liaison, and had opportunities to look at each other, I know my life would have been very different. I don't know that it would have created an ongoing homosexual lifestyle. It might have run its course of compulsion just as in the future many 'forbidden' fantasies would prove unpalatable when explored in the harsh light of reality. However, my roots in needing intimacy ran deep, and so did my fear of the same. Coming to grips with my fear and desire in an intimate sexual encounter with my best friend would certainly have been preferable to the denial I chose at that moment to live in.

Religious people I would later come to know would probably say something like "*G-d knew you'd die of AIDS, so He prevented the sexuality.*" Perhaps. Am I being cynical in thinking that kind of logic limits G-d's abilities? It's like the church testimonial that goes: "Aunt Edna was in a car accident, and they were going to take both legs off at the hips, but we prayed and prayed, and one was taken off below the knee. The doctor said it was a miracle."

REWARD – LOST DOG
Three legs, tail chewed off, blind in one eye.
Responds to "*Lucky.*"

So it was with a kind of 'kiss-and-don't tell' unspoken agreement between the both of us that our friendship and halting sexual efforts existed. I anguished within myself, or what passes for self - in the pubescent volcano between my ears, which, for lack of better terminology, had to be called my life. The post-handball game overture marked the last real sexual communication save one. Soon after moving (with my parents) to an apartment a mile away, Rick slept over.

"Hey Marty, let me try this," he said, smearing a sports ointment on my willing cock, and of course I pretended to be angry when the cream heated up uncomfortably. Just to have him touch my penis with a friendly hand was worth all the burning, yet even at that point I was too traumatized to come out. I think Rick also was using the practical joke as way to make an overture, trying to reach over the cultural barrier to intimacy, vainly attempting to touch, but, like myself, unable to do so except within the culturally accepted brutality.

High School

High school had been a horror of being ill at ease and girl crazy. I gambled a lot playing poker and sometimes cut school to go to the track. My only date in three years of high school was an interminable block of time filled totally without chemistry, in which I was totally awkward and ill-at-ease. We went bowling and I was consistently off just that little bit that allows a near blazing strike to turn into a difficult split, and every other ball is "almost" perfect. She beat me with her simple drop-and-roll technique. I encourage her to tell me about her social life, dragging out of her an admission that there's a college guy she really likes. By the end of this torture, I am haunted and taunted by the thought that I am ending our date as her girlfriend talking about the guy she really likes.

In my senior year at high school, I had arranged to deliver fruit and vegetables after school for a local merchant around the corner from our new apartment. I worked six hours a day weekdays and all day Saturday riding the store bicycle with a large basket around the neighborhood delivering fruit for a dollar an hour plus tips.

Willy was one of the few black kids in our neighborhood. He worked at the candy store next to the fruit store. One day in the Autumn of 1963 he came to the door of the fruit store. "Hey Irvin,' y'all wanna turn on daradio."

"Why?"

"President's been shot."

"You don't joke around with something like that!"

"I ain't jokin."

"Willy," said Irving, suddenly serious, "If you are kidding me, I don't ever want you in my store again," and Irving turned on the radio. Immediately I was treated to a different side of these people. Women customers started to come in as the news became final and wept in Irving's arms. Irving was a dirty old man with a wife and kids who grabbed everybody including (occasionally) me, and I was not unlike a curious alien from outer space wondering what were these people getting upset about? I mean, like really, *who cares*? It's not like anyone here actually knew the guy.

I saw lots of people cared. While I was loading my bike with boxes of fruit, a black woman walked by me with tears streaming unashamedly down her face. Within minutes I was negotiating between lanes of traffic, and in those days many car radios didn't work all that well. A young guy leaned out his driver's window at a red light.

"Hey kid," he yelled, "any news about the President?" What I heard in his voice I had been hearing all morning, People were willing to believe some nut might have tried to hurt JFK, but nothing more than that was conceivable. As I turned on my bike to look at him, I zeroed in on his calm yet concerned eyes.

"*He's dead!*" I exclaimed, not wavering in my stare. He disintegrated, and I felt much the voyeur as his shocked emotions poured out through his anguished eyes. Of course I also got very upset when I learned they would be closing the racetrack that weekend.

Spring arrived and I had saved up over $400 during the course of the winter break while the track closed for the cold months. This was at a time when you could buy a new Pontiac GTO for under $3,000, and a decent two-bedroom apartment in a nice section of Brooklyn could be had for under $80 a month. On opening day in the Spring of 1964, I cut my afternoon classes, took nearly all my savings, and, by chasing my losses, broke-out before the week ended. When the subject arose a week later – as my mother realized I had blown all my money – an interesting interplay occurred.

She totally freaked out, which was highly unusual. I said something like "*easy come, easy go,*" which was exceptionally stupid considering I had worked over forty-hours per week after school in snow, sleet and rain that Fall, Winter and early Spring to accumulate that much money. My mother turned on my father.

"*This is your fault! Taking him to the racetrack every week! I should have known!*" (duh!)

My father laughed, pretending anger the way a father does when he catches his son in bed with a girlfriend and is then supposed to scold him. You could tell there was a note of pride in his voice as he laughingly protested, "*I had nothing to do with it! What do you want from me?*"

Racism in Brooklyn

As I graduated high school I experienced what would become the worst ethnic or racial episode of my Brooklyn life. Usually, the neighborhood bullies were made up of diverse groupings of Jews, Italians, Germans and Irish, with the occasional Polock thrown in. There was no discrimination amongst those who might shake you down for money, a nice pocketknife you were too stupid to hide, or simply just push you around to make themselves feel better. That's when you're kids.

Now, it's that time of life and all the kids in my old neighborhood are graduating. It's that special weekend evening on a warm June night when school is over for most of the peer group. Although I skipped the graduation ceremony and Prom, I have won a New York State Regents Scholarship and gained entrance into Fisher College in uptown Manhattan.

The scholarship is the result of my high marks on a single test. I have the lowest average in my graduating class to win such a Scholarship and was occasionally tickled to hear other kids at school exclaim in amazement: "***You** won a Regents Scholarship?*" But it is also somewhat disconcerting as I find myself not unlike the nerd who's shocked to find out that others think he's a nerd.

But I am the toast of my middle class Jewish mother. She is walking on air as letters arrive from Governor Rockefeller, the local Senator and Assemblyman, and all the phone calls with busybody relatives now put her proudly in the limelight.

Consequently, I am in an unsettled glow of uncomfortable self-inflation as I walk around my old neighborhood on a June night after graduation. I am somewhat conflicted trying to force myself to look, sound and feel like a winner. It's a garment that doesn't really fit. Nevertheless, I am spreading myself around like cheese announcing to all who ask my impending march to uptown academia crowned with the word "scholarship." Rick and I arrive at Geizler's Ice Cream and Soda Fountain to treat ourselves to something special.

A local Italian kid who I've seen off and on around the neighborhood for years is crowing about the good news he had received. When asked for particulars, he announces that his uncle had gotten him a union card, and he named the starting hourly wage he would receive, bursting with pride.

Talk was made about our future as well, and I, being mean and unsure of myself, saw the temporary look of insecurity when he repeated:

"You... you're going.. you're both goin'... to college? And you won a scholarship?"

I pressed in. "Yeah, Leo, college. What's gonna' become of you guys, you Italians, if you don't go to college?"

"Ahh," he said, waving a hand at me, "if wee'ze so bad how come yuz sistahs awl gowout widdus, huh?

He had us. Both our older sisters dated Italian boys. Feeling like an asshole, I looked down into my malted, noting it had lost its allure. Thus concluded the worst ethnic confrontation of my growing-up-in-the-Brooklyn-melting pot. Sure we had *Murder Incorporated* and you could bet a number at almost any candy store, but burglaries and muggings were unheard of, and in our neighborhood most people forgot to lock their front doors at night, and I can't remember hearing of anyone regretting it.

Biting the Big Apple

Having taken the 7th, 8th and 9th grades in a special two-year program, I graduated high school at sixteen. I wound up getting a Summer mail-clerk's job at a famous department store in uptown Manhattan.

I was introduced to a supervisory mail clerk in his early twenties. After showing me my duties, he suggested we take a break, and within this time confided to me, with a surreptitious lowering of his voice as well as a peek down the hall to insure our privacy, that I would no doubt sooner or later meet Jerry, who was someone I should apparently know about.

"He's a fag," my assistant supervisor shared excitedly, and immediately alluded to the fact that he might have seduced the last mail clerk, or had tried to. My new boss then demonstrated his sensitivity to our libidinous co-worker: "I once mixed glue, you know that grey-color paper glue? I mixed some with water, and I held the jar up to him and licked my lips, and said, "hey Jerry, oohmm, we all jerked off in here for you."

He seemed somewhat concerned later when I shrugged my shoulders in nonchalance to his admonition to be careful. I appeared unmoved at the idea that the previous clerk might have gotten off with Jerry. *'Who wouldn't want to get his dick sucked?'* was my unspoken attitude towards being a sophisticate in the big city.

Jerry worked directly under the people who decided what the mannequins wore, and how and where they would be placed. He would work any hours without complaint pushing racks of clothing all over the store, dressing mannequins and working like a man possessed, which he certainly was.

About three days after starting there, I entered the area where he worked and, after placing some mail in the box, noticed a slim young man blatantly looking me up and down. He placed his hand to his throat and gushed,

"My Gawd! Honey, wait a minute. Who are you and where did you come from?" He swished over to me, continuing to look me up and down.

"Uhh, I was hired three days ago. I'm the new guy in the mailroom."

Exaggerating his words theatrically, he demanded:

"You *must* tell me *immediately* what your name is."

"Marty," I smiled shyly.

"Marty," he said, as he came close to me, his right hand held up by his throat in a feminine mannerism, his left lightly touching my arm. "Are you fucking any of these girls that work here?"

"No," I said, backing away almost defensively "I just started working here. But some are pretty nice," I added, not knowing what else to say, while another part of me thrilled over his fingers touching my arm.

"Do you get laid a lot?"

"No, but I'll be seventeen next week. Maybe that'll change."

"I'll bet your girlfriend... (He got within inches of my face while looking down the hall) sucks your cock all the time, doesn't she?" he asked, turning his face so it was real close to mine.

"I.. I.. I don't have a girlfriend."

Bet you wouldn't mind letting her give you a blowjob though, would you?

"Wouldn't mind at all," I added laughing a little.

"I bet you've got a big cock."

"Uhh..."

"You've got a big dick. I know you do. When you deliver the 3pm maildrop, try to come a few minutes early. I have to show you something. It's important. Be early if you can."

I found half my brain immediately froze and the rest of it was stumbling over my schedule so as to explain the ins and outs of being there at that time. The three-o'clock secret turned out to be a locked storage room that he had the key for.

Once inside, the atmosphere was claustrophobic with sexual excitement.

"Oh gawd, he simpered, "let me see it. That's all, just let me look at it."

"Are you crazy?" I said, exaggerating my surprise and looking around as if people could see us.

" No, it's OK, it really is. It's locked. I just want to see it, that's all."

I remained inert long enough for him to read my passivity loud and clear.

"Let me just *look*," he said, sing-songing the last word so it sounded like "loo-uhk." He came closer to me and opened his left hand so the palm gently caressed the growing bulge of my tight jeans. He moaned like he was feeling the most wonderful thing in the world. I gasped to experience the pleasurable jolt as excitement and the promise of more pleasure overwhelmed my consciousness.

He got the signal. Without waiting for any more response, he got on his knees in front of me. He proceeded to tug my belt open while I stood shocked still, amazed and watching as he unbuckled, unbuttoned and unzipped my jeans, and after pulling down my white jockey shorts with surprising force, murmured with approval as he took my semi-engorged state into his urgent mouth.

"I thought you were only going to look at it," I said, playing the simpleton for something to hide behind.

He looked up and smiled with his eyes, and I was grateful for his boldness, his sexual aggression. It might have been my cock being serviced by his wet and greedy mouth, but in terms of who the aggressor was there was no doubt it belonged to the man on his knees. As I approached orgasm, however, I was struck by the flood of aggressive feelings sweeping through my otherwise passive sexuality. The orgasm into his choking mouth was not only extremely pleasurable, but seemed to hold within it a sense that he would not only receive my bodily fluid but along with it something of my attitude as well. As he took me over the top, gagging and choking on my release, I was seized by a wild energy to use him selfishly in any way possible for my pleasure.

As I gasped with a total relief that made my knees buckle, he gagged and I sneered down when he looked up at me. I didn't know what else to do. While I was no doubt naïve and inexperienced, I sensed he was neither disturbed nor disappointed by my arrogance. Somehow, even within my dim teenage mindset, I knew that far from being upset with my sudden and surprising belligerence, he welcomed and was somehow gratified by it. His look back at me filled me with a curious sensation apart from my shuddering physical pleasure. With the peak now over, however, I couldn't help but feel I was the one being used – and as I suddenly wished I was anywhere else – he continued to urge the last drops out of my wilting unit into his hungry mouth.

There was an additional bizarre and alien quality to this sexual act taking place in this sterile storeroom. It's cold, lifeless walls filled with business paraphernalia stacked on metal shelving, the noise outside the door full of the humdrum tedium of big business and retail clothing, all contributed to the bizarre nature of what had just taken place.

As the days passed into weeks, there continued to be something "other-worldly" concerning this experience of stuffing envelopes and sorting mail one minute, then closing a door and having my penis sucked into orgasm the next.

I would leave for work with almost no thought of Jerry, just as if the entire experience had been a dream. Just as in a dream one can have the most emotional reaction, which turns into reflective thought upon awakening, so too my consciousness of Jerry when I was at home or on the way to work was only the most meager portion of what would later be a dynamic gasping experience. It was simply out of sight, out of mind.

I told Rick about it, and he didn't flinch. He came to visit me at work once, and didn't shy away from meeting with Jerry, especially after I told him that Jerry swallowed. Jerry was too busy with work to shake free that day to do Rick, but what became apparent to me only later was my refusal to see at the time that Rick would also like his cock sucked by a guy, but that somehow the idea of getting together with Rick never occurred to me.

Is it heaven or the hell that keeps me from diving in with my best friend? My denial of wanting to have sex with my best friend was now as bizarre as it was complete.

Fisher College and Young Love

In September 1964, I entered Fisher College in uptown Manhattan. It was just a building, and not as large as my high school. For all extensive purposes, the campus was Central Park.

I was still a terrible student and didn't care for school at all. Classes ranged from intimidating to tedious to boring. By cutting classes and/or not doing homework, the time spent in class became even more intimidating. I was running C's and D's and after staggering across the finish-line in June, received a note to meet with the school counselor. *"Take a year off,"* he said. *"Regents Scholarship winners shouldn't flunk out of school. He should see a shrink,"* he added to my mom when they spoke later. One was immediately produced, and I needed to see him badly. I had my first hot girlfriend, and my sexual chickens had come home to roost.

Not that I wanted to see, think or talk about these penile poultry, but I had to do something. My 16 year-old girlfriend's thing was so wet, hot and available that it was driving me crazy. Once inside, however, my aching rock hard extension would soon turn to rubber. My mind would start to enter territory that apparently was not acceptable to libidinous considerations, and what was stiff wood would turn to limp rubber the moment my mind hesitated to go down the road my fantasy envisioned.

In speaking with the shrink, I was far too traumatized to speak of these things nor my devastated childhood, but was able to apparently blurt out enough discomforting items to progress somewhat with the additional knowledge of jellies and condoms. I guess simply speaking about these matters to him even in a groping, stumbling manner helped somewhat.

I had learned some things and puzzled over others. My girlfriend's clothes – not to mention underclothes - had a magical effect on me. One night I became fascinated with a top she was wearing; a shiny-velvety snug-fitting thing that made her breasts feel like heaven through the material. I had been hypnotized by it all evening. Her parents finally went out and all our clothes came off. Later, when she was in the bathroom, I leaned over the edge of the bed and saw the top lying on the floor. I picked it up. I found myself stupidly surprised with the realization that it was just cloth. I couldn't get my mind around that… that I was somewhat surprised to find it was only…material.

When I asked her for some head, she replied "make me" in a teasing enough way that any normal male would have been delighted to pressure this willing and beautiful young girl into pleasuring him orally, but being aggressive was not my long suit. My after-date activity one night upon leaving her house shed some light on why neither of us were getting much satisfaction sexually at the time.

I was on the way home from her house, taking one bus and then waiting for yet another when a beautiful '64 Bonneville going the other way hit his brakes and hung a u-turn, slowing to pull up to me at the bus stop.

"Hi" came the drawn out feminine-sounding voice from the stocky young guy in the passenger seat. "Can we give you a lift?"

When I said, "OK," he got out and I got in the middle, all three of us in the front seat.

"Ooh, so where are you coming from?"

"My girlfriend's. Wow, this car is *so* boss. I've driven one just like this, and when you really punch it, and you feel that hesitation as the carb breathes in that four-barrel… *vhoom*, it just snaps your head back. This is like, so…."

"Did you get any head tonight on your date?"

"Uhhh, no."

"Laid?"

"No."

"Hmmm, that's too *baad*" he sing-songs, putting his hand on my leg. "Wanna little? he says in a low voice. "Go for a little head? We have a place."

These guys were really making me nervous. "Well," I said, hesitating to deal with that two-percent of my mind suddenly still working. "I have to be home before three."

All I remember about their apartment was the bedroom, which was scented very heavily and had all kinds of drapes and plumes and interesting artifacts. They also had a large parrot that had to have its cage covered with a sheet or else it gave off a very loud screech. They covered the parrot and took turns blowing me for a while but I was so nervous I couldn't come or even get hard. I could not relax at all. I think I spent a lot of time hyperventilating.

The short one called Freddie wore orange satin panties. The other guy was a tall blonde hardbody who was very well grown with a foreskin that had been snipped right around the slit, giving it a kind of grotesque attraction.

I found the texture of the foreskin kind of slimy and it made me gag and retch almost as soon as I put it in my mouth. My previous experiences were with Jewish guys. Even the two abusers from Pigtown were "cut." This guy wasn't.

I apologized that I couldn't seem to get into it. He asked me to jerk him off, which I did. That was kinda' interesting, as the sensation that it hardens and seems to get a life of its own is felt in a much different way than when my hand manipulated my own. The excitement on my part was heightened as his jagged breathing and gasping pleasure erupted in tandem to my hand's activity.

Freddie was also uncircumcised and I couldn't keep him in my mouth long either. He tried to sodomize me, but as I was a virgin there and very tight, I yelled that it hurt too much, so we stopped. On the ride taking me home they mentioned they could be found often late at night at Garfields, the all night cafeteria. They let me off at home, and I never saw them again, but would years later fantasize about going back there, Freddie's orange panties an occasional glowing reminder of temptations darkly imagined for a naughty and nasty night.

I never could remember where they lived, either. I was totally scattered about things like that. A friend of a friend took me along to a prostitute one night in 1963. I was 16. We went up to an apartment in the upper 90's on Manhattan's East side. The living room served as a waiting room with magazines for a bunch of us. Her uncle collected the $2 from each of us. Then it was my turn.

She was a surprisingly attractive young Puerto Rican girl with a pleasant smile and appeared quite mysterious in the seductive low light. There was heavy incense in the air and her perfume and lingerie helped make the scene intriguing and exciting. She pinned me for a virgin immediately, and seemed pleased at the idea. Her Latina accent worked the entire episode from a potentially cold sex-act into a low-light mysterious encounter. She really made an effort to put me at ease and gave me great head for a while and soon I was almost coming. She stopped and laid back, guiding me into her. The sexual intercourse was quick, uncomplicated and definitely enjoyable. I wanted to go down on her afterwards and started initial kisses and some licking, but – despite her words of encouragement – soon stopped. I think the sudden newness of everything; the touch, taste, odor and texture mixing with the idea of all the other guys depositing in there probably all contributed to my ceasing of what was to me surprising behavior. I had never thought about going down on the prostitute, and yet, after spending myself, was nonetheless attracted enough to the enterprise to actually initiate the behavior without much thought.

What before had been academic understanding of the rudiments of nature, reproduction and sexual pleasure was now affirmed into life experience, and the urge to sink deep into fantasy had not even been an issue. I had humped along unthinking in the missionary position and had achieved release with a pleasurable roller-coaster ride. It wasn't the screaming trips into other-world excitement that later sex would demand as its goal. But like I said, I was scattered about addresses, and could never remember where it was to go back again.

I went to a different whorehouse months later. While looking at a slim, fairly attractive brunette standing next to the pimp/night clerk at this rundown hotel in Manhattan, I decided to ask for a blonde. For some inexplicable reason, I had assumed my blonde would look like the brunette except for hair color. I had to walk up two flights past two very attractive Puerto Rican hookers smoking cigarettes next to their open room doors talking to each other on the landing. Their brazen and provocative looks had my head spinning as I arrived one-flight further up to find my blonde: A middle-aged lazy hag with a bad attitude. As soon as I walked in, her phone rang and the desk clerk spoke to her and she said to me "30 minutes." She was ugly and cold and when she smiled it was so phony you sensed that she wanted you to know it was phony. It's the hooker's hostile smile that steals your money while she takes your lust. Too lazy to take off her clothes – and me too tentative to say anything – she had me get naked and then hiked up her nightshift. It was awful and I couldn't wait to finish and leave, slinking out quickly.

Wall Street

I had been given a motorcycle as I approached my eighteenth birthday. I got a job in Wall Street as a Purchase and Sales clerk in the back office of a small brokerage house. Working was good for me, and it was fun to weave in and out of traffic on my bike.

I got to do important stuff for the manager of my department. After the nine-to-fivers left, he would call me over and peel off some bills, rhetorically asking aloud, *"Let's see, should we go for a Red Label, or maybe Black. Well, let's get six tall ones and a Red label. What d'ya think?"*

I would go down to the liquor store, and bring back a six-pack and a bottle of Johnny Walker. Often a couple of our brokers – the guys from the Exchange floor – would come up and drink with my manager, swapping war stories of the power players, who did what and which games, gimmicks and shenanigans were in the works. I understood little, and would occasionally have a beer, which would make me totally blotto, much to my boss's amusement. Before Christmas, one of the partner's came around handing out cash envelopes. Even though I had only been there since October I was given a week's pay, which I thought was pretty nice. My Wall Street education kept up through the late Spring, and I was ready to return to Fisher in the Fall. I was seeing the shrink and making some progress – towards what end I was not sure.

Red Flags and Stop Signs

It is a clear and warm June day as I am passing the Parade Grounds in Brooklyn on my Honda Scrambler. I am zapped by a sexual vibration from a blonde in tight Clam Diggers and a soft sweater walking towards me, and an energy burst seemed to appear, coming out of my midsection and into this creature. It was not unlike something from a *Star Trek* phaser-on-stun; a translucent field moving as a kind of glass funnel which came out of me. She was on the other side of the street walking towards me and I passed and turned my bike around thinking '*I don't know what I'm going to say*' and surprised myself even more by acknowledging that I didn't care. This was one-hundred-eighty degrees '*not-Marty.*' Although I had never picked up a girl in my life, I was just goin' for it.

I pulled up to the curb as she reached the entrance to her apartment house. I called. She turned and smiled, coming over. My heart and brain froze. She had me from the moment I heard the sound of her voice. Throaty and sexy, erotic innuendo peppered her easy conversation as I put the bike up on its stand and I turned around in my seat facing her. She climbed on the back passenger seat. Her scent, eyes, voice and outrageous attitude totally captured my consciousness. Sitting less than a foot away from each other, little red flags were going off in the back of mind. They dimly whispered '*something's wrong with this picture*' but I was only aware of the bulging excitement within my green jeans. She seemed to notice it as well.

As a sex act begins between partners new to one another, low lights are normal, but this was ink-black space. I knew deep down there was a reason. I soon discovered the most important one: I wouldn't see her tiny cock, for example, when she guided my hard-on into her ass after fellating me. I climbed heights and it seemed so right – and definitely better. There was no mental conflicts to deter my hard-on. It felt different. Tighter, hotter and greasier, I knew what it was and simply didn't care. I felt nasty, elated, realized, and alive. Playing by my own rules, I was suddenly a man-of-the-world, doing and taking what I wanted for my own satisfaction.

Now it is afterglow but now it is also after-wards. Low light is on, and the faint smell of shit wafts up off my cock as I turn under the thin covers. We are on our sides looking at each other. She is apprehensive, although trying not to show it. This is the moment that she knows that I know beyond any doubt she's a boy. She's been here before and sometimes men have violent reactions at this juncture when they realize they've been with a drag queen and not a female. Still heavily satiated from the powerful orgasm, I surprise myself how calm and at ease I am, sensing that something in me wants to serve something more in her. Whether out of rebellion or in tune with a kindred spirit – or both - I am pleasantly relaxed and satisfied.

I look at her face and raise up my right hand and gently calm away her flinch by stroking her left cheek, moving closer to kiss her lips gently, pulling back a little to touch her cheek again with my fingers, gliding them down slowly from her cheekbone to her lips. I keep them there and look at her. I feel good. I have done something forbidden and pleasurable. I see her consciousness fill with bliss and I'm thrilled to be doing something so different, naughty, nasty and rebellious, and at the same time making her so happy. Her return gaze impresses itself in my mind, and although I had climaxed a short time before, I sense a tingling anew even in my shrunken state. She embraces me with such a clenching bear hug of relief that even as an inexperienced seventeen year-old, I understood this was almost pathological in its intensity. I find myself in the strange position of the naïve teen having to calm down the worldly drag queen.

I soon close my eyes. She turns and we spoon, and I softly kiss the back of her neck before dozing off. I awake to hear her suggestion that she clean me with a warm washcloth she has in her hand. She's got on lingerie now and a black satin kerchief is attached to the wrist not occupied by the washcloth. I soon begin to arouse, blurting out to my own surprise "*you may wind up cleaning this twice*" as I pull her towards me. She does the "*Oh, my gawd thing*" in that teasing transsexual voice which seduces me into hardness instantly.

Progress

"You mean his cheek," Doctor D'Ambrosio says softly.
I don't get it right away, and wrinkle up my forehead.
"His cheek," my analyst repeats.
"Oh," I say, the dim light is getting a little brighter.
"You say 'her,' but this Brandi, is, a man," he adds softly, neutrally.

"Yes," I agree, as if to say *is there something significant to this?* "but I can only think of her as female," I add, laughing and shrugging, while I excitedly gush:

"And it's so wild, my dad drove by while she was on the back of my bike while I was talking to my friend Rick, and neither one pinned her. She's what's called 'passing.' Her friends at the apartment told me that's what her situation is. She also strips at some weird gangster place. She had me come one night. There are other girls as bizarre as her there, but you can easily tell they're boys. One introduced herself to me by jumping in the back seat as we pulled up to the place, giving me a big kiss – on the lips – saying *'It's OK honey, I'm a lesbian.'* But of course she wasn't a lesbian, she was like Brandi. There's all these characters at Brandi's apartment, too. I think one is a real woman, a prostitute. She's not there much though; kind of rents the other bedroom when she needs it. She was really angry the other day because she brought a 'John' – that's a customer – into the apartment but the bed and bedroom was all messy. She had told the guy that it was her apartment, but when he saw strangers had been using the disheveled bed he backed out and she lost the money and a customer. She was screaming about how much money she lost. I've been thinking of what it would be like to pay her to have sex with me, but I don't know if that would really happen with Brandi and all."

Are you interested in having sex with the prostitute? Doctor D'Ambrosio asks.

"Well, wait a minute; I've got to say something or I'll lose my nerve."

The good doctor makes a graceful gesture and I jump in.

"If I don't say it now it'll haunt me all week. I put his dick - Brandi's - it's real tiny - in my mouth. I wanted to try it. It was all slimy and I gagged and felt revolted, like I would throw up. But I do like having the other sex with her. It's so different, I like it," I add full of animated teenage excitement. "And she wants me to go up to Montreal when she plays up there. She's gonna send *me* a plane ticket!"

"But naw," I add, turning my head away and pushing away this point of view with my two hands, "I don't really care about the prostitute. She's not as good looking as Brandi anyway," I conclude, almost as if speaking to myself. I shrug my shoulders to make the point more obvious, not realizing the irony.

While I couldn't put it into words – to myself or to my doctor - was that a strange transformation was taking place by *not* taking place. The other fags who shared Brandi's apartment were waiting and wanting for me to fem out, and while in my previous fantasies (and real-life opportunities with the hitchhiking and to some degree Rick), the idea of taking the female role had appeared attractive, now that the opportunity was everywhere, I had no desire to.

Brandi had talked to me about meeting Jason, the mobster who owned the club she stripped at, and who apparently liked his girls to be guys, and I realized without thinking it through that he probably was not interested in me sticking my thing up *his* ass, but the reverse situation would probably be very much the case. I was too uptight to mention these concerns to Brandi or my shrink, of course. It seemed life happened to me only while I was unconscious.

Brandi had gotten me a plane ticket and I flew to Montreal to be with her for a weekend and watch her work at a bizarre transsexual nightclub. We stayed at a small apartment house that was guarded by some very hard looking guys. One night, as we returned to the apartment staggeringly drunk, I saw what-I-later-realized-was-a-guard standing there. I started to say something I thought smart in my drunken eighteen year-old brain when Brandi said in a most unBrandi-like tone that I should keep my mouth shut instantly. I muttered an apology and she again told me in a tone most serious not to say anything more.

Dr. D'Ambrosio looks at me differently. He is kind of smiling, I think. He then surprises me:

"We're having a guest speaker next month. I'm acting President of the Brooklyn Psychoanalytic Association this year and I think you'd enjoy hearing this speaker. He has a very different point of view on things. I'll have complimentary tickets for you."

"Sure, what's his name?"

"Tim Leary."

Leary is to fly into New York for the speech but is arrested in Detroit.

During that same time, I experienced a moment that broke through my sexual myopia. I had slept over Brandi's, and woke up first. The sunlight on his face revealing the facial stubble not yet shaven off, plus the makeup gone or smeared all contributed to a picture of reality that was affecting me in a new way. A light of realization was shining inside a (new) place that hadn't seen it this way before. I simply became aware in a deep and more complete way that Brandi was just a skinny boy with doctored tits, and the magical attraction was over.

Soon I no longer looked forward to being with Brandi. He would call me at my parent's house and whine and cajole for me to come over, but I soon no longer wanted to. And soon I no longer did.

Chapter 5 – Coming of Age in Greenwich Village

In the Summer prior to returning to Fisher I tried marijuana. I was at a frat club of sorts. Not like a normal clean-cut Fraternity House, this was a beat-up storefront converted to a low-rent party place replete with fisherman's net hanging from the ceiling below light bulbs of blue and red. Slow jazz was on the box and there were just three of us. I inhaled the smoke and soon felt a sense of expanded unreality creep over my consciousness in the dimly lit setting. Yet there was something about the unreality that held a promise of heightened insight over the old reality seen now from a different point of view. A sense of *"this is really cool"* became attached not only to the dim atmosphere with the bloozy music, but to the sense of the change itself. I felt I could sit here changed forever, just as Otis Redding was talking about the dock of the bay. I saw that not everyone reacted that way. Another first-time smoker was trying to stand on his head with a 'look-at-me' attitude.

It was the Summer of 1967 and I wanted to get my own apartment. The East Village was "in" and I found my own place for $66 a month.

Upon my return to school – and without any apparent effort – I began to be a popular guy around the college. Ever since my adventure with Brandi, I had an entirely new and easy attitude around girls. I wanted to have sex with them all, but I didn't care all that much if they shot me down when I tried to pick them up. I found I was seldom at a loss for words, and things I said were not what they were used to hearing. After being around all the raging queens, fags and prostitutes at Brandi's, these middle class college girls didn't seem very intimidating at all.

I had let my hair grow long, bought my first pair of Beatle boots the year before, and if I deigned to flirt with a girl in class or in the lunchroom, she was soon looking for my smile when our eyes met the next time. My confidence soared, and when I scored with a girl I had long sought after (albeit with a world record for premature ejaculation), I found she wanted her own key to my new Village apartment.

As for cannabis, I found what was to become my "gift" for my entire life when it came to scoring drugs (of any kind): I 'connected.' From simply being in the right place at the right time, I had found a great connection for kilo bricks from Mexico. They were filled with stems and seeds and sometimes still damp – as the water added to their weight – but I was able to sell nickels and dimes at Fisher, and easily recouped my money four or five times over, allowing me the luxury of smoking all I wanted for free as well as being able to dispense the weed socially with a certain carefree panache. Since I was on a scholarship to a "free" school, the check I received for a few hundred dollars a term set the snowball in motion. My middle-class parents were certainly not about to refuse me money if I said I needed extra for school anyway.

A kilo of pot was supposed to be 2.2 lbs., but after removing the more weightier stems, about twenty-five ounces were sellable. With a nickel bag equaling a quarter of an ounce, that came out to about $500 for a kilo if I was to sell it all in nickel bags. I was paying under $200, and could therefore afford to be both generous and stoned.

One Friday evening I left my apartment near Sixth Street near Avenue B and walked the few blocks to St. Marks Place, a block in the East Village that Dylan must have had in mind when he wrote *Desolation Row*. The *'circus was in town,'* as thousands of people hung out strolling around the various places sprouting up in time for the hippie revolution. I was in front of what used to be *"Balloon Farm"* when I heard someone call my name. It was somebody I knew vaguely from school. He was a friend of someone I knew a little better, and I had once taken a class with this guy. He was in a group of several people.

He was antsy and unsure so I immediately knew what he wanted before he asked. After looking left, right and wincing like he might get slapped in the face, he said in a low voice:

"You think you might have a nickel?"

"Not on me," I shrugged, *"but my place is just a few blocks away."* Noticing a tall, pretty girl with long hair and beautiful brown eyes in the group, I continued *"You want a nickel for all of you?"* I added good-naturedly with an easy laugh.

"Marty, all we have between us is seven dollars."

"Steve, it's Steve, right? *Joe's friend*?"

He nodded up and down, stuttering out, "Yeah, I'm Joe's..."

"Steve," I said, my tone quickly cutting him to silence, "it's Friday night. You've got ten people here," I waved, exaggerating the number in his party.

"Keep the seven dollars, I'll get you a dime, you pay me next week at school."

"Wow! Oh Marty, man, thanks!" he gushed. "Don't worry, I'll pay you as soon as I see you." He started to figure out loud when he gets paid from his part time job when I cut him off.

"Steve," I said, putting my hand on his shoulder. "I'm not worried about the money. I'll meet you back here in about a half hour."

"Cool, oh man, thanks!"

As I started walking away, I felt a soft presence falling into step next to me. The brown eyed girl.

"Mind if I walk along?"

"Not at all. I'm Marty," I said, gazing into brown eyes that I immediately longed to drown in.

"I'm Rhonda."

"Nice to meet ya." She was carrying a couple of large shopping bags. When she put them down and straightened up I could see her figure was to die for.

"So you're a dealer, huh?"

"Me? Nooo," I corrected with sincerity. "I sell some nickels and dimes just to be able to smoke for free with a little left over." I shrugged. "I pick up a key once in a while." My nonchalance was not an act. My racetrack experience had me betting this kind of money when I was in short pants.

"So, Steve's your friend?"

"We both go to Fisher. We know some of the same people."

We get to my place. A third floor walk up, it was typical of the East Village in the late sixties. A tiny main room with a half-a-fridge next to a bathtub with claw-feet and a scrawny nailed pipe coming up for a shower. The tub was covered with a board which could then double as a kitchen table. This main room had two large windows barred by iron movable gates to keep burglars from coming in off the fire escape, and a narrow door opposite the tub allowed for a tiny bathroom holding a small sink and a toilet.

The alcove to the bedroom allowed for a bed and dresser and I pushed aside the obligatory beads functioning as the door/curtain of the alcove and returned to the main room with a shoebox with about half-a-pound of pot, some coin envelopes and a postage scale to make the dime with.

Rhonda's eyes widened momentarily and I pretended not to notice. I weighed out his pot and we smoked and then got ready to leave.

"Do you mind if I leave these bags here? she asked. "I've been lugging these around all night. I'm supposed to be moving in with a friend but her phone got disconnected and I'm having a problem finding her."

"Sure," I said.

"I can come back and get them later."

"Whatever you *want*," I said, allowing the intonation of *anything goes* to creep into that elongated last word of longing. She took a small step to stand very close to me. We kissed, and her body was like nothing I had ever felt. It smoothed up against mine like liquid velvet, her soft wide mouth and tongue delicious, my senses melting into pleasure-filled mush.

We walked back to St. Marks Place and bestowed the dime on the eager group amidst hails and blessings, promises of fealty and everlasting gratitude. I asked Rhonda if she was hungry, and we narrowed down the possibilities to Perrogies at the Polocks, traditional pizza or the Italian sausage hero smothered in peppers and onions off the grill at a store-front pizzeria off of McDougal St. We decided on the latter, and we were soon back at my apartment.

"I'm in a bit of a mess," she said, coming out of the bathroom. I can't reach my girlfriend, and I don't know where I can stay tonight. My mom lives all the way out in Queens."

"Well," I said, reaching for the brass ring, "You can stay here," half-wondering if she'd insist I sleep on the floor, or worse, have us sleep in the same bed without having sex.

"Uhmm," she said, her brown eyes dancing mischievously while moving closer with a gliding sensuality. We embraced in another of those sensational kisses. "Sounds good to me," she added, walking into the alcove-bedroom. She smiled at me, and simply took her dress off, exposing her perfect teenage body, *sans* brassiere. She walked elegantly over to the bed, and with a panache I had never seen before, peeled off her panties and got under the sheets.

Getting in next to her, I was immediately aware of a certain comfort in the atmosphere that had always been missing before. As we kissed and embraced, and my hands roamed her body, there was such a sense of bliss that I just naturally hardened into the man I wanted to be. I would soon learn that Ronnie could felate in ways that would leave me breathless, and I found my premature problems simply vanishing. We spent the next couple of weeks fucking upwards of seven times a day (Ronnie said she once counted eight). I'm not sure if it was a result of a comfort zone developed because of my baby-step admissions to my shrink about my fantasies, or, as I would later discover, Ronnie had been a part-time stripper and hooker – but for whatever the reason – I definitely wasn't into sucking dick any more.

After three weeks of this Ronnie said she had something to tell me. She was three months pregnant. The father was not in the picture. She would have to go to live with her mother, she said, but she wasn't sure her mom would take her in, but she might get a bed in one of these houses for unwed mothers late in her term.

Silence. I thought about this.

I said, "If you want, why don't you just stay with me till you give birth? Ronnie shrieked, throwing her arms around me. It felt good. I guessed she had spotted me for a mark when we met, but we had gelled. She wasn't showing yet, was really great looking, said lots of cute and funny things and never complained. I didn't find out until after we broke up that she was only sixteen.

Psychedelic Conscious Expansion

I think it is necessary that the reader try to understand what is meant by my use of the term "psychedelic experience." While my earlier depictions of the experiences in 1967 might be helpful, their subjectivity could be off-putting. While terms such as 'Enlightenment,' 'Illumination,' "Buddhahood' have a certain meaning to most people, I have enjoyed the more pragmatic terminology employed by Alexander Shulgin in his description of the Plus++++ (Plus-four) experience written of in his first book PIHKAL ('*Phenethylamines I Have Known and Loved*" Transform Press 1991 pp. xxv):

> "*This is a separate and very special category, in a class by itself. The four pluses do not imply in any way that it is more than, or comparable to, a plus-three. It is a serene and magical state which is largely independent of what drug is used–if any drug at all–and might be called a "peak experience," in the terminology of the psychiatrist, Abraham Maslow. It cannot be repeated at will with a repetition of the experiment. Plus-four is that one-of-a-kind, mystical or even religious experience which will never be forgotten. It tends to bring about a deep change of perspective or life-direction in the person who is graced with it.*"

Chapter 6 – LSD Brings the Sexual Shadow[4]

    I had tried LSD a couple of times before. Or I thought I had. On two occasions I don't think it was real LSD. Probably weak doses or *Belladonna*, which was also making a brief appearance on the 1967 psychotropic stage. Brief, because in a matter of months chemists all over the country were discovering that with the right ingredients, you could make millions of hits of pure LSD in something smaller than your bathtub. Since LSD had been legal up till 1966, ingredients were not that hard to come by. Soon pure LSD was available everywhere for less than $5 a dose.

    I had gone to hear Tim Leary speak (finally) at the *Fillmore East*, a renovated movie theatre named after its more illustrious cousin, the *Fillmore West* in San Francisco. Definitely not the same lecture he would have given to the psychoanalytic group the year before, this was a *"how to take LSD to get the most benefit"* type of lecture. He was talking about the book he co-authored with Dr. Richard Alpert (aka Ram Dass) and Dr. Ralph Metzner. It was applying the LSD experience (*The Psychedelic Experience*) to the <u>Tibetan Book of the Dead</u>. It made no sense to me at all, and all I could remember was "'get in a quiet setting, and flow, don't react to thought, just flow out…" Well, that didn't mean too much to me at the time.

    A short time later I had taken what might have been a good dose of LSD but I wasn't in the proper mental set nor in the proper physical setting to "get off." Leary had explained that the "set" was your own mental preparation of quiet and introspection, and the "setting" was the physical scene you were in, regarding how conducive it was to propagating the potentiality within these drugs. My experience was like a rocket into outer space that didn't break free of the earth's gravitational field. I was still, however, several miles high. I was in fairly moderate energy transformations, and had that objectivity from the ego that – to a certain degree – makes one believe he or she can see all things clearly. It wasn't enlightenment, but it had me going somewhat in a spiritual direction.

---

[4] *Jungian theory speaks of a "Shadow" "un"conscious that holds all the things about ourselves we refuse to see in ourselves, as far as our accepted notion of our "personna," or as we like to appear to ourselves and others.*

Word around the East Village head shop was Tim Leary was going to be at some West Village haunt "doing something." I showed up at the *Café Wha?* and still surrounded by thick energy lines and a subtle wanding effect (called trails), I entered the jam-packed place to see Leary up on the stage. Jerry Rubin, Abbie Hoffman and people like that were there, and I got an "inside" look at politics, emotion and the group dynamic.

Leary started working the crowd.
"I know what you guys want to do!"
(Take more drugs?)
"Dance!"
(huh?)
"But we've got people killing innocent children on the other side of the world in Vietnam, and we've got to put a stop to it, right?"

A few voices in the crowd dutifully answered in the affirmative.

I could literally see the energy momentum of peer pressure working the room. To be acceptable, to be approved of, to rid yourself of the palpable pressure to conform, you had to go along with the emotional logic. The pressure was palpable.

Again, Leary from the stage: "We, the United States, are burning babies in Vietnam, and I think it's about time we stopped that, don't you?"

More support from the sheep this time, and I just watched it all happening, as people who had showed up on acid, or expecting to get some, were now being transformed into trained robots, yelling 'Yes' and 'No' on cue from the stage, bringing themselves into deeper states of commitment to further hypnotic submission.

Then Rubin or Abbey Hoffman came running to the stage in a fake army uniform with a big name tag pasted on it saying "General Waste-More-Land." I couldn't wait to leave.

I remember one guy in the crowd who was very highly vibed. He was like a live colored neon sign, while the rest of the people appeared almost gray. He kind of raised me up with a kind of telekinetic or telepathic scoping. It was quietly exhilarating. But the politicians soon extinguished our high.

The politically active had a tendency to do that. They wore hippie garb, grew their hair long and talked-the-drug-talk, but sitting down to smoke dope with these people always reminded me of the boring containment experiences I was forced to endure visiting my old Jewish Aunts and Uncles. These hippies - with their economic, political and social mindsets - often seemed to remain totally straight, no matter what drugs they did, or they became angry assholes like the guy who abuses Jenny in *Forrest Gump* - the Hunter Thompson types - who just simply never "got it." These people were bring-downs, plain and simple. Their idea of "bonding" was *"let's get mad at the man"* by reeling off complaints about society in a paint-by-number stereotype of "us" against "them." They were like Sheriff Wiggins' kids from the Simpsons, but with high verbal scores and Marxist-painted eyeglasses. It sounded cool to be angry and destructive, and these 'hippies' never failed to bring me down whenever they appeared. The guys from Yale who were deep into *Purple Owsley* wore sports jackets, but they were journeying into the cosmos.

Trouble in paradise on the home front.: The Puerto Ricans who ganged up the neighborhood outside my Lower East Side apartment accused us of selling grass without giving them any. They were 100% right. One had come to my friend's window with the threat of a gun, had robbed my friend of *his* rifle on this bluff, shook us up and we all decided to leave the Lower East Side for Brooklyn.

Now this "friend" was not someone I was simpatico with – the fact of the matter, which I had difficulty in admitting to myself, was that he made me uncomfortable – especially when we got high. Larry had been asking if he could stay with us in our new place if he couldn't find a place of his own. Since we were in the grass trade together and the robber had come to his apartment to hold us all up, I allowed that excuse to help intimidate or persuade, and I folded under the pressure. Nothing new in that, but it was a decision which was to have ominous consequences.

Rhonda and I find out we can only move into our new Brooklyn digs the day after moving out of the Village apartment. I discover we can stay at my Aunt and Uncle's house on Long Island for one night because everyone there except one younger cousin was out of town. We decided we would take some LSD at my cousin's house, and we are suddenly like hobos-on-holiday; feeling pretty excited and care-free. We will sleep in the same bedroom I almost murdered my cousin in seven years before.

I was expecting the same effects I had experienced in the past when I had "dropped acid." Some brief interludes of sensory alteration with increased emotionless insight. Maybe some "trails" where you slowly wave one hand and see a few hands following it. It would be a fun way to spend the night with Ronnie as we adventured away from the East Village and into Brooklyn dappled and starry eyed.

I had gotten the tablets from some guys I met who went to Yale. It was called *Purple Owsley* after a chemist of the same name. About an hour after swallowing our purple tablets, Ronnie and I were sitting upstairs in my Aunt and Uncle's living room, and as my cousin left the room, I realized I bore no ill will towards the young man A kind of unemotional and neutral state came over me, which, strangely enough, appeared perfect to seal the strange spiritual state stealing over me. I noticed that I wasn't thinking any thoughts in the way reverie normally enters consciousness, as if my mind had been emptied of its normal processes and mental chatter.

The Doors were starting up *Light My Fire* on Ronnie's boombox and a guitar chord took my thoughts along for the ride further and further out to the edge of the universe where I bade normal reality goodbye and sailed out into paradise. Colors that don't exist here on earth filled my mind, my consciousness, and my total *being*. Marty no longer existed. I found the more I let go whenever thought returned to *"me"* or didn't react to whatever thought returned to *"my mind"* the more dazzling shapes and colors I got – along with hints of cosmic understandings beyond any man's wisdom. As I allowed my mind to "turn off," I was taken into mansions of greater and greater paradise where mysteries of life were effortlessly revealed, but I would later see that these things could not be retained by my ego-dominated mind. What is "un" conscious cannot be made conscious. What is of the spirit cannot be handled by the ego.

I would mentally return to the living room filled with the understanding that all it took to go up into heaven was to remember to be effortless. By doing so, - or literally doing no-thing – not *doing* – a door opened deep in my psyche to a collective unconscious/heaven which nothing on earth could have prepared me for. It was like having the effects of the drug introduced into my system by *my own mental decision* to simply be effortless. It could all be "controlled" by turning off my "controlling" thought process, and by 'floating downstream,' as Leary and the Beatles had recently been telling me and the rest of the world. I was experiencing a universe unlike anything I had ever heard about, read about or imagined existed.

There was no way of telling how much time actually transpired before I "returned" to the radio announcer's voice on the radio. I was becoming aware of consciousness and mental concepts on an incredible cosmic scale, and I saw what Leary had been trying to say in his lecture: that the key to the entire experience is to just to let go and let your thoughts float off – as far out as you can, and I'd be suddenly *"tripping."* Far from the drug appearing to *"do"* anything, it seemed that it's entire purpose was to bring one to a doorway of sorts in which the stillness of the moment allowed a crack in time where eternity could be entered.

I was also inspired to realize that the *coin-of-the-realm* with which to navigate in this strange universe was love! The idea that *"all you need is love"* seemed to reinforce the spiritual logic that this enlightenment had nothing to do with any pharmaceutical element in the drug. It was not a kissy-face emotional love either. It was a state of trustful not-hating.

The colors and energy waves had dissipated somewhat with my eyes now open, and I glanced at Ronnie. I could tell she was in trouble. She was anxious and scared while her outer personality tried to put on a persona of cool control when she noticed my glance.

I was experiencing true joy and a real love for her, and I so wanted her to experience what I had just experienced that I started to communicate what she needed to do, but my personality/ego apparatus was not even close to being connected and working. Nor was my understanding. Hurtling on recklessly, however, I unthinkingly took on the role of "guide" while ignoring the egotistical indelicacy of assigning myself that role. The super-ego cultural sensor – by which I discerned Ronnie's ego-needs - was in another universe, and all kinds of mental concepts were being made known to various disconnected stages of my personality as I attempted to hook up my voice with what I thought I wanted to say. Finally, I haltingly and falteringly blurted out something like *"if you just relax and let your mind flow…"* and she whirled on me… smirked, and said in an airy dismissive tone, *"first time you've dropped acid, huh?"*

At first I didn't have so much "thought" as I did experience pictures with large letters spelling E-G-O and symbols of the game Ronnie was playing on me, and my hesitation to not respond spontaneously was the mistake which allowed for the intimidation to take effect. Hence I began to lose myself in the reaction to her, the resentment of her. I began to tumble mentally as under an emotional wave every bit the kind where the wave and the undertow flip you around helplessly. I saw myself filled with images representing lack of confidence on my part while I placed injustice to her part.

Somewhere my ego was scrambling and screaming *"Foul! I came down for you!"* I found love is a lot easier to consider when you're floating by yourself in a fifth-dimensional paradise. I was suddenly not a happy camper. My mind was literally tumbling with changing realities crashing and burning into unconscious worlds of *'good guy-bad-guy'* thought. Vivid pictures playing ping-pong with judgmental and highly troubling energies overflowed my consciousness. Dizzying fruit from the tree of resentment sent me spinning into terrifying images, suddenly bruised and out of control.

Rhonda, after giving me a patronizing look, continued to play the wise old hand at LSD. Placing me in the role of the confused novice, she took control. Bringing out the persona of the temptress, she purred a sex vibe to suggest we ascend to the bedroom with the rhetorical question, *"Ya' ever make it on acid?"*

   Our love nest would be in the same bedroom in which I had almost murdered my older cousin seven years ago. The walk upstairs was accompanied by the continued falling into confusion and inability to remember what had happened in my *'psychedelic experience.'* I was utterly unable to deal with these changes I was going through.

   When one has been 'far out' into galaxies unspeakable, the homecoming is itself a magical experience of a sort not easily discerned. Magical and full of potential danger, who can say how much of the personality is being accurately reflected and/or effected in these animated states? The colors and shapes had not yet dissipated. They were still more like thick confetti or streamers continually in the air around me. Magic was everywhere, but not gaiety. Rather there were wounded feelings; gloom, hurt and betrayal with my body feeling like grayish rubber – as this texture reflected what the walls and bed looked like – as I lay down with Ronnie. I believed that to dive into sex was the only course of action to avoid a possible emotional schism with Rhonda, which was unthinkable for me at the time.

   I was surprised to realize that the phenomenon I could only discern as *colors* - were in reality much more. They were like signposts or buttons that grew into full-blown energies as I delved into the thoughts and emotions which they symbolized. They had dynamism in that way. They in turn formed sub-dynamisms of groups forming a *complex*. As I realized what was necessary for me to perform sexually, the colored air itself within these thin lines of energy began to come alive with the spirits that enveloped and ingested the fantasies of my sexual bedroom.

   The heavy outlines of multiple energies – not unlike neon – surrounded everything. Compared to the free-flowing jewels of my previously enlightened state, it was deadness now coming alive, but there was an electricity, a telepathy, that was not only unmistakable, but rapidly making me aware of my new realities. I had left heavenly realms to be seduced by the tawdry storefronts of 42nd and Broadway.

   There, amidst the dripping, melting browns and rubbery grays of my bum trip, Ronnie is pretending bliss as we embrace naked on the bed. I'm very far away from being excited sexually. But excitement was all around me, tempting me to allow it entrance. '*You know what you want, you know what you need*' seemed an ungrammatical tempting advertisement for hot sex 'on the edge of town.' It was as if the only way I could embrace these tempting sexual excitements was to pay them with my attention, and then that would lead to SUBMERGENCE. Living quicksand? Oh, it looks *way too dangerous*. I can't believe this is really happening. A thought sizzles through the soul: *'it's all real.' Yes, you. We're here for you. This IS you. The inside you. This is your sexuality!'* It was as if these small slivers of pastel colors were a jet-engine fuel and all it would take would be my spark of sexual submergence into imagination to make them come alive. The jet-fueled-mist was everywhere, spiritual energies just beyond my sight, but showing their presence in occasionally glowing opacities as I turned to give them attention. But I dissociate from them enough to know that to submerge into them is to offer my mind and body to be ravaged, invaded, to be re-created by something and in something over which I have no control, not even a separate *being*. These are infrahuman spirits that no self-system in this culture has ever been identified with.

I try to barter the degree of my own submergence; my worship, my becoming... in a world that's not so much imagination as it is subconscious complex, collective unconscious, or, in this deep reality, perhaps the truth of the matter is that all these concepts represent simply another name for the spirit world. *Can I just dip my toe in enough to get the job done*?

Ronnie had started to give me oral sex, which did absolutely nothing for me, and I immediately realized with horror that I was actually *shrinking more* under her skillful ministrations, until I decided to stop arguing, and... *capitulate*.

I surrendered my lust to the energy flow. I relaxed and in doing so crooned inwardly for deliverance by my unseen spirit, seeking to allow all those imaginative vulnerabilities to a lust which will marry my sexual submergence into hard body deliverance. I sought these tempting forces without censorship, without a thought for inhibition. As they entered and filled me I heard Ronnie moan even though my cock was still small and had not yet started to enlarge. I understood. The confetti colors of strips and spots grew quick and large into three and then four dimensions, and an inspired collection of live beings began to grow out of the air. A budding petal started to open peeling off its outer shell to reveal the emergence of something like a giant chute or pod with a Chiquita-banana pornstar emerging from the fruit of its upper center. Nothing laughable, her burning red-eyed gaze looked so deep into my soul there was no question of disobedience.

I surrendered and became that female spirit that was part of this fiery demon madam, and I assumed an identical role to that which Ronnie was giving to me. The pleasure, however, was being received by someone (or something?) else but using my body as a channel for that somebody (or something) else. As I became Ronnie I could feel how much I pleasured him, and cared not which name or real-world identity the demons threw out to put on the mysterious 'other.' Was it an enemy I was submitting to? Another male who intimidated me? I knew I dared not turn back into more culturally approved imagination, but wallowed and swallowed into the humiliation of seeing a boy from my class, then a social nemesis; each taking a turn, pleasured by the not-me of my feminine libido. I knew I would shrink to rubber the moment I took this soulish commitment off the accelerator to question what I was giving myself to... what I was really worshipping.

Now I was past such concern. With devotion I dove and drove deeper. I took them all, serviced each with gusto as the spirit willed, and the spirits coming up through this plantlike opening were unlike any representations I had ever seen on earth nor are their likenesses portrayed in any media ever created in the history of man.

The sexual energy-imagery was a plethora of spirits of wickedness, sadism and masochism, submissiveness and humiliation, degradation, domination and mischief; cuckold betrayal, half human, half demon, half male, half female and their hermaphrodite nature a mere signature of their inhumanity within all of us.

Shameless scenarios linked up to delirious excitement hardened my body bringing Ronnie's energy to a now raging life as well. As I entered her, endless faces of sensuality, sexuality, cunning, enslavement, humiliation and betrayal enveloped me, abused me, cuckolded me, and as the height of excitement and physical release approached, demanded greater commitment and a total submergence into this eager worship. As I gave up my mental, emotional and spiritual soul to it, Ronnie was crying out uncontrollably.

As I poured out my release into her eager body, a spirit which was to haunt me for forty years showed itself. As the orgasmic satisfaction plateaued my consciousness free of anxieties, a dramatic, devilish hermaphrodite with an intense opacity of yellow, red and fleshtone showed itself. It's blue eyes burned with a temptation that turned from teasing concupiscence to coldly hateful. It is part of the multidimensionality that I could realize two truths simultaneously:

One, it came to stay within my inner world, and it let me know just how it was going to set up residence, and/or

Two, it had been there growing as psychic larvae since my trauma at age five; I was just visiting it momentarily. *Hello there, see you in hell.*

It completed its demonstration and declaration in front of my eyes by turning and showing me its two perfectly round childlike buttocks as if in a desire to be sodomized, and then, bending slightly over as if in invitation to be entered, spun the one butt cheek on its left in an east to west 180 degree spin and the butt cheek on its right going west to east in a minus 180 degree spin; both staying in place anatomically but as if each butt cheek was spinning on its own axis away from the other; and so in doing so tore its own anus to pieces from its ripped-open dark middle, introducing the entrance of a greater spirit that it served by having its master emerge through this opening into my reality and thus acquaint me with true terrifying hellness with a hate the likes of which I am unable to describe. I tore silently shrieking like wet toilet paper shredding apart, and became deeply psychotic, finally finding a quiet place of relief by accepting my insanity and staying there throughout the post orgasmic afterglow for hours afterward.

I had fallen into a state of dull catatonia in which my mind stopped raging. The word "psychotic" floated across the theatre of my mind in big thick letters, but there was nobody left in the audience to care. I didn't have the energy – or I no longer existed – to care any more. I reintegrated into "reality" within a few hours.

The next day we moved into our Brooklyn apartment. We decided we'd been through some *'pretty heavy tripping,"* so in order to be responsible, we agreed to be prudent and wait another two weeks before doing it again. We wound up making that about four weeks as Larry, – the roommate I didn't like – moved in. I hadn't a clue why I got myself into these situations.

Before Larry moved in, Ronnie and I set up housekeeping and it was pretty nice. We could sit out on the large window-sills overlooking a backyard with some grass and a tree or two surrounded by a fence. We would walk to Prospect Park.

Ronnie wasn't hardly showing, still smoked cigarettes and lots of pot. She once asked me to try some S&M. I tried hitting her on her butt with a belt while she laid down on her stomach naked, which she seemed to enjoy. I couldn't get into hitting her, though. She encouraged me to try hitting her harder, but it did nothing for me sexually, as I couldn't put together a good fantasy. It left me physically limp and mentally uncomfortable, but it seemed to turn her on. So I said, "let me try your position." Ronnie raised her eyebrows, "it really *hu-uurrts*," she said, singsong-ing the last word as her eyes laughed and sparkled.

'Well,' I thought to myself. *'She seemed to handle it like it was nothing at all.'*

So I laid down, started to get a little fantasy… and WHAP!

"*Holy Shit*!" I screamed, my body jumping about 10 inches off the mattress, the stinging pain on my buttocks effectively ending my days in

S&M. Ronnie had a good laugh. She was a nice street kid who'd had some hard knocks, and while she was playing me for some 'shelter-from-the-storm' when we met, we really warmed to each other as time went on.

We had a brief time for just the two of us before Larry the roommate would be moving in, and someone who Ronnie described as *"a friend from the place I used to work at"* showed up. He was different from anyone I had ever met before. Upon entering our apartment, Jim asked who else was in the apartment.

Just us, was our response.

He asked if he could check.

We said sure.

He did. When at last he was ready to sit in a cushioned chair in the living room, he pulled back his jacket, revealing a large revolver. Placing it underneath the cushion, he explained: "I always feel it's impolite to carry it on me when I'm with friends."

We smoked some dope and I saw it would be in my best interests to avoid saying anything that might be misconstrued as insulting to "the big guy" which included a lot of verbiage I could see he construed as potentially suspicious when my words had nothing to do with him at all. He had a much higher level of tension than I was used to, and when coupled with that 'violence-just-below-the-surface' mentality, it was enough to give one pause. When someone knocked at the door in order to buy some pot from me, the gun came out from under the cushion and into his belt. He remained at a stage of high alert throughout the pot transaction, and although it made me nervous, it was such an unusual situation that I can't say I really minded it. I found it amusing that this guy – who was a genuine gangster – was so on edge over a middle-class friend of mine from school who would shit his pants in a heartbeat if he ever knew what Jim was about.

Jim returned again, and he was one of those people who would smoke pot, alternate between feeling good and getting very anxious, and then decide to smoke more. He would think so hard to ascertain whether or not he was stoned, then relax and say things that made it obvious he really was stoned.

He had come over to propose to Ronnie that she should consider a deal to sell her baby to a couple willing to give her $2,000. While I recoiled at the idea initially, Jim went on to say that some people have trouble getting through all the adoption red-tape, and their sincerity to want a baby was definitely showing with their willingness to pay cash.

"Good people," he assured us.

"Good enough for me," I added, but quickly volunteered it was all Ronnie's choice, and it would be all Ronnie's money. This appeared to earn me brownie points with the big guy, and might have been the difference between me later getting hurt when I almost ran into some trouble with him.

It turned out over the next week or so the perspective parents asked if Ronnie smoked or did drugs, and the hoods answered honestly. Ronnie said that was because the baby was *for* one of those connected. It was discovered that these habits were considered unfavorable elements in their decision, so we got "no sale."

On the night Jim came over to tell us the news, he brought a 'guest' with him. A highly nervous package of tight bristling muscle in the form of a Doberman Pincher. He was being trained as an attack dog, and it was not to be petted or fed.

We sat in the living room, and moved the furniture around a little so there was a four-foot radius for the dog to have as "his" space. Jim explained that the command to "stay" was counterproductive, especially for a young dog as this.

"A dog needs to know it can get up and stretch, and rearrange itself within a small area," Jim went on to say, with the dog now less than three feet from my legs as we get high with this attack-machine-in-training seated with his yellow-amber orbs from hell one jump away from my lap.

After averting my eyes from the dog's own satanic lamps, I couldn't resist sneaking a peek. To look into the dog's eyes was to experience the terror that the dog saw how scared you really were, and was about to – in the very next instant – rip on you with those razor-like teeth. It was like the situation where you tell yourself "don't think about something," so of course you can't help but be aware of thoughts concerning that "something" sneaking into your head. It was like this with the dog's eyes. They were so other-worldly, they had a certain golden evil beauty that I found both mesmerizing and terrifying at the same time. Added to this was Jim's voice saying dogs could definitely smell fear, etc.

The animal was very young, and was constantly licking itself. This is what my parents euphemistically referred to as a dog 'cleaning itself,' but Jimmy told us that at this age, the dog masturbated all day long. That's what it was. During the hour or so we smoked and talked, the dog must have done it a half-dozen times. While I was terrified I would be moving too quickly even uncrossing my legs – and I kept them crossed through fear that my genitals were what the dog would rip from my body first, the dog would react to my every sudden move. The tense, savage animal didn't bother Ronnie at all, and she waxed philosophically how wonderful it was that the dog was just so free to release itself sexually without a care.

Jim seemed to warm to the pot a little more, and I found myself loosening up as well.

"Jim," I said, "if I'm out of line here," just tell me, and I won't ever bring it up again," I said, noticing his eyes narrowing. His body had a way of drawing on itself that violent readiness to spring which always rode like an inner lining just below his surface.

"Ronnie tells me you've been given a Laundromat. Am I correct to offer 'congratulations?'

"Aah, it's nothing," he said, relaxing. "I was hoping for, well, something more…" I could tell, however, that he was not all that unsatisfied.

I shrugged, adding with a smile: "Well, we're all still young. Life's not over yet."

"Y'know what I regret? he asked rhetorically. "If I had it all to do over, I would be a cop."

"Really?" I asked with genuine surprise.

"Oh yeah, the money I could make as a cop would be tremendous."

So we kind of bonded, and he asked to buy some pot from me. I gave him a very generous and clean amount for $20.

A week later Ronnie tells me there's a problem with Jim. He thinks I sold him something that wasn't even pot. I had seen this with some people who were new to smoking. They were so eager to mentally measure the effect of the pot, that this low grade Mexican stuff would sometimes appear useless if you didn't relax or were familiar with its effects. Jim was unhappy. I was nervous. A few days later Ronnie reiterated his displeasure, as he had phoned her earlier that day. I reached him at the midtown bar they all hung out at, and where Ronnie had worked as a stripper and part-time prostitute.

The bar phone rang and I asked for Jim.

"Jim?"

"Yeah."

"It's Marty."

"Oh Hi Marty. How ya doin?" I don't like the tone at all. It's was way too superficially friendly.

"I understand you're not happy with the grass."

"Yeah… I don't think it's the same…"

"OK, Jim, but this is the same stuff I sell to everybody, and I gave you a lot more than I do normally for that amount of money. But if you don't like it, I want to come down to your place and give you your money back."

"A lot of that stuff is gone," he says, a little perplexed.

"I don't want you to give me any of it back. I'll just give you your money back. I just don't want any problems between you and me. You're Ronnie's friend and I don't screw anybody, least of all Ronnie's friends and least of all somebody like yourself. I am just a college kid, I'm not a tough guy drug dealer, and I don't want I should be afraid to open the door if it knocks." I add in Brooklyn yiddishkyte.

"I'll tell you what, he says. Don't do anything yet. Call me tomorrow,"

Ronnie tells me the next day that it turns out he had given the dope to some friends of his and they were raving to him that morning that they all went out and got stoned out of their heads.

I am now reprieved and relieved. I called the next day.

"So, we're cool? I can answer my door?"

"Yeah, you can answer your door," he laughs. "Everything's ok." We ended on a good vibe. I never saw him again.

* * *

Weeks later we dropped acid, or at least Ronnie and I did. Larry said he would but didn't. I wandered into the bedroom, leaving the two of them in the living room. I went "out" again, out into the bardos of pink and blue creations, of colors unknown on this earth and magical visual understandings of secrets unmentionable which the "mind" cannot hold upon returning to its ego state.

I found a love for G-d in my heart, as it became revealed that it was only with a love for G-d that one could enter paradise. I, a secular Jew who had never read a bible nor knew anything about Christian doctrine, confronted a shining presence and a symbology of G-d the Father and His Son, the Messiah to mankind. It was a presence, a totality of reality making itself known to my mind.

I know when I *came out* of that presence, because I had to think; or *I left* (got booted out) *because* I (embraced a) thought. There was a blinding glowing gold cross, and an innate understanding that salvation is real as I left the presence of G-d. I know and vow to return here, I sense this in a way more foundational than mere thought. I will dedicate my life to this journey, this spiritual quest; I determine to return to this light.

One cannot have a thought, after all, and be in THE PRESENCE, THE LIGHT. G-d does not share his throne with such carnal trappings as thought. I find thought to be the tease, the robber, pulling and leading me to follow its own subtle innuendo, tempting in its implications to greater emotional energies and deeper commitments to darker realms. I gain understanding regarding the *Tree of Knowledge*. Our best thoughts are at most fingernails in the spiritual world. Effort becomes the enemy of clarity, analysis the undermining of understanding, thoughts of past and future a fleeing refuge from the pure awareness of the here and now. The repeated thoughts have led me to something, however. It's making its presence known. There is some *effect*, some communicating entity known as sound and it is meant for me from another. Someone is calling my name.

This diagnosis of my personal pronoun carries its own attraction to deeper roots. Roots of self which include ominous emotion (this "self" cries out to be attended to with devotion). I fall within its gravity from the pure gold light; the shining cross of the Jew who defeated death; a notion of *"Marty, Marty..."* that they call out to me from far away, stirs energies. Seemingly at first far apart from me, then by my very acknowledgement of its reality brings it into existence and creates form in my mind. I'm coming back. I'm returning to the flesh. I am the quantum physics created in and by its own attention.

After all, what is a *"Marty?"* It is not music, which exists within me and outside of me in colors and dimensionalities without boundary. Music is its own light and color bending in texture and creating brilliance moving through the air. Energies all around me are bending to this four-dimensional "music" that I'm *seeing*. And I'm seeing the sound with its own other fifth-dimensional world too impossible to describe in terms we use and understand in our three dimensional world. It is not simply colors, which exist beyond the common spectrums seen in everyday life, but these three and four dimensional pastels color my world with a significance the soul understands but the mind cannot grasp. My mind's attempts to conceptualize the experience busts and pops soap bubbles of angelic wisdoms as if groped by the ego's crude and calloused fingers. *"Marty, Marty,"* the sounds from the callers pull me back...

Oh, I see it now... that stuff. Marty is the identity, the personality, my ego - attached to that name that now appears to be gaining its own reality, emotion begins to run as the river of gathering, a cohesive herding of its own energy, bringing all my parts together; the large foundational pieces that form the base, the keystones, the bottom-most foundational structures living un-consciously, bringing the ego identification into life. It is letting me know about the re-birth with bold 3-D type. An ugly brown planetoid ego; the 3-D dripping quality, oozings toned with pride and conceit; bring the complexes into being – these wounded, traumatized energies from my infantile and childhood conflicts are merging into a trio of pie-like pieces creating my own complex of insane energy relationships, bound by reaction arrows to and from each other, fueled by rivers of emotion.

A horizon of awareness brings an instant glimpse into energetic foundations of anger and guilt, denial and fear all buried beneath an insanity called "normal reality" and then I am no longer above and aware of it all, at all. I am in the river and drowning in it myself. My legs transport my body into the living room, filled with my hostile roommate and nervous girlfriend.

Larry is making an unkind remark about my state under the influence of LSD. He has said something in a slight deprecation that under the insane guidelines of our everyday reality provides a challenge that I am supposed to respond to. I find myself simmering with a resentment that steams and boils over into my life's blood. It has every intimidating nuance delivered to my mental acuity with microsecond speed, howling to be heard in my mind's courtroom of injustice. Like room service in the hotel of the damned, it delivers teases with illustrative wallpaper on these corridors of hell where I mentally wander. I am struck by the fixtures – the mirrored nuances of my reflection; they tease me to argue. My mental radar picks up the nuance and transforms itself screaming into my own emotional hurricane.

I must do something, say something, fix something… And I follow, defend and argue silently with wooden railroad ties of lumbering thought, laying down the future tracks of structured behavior. What the actual behavior will be suddenly appears superfluous. I lost the minute I tried to win, and now am truly lost.

Yes, my guard stood hard when abstract threats
Too noble to neglect
Deceived me into thinking
I had something to protect…
                      (My Back Pages, Bob Dylan)

I find myself in a type of cartoon town and I walk out of the trip and into a telephone booth on 'Come-Down-From-Acid Street,' and what am I doing with these coins in my hand? Just like the chocolate coins wrapped in gold foil that are from the land of Willy-Wonka, the phone booth itself is also right out of ToonTown. It reads "Attention" where is should say "Telephone." I'm in the booth paying into the phone, but what am I paying "Attention" to and what am I calling?

I received *attention* from these two other egos, and now *attention has to be paid*. I have to give worship and adoration to this magnetic and intimidating ego-reality by my presence at pride's alter. Like a god on earth, I pay with my soul's attachment to this game, this reality.

Hypnotized by the cultural normalcy, my soul seeks to play the "function" game, and cover, protect, please and pretend. I live now to reinforce my illusion. This is reality, and one plays the game and/or pays in shame for illusionary equality.

    I am pasted-smile normalcy, an acceptable sheep within whatever uncertain pasture I now find myself. And now the snake from that tree in the Garden has got me. With my treason, with whatever corruption I embrace so eagerly, evil puts its claim on me, on my pride, and I march and salute, dance and play the game of one-upsman-ship, where the female roams the land as Tyrannosaurus Rex.

> *Oh, hello Mr. Soul,*
> *I dropped by to pick up a reason*
> *For the thought that I caught*
> *that my head is the event of the season.*
> *Why in crowds just a trace of my face*
> *could seem so pleasin'?*
> *I'll cop out to the change,*
> *but a stranger is putting the tease on.*
> *In a while will the smile on my face*
> *turn to plaster,*
> *Stick around while the clown who is sick*
> *does the trick of disaster*
> *For the race of my head and my face*
> *is moving much faster*
> *Is it strange I should change?*
> *I don't know,*
> *why don't you ask her?*
> *Is it strange I should change?*
> *I don't know,*
> *why don't you ask her?*
> (Buffalo Springfield)***

I've offered it my mind, it's given me its bondage, and I'm in the hole for good. I'm B-A-C-K.

> *"If you want to wrestle an alligator, you don't jump into the water with him."*
>
> Roy Masters

Larry was continuing to insinuate and tease, giving additional subtle insults. I could see instantly they were based on his jealousy of me and Rhonda. I simply didn't know how to negotiate that intelligence into a workable verbal response, nor did it occur to me to ignore him. This anxiety I suffered from his intimidation had always been a problem for me, and now realizing that I had invited this problem into my life when I hadn't had to gave me an even greater measure of violation to add to my sense of helpless frustration. I was humiliated into thinking that he 'owed' me for that help, and now, like a little girl stamping her feet that someone she gave a lolly to wasn't being nice to her, I burned in resentment that I hadn't kept this asshole out of my life. What we expect and don't receive...

I was confused and only aware that I couldn't defend myself properly. I was *losing*. Feeling ashamed as the apparatus normally at my mental disposal no longer appeared to function, I literally could not remember the point of what I was trying to communicate any more, although I was starting to become very anxious, and my trip was bumming into a burning horror.

Rhonda was scared for her own security and said something in an obvious effort to agree with Larry's position on whatever his rant was (which included a vague insult toward me), and I saw him extend a kind of castle landscape – or territory of himself – into her space by approving her effort, and noting – within the timber of his voice – his pleasure in hearing her submit to his point of view. She had paid respect without acknowledging any fealty towards me, was seeking his approval in obvious solicitude, and he would reward her slight disloyalty by not using the same hostile game toward her as he used toward me. She had bargained for an alliance, and loyalty to me was the chip she brokered. How long before her body would follow in the bargain, I wondered? I had to wonder at this imagery I was seeing. This game was afoot before my mind's eye, and although I knew many a professional would call it hallucinatory, I knew it for the reality it truly was. Even paranoid people have real enemies.

I tried in vain to say something but was so many levels off of communicating effectively that Larry just howled. I was too high and it was interpreted too low.

"He has no mind," Ronnie treasoned, and in doing so, pulled the plug on our relationship.

I wondered if Ronnie saw things at all like I did, so later when we were alone I brought up the subject of Larry to her. "*He has a beautiful mind,*" she said. I allowed my resentment of her to fester and grow. I hated Ronnie for being intimidated and it felt so much better judging her for her fear than having to see the same weakness in myself.

Perhaps as a consequence of this, or perhaps because I wanted to show off in a particular way, I was disappointed with her attitude at Fisher when I brought her up to visit weeks later. I wanted her to be the street-wise sophisticate; cool and superior to these little momma's boys and live-at-home girls; but Ronnie was impressed with the college, and totally intimidated by what she saw as all these "smart people." I secretly fumed, as I was beginning to despise everyone.

Larry moved out as she was ready to give birth. She would be staying at the home for unwed mothers for two weeks prior to her due date, and that soon came and went with the new-born baby up for adoption. According to Ronnie it had excellent prospects to be taken, as she said it was the prettiest baby there. I had not been allowed anywhere near the place, and that was fine with me.

Chapter 7 – Schizophrenic Processes_Beginnings

I was very much at ease starting a conversation with girls at school. It was fun to flirt and overcome their early resistance to my overtures. I had a motorcycle, a car, my own apartment, first in the East Village and then Brooklyn. I had taken a year off and now was running almost a B average. I read Hermann Hesse, had Mao's Lil Red Book, and by getting nickel bags for the right people I had wound up with great tickets for *The Doors, Cream,* and *Jimi Hendrix* when they played at Fisher.

When I walked into the cafeteria – which pretty much served as the central gathering place socially – I was almost always waved at, called to, and asked to sit with somebody. I would be asked if I wanted to come to a party with the caveat that it was probably nothing like the cool get-togethers I was (in their minds) used to. I was slim and good looking with natural curly baby hair which girls liked to run their hands through. Some girls asked me if I had a perm. So what did I need this bitch at home for? Especially after she got back and went into post-partum depression.

During the two weeks she was away, I felt like a bachelor with the wife out of town. I also began to have more and more contact with a strange guy around school. He first appeared at the fringe of a crowd of one or two guys I knew who had their own apartments uptown, who were also seeing shrinks and had their own connections to guys at Yale who had this great acid.

Psychedelic drugs had once seemed like my mountain that I sat atop of, but lately nothing good had been happening taking them with Rhonda, and I saw that as the measure of all things. I looked to find some excuse, some compensation, and I found myself becoming mesmerized by this homely and unusual individual at Fisher. He was ostensibly on a path to reach an ego-less state by understanding post-Freudian psychotherapists, notably Harry Stack Sullivan as well as CJ Jung, - using as an integration factor all kinds of psychedelic drugs. This was considered tantamount to the goal of having the LSD experience without having to take the drug. Morgan was bringing in some kind of assurance that the road to Nirvana lay in understanding where the anxiety was and then, using LSD as a tool, one would achieve self-hood, individuation, enlightenment, Buddha-consciousness.

He seemed to appreciate everything I said in a novel and increasingly insightful way and would build me up with his amusing reactions regarding my ability to pick up women. This, in turn, would usually have me bringing up the subject of Rhonda, and it seemed he never missed an opportunity to let me know what dark forces women seemed to generate in order to get in a man's way when that man was seeking spiritual truths.

"Jealousy," he muttered once, "It's as if they try to make you jealous. But I think it's *they* who are jealous of our trip." My jaw dropped open. I had never even brought up the subject of Larry, Ronnie and me with him, yet I assumed without thinking that he was referring to that exact situation.

"I know what that's about," I smiled grimly. "It was on acid that I picked that up."

"Do you ever get into that ESP? He asked with a blank face. I overacted with the psychic overpayment of positive projection, allowing myself to believe he had powers he didn't have. I regarded that last statement of his **as him communicating to me that he *had* this extra sensory perception, and was therefore able to see what was transpiring in my mind**. I sensed a nagging indication in my mind that this was what he was subliminally communicating to me by speaking these words at that exact time. I had an overwhelming "sense" that he could see into my head and "knew" what had taken place with Rhonda and me in our first two LSD experiences.

In addition, he was soon acting in a different way around me than others did. For example, in general, if I mentioned that I had studying to do, or had to be leaving soon, or hesitated over a suggestion to do something with someone, people got the hint and left me alone. Morgan would just stay, nagging me to do something with him, and soon it became my will against his, and I found myself giving in to his pressure, a weakness for which he eagerly rewarded me by telling me that *I was a great and caring friend*. I had no sexual notions towards Morgan at all. He was a homely young man with thick Jewish lips, fuzzy facial hair and a disgusting habit of "French inhaling" the cigarette smoke from out of his mouth and up through his nostrils. Yet I couldn't seem to say *"no"* to him, and began to spend my part in the relationship trying to "measure up" to what I assumed to be his personal and superior insights.

In my mind, the question of *"what do I need Rhonda for?"* began to fester and make a lot of sense. Besides, I would have been embarrassed to let her see how I was evolving into a student at-the-feet of this spiritual "teacher."

Things with Ronnie and I could have been nice, but it was as if I couldn't have any of that. Happiness is not on the menu; or if it is, only as an appetizer, and with a *"Sir, we watch our portions carefully."* After all, where could I find a better source of real pain and despair than to throw away a nice partner that said funny things, really didn't do anything to hurt me, and was only guilty of having the same vulnerability to intimidation that I suffered from?

Her eagerness to please me was altered by her Post Partum Depression, and she now had her figure back – which was killer with her boobs swollen with milk – and in addition I had Larry out, so everything was going for me. So of course I dumped her. Hard. She threatened suicide, and I was on the phone to my shrink on it. He pressed me to have Rhonda stay, and for the first time in our relationship, I got annoyed and "righteous" behind my anger, voicing the opinion to my doctor that it was my life, etc. I was casting off my safety moorings just when I needed them the most; as storm clouds were shaping up big-time on the horizon.

Hiding From the Shrink

What was suddenly new, strange and uncomfortable was my inability to admit to my shrink why I insisted on dumping Ronnie. He asked me flat out. The answer rose up from my conscience but I couldn't give it its voice: it was Morgan. I saw my subjugation to Morgan's leadership as something too humiliating to bear in the presence of my girlfriend, and apparently, now too humiliating to bear in the presence of my therapist as well. I imagined a competition and a jealousy between the two of them.

I secretly believed that Morgan had these "answers" that I couldn't say "*no*" to. I had been using LSD and concentrating on these Jungian archetypes, and somehow – probably when ingesting psychedelics with Morgan – had concluded that Morgan had supernatural insight. What was transpiring was I was seeing Morgan as a god of some type, and this was some kind of objective truth, as it reinforced the greater insight I believed *he* had. I came to believe that he had actually more insight than my shrink; or my shrink saw the same truths as Morgan, but yet, through some mysterious twists of spiritual logic, was unable to say as much. It was some kind of 'secret' that we all shared. It was an uncanny "feeling" – a schizophrenic process gaining foundation within.

My shrink had already suggested I should stop taking LSD for a while. There was another reason that played just below my consciousness: sex with Ronnie seemed to always necessitate a deepening submergence into those imaginings that related to some things I saw (but couldn't quite put my finger on) back in that first bedroom with LSD. So without giving it any conscious consideration (thereby keeping it from my shrink as well), something in me was leaning towards the conclusion that to avoid Rhonda was to avoid these disturbing sexual identifications. All this I kept inside and well beneath conscious consideration.

As soon as Rhonda left. I met the perfect poster child for the sixties Flower Children.

Marnie

Reading the words of the ancient Hebrew scriptures, we are told there are different levels of punishments for different offenses. We hear Jesus telling his disciples *"it will be better for Sodom and Gomorrah in the day of judgment than for THOSE people."* He was referring to those who didn't accept his disciples – the *"wipe the dust from your feet when you leave"* scriptures. Given that Sodom and Gomorrah would be punished as well, one is left to deduce that theirs will not be as harsh an eternal torment. So apparently there are varying levels of punishment in Hell.

Likewise, there would be a certain poetic beauty in the architecture of my psychotic disintegration after my demonic treatment of Marnie.

Marnie was *the* poster child for the best the 60's would have to offer. She was fresh and happy without being phony or foolish; she was clean-faced and beautiful. An intelligent, demure natural blonde with straight beautiful hair, her smallish breasts anchored a vision of perfection into a flowing hourglass figure with a great behind atop peasant legs. I fancied her as my "next" and swooped her up.

We had gotten to know each other when I was still with Ronnie; once taking a very pleasant walk to the park talking about life and school, etc., but really just enjoying each other and making noises with which to do so. In spite of her words of how sorry she was to hear of my break-up I could tell she was pleased that I was available. I mentioned vaguely about us taking walks in the park and now not having to feel guilty. I could sense all the lights were green.

She was with another guy at a break between classes climbing a large boulder in the park. I put my arm around her and waived at the guy who was up on a rock. "We'll be back soon!" I laughed and quickly overcame her objections, "No, I have to talk to you. This is very, very important." And I gave her the look that had worked so well before. The yes-we-have-to-pretend-this-is-all-very-important" goofy look. "And then you can go back to what's his name…?" I added.

She hesitated…. laughed, and said, "We weren't really doing anything…" and trailed off.

"See? Then we're doing the right thing. Cause this is really, really important."

"What is it?"

"Well, first, you know the animals at the zoo are gonna go around in five minutes."

"What animals?"

"Monkeys and bears and stuff… You've never seen…?"

"No," she says warily."
"Today's your day, Marnie Appleton."
"Because Marnie," I swung her around to look at me as the bells in the Central Park Zoo tower struck the hour. "You are the most delightfully impressive girl in this whole school. I mean it. I find myself looking at your face and I can't look away. I feel I stare like an idiot. And it's important that you know this Marnie, because now…" with the chimes starting, the metal monkeys, bears and elephants went up and down and moved around the clock in the Central Park Zoo tower to signify the hour.

"I had a dream that when the animals go on parade, at that *fateful moment*," and I took her in my arms, and with her eyes dazed swung her around, "*I'd be kissing you*," and kiss her I did. We started to 'date.' When she shared her creative, impressive, well-off family, I was more than a little jealous.

Then it was time. Makeout extremely nice. Excellent green satin panties covered her beautiful ass, and came off to reveal her natural blonde hair. Right before we had sex, she had momentarily made a motion towards my rod as if to say "protection?" I waved the issue aside easily: "I don't use those things," was my explanation. It was enough for me to communicate the fact: I don't use them. The world is about me, isn't it?

Her body is flawless. She's calm, sweet, and genuine, and as her small warm hand squeezes my hardening tool and she is happy and is getting turned on and is moaning and then… she is a virgin. But my world is suddenly about 'worse.' The submissive demons of hell are back, "*If you want the wood, you'd better dive in us good.*' I thought these things belonged to Rhonda! They're in me just as they promised they are, would be, and were that night in my cousin's room on LSD.

From that moment on Marnie is an afterthought. I am not interested in her in the same way at all. I have bigger fish to fry. A world outside the three-dimensional is now becoming all important, all pervasive, and all threatening somehow. I have arrived at a crisis not unlike the horror movie where the monster – thought defeated and left behind – turns out to be hiding with you in the escape craft. This schism is more genuine than I had believed possible, and my shrink was going on a month's vacation. I couldn't begin to tell him what my consciousness was only vaguely sensing anyway. The wheels of my life were beginning to come off.

Within a couple of weeks Marnie and I are in the park with two big capsules of Mescaline. I'm the expert. I'm telling her all about what to do, what not to do, just relax, float along with it; and once in the park (we had dropped the Mescaline at the Fisher cafeteria and walked to Central Park),

I was bothered by everything. I got caught up in my role, my thoughts and simply never got off.

I was now where Ronnie and Larry had been on all the other trips where I had gotten free of the normal waking, ego consciousness. I started to say something that was indicative of my state, and I heard the surprise in Marnie's voice as she spoke: "*I thought you were with me*," and I knew where she was. It was where I had always been before on my psychedelic drug experiences, and now I was on the outside in the ego trip. It was horrible. Humiliated in a whole new way, the karmic torment of the judgment vision played below the visual hallucination as my self-concept twisted in a fiery hell of self-damnation.

She is good and nice and kind and loving and all I want to do is run. By now the sex is work and the relationship akin to a chore. I am aware in a general way of a dissatisfaction that I had not had with Ronnie. I knew something was wrong, but I couldn't put my finger on it.

Now more wheels are starting to come off as it's my turn to step up, and fleeing reality has become my main objective. I'm falling behind on rent and had gotten rid of my motorcycle and car. Marnie is pregnant. I had gotten another girl pregnant months earlier. Her family was wealthy and we wound up flying to Puerto Rico to an abortioner's hide-a-way house.

For Marnie, however, help came from an abortionist on Fifth Avenue, and her sister stayed with her during the operation while I waited downstairs and drove them both back to my place. The doctor had given her pills, some of which were for pain and to help her sleep and I vaguely pouted inside my head over the fact I couldn't have any. Once settled into my apartment with Marnie asleep, her sister suggested I go out and get a pizza for us and perhaps Marnie could eat some when she woke up. With hours ahead of me with nothing to do, I had decided to drop one of these pills Morgan had given me called STP (real name DOM). When not much was happening, I took another. Thirty years later, its creator, Alexander Shulgin, would describe the DOM situation in a most unique book.[5]

> "Through the year 1964, DOM was being evaluated by several of my allies, in the dosage range of 2 to 4 milligrams I was still dedicated to marginal threshold dosage evaluations, unwilling to dip into the spring deeply...

---

[5] *PIHKAL [Phenethylamine I Have Known and Loved]–* **A Chemical Love Story** *by Alexander and Ann Shulgin - Transform Press. 1991 pg. 56*

The first full "psychedelic" experience of DOM was reported by another friend, Mark, at 4.1 milligrams. For him, the effects were noted at about half an hour, and between 1 1/2 and 3 hours there was a matter of fact but impressive recounting of visual and interpretive effects similar to those of mescaline. It wasn't until his fifth hour that these really broke through, and his notes are replete with superlatives. For him, there were colors and textures without precedent, as he had no past experience with color effects with mescaline.

It was many years later, in 1967, that some unknown enterprising chemist introduced DOM onto the street, where it was called STP and, unfortunately, it was distributed in doses of up to 20 milligrams. When you consider that the active level, a plus three effect, is closer to 5 milligrams, it is not surprising that the emergency wards of numerous hospitals began seeing young people in states of confusion and panic.

They had taken the new drug, and, when nothing seemed to happen within the first hour, some of them believed they had taken too low a dose, and took another pill. The hippies and street people were used to drugs like LSD, which come on relatively quickly and are completely developed by one hour.

...In going through my files recently, I discovered a hand written note that had come to me not long after the first trials with this material. It was short and impressive. I have no idea from whom it came, so no answer could ever be sent. It implied an experience that had several faces:

"If on this page I shall have expressed it to you, then it is true that DOM has the glory and the doom sealed up in it. All that's needed to unseal it is to surround it with a warm, living human for a few hours. For that human, for those hours, all the dark things are made clear."

Intimidation, Breakdown and Treason

I spoke to Morgan from a Pizza parlor pay phone and he insisted I come up to see him in uptown Manhattan, an hour away by subway. The part of me that realized I was on a mission for the welfare of the young girl did not have a strong enough voice. I introduced it feebly. I verbally put forth my chivalrous and duty-bound obligations while on the phone with him. But just as the man who needs what he needs sweeps away the polite protests for the fleshly prize, I yielded for his pleasure, did I not? I blinked and found myself on a subway on my up to see him. I started to realize the strange fascination of it, but upon realizing, simply remained in the motion I was in: not unlike a dream over which I had no control. I was soon in an apartment with him and some other people I knew from school in the upper nineties on Manhattan's East side.

In response to the innocuous *"what's goin' on?"* from someone, I heard myself describe the situation I had come from, and saw the look on one guy's face, and my conscience flooded back in. I heard him say *"What the heck are you doing here?"* and upon hearing my own words and his validation of what they entailed, my situation became more real to me. I prepared to leave. Morgan however, became very annoyed and adamant in his demand that I stay longer for one reason or another that hardly seemed appropriate in light of my circumstances.

Then the beast showed itself. My quadruple dose of DOM (STP) was becoming activated. I saw something not of this world. It was something many people would call a hallucination. Others a 'projection." Others dare to know it as *seeing into the spirit world*. Around, in and through Morgan an energy took shape: a controlling bestial thing, fascinating in its ugly cruelty. Too easy to dismiss its terrible meaning, its presence immediately reflected horribly on my self-esteem. Reality. I had to flee from it, and the requisite words of succor from that most subtle of all creatures whispered loudly in my mind: *'Oh, forget about it; it's not real.'*

I continued to break apart as I caved in for about five more minutes. In the eternity of those five minutes, the *"not-me;"* – that *'slave'* role that I had just fit into – was overwhelming my consciousness. The belief that I was a separate human being capable of making my own decisions was stripped naked in the consciousness that I was existing in that moment only because I couldn't say *"no"* to Morgan. He had made a complete and utter fool of me simply to demonstrate to these boys from school (who, I later found out, did not think too much of him) how he could control me. They had previously held me in high esteem, and so my humiliation served Morgan's own sense of who he was; a superior controlling beast (which existed in him to shroud his own sense of helplessness). I was a 'prize' for Morgan. The dissociation (that unseen part of my unconscious submission to him) was failing to remain "apart" (dissociated from my consciousness) and failing right at the moment the unheard-of-dose of DOM (STP) was rushing in to picture it all for me.

There were two boys from school at the window looking out to the many floors below.

"*Look at the long leash on that dog,*" said one boy to the other with a nod out the window. Was it an auditory hallucination? All things were suddenly uncanny. All reality revolved around those words just spoken. Something was DIFFERENT.

"*Good looking dog, too,*" said the other boy.

They were talking about me! That demon of control (the "leash") in my relationship to Morgan! Of course! I was the 'dog' called off his sacred watch in Brooklyn in order for Morgan to show these boys who was boss, me being one of the most popular "hip" kids in the school? Here was Morgan, now putting me in the place of submission. Hence the '*good looking dog*' in their conversation? I am!!! Their voices (EXACTLY reproduced in in my head) are telling me they are! Why was it not then possible to say:

"*I'm sorry, I am on a double dose of 40 mg of STP and have abandoned my needy girlfriend cause I'm stoned out of my mind. Goodbye.*"

Why could I not use the rationalizations we all do when we notice we've made asses out of ourselves? Instead, I refused to consider that remark in any vein but through the overwhelming vulnerability brought on by a wave of horrific emotion so total that all understanding was swept away. It was exposing my weakness: my dissociated but "factual reality" state of submission and humiliation that I had been running from seeing; first refusing to see its essence within my sexual fantasies, and now in the 'fate' which that refusal had prepared for me in my reality.

These circumstances are ripping my soul apart. The pain of the shame is unbearable. I cannot face these representations of this loss of self-esteem. It's '*not-me.*' That little slave-person was "*not-me,*" and the awareness that this entire episode exists, the awareness of what it must mean for me has to be erased. It has to be fled from. Therefore, the autistic nature of my own perception, once insightful, was now utterly betrayed; ultimately made a slave of lies in order to prevent truth from shining in.

There was a new force coming through Morgan and into his relationship to me. His need to have me stay was a "coming out" of sorts.

A demand for me to recognize his authority by my sacrificing Marnie on his alter. Who do you serve? For *"you got to serve somebody."*

I burned alive, while allowing a constant denial that all this was happening. A new understanding of "what's what" supervened[6] within the personality and allowed a return to a modicum of my senses, and muttering and confused, left the apartment to return to the searing anger of Marnie's sister, and the heartbreaking disappointment on the face of my de-flowered flower child.

That set the stage for the disintegration. There is always a balance and a judgment that only G-d determines within each moment of one's life, and having seen the beast with its mouth wide open and yearning for me, my only alternative seemed to be to avoid dealing with it. Michael came back for more of me. I craved more drugs to avoid dealing with the reality. I was on a suicidal downhill slide into more and greater darkness, the drug experiences themselves now only exercises in different but greater anxiety.

Before leaving on a month's vacation, my shrink had cautioned me about further LSD use. You've done enough, he said brightly. *You've had the trip, the insights, but give it a rest.* I agreed with all the sincerity of a child agreeing to *'be-good'* as a parent leaves on a trip.

After immediately taking more LSD, I begin to get really scared after bonding to one extremely moving revelatory heaven and hell experience. I found myself in a Christian Science Reading Room staring at the Bible

---

[6] *"In... adjustment to the uncanny; ... one literally steps out of the world as it is and into the world of some mythological system and for a while plays a role in that.*

A few people have had experiences characterized by these extremely disquieting and extraordinarily repelling uncanny emotions, in which, for a while, they acted as if they were one of the demigods or demi-devils or what-not, and got through it, and so from then on knew more about life on the far side of it."

Footnote from Sullivan's 1945 lecture:"*After an uncanny experience there then supervenes a total state of personality, one might say, in which one says. 'Well, this is it, for good or evil, for better or worse, it is so.' And this acceptance of something – even though one cannot think of it or analyze it – as being so, to be survived or not as the case may be, is what I mean by the peculiar expression, adjustment to the uncanny."*

"Interpersonal Theory of Psychiatry" (Sullivan) pp323

passages from the Garden of Eden and then from Jesus. Tears start to fall down my face. I am obviously spaced out and am wearing hippie garb. I believe G-d is trying to reach me through these words. I start to leave the establishment and am struck with a powerful momentary presence of the bookstore clerk behind the counter, I sense he is going to talk with me, or maybe I should talk to him. There is hesitation, both of us lacking the courage (or the obedience) to deal with the moment. I leave. I fall.

    I begin to become filled with a panicky anxiety-ridden reality whenever I was around Morgan. I notice relief flooding through me every time a telephone call determines he may not be coming over that day. I really didn't want to be there with him, yet I believed I *had to be there*. A better description than 'friendship' might be 'fiendship.' I find myself continually unable to refuse his presence. Hypnotized and intimidated, the more I fought it, the more I'm tied to it. He represented an authority, force or presence I didn't like but was somehow compelled to please.[7]

---

[7] **The following is again from Dr. Sullivan, who experienced his own schizophrenic break as an undergrad at Yale**: "*I now want to consider a particularly important situation which arises as a special instance with these people with chronically low self-esteem who have advantage taken of them. And this is the situation in which the weakness which is so revealed actually includes some evidences of a dissociative system in the personality concerned. And, in these instances, the experience of being led to reveal one's weakness is, briefly or permanently, attended by some measure of the uncanny emotions–awe, dread, horror and loathing. These emotions are, in many ways, the nearest that anybody comes to the reality of dissociated components in the personality, unless a person plunges into the waking bad dream that is schizophrenia. These then, are instances of momentary representation within awareness, or of more durable representation within awareness, **of the 'not-me' phase of personality**, which I can scarcely say is ordinarily personified, but which under certain unfortunate circumstances can now become personified.*"

"*As I have noted briefly before, these situations may be accompanied either by such fascination that the person, despite dreadful feelings, cannot seem to avoid being entangled with this unpleasant person who has taken advantage of him; or else by revulsion; also joined by the more chilling awful suspicion by which one begins to build up structures of probability – or improbability – which become more and more uncanny.*"
"**Interpersonal Theory of Psychiatry**" **(HS Sullivan) pp358-59**

I tried to configure pleasing mental images – within this conceptual framework – to him, believing he could "see" them supernaturally. I began to believe his words related to this activity; my unspoken effort. This madness soon accelerated my persecutory delusions into the red zone.

I assumed Morgan had paranormal abilities to see into me and all other things. I began to see my desire to be away from him as a rebellious "resistance' to enlightenment.[8] I began to "see" or assume a reasoning whereupon Morgan's utterances were just too deep for me to understand, but a voice in my head would suggest I could understand better with just one more dose of LSD, or STP, or a double dose, mixing them together, forgetting whether or not I had even taken any a few minutes after taking a mammoth dose, and then retaking more just to be sure, and then the breakthrough would surely come. Then I could 'meet up' with Morgan on that plain of ethereal perception. My adoration forced me to conclude (within a hazy "sub" or pre-consciousness) that both my parents and my friends – who could only see Morgan as slow, low and unattractive– were obviously against us, as these old-world acquaintances were working against my attaining these paranormal abilities and insights. They were just lame middle class straight people, not able to "see" what special forces were at work here.

Around this time I dropped over someone's apartment from Fisher who wanted some weed. A girl in this group had a startling physical similarity to my first real date from junior high: she was short, almost-pretty, pudgy and Jewish. I had not enjoyed my first make out with her look-a-like six years before. At fourteen, the girl's kisses mixed with her armpit odor to the point where it left me flaccid and eager to go home. After getting home and starting to masturbate however, it was impossible to avoid the fact that my imagination was far from her or anything heterosexual as I approached the "big O."

Now a certified stud six years later, I find myself surrounded by first-time smokers and wannabee hipsters. It's someone's first apartment and he is eager to show me his posters and record collection with shameless expressions of approval-seeking as he reels off his counter-culture accessories. I tried to accept their idea of me and was waxing stoned about something when this girl who bore this uncanny resemblance to my first fourteen-year-old date says to me *"you're weird!"*

I was about to let her know how she reminded me of my Aunt Dora's plastic seat covers which we were forced to sit on every time we visited those relatives in Bensenhurst, and why did she think that was?"

---

[8] See Britneyzian Prophecies www.trailopen.com/index-3.html

when suddenly I was seized by such overwhelming panic that I could no longer remember what I was saying or why. I just knew I had been vaguely "punctured," or in some way reproached and attacked somehow by this girl's rather innocuous remark. I was suddenly out-of-control and in the grip of some horribly overwhelming "space" in which there was only panic. If I was a person inclined to think in such terms, I would cry out that there was suddenly no "G-d" in this new place of existence. Overwhelming vulnerability infused itself with such totality that I was outside the normal space-time arrangement of consciousness.

There was still, however, consciousness of the fact that I was shaming myself in the *here and now* and even worse, the horror that *"this is all real"* became suddenly validated. There are suddenly shocked, sympathetic and caring faces around me. The same people who minutes before felt almost privileged to be hanging with me and buying pot for the first time from this "cool guy" were now sympathetically staring. One looked at me sympathetically and said, *"It's all right, man."*

As minutes tick by, I am sure now that every sentence communicated between members of the group has meanings within meanings related to my condition. The vulnerability of my state appears endless as the reference processes of their thought and logic pertain more and more to these thought-filled entities, my unconscious realizations which dovetail into each other in a downward spiral. I try to stabilize myself in this freefall. I must understand and make sense of what is happening. They are, therefore, by this new subjective reasoning and logic under which I am now standing, able to READ MY MIND. What else could their words possibly mean?

"Oh, that's old stuff," I hear PERSON ONE say to another (as part of an ongoing conversation they were having but I only started to just listen to). *He's commenting on my conclusion! He's mocking my realization that they can read my mind! They know and understand that already. I'm lame and slow here! I'm so open and vulnerable!*

"Have you seen his new stuff?" says PERSON TWO to the previous speaker.

"Well, that's what I'm waiting to see," says PERSON ONE.

I "think" the following a little below consciousness: *They are waiting for me to "give them" my new stuff! I must figure out what to say; what this "new stuff is" and give it to them! It must be an expression to communicate my transgression somehow.... that being condescending somehow to the girl?*

"*Lost in Dora and smoke,*" I blurt out. I panic as everyone looks at me pitifully. Psychiatry calls this a "*neologism.*" It's basically saying a few words as a response, but they don't relate to other peoples' experiences or references. I appear to be simply murmuring nonsense. I finally flee the premises, immediately seeking ways to live as if that entire experience had not happened. I return to a modicum of reality as the schizophrenic process subsides.

> *"Individuals come to a certain age with implicit assumptions about themselves and the universe. We all depend upon a large number of things that we are really not justified in depending upon, but we have never had any reason to suspect them. The sun rises regularly, our alarm clocks work, and so forth. A great body of assumptions is the foundation upon which our life processes rest. In a remarkable number of young people, however, there comes a time when their faith in this background of implicit assumptions about their own abilities or about the consistency of the universe, and so on, is ABRUPTLY SHATTERED. Then instead of building the rationalizations that we do when someone points out we have been an ass, these individuals go on feeling terribly upset about things. From that time on, instead of building the types of rationalizations with which we normally heal the wounds to our self-respect and all that sort of thing, **these people are different from what they were before**." ("Schizophrenia as a Human Process;" Sullivan pp 243)*

Let us diverge and enter into the etymology of this neologism, thereby allowing those capable of reasoning outside-the-box an opportunity to do so.

I'll use the example mentioned by RD Laing in "*The Divided Self.*" He scratches the surface of something now worth pursuing more fully.[9] He points to a patient who states that "*he doesn't make love to his wife but only to his image of her.*" (Laing, pp86)

Let us, in order to better understand schizophrenic processes, proceed to undertake the subjective experience here. "*I don't make love to my wife, I make love to an image I have in my mind.*" There is an existential truth to this matter: When engaging in coitus, the man "existentially" is not making love to anything "really" but his fantasy. As Laing puts it, "*... there may be loss of the 'sense' of realness in that the individual expresses the existential truth about himself with the same matter-of-factness that we employ about facts that can be consensually validated in a shared world.*" (Laing, pp87)

Although the entrance into the "Mirage" of schizophrenic processes (as I call them) may be as varied as the individuals having them, I believe

---

[9] "*The Divided Self*," RD Laing (Pelican) 1965

the following remains an entrance gate for many. Imagine you are in a social situation with people of long acquaintance who understand the artistic, autistic and existential meaning of your words when-using our example- you say, *"I don't make love to my wife."* They understand that you mean *'I make love to an image I have in my mind.'* Let's say an individual new to the group hears you say *"I don't make love to my wife,"* and in turn responds with,
"What the hell are you talking about? You have kids. Are you letting other men have sex with your wife?"

You, as the existential speaker, **could RATIONALIZE and say**:
"Within the spectrum of sexual relations, one can imagine submerging so deeply in imaginative worlds of lustful pursuit that it hardly seems appropriate at times to say that the resulting eroticism thus created or engaged in is tantamount to making love to the actual woman one is in bed with. Therefore, I occasionally – with people I know – allow myself a certain creative license or existential motif regarding these sexual relations."

Instead, there could be a schizoid "failure to react to "rebuff:"

*"One finds that the individual who has had a schizophrenic illness has not, in the first place, developed the abrupt manifestations of hereditarily-determined deterioration in the life processes. Instead, he has stood in a significantly and **distinctly difficult position in the social situation** in which he has lived; ... he has come upon certain situations which were **most serious in their negative effect upon his self-esteem**; and after encountering these situations (which include as significant factors only other people), after perhaps**, a rebuff to his self-assertion**, he has shown a significant and characterizable failure to react by any of the methods of reacting to rebuff which are more or less well known to all of us from our personal experience."*

*"We find that the stricken individual, following the peculiar and **characterizable failure to react to rebuff**, has lost a great part of that confidence in the integrity of the universe, the goodness of G-d, and so on, which is our common human heritage from infancy; and that from thence onwards he goes on feeling decidedly uncertain about life. **Apparently, if one is sufficiently uncertain about life, one loses the cognitive assets which serve us in distinguishing products of autistic or purely subjective reverie from products which include important factors residing in so-called external reality; and when one has lost this ability to distinguish***

between such reveries and such objects having more external points of reference, one begins to sink into mental processes significantly like those we experience when we are asleep.

With the appearance of a partition in which considerable waking time is spent in a condition in which one is without the ability to tell what has true, genuine, and consensually acceptable external references, and what instead, is purely personal fantasy, there appears a peculiar disorder of social activity (and I might say of even non-social activity), and it is these peculiarities that seem to constitute the essence of schizophrenic behavior.[10]

Consequently, the social pressure of the rebuff might send the sufferer into schizophrenic processes; that is, into the mirage of trying to communicate the actual content of (in this case) the sexual fantasy itself. This often results in a *neologism*, for example. "Ted called me up," he mutters in response to the question *"are you letting other guys fuck your wife?"*

This content refers existentially to the ACTUAL FANTASY ITSELF that he is having when involved in the coitus under discussion. The sufferer "backtracks" (regresses) within an ever-increasing compulsion to become UNAWARE of what, for some inscrutable reason, he does not wish to become aware of.

"**Lost in Dora and smoke**" reflected my own reference to my Aunt Dora and my admitted confusion under the effects of this marijuana. Obviously, no other humans are privy to this inner *circle of thought*, so there is no possible way *"consensual validation"* can take place. The failure to deal with 'rebuff' has sent me into a regression to an earlier time in my personality growth. This "breakdown" mixes such powerful and overwhelming emotion with current (adult) life-situations that verbalized expressions can often only be defined as 'incoherent.'

---

[10] *"Schizophrenia as a Human Process"* (Sullivan) pp221. You will find no greater example of this than in "The Britneyzian Prophecies" (www.trailopen.com)

The Army Induction Center

I got my token and a letter from my shrink. This was the moment... at last I would find out what he thought of me. To those not living in New York City in the late sixties and thus unaware of the significance of *the token* to all draft age males, let me help you. The Draft Lottery was in the world, and I had dropped out of college. When the draft board called you for your physical, they sent you an official letter with a subway token or two - depending how far you lived from the induction center - so you could use the subway to get there. So you had no excuse. You had to go. You had to show. You had to tell your friends, "*I got my token.*"

Soon I am riding the IRT subway courtesy of the army's largesse. My acid-and-analysis friends at Fisher have assured me I will get to read my shrink's letter afterwards. "*The army medical officer hands it back to you,*" they say.

Entering the Army Induction Center, I am in heavy energy lines, with thick bars of massive sheets not unlike thick liquid glass appearing as I think, look, and ambulate about. Pictures shoot out from thoughts through my eyes to the horizon but it is impossible to perceive these images fully, only their shadows. I begin to wonder if others around me can see them and my paranoia eagerly entertains this psychotic assumption. While not 'hearing voices' in the sense that I'm hearing things others are not, as when voices in my head would be speaking only to me (that would come later), but am instead experiencing the birth process of that state. The voices of people around me appear to have emotional impact on me as if their words have something to do with me.

If one says to another "*It is really a long fucking wait,*" I feel somehow he is speaking about something that relates to me; his perception of me; or what he is expecting of me (and I am 'late' – autistically speaking – in 'delivering'). It is uncanny, and find myself slipping into a quasi-shell best described by that Springsteen lyric to come of:
"*just like a dog that's been beat too much,
n'spends half its life just coverin' up.*

Consequently, it is safe to say paranoia exists, but not about going to Vietnam. Considering that the army might be an exciting change, I am ready to shoot at people and throw grenades and stuff, but I don't like the sitting and waiting, and decide I really don't want two years of this type of thing. The directions to wait on painted lines did relieve my anxiety concerning what to do, however. *Follow the Yellow Line. If you have a shrink issue, you can speak to the Army Medical Officer, so stand and wait here on the Green Line.*

The room for the army shrink held an Army Medical Officer behind a desk, and maybe two dozen chairs half filled with truly terrified young men. It was not private. You were called up to sit in front of the Officer, but it was easy to hear what was being said. Most were hippies with little more than truly pathetic notions on how to avoid the Army.

"*I'm really freaked out on acid*," said one middle class momma's boy, apparently mistaking the Army Captain for one of his parents. "*I recently gave someone a blow job*," murmurs a tall skinny kid with greasy long hair, and I could see him stiffen at the idea of having to turn around and face all of us after his big confession. These pathetic admissions were all they had to offer in their attempt to extricate themselves from being tractor-beamed into the meat grinder. It was apparent to me that the army shrink might as well have said "B-o-r-i-n-g." Nobody made a dent, and every one was sent down the hall to continue his processing.

I didn't think at all about what I was going to say.

Sitting down with the uniformed army captain, I handed him my file and shrink's letter. He glanced at it, saying, "So what seems to be the problem?"

Thoughtfully considering his question as though I had never considered it before (for I truly hadn't), the answer immediately appeared in the form of his assistant who came to his side with a cup of coffee for him. The gofer then vocalized an offer to get milk or cream for this hot liquid. He had something like MOO stamped on his name badge (I couldn't read his name clearly), and the Captain says "No thank you, MOO" and I answer, "*I'm not seeing reality correctly. Like here, this soldier who just brought you coffee, I think his name is like MOO or something(?); and when he handed you the coffee, you said 'no thank you, MOO' as far as his offer of cream for your coffee.*" Getting the officer's full attention now, I add: "*and he turned into a kind of cow.*"

Putting my hands out while smiling a little in a "wait, I know what you're gonna say" gesture, I continue, "*I don't mean a REAL cow like you see in New Jersey, with flesh and udders and smelling. I mean like a commercial, like the cartoon of a friendly Elsie-kind of cow selling milk or ice cream on a billboard. But you said,* and I lean forward excitedly to make sure he understands; *"YOU SAID you didn't WANT any milk."*

The captain was with me now, he's *Ghost Ridin'*. "*I don't think I'm really seeing things; reality, correctly,*" I went on, "*because cows **give** milk.*" I nodded. "*I mean some of these are archetypal,*" I add as if to whisper out of the side of my mouth, "*It's kind of like some of these bills are hundreds, you know,*" I laugh a little with relief cause I realize how nervous I am as I continue to pour out what the problem is. "*So, to line up with reality, where he gives you milk for your coffee, he turns into a cow, right? I mean he should. That **is** reality. But when he **doesn't** give milk, then he turns into a, well, what*?!"

My voice starts to get a little raised, a little more annoyed, my head turning to the left and right quickly as if to shake cobwebs which prevent me from seeing the symbolic alternative correctly.

"An uhh, what d'ya think? A shriveled old Indian tit from some old Harold Robbins novel, a desert scene? Yeah, yeah!" I add loudly, my hand bobbing up and down with a 'call-on-me-teacher-I got it!' attitude: "*With the sun-bleached steer's head in the desert cowboy movies! I mean, that's what I should have been seeing! What do you think?*" I look straight at the army officer questioningly.

"*I think it's time for you to go*," he says.

Scribbling some lines onto some forms, his hand carries out the authority vested in him by the most powerful organization on earth. ***Stamp***! ***Stamp***!! ***Stamp***!!! I am bureaucratically authorized more years on earth. More open paths of tree and rock appear next to my running stream, as my angel, my fate, my destiny, my plan continues to unfold outside the Russi*an Roulette of Vietnam.*

"*You're classified 1-Y. Take it easy*," he intones, (a bit) sincerely, I thought. A warm feeling flows through me with the realization I could receive pity from this stranger trained to have no pity.

"*So you don't think you'll be calling me*? I ask redundantly, just to hear him say it again, so my ego can roll in it, savor it, suck every possible nutrient of victory there is from it.

"*We'll call you if we need you*," he says, and with facial body language indicates again that it is indeed time for me to go. The dismissive and sarcastic quality of this remark detracts from the sweet boost I was seeking, but I rationalize the pain from his implied sarcasm a small price to pay for being released from the army's grasp. In spite of my visions to up the ante from my pillow case saddle and air-rifle childhood fantasy days with *Ghost Rider's in the Sky* playing on the turntable to real guns and shooting, I conclude I am happy and relieved not to be going into the army. He gives me some papers and the letter from my shrink.

'G-d, *those acidheads at Fisher really know what they're talking about*,' I think. '*I got the letter*!'

As I get up, I feel like I have just emerged victorious where many others have failed and I turn to view those preparing to engage the army officer in their own battle for what may be their lives. I am very paranoid that the captain will see my self-satisfaction and reverse his decision (*what would the neighbors think if they saw that smirky attitude?*); but assuring myself that not only was my back to him, but at the very least I needn't be *ashamed* of attaining my objective, I look up at the other supplicants.

Their eyes are full of wonder; their own travail forgotten as for a moment they are lost in their admiration and awe of the *Marty*, the crazed mountain-king they would like to be. I am their sudden rock-star, and for a moment I dig it; but am immediately struck by the image of a cell full of condemned men, and me walking out with a pardon. The despair and desperation creeping back onto their faces make me somewhat ashamed of my mad freedom, but I quickly replace the guilt with the thought that my room at home is full of drugs and music. I can go home and escape into these comforts, jump on the phone and tell everyone what happened... Death was in the room as well. In one teenager's persona of helplessness and despair, I will always remember his face as 'my Vietnam.'

The End is Coming

I moved in with a roommate to share an apartment across the street from Prospect Park. My room had records, a record player, a mattress and little else outside of a dresser and some boxes. I again try to pull away from Morgan but am again too weak, and am easily talked into doing more drugs which he promises are so good I won't believe it. I can't pay rent.

I needed physical relief in the form of sexual intimacy in the worst way, and (later I would realize) Morgan was a real-life personification of the sexual fantasy: ugly, controlling, manipulating and demanding. Although he fulfilled my sex partner's psychological profile, he turned me down, nervously stating "*I don't go that way.*" When I told my shrink (upon his return in September), he encouraged me to cut Morgan loose. "*Why keep him as a friend?*" He asked.

For the second time I rebelled and argued against the advice, ignoring his suggestion. This is *my* madness now, that would be overwhelmed by my embrace of a confused companion but stand-right-up and confront the shrink.[11] We "*embrace that which corrupts us,*[12]" says Roy Masters. First

---

[11] *As I have noted briefly before, these situations may be accompanied either by such fascination that the person, despite dreadful feelings, cannot seem to avoid being entangled with this unpleasant person who has taken advantage of him...*" Interpersonal Theory of Psychiatry (Onset of Later Mental Disorders _Sullivan) pp359."

[12] *Roy Masters, Foundation of Human Understanding; www.fhu.com ("Embracing the Corrupter")*

it had been his suggestion I stay with Rhonda. This second separation from my shrink's good advice resulted in the unintended effect of letting go the last rope holding the ship to shore. It was now cut. Having rejected my shrink's advice to leave Morgan, that left me alone *with* Morgan. This caused the greatest of anxieties, as I now found myself suddenly alone realizing an extreme sense of vulnerability. I went into a state of panic. I was constantly anxious, twisting on the hook of submissive tutelage and "less than" status, while getting no satisfaction of any kind.

In the *Screwtape Letters* by C.S. Lewis, the author describes a more accomplished demon tutoring a novice demon. The more experienced one points out the goal of bringing the human into a state of compulsively desiring something so much that he will ruin his life in the pursuit of it, and the *coup de grace* being the inability of that human to receive any pleasure from getting it. Using alcoholism, for example, the reader sees the alcoholic get to a point where he receives no pleasure at all from a drink that he ruins his life to get.

Breakdown

I move back in with my parents. No longer on my own, I have somehow lost my apartment, my live-in girlfriend, car, motorcycle, scholarship as well as the ability to function in an uptown college; along with whatever unconscious (yet assumed) esteem and prestige I had heretofore unknowingly possessed. I didn't know how much of my security – my freedom from anxiety – had been tied up in that, and now "*it*" is gone. Instead of the normal spirit, or energy which rises up to meet the day's trials, I am lost in confusion. I am also unable to avoid placing myself in this societal 'two-group' of subservient-adoration to this strange, low, unpleasant individual who somehow pushes buttons of intimidation within me that I am powerless to ignore. I spend much of my time escaping into masturbation fantasy, my only relief from the growing all-present anxiety which seems to enter every aspect of my life.

In seeking sexual relief, I find myself compulsively visiting submissive and humiliating energies within a deeper and more committed masturbatory submergence. I am drowning in the vortex. I am frustrated in being will-less. By not pulling away, I strengthen the hold of the very person who is causing me these anxieties.

My shrink has returned from a month's vacation and freaks out at all this, insisting I try to get out of my parents' house. I am too paranoid to attend classes. I cannot make enough money at the low jobs I take and am soon back in my boyhood bedroom. I see intense hatred on the face of my father and am unclear if it is my projection onto him or his reaction to me.

In the Fall of 69 I take my last combination doses of LSD and DOM, then take still more DOM when I don't feel high only to find myself in an ongoing hallucinatory dialogue with demons.

I allow them to direct the thoughts I cleave to as my own and cry out energetically in my mind "*I hate you, G-d!*" I repeat the silent but energetic curse at the creator, and make a willing conscious decision to scorn my conscience just to show these demons they don't scare me. I invite them all in, and legions flood into my mind from the left side of my head. I am lost in the most intense acknowledgement of reveries demonstrating through imagery my ability to have paranormal capabilities.

After a couple of days lost in this world, I get a full night's sleep. I wake up thinking, '*wow, that was a weird trip.*'

"Oh?" comes the voice, "*it's not a trip, it's here and now.*" I now have a special burden of existence. People say things now that refer to the fact that they can see what I am thinking, but we cannot speak of this directly. That would only embarrass all of us, and something so terrible would transpire as a result of it that I would never be the same again. That would be so unthinkable that one cannot even go near that line of thinking without incurring the most severe anxieties: awe, dread, horror and loathing... the most eternal damnation.[13] *And it's all an open secret. THEY all know, though...*

Within minutes I am sure everyone in the neighborhood can see what's going on in my head. When I think "*Oh, that's nonsense,*" I hear the response of my neighbor's voice, "*Oh really?*" along with a picture of that neighbor in their apartment with a cone-like funnel that attaches from their inner ear to my mind. Then I think, "*Well, if you can really see in my head, what about this?* – thinking now about something sexual – and the voice chimes back that they can see that too – this voice is joined by others, and everything I worry about "*them*" seeing is "*pointed out*" as being seen, with laughter and mocking intonations about my images, attitudes and ideas.

The mocking logic assumes a reality over these images that has them "reflecting" an acknowledgement of their reality by voices I assume/presume to be my own. They persecute me by finding fault with

---

[13] *See HS Sullivan's masterly work on "Dissociation" in "Schizophrenia as a Human Process" as well as "Interpersonal Theory of Psychiatry" pp 275-6; 288-9; 325; 327-8; 331; 379. Also Evidence of (316-22); Failure of (359-63); Maintenance of (357-8); Reintegration of (322-25).*

images they ask me to take responsibility for.[14] The voice talking to me uses the "I" logic. That is, the image is "you," and the logic sets the stage for you to believe it's "you" thinking about that image. You think as – or in – the first-person singular. It's the one-two punch; the good-cop/bad-cop logic of thought and reaction to thought. Although in this case it might be termed "image" (hallucination) and "reaction to image," (thought and feeling), I believe it is all "me," allowing a self-concept as stable as leaves swirling in the wind.

My situation is explained to me through these communications, replete with visions to demonstrate these 'truths,' along with the corroborating voices. When I think of something sexual, old Mrs. Farber, my neighbor below, murmurs "*Ooh la-la*," and if I think of masturbating, other neighbors throughout the building chime in with "*Oh yeah, we can get off with that*," as it's explained to me that they get fantastic, 'out of this world' relief when I do, and I would be a nasty little shit to deprive them of it. In fact, if I don't do it, they have ways of invading my mind and making it *worse* for me. *Well, I don't have to do that*, I think. "Oh yes, you do," blurts out a voice of some nine-year old boy who lives in the apartment building. Mocking laughter of the others (all who live in the apartment and how far beyond?) reaches my inner ear, with a barely nuanced "*Shhh*," as if the mother of the boy was yanking her little boy's ear to keep him from talking any more to me and '*spilling the beans*,' so to speak." There was obviously a conspiracy of them to all be able to look inside my head while pretending they couldn't. I could hear them all laughing as they waited for me to basically have sex for them (by and with myself). This world has had fault lines crumble within it, a paranoid adjustment is trying to take shape to keep one making sense of what is going on understood, and the personality has broken down.

I am unable to verbalize this, however. My shrink is full of shock and chagrin. I make scatological comments about his asshole. I don't want to, but I think I am being "*up front*" and compulsively "*honest*" in doing so. A voice in me compulsively demands expression. I am not sexually attracted to him yet I speak about licking his butt. While arrangements are being made to send me to a hospital, I find out Morgan has disintegrated as well, and is already in one. I am strangely apathetic. I know without considering it that the ties are broken between him and I. His destructive

---

[14] *While "autochthonous thoughts" which appear to come from outside oneself have been noted by many practicing psychiatrists (Sullivan ITP p360), their working-in-tandem with hallucinatory imagery (especially auditory) in order to complete the "logic" of the delusion has not been noted before now.*

mission was complete, and the energy that had made it happen between the two of us had moved on, leaving me as roadkill. I am to go to Hillside Hospital, a part of Long Island Jewish Hospital.

It is expected I would stay a few months. I was there almost two years. We are two-in-a-room, co-ed, and we wear our own clothes. The wards are unlocked at all times save after midnight. My roommate is a pediatrician, and he had brought a great sound system into our room. He would later commit suicide upon leaving the hospital. I certainly was not a good roommate, and I must admit my behavior did nothing to help him.

It's interesting to note the difference between the inner workings under psychosis and the outer. Inside my head, for example, when involved in reverie, there was always a strong compulsive component. I *had to* say a certain thing, I *had to* respond to some delusionary belief. I was apparently helpless to avoid making myself helpless in the eyes of everyone I met; even small children. I was helpless not to, and as far the "outer" behavior was concerned, I was even more helpless in my inability to discuss such matters with the shrinks.

I am becoming "trained" by these voices into delivering tortured, compulsive communications concerning inner dialogues as if the person I'm speaking to was privy to them. I developed a series of inexplicable, unintelligible "inner rites" – of a nature difficult to retain in memory – by which I helped adjust myself "to the uncanny."[15]

It was beyond logic. It was as if one could not speak of simple basic matters using simple English. It was too gross, too juvenile, too immature. It would embarrass everyone and I would be miserable and humiliated (the awe, fear, loathing and horror Sullivan speaks of) for doing so. The destruction would be cosmic. It was anxiety of such an overwhelming nature that I was oftentimes literally speechless in its presence. The proximity of the breaking point caused so much anxiety to be raised that it was not unlike having an electronic high-voltage fence surrounding my mind as far as options of thinking and living might be concerned. The fence surrounded the delusionary property, and kept me in a mind-loop of submission to the delusion with thought too overpowering not to react to. What was not outright terrifying in its assault on my esteem-security-censor of inner decency/acceptability was made controversial with good-cop / bad-cop points of view – each with images and voices - I was so close to hell I was living with the demons saturating my thought-processes. The short-pants trauma and the hostility it created were never

---

[15] *Interpersonal Theory of Psychiatry (Sullivan) pp324*

so achingly exposed to a mind terrified to see any truth at all, let alone the big enchilada.

I was masturbating one afternoon on my bed in the room I shared with my roommate. In my fantasy – which I believed was being aired through the cosmos to everyone in the hospital and the surrounding area – it was necessary to show more and more of my humiliating desires, and come to orgasm doing it. I was having a difficult time completing my mission but voices were encouraging me to *just keep it up*. Hence when my roommate came in with a visitor, I just kept on going. I wonder how that played on his mind when he decided to commit suicide later, after leaving the hospital for good.

Sullivan speaks much concerning the patient's occasional violent outburst or physical assault as actually a statement of the patient wishing to make contact with that person. I remember once wanting desperately to reach out to a black attendant, but could only find myself wanting to strike him and call him "nigger," a word I didn't use or consider using in my ordinary speech.

Chapter 8 – Mental Hospital Life

Anybody who came into my presence was uplifted out of themselves somehow into a different state which was tied into my head. This was continually demonstrated to me by the words they spoke. How they perceived their new state had something to do with how they "*saw*" me as they **entered** into my "***inner world***." They were instantly seeing me in a unique, spiritually insightful manner, as their own well-being in this – their new "wonderland" – depended on them communicating to me effectively about it. So they would speak in coded words of insight that I tried to match up with my own thoughts and images as I perceived these people were seeing them. *I was incapable of measuring their words to mean anything other than this; filtered through the delusionary architecture.*[16]

The thoughts that I had often reflected images that were kind of "*on the edge of town*." That is, images that were just on the outer edges of my consciousness, not unlike those dust mites that land on your eyeball and when you try to see them clearly they whisk away. It was assumed that these people who were speaking around me, however, could see these images that eluded me. I heard thoughts speaking clearly in the **PRECISE VOICE** of the other person speaking to (or about) these images of mine that they (apparently) could see and therefore understand better than I could. Ergo, my mental, spiritual and psychological health depended on me working out this situation with "them" verbally – in order to be "alive/right/ human/correct." I had to try to "give" of myself in contorted (i.e. submissive) ways so that "love" could be established. In this manner a truly transcendental experience could be enjoyed by one and all. That this aim was "understood" and "never-to-be-discussed" was so elemental that the entire weight of awe, loathing, horror and dread attached itself emotionally to any thought of speaking about this delusion. That was immediately "blocked' by *substitute processes*.[17] To think of discussing it

---

[16] *This inability to distinguish alternative meanings to what is often –in the light of reality–no more than innocuous statements by others is the basis for Sullivan's remarks that it requires 'remarkable and fortuitous circumstances' by which such awareness takes place in the sufferer. If these circumstances can be made to exist, this "light" of awareness triggers recovery and reintegration of personality. It's possible anti-psychotic drugs actually prevent this from occurring.*

[17] *To speak of "substitute processes" in the Sullivanian sense is to speak of an entire linchpin within his interpersonal psychiatry (ITP: pp346-358) My seminal*

– i.e., especially mentioning it to my shrink – was met by overwhelming anxiety. I was commanded more or less to believe that the idea of admitting where I was wrong in my thinking was a constant and necessary part of my interpersonal relationship. I lived in a world of coded messages. Walking into the hospital dayroom, where perhaps a dozen people are sitting around talking, a typical experience (of me hearing words that are being spoken around me) might go something like this:

"*Look out!*" laughs a boy in the middle of retelling something in a conversation to someone on the couch, but in the "*look out!*" what I hear is a comment warning me that he can see I'm about to make a dangerous decision regarding something in my thinking process.

"*I thought she looked terrific,*" comes a comment from one of two girls sitting together, talking about who-knows-what. The other responds, agreeing: "*adorable.*" I reason their words must refer to one of the many female figures or creatures of the collective unconscious I must be exhibiting, perhaps as a source of female consideration regarding what I should "*look out*" for? Is that a good thing for me to try to be, I wonder, as I get a hint of that image evaporating over my interior imaginary horizon. What mindset of complex of emotions are necessary to bring that back? And do I want to? Does it have something to do with "*look out?*" I imagine a *femme fatale* which would bring out that kind of exclamation from a single guy. The other said she was '*adorable.*' But do I look like a fag if I look "*adorable?*' Should I be ashamed? I look like a fag! Now I am ashamed of myself.

"*No, that's so bogus,*" a young kid says loudly to someone on the other side of the room. Is he talking about me, and my concern over the "*adorable*" attribute given by the lady across the way? That it's bogus to think of that? The pressure builds to the point that I *have* to say something:

"*It's better for me to figure out which…*" I blurt out. People stop and stare, some laugh and shake their heads.

This was the kind of torment which made up my existence for almost two years in Hillside Hospital. I was overcome once or twice, fleeing into my room, curling up in a ball with my hands pressed hard over my ears, my fingers pressed into my temples, silently shrieking. This latter behavior had its own dark terror in that it did offer a kind of relief. I knew I had to flee from this succor as well, lest I allow myself to enter its silky darkness, and embrace too completely this respite from anxieties and demons –

---

work in Britneyzian Prophecies (trailopen.com/index-3.html) takes the vague blur of conceptual monologue and places it into sharp psychological relief.

suddenly realizing – that should I embrace this 'relief' of pressing my fingers into my temples, I would never return. It's amazing what "awareness," even within that psychotic maelstrom, can do for one's survival.[18]

Apparently functioning" in the "real world" would not only place me in a better position to avoid this paralyzing anxiety which came from my interpersonal world-view, but would keep me from the inner temptation to slide into a mental state known as *hebephrenia*, in which concentrating-on-my-fingers-pushing-into-my-temples would become my only reality. That can lead a person to spend attention exclusively on bodily functions to the exclusion of everything else. In 1969, when Thorazine didn't help, they tried a small dose of Fluphenazine Hydrochloride, at that time carried under the brand name of Permitil in 10 mg. doses. That didn't work either.

Staying Alive

What people say must mean something. Something is happening behind their words. I am in turmoil. *'That's a long leash'* they said… *They're talking about me*! "***I am now.***" responds THE PERFECT VOICE of that guy I knew for less than five minutes at Morgan's apartment (that day months before). He is here again somehow. He can see me thinking of this very thing right now! Inside my head! I just saw a picture of him/it; the entire scene, organized from realities and now presented in the fourth dimension popping up again speaking in my head as in *'here and now.'* He has (been hiding and?) been able to re-appear in the here and now. He's connected! "*Good lookin dog, though.*" I cannot bear to see what this is. I break-down; I break downwards, for my "personality" can no longer admit 'autistic references' which in any way, shape or form damage what imaginary self-esteem I imagine possessing. Therefore a superficiality and I'm "*wound so tight I never admit I do anything wrong*" dull paranoia-catatonia envelops me; protecting something I really don't care about protecting. I have become lost, helpless and react to everything.

We all have within our personalities the ability to read "in between the lines" regarding the manner by which we communicate to others and they communicate to us. All our realities dictate that we see more than simply the light of other beings bouncing off their physical presence and hearing their words as they begin interpersonal 'entrance' into our lives. There are motives and meanings within meanings that we all reference within our communications. Body language, varying tone, the use of assumed sub-personality by which to make our points, as well as referencing past and

---

[18] *See "Awareness" video (www.trailopen.com)*

future is all done effortlessly by one and all in order to reinforce a "position" in the present.

The staff in the hospital were always trying to get me to *"function,"* a word some of us patients occasionally sneered at with derision. We were forced to leave the hospital to go out on weekend stays with friends or relatives so we could attempt to perform acceptably (function) in the outside world. We also played in a softball league and the teams we played against didn't know we were nut cases. They thought we were factory people like them. Sometimes this provided us all with a few brief laughs, and once even a few beers. I was pleased to be the ringleader in this effort, having sauntered over to the other team's cooler in search of a match or something, and easily accepted the proffered can of brew. I called over some of my teammates, and the guys with the beer were too polite to say anything as a few more lunatics came over and indulged, all of us smiling and bonding for two or three seconds. I was reminded in no uncertain terms back at the hospital that alcohol didn't mix well with some of the medications my teammates were on, and thus I agreed to not pursue such activities in the future.

I did not like to leave the hospital at all. It was an emotional asylum, an escape; a haven. It also had beautiful grounds and trees. I had my pillow and my bed, my records and record-player and my books by Sullivan, Jung, Clara Thompson and Karen Horney. During my stay I became totally institutionalized and quite used to talking with shrinks. Sometimes once a day, sometimes three times a day, sometimes three times a week. Shrinks rotated, with some residents alternating on-and-off in between new shrinks possibly doing their internships..

The hospital was, above all, staffed with sincere and caring people. From the orderly to the head nurse, people genuinely cared even while being highly professional. Even I, totally psychotic though I was - could feel that. It was one-hundred-eighty-degrees opposite of *"One Flew Over the Cukoo's Nest."*

A pretty blonde nurse came in with her husband to play guitar and sing for us, and I got so confused in my mind I thought she was telling me to leave during the playing of her songs, so I got up and walked out, totally insulting her without meaning to. I think I was able to share that with her later. It never occurred to me that I was insulting her when I did it.

One weekend I was to stay with an old school friend in the Bronx. I got up there hours early and went into a movie. I sat terrified through a Clint Eastwood picture, sure that everyone in the theatre was in my mind criticizing me for not watching the movie 'correctly.' I was vilified with audio hallucinations for identifying with low characters, and of course not rooting for Clint would earn lots of tormenting emotional jabs.

As I walk out surrounded by the buzzing crowd I would hear something innocuous from a woman saying: "*Gee, shouldn't he have known that?*"

What does she mean by that? Thinking on the first corresponding image to surface in my head in relation to that remark, I entertain the delusion further: She must mean '*shouldn't I have known that people can't see into my head during a movie?* But then how could she know that without she herself seeing into my head?

She must mean what I was just thinking but that nobody really was "*in my head*" so she must be a '*friend*' trying to help me to understand that. The obvious inference then is '*she's now in my head*' but somehow is trying to tell me that although she's in my head now other people can't see *that far* into my head (i.e., as in during the movie, etc). Somehow she can therefore tell I'm troubled about thinking about people who were '*in my head*' during the movie because either I'm not that "deep" in my head any more, or they are not that deep in my head any more, and is there a relationship between the former and latter states. I start to figure out a way to acknowledge some gratitude towards her.

"*I guess I'm learning all the time,*" I blurt out to no one in particular, stealing a glance to see how that worked. Did I "trip her out?" When I speak I see a great burst of energy shoot out from my forehead and splash-out all around me.

I then start to re-think all the disturbing thoughts I had during the movie. A young couple walking by are discussing something: "*Man, that scene was too much!*"

Do they mean that great burst of energy I saw irradiating the air when I just spoke was "too much?" (I can't remember that any more). Oh my G-d, I think, I must be letting people in to my head "too much."

"*I didn't think it had to be so violent,*" the girl says to him. Oh, that must mean I'm being too hard on myself, and these people can see I'm just beating myself up because I myself glance or suspect an image like that. I feel guilty that I can't lose myself in the magical lands filled with images and archetypes like that last one I just "suspected" on the outer images ("on the edge of town" imagery.") I'm spun around in it, anxious in it, while others, strangers, they can see my imagery, and prosecute, and persecute, and on and on it goes.

Even after learning not to react verbally (psychotically) to this "assumed" reality, for years after my release my mental apparatus still functioned in this way. I flinched inside when, lost in reverie, I would suddenly overhear people's words to one another. I had, however, learned to "function" by simply cutting the cord to my own verbal response. I simply wouldn't respond with the paranoid thoughts I was thinking, and, in doing so, began to create a foundation for some sort of remedial personality.

Lesbian Brother

In the movie "*Das Boot*," the submarine is sinking out of control and will soon be crushed by the mounting pressure of the ocean depths. It is saved from this fate by a small spur of sand sticking up from the ocean bottom. It rests there until sufficient repairs are made and it can then resurface.

There was only one activity involving other people that kept me from free-falling into catatonic or hebephrenic madness. There was one "space" that I could enter, one cave of safety which allowed me anxiety-free relief and self-repair for oh-so-brief a time. This activity reinforced "life," and reflected a sense of intimacy with another. It had definite meaning and for the briefest time allowed a sense of relief from the tension of my illness.

It was only by submerging myself into the world of the female, losing myself in them – giving myself totally to them, that the nurturing nutrition of intimacy could occur. Like a filling station for my collapsing soul, it helped cushion that knock-out punch of utter hopelessness; *you couldn't cut it. You broke. You're hospitalized. You failed. You're too weak. You are shamed. No amount of back-slapping will change that…*"

* * *

She had been talking with Wendy and JoAnn when I walked over. Susan stopped talking. I took a step back and lowered my eyes,

"If you don't want me, uh, staying here, I… underst…"

"Oh no, its OK, Marty," Susan said quickly, using a hand motion to placate my timidity before returning to the other two girls in pained-face mode.

"These people…" She turns to me to bring me up-to-date – "I'm on the bus coming back here from visiting my Aunt for the weekend, and all the seats are taken, and these two women, I think mother and daughter – I don't know, they're standing right next to me – I mean they're as close to me as you are," Susan motions to the three of us surrounding her, "and the older woman says, 'now look at the bust on this girl.' And after they stare at my chest like I'm some kind of mannequin, they start talking about bras or something, and I'm standing right there! It was horrible…"

Eleanor, who has a face like a small animal, would much later be giving me oral sex when we would be discovered in a supply closet by a doctor looking for supplies. However, in this (the before-that-time), she is skittish and looks like she's about to burst into tears. She shakes her head slowly in sympathy, while Wendy, who is rather pretty but totally flat-chested, also clucks her eyebrows with '*Ohs*' of sympathy. Susan is prettier than both of them, is very short with a tiny waist, a smallish yet symmetrically round almost Negroid butt (that some Jewish girls seem to have) replete with a bust and bra combo that resembles two artillery shells in the full bloom of youth. Eleanor and Wendy get called over to the nurse's station.

"I don't know how you have the courage to do it," I share sincerely. I find that when I say that my whole being warms up not unlike an electric blanket. I myself had made an excuse and stayed in that weekend.

"I couldn't go out," I add.

"Marty, you have to start going out."

"Yeah... I know. Well, you seem ok now..."

"I was freaking out," she says unsteadily.

I make just enough body movement to show I am considering a suggestion of sitting together in an area designed for such things. An image of me pinning a corsage on her at her doorstep/prom emerges as I say "I'm sorry for what happened to you." I'm satisfied by my sincerity, and I feel choked up by emotion after I say this. It is not unpleasant.

Sue and I make enough eye contact and head movement to acknowledge in body-language an agreement to walk into the dayroom area together. There are maybe a dozen people in a few different groups, some sit alone.

"*Well, you can kiss off, I said! You can kiss it right here!*" John is almost shouting as he recalls a story loudly to a couple of admiring toadies, who dutifully laugh as he bends over and in an obnoxious and obscene manner points to his own behind. Although John and his admirers are seated on the other side of the room and their words have nothing at all to do with us, I sense Susan flinching. There *it is*.

We sit in the corner of the dayroom, and I feel the warm patience slow over us like a blanket. We are curling up under a sea-blanket of some kind. It's like a virtual football blanket a guy and girl can both canoodle under together. Such was the climate for me and my sister in this sudden, magical place. The drawing out of her pain was in the timing, and the gentle suction; luring her irritabilities – her dis-*ease* – to flow out into me like a stream of acid rolling down into my silent absorbing nutrient.

"It's like arrows," I flow out to her on the empathetic wave, "these almost piercing, fear-rending pins… and we're cushions before we know it… it's like; wait! That's my pain… like *you're the target*…" I nod in the direction of John, watching Susan's brown eyes grow wide as I ghost-ride with her now. It has started to tingle and as I bring attention in my mind to that fact I am momentarily aware of an image of her mouth covering the head of my penis. "Am I making any sense?"

"Oh yes, Marty… please…. I want to hear what you're saying. It's good for us…"

"Y'know, we're not targets, I have to *choose* to remember that," my voice almost breaking. It's like we're pin cushions, that's how I think of it, and I think you also are… are… also suffering these bitter arrows. I know we're both realizing its *all* illusion. We're supposed to, anyway."

She laughs. I can no longer remember why. I think that's good, nor can I remember anything of what I have just said.

"I get so scared sometimes, Marty."

> *I'm sitting on my bed, speaking more comfortably to my sister now. I'm her younger sister and wear flannel jammies in the bedroom we share. I love talking to her, kinda look up to her in a way, and imagine I'm holding and hugging a stuffed animal while doing so. I can just listen to her talk all night.*

"All the time for me, Sue. I know, I feel like there's no difference, or that's not the right word, there's not… not enough *separation* somehow… But for you to be able to go out, and deal with all of that… it's over for you this total tension of pain, I know it's ending for you this panic; I know that somehow, now there is kind of … hope; after what you took on today being fuckin' burned on the bus."

I am getting hard as I gesture with an arm flung out to capture the disdain for the bus-riding automatons. What had warmed me up like an electric blanket before was now ghost-riding with the opportunity to be her sibling. I became full of that reckless patience that stretches out the potential for humiliation, I blurted softly:

"*I know it is; cause it suddenly seems to mean a lot to me.*"

Her eyes filled with such softness that I feel my heart melt. She reached over and squeezed my hand so nicely. It wasn't that intense grasp - almost in desperation - that so many of the other girls gave. She angled her head just enough towards the door, and we took a deep breath, got up and walked down the hall, stepping outside into the lovely evening. It was blissful to experience even these few moments walking out into the courtyard area, totally free from anxiety of this place somehow. The sense of peace and patience mingled with the quiet excitement of a fresh female. It was like a dream but better. We walked into that warm scent of a summer night amongst trees and grass to a bench near a tree by the side of the pavilion, giving us some measure of privacy. My heart raced as I leaned over to kiss her lips. I touched her so gently and it was just barely a kiss. But it was a kiss. Her lips were so soft.

This seemed to fill her with a kind of calm, and I knew she had made the decision to have me if circumstances permitted. Her eyes seem to soften even more. She asked me about me, and I asked her about her, and when we ran out of things to say we kissed some more, and her magnificent breasts felt marvelous through the sweater and bra. Although we fucked the next night, I think we both felt it was somehow obligatory, lest we insult the other person. Truth be told, I loved the holding and the kissing more. I wanted to kiss her, stroke her face, neck and breasts for hours, burying my face in her neck and hair. Wanting to give her bouts of oral sex, I imagined her face crying out in ecstasy, with or without copulating.

But I usually had to get to the latter act fairly quickly, lest the lack of time we had to ourselves catch up and prevent the deed from actually getting done at all. Also, fucking quickly prevented all the people from getting into my head and then dragging the girl in with me, and that became so complicated that I never really had good sex in the hospital. Much to the staff's surprise, I found flirting to be a relatively anxiety-free activity, while the actual sex act often ran aground if I didn't conclude quickly. Too many trains on too few tracks there...

This same scenario had played out in similar fashion with three other girls before Susan, and one afterwards. This activity drove all the staff into a frenzied comparison of notes to see what was going on. Since all the girls reported that I had never been forward or pushy, there was no small stir amongst the residents and interns regarding what was going on with *"Marty and the girls."* All except Susan had left after the standard three-month stay.

After Susan and I had been conjugal for about a week, a sudden change came over her after she had had a session with her regular, private shrink. It was then that she decided to take a break from our sexual relationship, and I received the innocuous euphemism that I was now being loved *"as a friend."*

Soon afterwards, I found – for the first and only time – a second shrink sitting next to my current, assigned shrink in therapy. It took me a while to realize it, but even though she introduced herself as such, I really didn't become fully aware she was Susan's psychiatrist from the outside. She was in as a visitor, apparently in just to see me. She is introduced in what seemed to me an oblique manner, and is immediately speaking in a hard tone for quite a while before I realize she is talking about me. This is probably the reaction on my part most in keeping with the psychiatric observation that schizophrenics handle emergency situations extremely well.

A quick note needs to be injected here on the nature of "oblique" communication: The first few words engaged my brain which was already uncontrollably flowing with uncanny emotion. From there a projection of an unnatural hostility and intimidation may be attached to the imaginary impressions received from people's words. My world is one in which I assume they are seeing into somehow. The delusion is reinforced with words and pictures echoed by voices in my head. So by the time a dozen words are spoken I have effectively ceased listening and am grappling with the ramifications of psychotic re-scanning of the first four or five words again. Once in this delusion, I can be tempted to believe that words that are now belonging to an entirely different frame of reference can be picked apart to enter the mental puzzle of understanding the first few. This is like a train that you jump off of after the first five words are spoken. The train keeps moving. That is, the words and thoughts of the speaker are moving. As you stand on the sideline, locked in your psychosis of anxiety, the persecutory nature that is enveloping you grabs hold of a few more words here and there from this "train" that is continuing to roll in your presence. They may be likened to a moving conveyer belt that one is grabbing parts off of that really don't belong together.

So as I began to relax enough to hear what she was saying, I thought at first she was like, some kind of public health speaker communicating about things like venereal disease similar to the films one sees on documentaries of WWII army life in the 1940's. I figure they're visiting all the patients to warn them about the dangers of sex and venereal disease with a slant "on the mind." [19]

Then it began to dawn on me that she is speaking in detail of me and some old, long ago sexual activities. It seemed so long ago that I had had sex with any of these girls. I couldn't help but focus now on the shrink herself. She had hawk-like features, reminding me of a hand-held old-fashioned can opener. Like her lower teeth and sharp jawline could be that part of the can opener that grips the bottle cap under its edges, and her

---

[19] *Apparently, Hillside had no female shrinks, interns or residents at that time, and Susan's shrink was here after making much noise concerning this lack of diversity, and saw herself as protecting patients of the female persuasion.*

hard severely hooked nose could function as the leverage part that saws the can.

I wasn't sure if what she was opening in me for all to see was *me*, or a reflection of *her*, or what *I thought of her*. There was a sense about her with an uncomfortable memory I had when I was twelve: I was sniffing my sister's panties and it must have been her menstruation time because the searing, pinching stench emanating from the soiled crotch burnt a howling hole through my brain. It was like a booby trap. Something about this lady psychiatrist was bringing this imagery out of my own mental bottleneck as her birdlike beak snapped off my bottle-capped mind with her overbite.

Something kind of wonderful happened then – as it was wont to do on occasion. I totally snapped out of my psychosis and wasn't thinking she or the male doctor were reading my mind at all. I wasn't even thinking *about that* at all, and started to respond to what were obviously some wild accusations on her part. I figured there was still a possibility that she was in the wrong room, and I could be a hero – or at least lend a helping hand – to point out that she really wanted to be speaking to someone else. Sgt. Pepper lyrics played in my head: "*Someone needs to know the time; glad that I'm here.*"

She talks about "Don Juan*ism*," with a kind of sneer. I turn my head to my right just to see if maybe there was somebody else in the room she might be talking to.

"*Are you… are you talking to me?*" I asked with incredulity all over my face. I notice my shrink – a young resident with whom I had had perhaps a dozen sessions – suddenly becoming undone as if he was experiencing electrical shock. His eyes actually grew larger. I straightened my position in order to 'straighten' *them out* now as the aggrieved party. It is dawning on me they are definitely here to talk about my soft, troubled sister of long ago.

Perhaps because I appeared a tad more forceful whereas before I had sat in befuddled timidity, the gal doctor backs up somewhat with no small amount of curiosity.

"I never, **ever**…" pointing my finger at her, "pushed those girls into anything! I never get forward or pushy, or come on to them….like some kind of pick-up… *bullshit*! You can ask him!" I point to the shrink who is still trying appear composed and keep his jaw firm.

That part of me that has loved so many of these girls will not be denied. She may be in flannel jammies and pigtails, holding her stuffed dog against her chest with her arms crossed, but within the acceptance of her magical realm there exists power that these here know nothing about.

I am on some kind of ethereal railroad track defending this world of teddy bears and pony tails, of holding small pillows against my pajama'd bosom, and listening for hours watching the others' facial expressions change and body-movement posturings. As I determine the good of it, the safety of it, the temptation to submerge into it becomes too much. The lady shrink is also full of pain, tired and forlorn. I'm attracted. Why deny her that full hug, that tucking in, that kiss on the cheek goodnight, the sense that it'll be alright? I'll draw out'n, listen; take her pain all night.

"What I do..." lowering my voice and sighing, *ooh, riding the timbre'd voice*, "is see, like, I see the pain and the hurt" (I am amazed within myself that I can watch the lady doctor narrowing her eyebrows, her face showing the tension over the possibility that I'm referring to hurting her patient, and yet I myself am no longer frightened by that hostility. I am behind some kind of wall, not unlike a one-way mirror, and they are all moving *so* slow...)

"Like with Susan, what she needs... with communication... not sex." But it is not Susan I'm seeing in my mind. "When she was frightened in the dayroom," I hesitate abruptly, taking it all back, holding it in my arms sitting on the edge of my sister's bed.

The female doctor almost falls over (mentally) as if she had been pushing against something that suddenly disappeared. It was reflected in imperceptible body language. In that moment the words we pretended were for Susan were repeated, but the soothing balm took on the reality now only as the can-opening hawk accepted it as the unguent *she needed*, and could smear it on and in; becoming a cloak, for she was raw with pain inside and it (her pain) came out easily looking for autistic salve. Looking at the lady shrink softly for permission, my voice a little more than slightly-above-a-whisper, my body language a subtle "may I continue?" she rushes back in, assenting with a nod, her demeanor changing.

"*Please, go on,*" she says more softly, and I know we're lookin' to the ghost-ride soon... Slightly above a whisper, my voice repeats my tale of the dayroom. Oh, I speak to her... now it becomes clearer: it was just us two sisters now, sharing confidences.

"*So Marty, you felt you could help Sue with her anxieties?* She spoke more, but I remained open to receive more than the meaning of the words, as if the shrink started to sing back to me, a small stream in this unimaginable psycho-spiritual landscape watered both our souls; inextricably, unintelligibly. Words resembled more scarves floating lightly on the ether of longing than depositories of "meaning" in the harsh light of consensual validation within the cultural consciousness.

Here I am eager to hear her tale of travail, coming off my own bed to sit on the edge of hers, and just as eager to assuage every fear, encourage every hope, I sit still, patiently hanging on her every word, pony tailed in flannel, holding a stuffed animal in my lap. I am love; I am listening; I am silently giving as I am totally receiving. Her voice not unlike musical notes, I am soaking up all her acidic energy, all her jagged anxieties as a sponge, as a million magnetic air molecules I allow the acid of her angst to be neutralized in my silent still vacuum. I am hers. I don't need or want anything. The privilege of being here fills me with serenity and peace. That is my sole purpose for being in this existence. This is our moment. Something is happening softly with the shrink's energy just behind her hazel eyes.

"the pins that hurtle into you like you're the target. We're realizing that's all illusion from our own early hurts, and it's ending, this pain... it has to, it simply is, and it is because of your courage, your effort, that now there is some hope.... for us... both"

I am also suddenly aware how truly wonderful this ugly lady looks, in that way that the unique look of a gaunt, hurting soul often can, and that indeed the shrink, had I been a doctor or other 'on-your-level' professional, *would be ripe for a kiss herself at that moment.*

I am suddenly living in a giant moment of silence as I realize I've gotten extremely courageous in my recklessly deep, profoundly brazen spirit of love and have said something just like that to her out loud. Her seconds of silence in stunned shocked non-response seals the verdict involving what her response would have been. I see her in my mind eyes closed, speechless, rapt in pleasure, the soft lips now parted after the sudden, wonderful kiss. Had we not been trapped in the doctor-patient relationship, I would be leaning back from it right now. I should really tell her that, but lack the courage and/or arrogance. As for what the lady-shrink's response would have been, that reality lives in a space deep inside that defies logic: for the briefest of never-to-be-admitted nor-spoken-about moments, all three of us just *know*.

Not unlike Ed Norton's character in *Fight Club*, I'm suddenly mentally back from the land of *'wannabe.'* I see myself hellaciously guilty and I appear to myself a trickster and a fraud. Worse, I'm now uncovered as such, appearing a pathetic fool, a mental patient talking about kissing a doctor.

There's clearings of throats, and time becomes a big block of unmoving anxiety as words in my head become like annoying insects flinging themselves against this wall of ice or glass trying to recover, build, and gain some measure of self-respect from this shameful debacle, but I am too undone, and now she has to have her way with me. I have to be eaten alive under her probing. The whole world changes as I burn as a living offering.

The session ends with me saying I understood that these girls were under a lot of strain, and having sex was sometimes something more than they could handle, and it was all logy and groany-down depressive, like she had to whack my pee-pee with this rule stick and I had to obey like the emasculated little wiener I was.

After the session ends, I have to go to the nearest bathroom as I have a really bad stomach ache, and I have to push so hard I feel my brains are coming out of my ears to the point where people can probably see my thoughts all the way to New Jersey. Relief itself brings with it unusually colorful and pleasant hallucinations, which I attribute to the release of euphoria in emotionally re-experiencing the successful toilet training of the toddler state. My body is free of that tension, and the relief is palpable. I spend a lot of time washing my hands and face, and leave refreshed.

I'm walking down the hall on my way back to the resident's pavilion and I pass the doctor's lounge. I see three young doctors sitting there, including the guy who was just in the session with me. It is obvious by the look of unrestrained glee and high pitched laughing exclamations that they have just heard something of intense good news. I do not see the female doctor there. They turn to look.

"*Marty*!" they all shout loudly (and somewhat raucously), grinning and waving in unison. They appear jubilant. As I pass the door with my return wave, I am a step or two down the hall when I think I hear one say "*You are G-d, man.*" Another says "*shut up!*" That bothers me for a little while, but these auditory hallucinations happen all the time, and I soon forget all about it. I have more important things to worry about. The negro janitor will be by later to clean my room and I'll have to deal with thoughts that rise up in my head screaming: "*don't think the word nigger.*"

Outpatient Heroin

It was time to leave Hillside. They had been telling me this was coming, and I had tried to stay out on the weekends, but I'd really rather not leave the hospital.

After about eighteen months, they explained to me that they can only keep a patient so long. My alternative is to go to the State Hospital, which – even in my deluded condition – I can sense (thanks to the sincerity of the staff) that it is a place I do not want to go to.

"Our charter says you're at the maximum," I was informed by Dr. Arthur Rifkin, who I would get back in touch with 30 years later. He let me know that experimental dosages of Fluphenazine Hydrochloride (in 1970 marketed under the brand name of Permitil in 10 mg doses) was showing some good reports. But instead of the recommended dosage of 10mg-30mg, I would be taking 300mg.

"Let's try it," I agreed. I had to be able to function outside the hospital setting, and taking lots of drugs had an appeal in its own right.

Three hundred milligrams meant taking 30 pills, as no higher dose than the 10 mg. Permitil was in manufacture. There was slight improvement, but not enough to allow me to get along inside or outside of the hospital without sliding into severe psychotic episodes. We upped it to 400mg. A little better, so we pressed it to 500 mg. Seeing improvement, we ratcheted it up to 600, then cranked to 700 and finally topped off at 800mg. This seemed to allow for a functional Marty. More than a little dazed and sleepy, and perturbed to have to swallow eighty pills a day, I bid farewell to my safety net, and left the hospital to stay with my sister.

My sister had married and had a young daughter by this time and a new house on Long Island. Her husband worked hard as a diamond-setter apprentice. While it is safe to say without their helping hands I would have destroyed myself, it is also safe to say he needed his crazy brother-in-law coming to live with him as much as he needed a new hemorrhoid. His father helped to hook me up with a job driving a cab in New York City, but it took over two hours traveling time from the house on Long Island to uptown Manhattan.

I began to sleep in and skip work. I could sleep twenty hours a day on the 800mg of Permitil. Always good for tough love, my brother-in-law announced he wouldn't support a loafer, and I soon had a dingy apartment in Brighton Beach; a half block from the El (the elevated subway). I could take the subway straight into uptown to the taxi garage, so transportation to the job was no longer such an ordeal. I couldn't understand how my upstairs landlords could read my mind, say such provocative, insightful things to me deep in my skull, yet prove so superficial, petty, hard and unfeeling in the light of day.

And then there was still the issue of work. I was paralyzed with anxiety, and sometimes felt I couldn't take a deep breath until the passenger left. I got lost a lot. I understood that North meant the streets took on higher numbers; and East was like 2nd Avenue, and West went over to 10th Avenue and stuff like that. Nevertheless, when somebody would bark *"Northwest corner of 57th and Broadway,"* I almost never got it right. The pressure of having to do something correctly it in front of someone else was overwhelming, and I found myself on my twenty-second birthday walking back to the scene of my old cosmic living days in Brooklyn.

I ran into Max, a pained soul-searcher who had (back in the old days) made an effort to let me know Morgan was a zero and the sooner I figured that out, the better. I hadn't listened. I should've loved Max.

We greeted each other near the entrance to the park.

"Whatcha doin?" he said. The atmosphere was so ghostly. We were like the after-torture time in Orwell's *1984*.

"Out of the Hospital, drivin a cab… on a shitload of meds."

"Oh yeah, I've been in one too."

"A hospital? No shit?" I said, unenthusiastically.

"So what else ya' doin?"

"Just hangin out," I twisted. I was feeling very anxious over this conversation cause it was bringing up the delusion that he wanted me to 'open up my mind to him.' I knew him when I was doing twenty, forty and sixty milligrams of DOM mixed with LSD, and lived in a magic kingdom, before and after it all turned to hell on earth. I was fond of Max, and although fondness brought with it its own anxiety, I vaguely rued the fact that, had Morgan not been in the picture, Max and I could have gelled very well as pals.

"Just hangin' out? He sounded angry. "Just hangin out!… he stammered as he would over a champion who has crashed and burned. "I remember when you were something!" and he nodded over to my old apartment.

I froze in catatonic anxiety. It became impossible to speak.

"Ever shot up?" he asked.

"No… ya mean, like heroin?"

"Yeah, ya' ever done it?"

"No, but today *is* my birthday," I mused with all the subtlety of a girl looking to get naughty. Strangely, as if in anticipation of the dark relief to come, I found myself not all that uncomfortable with the imagery.

"Then it's no charge. Let's go in the park. How old are you?"
"Twenty-two."
"Happy Birthday."

I found the pre-shot ritual of mixing the powder and water, along with the technology of heating, drawing and injecting literally fascinating, and the relief from my omnipresent anxiety left me breathless. Suddenly I am in love with the sudden possibilities of life, Max and the world. In a strange way, I was suddenly hopeful. There was, apparently, a reality in which the hellish torment of my psychosis could be relieved. In addition, the slow exciting mystery of mixing the illicit powder with water, the heating, loading and injecting of it offered a delightful ritual with a powerful effect that narrowed the world to something negotiable. Yes, life took on a purpose: Take money, and then worry through the illegal, tormenting excitement to get the stuff, then enter into the mind-narrowing atmosphere of the pre-shot ritual, see the blood jump up into the syringe, know that you will then "change" your existence; and with the push of a finger, you do so.

Over the course of the next few months shot led-to-shot led-to-shot led to my completely substituting heroin for the anti-psychotic medication and stopping the out-patient treatment completely.

I drove a cab and shot up the tips daily, leaving the bulk of my paycheck for my rent and small bills. I often ate cookies and milk for dinner. For the first time in my life, I found myself hungry and unable to afford a meal.

While shooting up in the Prospect Park, I came across a friend of a friend from high school. Jerry was now into smack as well, although we all worked 40 hour jobs. He was the same guy who let me tag along to end my virginity with the Puerto Rican prostitute five years before.

We were instantly simpatico. He spoke in overly sarcastic, self-deprecating witticisms, and would surprise me with an occasional biting piece of prescient self-examination. This helps enormously when one is as vulnerable as I was. We soon found we had to forsake the convenience of nearby Prospect Park and take multiple busses to get to Williamsburg, another section of Brooklyn, where the supply of heroin was more plentiful with a lot less heat from the cops.

The middle class surrounding Prospect Park in Brooklyn had reacted with objections loud and clear to the authorities regarding the debilitating state of the Park, and it became increasingly difficult to score and shoot there. Cops were now everywhere and searching everyone. Consequently, Jerry and I would trek to the new Mecca via public transportation.

Williamsburg was interesting. It had the remnant of the Hassidic Jews, the ultra-orthodox with the long sidecurls, beards and the long black coats.

I mean, they would never think of moving simply because blacks and Puerto Ricans flooded in. This was where their Rebbe lived. This was where they prayed. Even when, years later, one of their number was murdered by a gang of blacks and Puerto Ricans screaming anti-Semitic taunts (with the resulting all-black jury letting the killer off), they still stayed.

Another good thing about Jerry – although I didn't realize how good it was at the time – was that he took his chippy[20] like a man. He didn't whine aimlessly or repetitively like a dog in heat. He was a good guy to shoot dope with. Waiting for the interminable bus and the nerve-wracking transfer-bus that you hope you won't have to wait too long for, the heroin craving can be particularly difficult. Consequently, Jerry's stoic capabilities were a boon. These were slower days anyway – you waited for transportation as part of life. We moved slower, I guess, using public transportation without cell phones and the internet. And you were hurting. You were nervous and anxious as only the junk-sick know. And you're in Williamsburg and you cop. You don't have time to shoot or take a snort (and you get really paranoid doing it on the bus, cause you worry that the driver knows you did and is even now calling the cops).

A few blocks from Division Street in Williamsburg was a square block of schoolyard called "the park." If you had just gotten off, it was a pleasant Disneyland, and if you had more in your pocket, you could even bestow a smile on all fellow travelers who hung around on benches looking to get high as well or sell. One day, I was on my way to the bus stop by myself in such an atmosphere when I smiled at this black guy sitting on a bench. He smiled back, and we each saw the other was high on the same thing. We grinned with an *"ain't this shit great"* look as we both floated pleasantly by immersed in the quality of that day's product.

A couple of weeks later I was looking to cop and arrived at the Williamsburg "Park" alone. I walked over to two Puerto Rican guys I knew, having been previously introduced to them by Jerry.

"Hey, what's happenin?"

"Manny should be by in a half-hour, says Marco."

"Any good?"

"He had three-dollar bags, shoot two n' you're definitely down."

"Definitely," adds Miguel.

"Half-hour?" I mutter stupidly, as everyone knows you wait as long as you have to.

---

[20] *"Chipping"* - A small heroin habit; defined loosely in this manner while the addict still holds a job and/or the appearance of a normal lifestyle.

"There's Hector!" Miguel half-shouted, and was three steps ahead of us making a beeline for a guy on the other side of the schoolyard.

"Hectors always got," Marco responds to my questioning face as we both fall into a quick step behind Miguel. Halfway to our oasis we notice a black guy come up to Hector and within half-a-minute a deal is made between the two of them. The black guy appears familiar but I can't place him.

As we approach them everyone's neck starts turning to scan for cops. We are five guys standing out in the open.

Hector looks at Miguel and casts an eye on me.

"He's cool," Miguel says as he nods his head slightly in my direction.

I nod with the respect becoming a new guy accepted on trust while Hector speaks in rapid-fire street Spanish. Something about his dope and the black, who is still standing there. I see it is the guy who I shared a stoned smile with weeks before.

"This is Reese," Hector says. "He just bought all my shit. So deal with him." He slaps hands with Reese and walks off.

(beat)

Nobody says anything. Apparently Marco and Miguel don't know this guy either.

"Hey," I say, nodding to Reese. "what'cha got?"

"Treys. If you wanna cop, let's move over there," says Reese, nodding towards some new construction of a street level apartment about 50 yards away. We all move along, the heightened, brightened energy obvious in our walk, voices and faces.

I'll take four, I say, as soon as we get into the half-finished construction area. I look left and right and down the block for any cruising cops, then take out a ten and two ones, handing it to him as he looks at the money and hands me four small folded packets. Marco and Miguel take two apiece.

"Can we get off here?" I ask.

"Fuck yeah," says Marco.

"Let's do it, man," adds Miguel.

"I could go for another," Reese says. Anybody got water?"

"Right here, *essé*," says Marco as he pulls a small bottle filled with the clear fluid.

"My man. Let's get down," Reese says. He has a softness, like an evenness, that's unusual in his voice. It's closer to vulnerable than what one normally finds here on the streets. It doesn't mean he wouldn't rip you off or he was incapable of violence, it was just an indication that he *might not* be inclined to do these things. We sit in a kind of half circle, everybody's back to a piece of wall in a space that would eventually be a small kitchenette or laundry room. There is not yet running water in the place, and we find a can to squirt our residues into.

"I need a dropper," I say. "I have a point, I just didn't have time to get a dropper."

"You can use mine after I get off, Reese says.

A dropper is the same simple plastic dispenser – essentially a plastic tube with a rubber bulb on top – that you buy at a drugstore with iodine or something like that. You have to make sure, however, that it has the tapered end, not the bulbous round end. This allows it to almost fit into the cone-shaped end of a "point," which is attached to the needle. The 'almost' part of the equation is solved by adding a "collar" to the "neck" of the dropper. A torn off corner of a dollar bill works well when dipped in water. It tightens and stretches as a gasket to allow the dropper to function as a syringe above the attached needle.

Reese pours a little water into his bottlecap and squeezing the dropper's bulb, draws up about three-quarters of the way up. He dumps the excess water out of his bottlecap. He then pours one envelope's worth of the same stuff he sold to us into the bottlecap. Squeezing the bulb of his dropper, he adds the water from his dropper into the cap. He has a Bobby-pin wire assembly that acts as a handle to hold the bottlecap while he heats the mixture with a lighter. As soon as it shows a boil he places it down and drops a small piece of cotton in. Squeezing the bulb on the dropper to remove any air, he places the needle into the cotton and releases pressure on the bulb, resulting in the liquid heroin climbing up into the dropper. He pulls a belt tight around his bicep and poking the skin above his bulging vein with the needle, he pierces the skin and flicks the dropper's side with his finger, moving it a tiny bit. That appears to make the hit as blood rushes up into the dropper's neck and he releases the belt. The buckle makes a tinkling sound as it falls to the concrete floor. All our eyes are on him as he slowly squeezes the dropper, sending the heated brew into his vein. He exhales wonderfully, and his eyes go glassy and a small smile appears. He's in a nod from a three-dollar bag. This is indeed a wonderful sign if we are going to be shooting the same dope. There is always the nagging suspicion he sold us something different than what he's shooting, but it appears to be Hector's stuff all around.

He is still holding the used syringe. I need the dropper, but I see Reese's situation. I make eye contact and pantomime my taking the syringe. He smiles, and I take the syringe from his hand, screw off the needle, uncurl the collar and, pouring some water into an extra bottlecap on the floor, proceed to fill up the dropper with clean water, squirting out the residue of Reese's blood into the can that we set up for that purpose. I also squirt out clean water through his needle, which is an extra bit of compassionate courtesy outside the normal ethos of junkie etiquette. There is always a danger of old blood clotting up a needle, and one of the most excruciating situations for any needle user is to find, upon hitting a vein, that your needle is clogged, and you can't get your heavenly ticket into the vein for the ride. By taking the extra time *now* to squirt water through his needle I am eliminating that danger from occurring in the future with Reese's just used needle. I feel Reese's warmth from his heroin energized soul enter into my raging psychotic anxiety. Reese looks at me with dream-filled eyes and I intuit that he is remembering our smile towards each other weeks before. That memory is now stirred-in to warm whatever bond might be brewing between us.

I mimic Reese's behavior with my own dope and the result is the same. The shit is great, and I happily leave Williamsburg with three bags in my pocket, my immediate evening's future assured.

Two weeks later I get off the bus and am walking towards the park when I see Reese going into a candy store near Division Street. Hoping he was carrying, I quickly enter the little Bodega and find him having a coke in a back booth alone.

I was still psychotic and terrified of everyone, but black people could sometimes hold an extra tension. You never knew how much anger they felt towards you for simply being white. The Puerto Ricans, on the other hand, were much more laid back and probably my favorite group. They often spoke Spanish, which I found to be a marvelous balm for my mental state. Because I understood little, I found their words to be more like musical notes than communication, as it was impossible to misinterpret their meaning, which was the constant source of anxiety when around humans using English phenomes.

But Reese and I had gotten along so well in our last two encounters, I figured I could at least approach him to buy more dope.

"Hey, what's happenin'?"

"Hey, my man," he answered, offering a wave of a hand towards the empty bench in the booth opposite him.

(beat)

"Ya got?"

"Waitin, maybe half-hour."

I grimace. A half-hour seems like a lot of time, but it's a 15 minute walk just to the schoolyard.

As we talk it becomes clear what Reese is looking to do. Buy twenty or thirty dollars worth of dope at a bulk discount, then resell to make a few free bags for himself. As we talk, I tell him I drive a cab, and am switching to days in order to make it easier to cop. He finds this interesting, he says, that I have a constant flow of tip money and am looking to cop every day, and he is looking to buy small weight every day.

He looks at his watch and says it's time for him to go. He adds that if I want to front him twelve bucks, he'll return with four four-dollar bags or maybe five three-dollar bags for me.

I look at him and laugh a little, making a weird face.

"What's funny?" he asks.

"I guess this is the '*I won't come in your mouth time*,'" I say, looking down, terrified now that he thinks I'm looking for a homosexual liason. As a result of this self-conscious review of my words, I am immediately engulfed in the homosexual imagery. I am not turned on sexually at all, however.

"*I won't come in your mouth*," he deadpans.

I couldn't help it. Wanting so badly to trust someone – and win their approval by doing so – I wind up sitting around that candy store for almost an hour, sure I've been beat for the money I fronted Reese. Now my heroin withdrawal meets my self-critical thoughts about letting this guy take all my money, and I'm flirting with suicidal imaginings. My decision to give him the money as seen as further evidence of my wimpiness, and my brain reels with fiery notions in which the pathetic meets the helpless.

I imagine his reaction upon hearing I've killed myself. One part of me sees him chagrined, the opposing and mocking viewpoint shows him relieved that he wouldn't have to see me again while owing me money, calling me a honky fool. Suddenly the door to the candy store opens and Reese comes in.

"Good shit," he says with a smile.

"**What a guy**!" I shriek.

Reese suggests going back to his place to get off.

"I live with my mom and sisters," he says. I'm relieved to hear that, cause I am not looking for a sex scene with him, but I am also thinking perhaps he's lying and am somewhat anxious at the thought of a bunch of black guys beating me to death in a ghetto apartment. But the old Lenny Bruce comedy bit about the idiot kidnapper who grabs junkies that nobody wants also crosses my mind.

I'm tempted to ask him for my share of the dope on the way to his place but it doesn't feel right to do that. Neither does *not* asking. I see myself as a little bitch-boy tagging along behind daddy. We climb two flights of stairs in a building not unlike my earlier East Village apartment. As we get to the door we hear loud female voices arguing inside.

"Don't worry, it's cool," Reese says reassuringly as we get to his door. I find the empathy useful. *Oh please don't steal my heroin*, I worry.

We enter and his teenage sisters turn and look at us briefly. Small talk is made between him and them: Have they seen so-and-so? Has what's-his-name called? I am introduced and accepted with a nod.

A dismissive twist of the eyebrows from the older one allows me to know what she thinks. The younger one smiles shyly. The mother comes into the living room from the kitchen,

"This is my mom," says Reese,

"Nice to meet ya," I say politely, realizing I don't know anybody's last name.

"Hi," she says, looking me over. She knows what we're doing here.

She returns to the kitchen, and we retire to Reese's bedroom, where I get my dope, shoot up, and am happily ensconced in a heroin cloud as Reese's mom calls out to say she's going out. The air conditioning is better in the living room and we go out there. I am in a profound state thinking that the only thing better than being on heroin is being on heroin with a bunch more in your pocket. The smack has totally relieved me of any awkwardness towards the people and the situation I'm in, reinforcing in my mind the wisdom of my choice of medication.

Reese has proven himself, has accepted me, and I am floating free. We work out a deal wherein I agree to front him at least ten dollars each time I come down to the neighborhood. This allows me to book over to his place as soon as my taxi shift is done, and my stuff will be there hassle free. With daily tip money for dope and my salary for rent, I have to admit to a certain amount of satisfaction about my new state of affairs.

As the summer of 1971 drags on, I am an almost daily visitor to the Jackson apartment. Evette and Maddy are used to me, and are easily amused by my self-deprecating comments on myself and white people in general.

They were once showing each other some spiffy dance move and then looked at me. I would say "you know white people can't do that. Here, let me show you how I would do that," and I would imitate an early 60's frug move with the fists and straight forearms going up and down with the head in time, and then rotating my backside real slow while they howled with laughter. Their mother came out of the kitchen to see what was happening and smiled at the sight. Of course I was high on heroin at the time. Had to be. Nevertheless, it was the most fun I had had in years. Good therapy.

Between the dropping of the Permitil, the current intake of heroin and my shrieking psychosis, my libido was generally in shambles. I hadn't had sex since the hospital over a year before. I did long, however, to get enough heroin to invite a local female junkie I had met in the park back to my subterranean apartment. She was kind of hot in a skinny, street-tough Juliet Lewis *Basketball Diaries* kind-of-way. She had a very interesting face. I couldn't tell if she was pretty or homely in that she looked different from almost every angle. She had a kind of cute button nose with thicker lips than you'd expect from such a thin-boned face. Her eyes sparkled with a critical cynicism that she would occasionally allow to flash, and then they would soften into that '*seen-it-all*' thousand yard stare. She was my Dylanesque "*Sad Eyed Lady of the Lowlands*," and I yearned for her on certain occasions. I loved her intensely at those moments, although we never really had a chance to even speak to each other outside the most perfunctory remarks. Her visage was usually drawn by anxiety and junk sickness, eyes narrowed and nervous.

I longed to relieve her travail by giving her drugs and oral sex. I imagined giving her dope, and then oral sex right after she shot up. I could realize my face between her legs awash in her juices, and when that image would come over me I would find my nostrils widening to catch her scent, and find a slight moan escaping my lips spontaneously, even though I was alone and she was nowhere in sight.

My mom and dad had moved to LA while I was in Hillside. My mom had suffered through her second open-heart surgery and was told the cold weather of New York was not good for her at all. They had a pretty nice setup going in LA and wanted me out to visit. I went.

It was almost glorious. The warm sun shown every day on clean streets. Everywhere there were swimming pools, the ocean and then there was the most incredible thing of all: *California girls*! Whether it was the Hollywood mentality or the warm weather, it seemed almost every female wore almost nothing and had a look that snapped your head around.

I was off the medication, had acquired the ability to somewhat muffle and mumble my way through social conventions, and, taking the path of least resistance, found myself agreeably open to my mother's idea of returning to college at the University of California at Northridge.

I returned to New York with the idea of moving out to LA firmly established in my mind. As I mentally prepared to leave New York, I played the guilt card on my mother by calling her soon after returning.

"Listen, mom. Let's be honest. You and dad have a nice thing out there, and I know… the hospital and stuff… You don't have to say you want me out there… I understand."

"What are you talking about? We both want you to come out," she said with alarm in her voice.

Well, I owe some money and stuff here. Can you help me?

In order for my mother to prove what an embarrassment I wasn't, I wind up getting hundreds to party with. I'm spending quality time in Williamsburg. On my way up I occasionally buy a large take-out bucket of chicken for Reese's people, and when I knock on their door and they ask who it is, I simply say *"it's me."*

I can't find Diane the junkie date I wanted, and the money simply evaporates as I quit my job and stay liberally fortified with Williamsburg wisdom. It is during these last days of familiarity that a political face normally unseen comes out of the dark red mist to stare me right in the eye, and I wonder why no one else is seeing it the way I do.

Somethin's goin' down in the living room. Evette and Maddy are serious about something.

"Y'know Charlene got it bedder den Momma," say Evette, in her fifteen year-old wisdom.

"How dat?" say Maddy, the shy fourteen year old.

"Charlene only got her 'n dababy. Momma got you, me, Reese n'herself 'tink bout. Charlene got it made, dat fo' damn sure."

"What's Charlene got? I ask."

"Her own crib!" Maddy exclaims excitedly, *Gone With The Wind* wide-eyed. It seems Charlene has been their life-long friend and neighbor, had just turned sixteen, had a baby out-of-wedlock, and has assumed the full mantle of womanhood with all the perks the government could bribe her with in order to enter such a state "accidentally" (of course).

I see in Maddy's wide-eyed amazement an eager acolyte for a similar fate, and my heart sinks a little.

"But she's tied down with a baby now for eighteen years," I counter. "Her possibilities in life are really limited."

The heavy effects of my last injection haven't completely worn off. I was still feeling no pain, and my sudden ability to speak about life and opportunity was too tempting to ignore. Without the heroin to dull the paranoia, it would have been impossible.

"Possibilities? Sheeyettt..." Evette offered. Wha' poss-bil-ties? Work at 'da market? You can' get no place doin' dat! She **on her own**, got'r crib rent **covered**, **cash in hand**, **food** stamps, **medical** taken care of fo' dababy... Sheeyett. Besides, what you know, man? Real woman, *she* **have a child**." (emphasis Evette)

"Hey, I may just be a honkie on dope, but you're giving up your (lowering my voice to tick off a list of stuff) virginity (Maddy looks down embarrassed) – you can't live with the guy – and sure, you can't get the same benefits working at a low paying job *right away*, but if you hang in there, they'll pay more, and if you learn the job good, they'll *want* to keep you, and they'll pay you more to keep you. After a few years at some convenience store or fast-food place as manager, you'll make three times as much getting a job with a Fortune 500 type of outfit. Especially as a black woman. What seems like a lot of promise now with some green, food stamps and some project apartment is gonna turn into a weight 'roun your neck. You're gonna find your life is over before it begins."

"You mean like yours?" Evette says, her eyes scoping derisively at me over the tops of her glasses while her younger sister squeals in shock.

"You got me," I say, and I say no more, throwing up my hands as pantomime shields to protect myself. Sliding back into the old overstuffed chair, I note to myself that if I keep my hands up between me and them just a little longer, maybe they won't see my face flaming so very red.

I corresponded with Reese twice after moving to LA. The second letter was a Christmas catch-up piece. Both his sisters were pregnant.

People with their heads-up-their-ass call this 'compassion' or 'welfare-abuse.' When fourteen year olds with third-grade reading levels are encouraged to go out, get fucked and get pregnant, the correct word is "targeted."

Maddy and Evette picked up some cash stuffing political flyers, while Reese indicated in his between the lines sarcasm that their service to the local party leaders might have been of a more intimate nature. Maddy, I was pleased to see, was eager to share her newfound political acumen in the last communication I was to receive from them. She scrawled out her message in her own hand below Reese's PS: *Don' ferget tavote least once (haha) at da lection fer da gummint. Evette sayin Democrats wanna git us anuder 2hundrid on top of what weeze git now if I'ze have 'nother chyle. Daze da fren of da black foke. dat fer sure.*

Love, Maddy.

Chapter 9 – Hell Puts on a Smile – Los Angeles 1973

I arrive in LA and my folks have an extra bedroom. I know no one and I hit up the last of my heroin on one of those often-useless patios that look so charming when you rent the place. Then you come to see it as the tedious receptacle of fake shrubs and a shocking amount of gritty dirt comes from nowhere. The wrought iron flowerpot holder scrapes and shrieks on the gritty floor.

So now two years after the hospital, I am in LA. I am on SSI (Supplemental Security Income) for mental disability. Enrolled at Cal State Northridge with dreams of a degree in psychology, that doesn't last long. I soon need something to replace the relatively small heroin habit I had going in NYC. I soon come to find Tuinols, Seconols and especially the methaqualone phenomenon. There appears to be a new psychopharmacological niche in the form of a drug called Quaalude.

An interesting form of soporific, Quaalude translates an extremely pleasant and heady reality for 15 to 40 minutes (depending on how much food one has in the stomach). In the unusually pleasant head-space this chemical introduced, sexual activities came to be regarded (sometimes suddenly) as a surprisingly amenable activity. I say "surprisingly" because females not intending to have sex would often be searching for their panties after the drug wore off. The amount of females heartily attesting to this fact would make this drug legendary within months.

The basic truth was that – in most cases – unless the girl was unusually virtuous or actively disliked you, you were probably going to get laid. Not only did a single dose of a Rorer-714 (Quaalude 300 mg) create a mellow and euphoric state of mind, it so increased the natural pleasure of tactile sensation that a kiss and the promise of naked skin was just too heady a euphoria for many females to say "no" to. I even had a doctor and later a pharmacist ask me (not without a little guilt in their expression) if it was true what they had heard regarding this drug and "...*ahem, sex*?" Kids wore T-shirts with the Rorer-714 Quaalude logo on it.

I could sense this was my direction. Like a future astronaut approaching Cape Canaveral, like Robert Redford's character in "The Natural," I "knew" there was a place for me in this niche. And gold there was, in the form of a stomach malady that I had learned to control and live with.

You see, except for a few "script doctors" here and there, it was becoming almost impossible to get doctors to prescribe these anymore.

The FDA had sent out warning letters regarding their addictive properties and propensity for abuse and Quaalude prescriptions were being monitored by the medical governing bodies.

A typical doctor patient conversation would go something like this. Having honed my skills as a patient with thousands of hours of therapy, I actually geared up for these confrontations.

"What seems to be the problem?"

"I just came out from New York and I've started this new job with a sales organization. I can't sleep lately, and my ulcer is acting up.

"You have an ulcer?"

"Yes."

"What kind, do you know? It's been diagnosed?"

"It's duadenol. I am in the process of getting engaged, and lately, I lower my voice and almost imperceptibly looking left /right in the examining room, I've been failing sexually."

This usually causes a shift in the doctor's comfort level.

"In New York they gave me some long-term antacid for during the day and Quaaludes at nigh…"

"Oh, no! Those pills have been re-designated as Class 2 narcotics, and.." he says, peering at me over his glasses and changing his voice tone, "*it's considered evidence of drug reliance to ask for pills by name.*"

I roll my eyes. "*I'm* not a drug addict. I have an ulcer, and…"

He cuts me off like he knows what I'm all about. Even though he is basically correct in his estimation of me, I do a slow burn.

"We'll schedule you for an Upper GI. In the meantime I'll write for Librium and some …" he would go on to mention some other limp-dick drug that I would only cash the prescription for if the Medicaid paid.

I was a warrior. A warrior doesn't shrink from doing battle with those forces that would seek to thwart his heroic goals. Two days before the X-Ray exam known as an "Upper GI" – which stands for "Upper Gastro-Intestinal" (meaning the X-ray would detect ulcerated lining in the stomach area) – I go into battle mode. I am like the screaming football player smashing into the tackling dummy.

No milk and cereal for this boy in the morning. Cigarettes and two cups of very strong coffee start the day. A short walk to the Taco Belle in the warm LA mid-morning sun continues this punishing trial. I return armed with the ammunition necessary for the task at hand: tacos on the hard shell smothered with Extra Hot sauce, and wash it down with a beer.

The dull persistent ache starts below the rib cage. It doesn't diminish now with my breathing as it normally would. *Is that all you got*? I sneer at my own inner fissure, the sore that was eating away part of my stomach lining.

'*See what you can do with this.*' I dare it as I tip back some Tequilla and chase it with a beer and more cigarettes. *Marihuana*? What a great idea! Add some anxiety too, bitch! Like Rocky Marcianno willing to take two punches just to give one, I wade in daring my opponent to give me more. The next 36 hours pit a man accustomed to pain against a sore determined to give him more, ultimately uniting as one in the drive for supreme discomfort. Then the eight-hour fast prior to the exam.

I drink the evil tasting potion at the Radiologist's office and they take their X-rays. A week later I'm sitting in the same exam room I had suffered the humiliation in at the hands of this pontificating MD.

As the doctor came in, I looked up to see an added bonus was in store for the Marty. He hadn't seen the chart with the Radiology report yet!

Dr. Samuels, young father of two, an active volunteer at Helping Inner City Youth and Big Brother, flipped open my chart after glancing at me with a barely disguised condescension that said '*oh, you again.*'

Your expression's changing, bee-yatch! *What have you got to say for yourself, now*?

"You've got an ulcer!" he says now. Genuine alarm is in his voice. "This could bleed if we don't take care of it!"

"It hurts… almost all the time, now," I murmur pitifully, not without a little intonation of *I wouldn't have had to suffer this whole month if you had believed me*" thrown in to a point where I became paranoid that I was overplaying my hand.

"I just don't know what to do. In New York, they tried the same pills at first that you prescribed… just like the ones you gave me last time (*see, boychick, mama is acknowledging you tried, yes, you were a good boy, you did the right thing given your state of understanding at the time, but now…*), but.."

"What did you say worked? he broke in quickly. He was not about to screw up what obviously had worked for the previous medical men. That would have appeared *negligent* and could be construed as *bad medicine*. "What finally worked?, he asked, although we both knew the answer.

"The qualludes and I think Librium and something for long-term antacid relief."

Well, I'd rather you take 5 mg Librium and you'll take one Quaalude at night for sleep.

"Sometimes one-and-a-half works better." Seeing his doubt, I comforted him with "sometimes no pill at all, if I'm tired, I just fall asleep." But a good night's sleep just seems to diminish the effects of the ulcer so much…"

Sometimes one of the doctors – especially after a few months of this routine, would write for 45, and then I would come in again after 30 days. He would occasionally notice the discrepancy between the 45 days worth of pills and the 30 days in between visits.

They would often have the same look on their faces as they'd remind me not to make a return visit until the full amount of time was up, but they'd let it go "this time." It was the kind of look a girl gives you on the first makeout when you squeeze her breasts and she gives you that "I don't want you to do that," but keeps kissing you anyway.

After a year in LA, my ongoing, continual monthly score from all my doctors included one 60 Quaalude script, another 45 day prescription and 2 more for 30 days, and another prescription for Parest, which was a competing Methaqualone product (same ingredients as Quaalude) 60 tuinols (a two month supply), and of course a steady but shrinking supply from the Hollywood doctors who were fighting with their lawyers to continue their pill mill. Nice guys though.

One of the advantages of Medicaid, at least in California at that time, was the unlimited availability of top-quality medicine. There was literally no limit to the amount of doctors and meds you could put on the card, and whether I had a headache or a heart attack, I could go into a hospital Emergency Room and be seen. It was literally "money's no object."

I had moved out of mom and dads and now within months had over two hundred Quaaludes plus barbiturates coming to me legally every month, with the government check to help pay my rent and extras. I would pick up some short money selling wholesale belts at swap meets up and down the California coast, and I was just never lonely with all this dope continually on hand.

People were genuinely happy to see me in social settings. I do not know how important this was to my ability to stay therapeutically "functional" during that time. Before the hospital I was around a college-hippie crowd. Before that Brooklyn middle-class. Now my social set consisted of heavy drinkers working low-paying jobs, in and out of trouble, marriages, pregnancies, jail-time, drug-addictions and drunken binges, and they regarded me as a 'person of prestige.' If I met two young couples at a party, for example, and asked them if they had ever tried Quaaludes, and they eagerly responded they wanted to, but had little or no money, I would give them each one. Within twenty minutes I was looked at by the four as something Messianic, and the hugs were genuine, and soon I had girls in my bed. I don't know how much value to attach to my post-hospital out-patient "social treatment" under these circumstances.

It definitely made my psychotic mental state more tolerable. Although I was never comfortable around people, I was certainly more comfortable on soporifics relating to people who were smiling warmly at me. They always appeared eager and interested to know how I was. I found out that – as with many drugs – the more you're into them, the more often sex can slip through your fingers. You start off sure you'll get laid, then you and the willing girl take too much, and wind up too stoned to do the deed.

Before plunging into the pills in this heavy way, however, months before a Beverly Hills shrink had been arranged for me through family connections. After the interview, he agreed to see me at a reduced price. He made sense, we communicated well, and he convinced me to stop all drugs and to try working. At the very least, we could get an idea of 'where I was at.'

I took a part-time job for the Christmas rush at UPS, simply looking up weight and zip code info and charging the customer appropriately. I simply gave UPS a different social security number to avoid any problems with my government SSI check. The first day was torture with the anxiety so high in the red-line that I could barely speak to anyone. I was so terrified that I considered suicide the next day on the way to work. I actually pulled my car over to the side of the road on my way to the UPS depot, and purposely banged my head onto the steering wheel like some cartoon character accentuating his frustration. I burned alive with an anxiety so overwhelming I could barely look or speak to customers without becoming totally psychotic. I also sat down when I shouldn't; smoked when I wasn't supposed to and fantasized that I was a hero there while hoping to get fired so I could go home, get into bed, jerk-off and turn on some music. Monday and Tuesday were done, and now it was time for my Wednesday shrink session in Beverly Hills.

A wealthy relative had outgrown my size in clothing so I had this one expensive sweater and slacks outfit which was my uniform for the 90210. I arrived a half-hour early at North Bedford Drive in the center of Beverly Hills; a short walk from some of the most elite and expensive stores in the world.

I went into this little "coffee shop" thirty yards down the street. They also served wine and quiche, and were frequented by probably some of the most beautiful and moneyed people in the world. I entered to see one of the most beautiful women I had ever seen in my life serving as a waitress. She was new, and a glance told me her story: A fight with a boyfriend or similar circumstance finds her temporarily working.

An Asian beauty in her early twenties, she was nothing short of magnificent. Her waist-length hair alone made you catch your breath. But her brow carried a posture of such dignity that it not only accentuated her fantastic figure, but outshone it. A potential haughtiness infused her bearing, one that could cut you so deep you had to approach it. A trophy wife in the making, her proud carriage announced for all the world to see that she would be perfectly at home in any club or mansion.

    I am outside myself in adoration. I notice her five-second interaction with the chef and the manager and immediately I "know" what must be done. She is downhearted, her current efforts to survive happily and successfully at life being blocked by these miserable, inconsiderate people. My heart empathizes. I'm going for it, and look forward to the effort. She is standing at my table. I press on the accelerator and I don't look back.

    "They always do that to you, don't they?"

    "Wha...?"

    "Them." I nod imperceptibly towards her bosses. "Listen, " *I make like OK, I'll share this with you.* "As far as beautiful women go, you are head and shoulders above all the models and actress wanna-bees that come in here all day long, and look at *them.*" I nod my head in the direction of her irritating superiors. "They probably don't even know how unfair they are to you. I'll bet you've been getting that all your life." Casting my eyes down with a bashful smile, I am half-a-second in front of her question as I add, "and I'll take coffee and a croissant."

    "Thanks" she says in a warm open tone. I smile older brother.

    When she returns with the order, I am totally in love.

    "Y'know, if I don't say this, I'll feel like a coward all week. You *know that,*" I add, with my eyes laughing as if we've been familiar for years. "I know everybody hits on you, and there are a lot of nuts out there, *I know, I know,*" I mime silently, putting up my hands in defense, "but I was thinking with all these outdoor café's on Sunset..." (*the image comes with my words, and now I am standing outside this workplace, dressed in a beautiful sports jacket and slacks. I straighten up from sitting on the fender of my Mercedes to greet her as she gets off work*) "if you wanted we could meet for a coffee, a drink or whatever you want in an *outdoor place*, surrounded by other people, and you could see if I'm like... nuts, or whatever," and we both laugh, as I notice she is allowing me to continue. "If after a drink, you're still inclined to, uhh, speak to me (small shrug), maybe we could go out to Santa Anita for a few races. Maybe, y'know, get a table in the Clubhouse, just stay for *few* races," I shrug again over the word '*few*' "and, y'know, that's all..."

    Y'know, it's not a good idea to see customers..."

"Of course, you're right. I shouldn't be bothering you." I add shortly. I shake my head, annoyed with myself.

"Oh, no," she added very quickly. And when her words came gushing out that rapidly, my dick tingled.

"I've got other orders," she said with an apologetic face, as if to make sure I found her excuse sincere. A thrilling sensation shoots through my chest.

She came over with the check.

"Never say die," I add with hands out, smile on, palms up in a 'what am I gonna do' shrug. "Sometimes... and I don't want you to think I'm a drug user, cause I'm *not*, but my doctor gave me a prescription for Quaaludes (*is that how you pronounce them*?), about two months ago. I don't take them any more, but once in a while, they're kinda' fun." Her expression still open, I move on. "Again, I'm not, y'know, *into* drugs (*really, I haven't shot up in weeks!*), but sometimes I snort a little coke, and it's fun at the racetrack sometimes. Well, Just a thought."

I gave her a ten dollar bill for the under five dollar tab, and when she brought me the change, I make a face as I put up my hands in a *'puhleeze'* gesture; indicating I wouldn't dare take change from ten dollars for a four-and-change bill. But there was something else sitting on top of the five, and it wasn't U.S. currency.

"**Here it is**," I showed my stunned analyst the matchbook cover a half hour later in our session. I handed the torn off matchbook cover towards him with the girl's name and phone number on it.

"You can pick up women on a dime, so what is driving you so crazy at work?" he says, his voice still full of wonder, his face working to lose the traces of genuine astonishment. It struck me later that he had been in the coffee shop himself at least a few times prior to my adventure, and had seen my trophy – in the flesh, so to speak.

"I don't know," I answered honestly.

The next week I felt like I had planted a land-mine with my overture. Since I was living at home with my mom and dad making $6 an hour, I purposed to simply avoid going back to the coffee shop. Fortunately, the girl had left this employ before my next visit.

The Valley Drug Store

I became friendly with Ray, who had rented a three-bedroom house in the San Fernando Valley and was looking for a roommate. He had been the apartment manager in the previous place I rented. Being the manager, I had plied him with ludes, and it turned out he was a great "T and A" man, so we became good friends. I was the first Jew he had ever met on a social basis, and I learned what subtle anti-Semitic foundations were laid in this good-ol-boy from the Midwest. What was most interesting was they weren't personal, nor to him even important. Assumptions and pre-judgments concerning my people existed which were simply, to his mind, no big deal (*The Jews must've done something wrong to piss off all those Germans...*). He agreed they were wrong, but like, really... (*in his mind*), what's the big deal?

It was a San Fernando Valley three bedroom with a porch that ran off into the fenced backyard that had enough cover for a fourth visitor who was to introduce me to a new slant on sex. Fat girl sex. Mammoth, gelatinous thigh, fat-girl-sex. These people are *so underappreciated* as sex objects. They are possibly the best natural sex partners. I could just lay on top of her forever. So comforting. But she moved out.

But soon there was Billy, drugstores and heroin.

Billy arrived on the scene from Alabama with an affable grin, the ability to spin an interesting story while whittling wood with his bucknife, sing a good song on his 6-string, and with hardly a penny to his name. There was a girl in our crowd who I was always trying to make but never could. We just had no chemistry; probably stemming from the fact that we were both unconsciously attracted sexually by the same type of crude male. But she was a great looking stoner party-girl and had a figure to die for. Billy bagged her the first night, and by the weekend had her crooning along to his rendition of *"Big Ten-Inch"* on his six-string, which was a somewhat below-the-radar song of the day in the early 70's.

One morning soon afterwards Billy shows up in a Baja-bug dune buggy, a fistful of cash and a cardboard box full of drugs. Drugs in their pharmaceutical wholesale bottles.

"These are what I *haven't* sold yet," he announces with a grin.

Vinny had cashed in on what was, for a brief period of time, the easiest score in Los Angeles. Burglarizing drug stores after-hours for narcotics. In the early seventies, drugstores had the simple minimal security just like any other small business. If they got robbed for drugs, their insurance took care of most of it, and their deductible was small compared to the cost of installing an upgraded security system.

The problem for the drugstores – and the opportunity for the drug robber – was that in California, due to the unique earthquake potential, the legislature had mandated that all narcotics must be able to be reached by paramedics in case of emergencies. They could not be locked securely. Consequently, the narcotics cabinet opened with a swift yank. By sending in a minor to burglarize with a pillow case or two, one could hit a terrific score with very little chance of getting caught. If the minor got caught, he was out of Juvenile Hall in days, and he knew it. When he didn't get caught, the haul was enormous; not merely for quantity but from a quality perspective: Dilaudid, Morphine, Opiates, Barbiturates, Hypnotics, Amphetamines, Methamphetamines of all types, along with surprising exotic stuff that nobody normally ever heard of.

Billy had hooked up with people who knew some Hell's Angels who were into this, and when the minor they had chosen didn't show, Billy said "*fuck it, I'll do it*," and after having to split his loot with them, he simply took off more drugstores on his own.

Plainclothes soon showed up looking for Billy. I had only seen cops this way on TV shows. These were not TV cops. They were like ordinary looking people, only much more mean and scary. Ray, who was a solid 6'2", said, "Hey, hold on a minute," as they started walking throughout the house. "You guys have a search warrant?" One of the detectives shoved him so hard into the wall that the entire room shook. He asked Ray if he wanted some trouble. Ray responded that he did not.

It was therefore with some trepidation that I received a 2 a.m. phone call from Billy. They had hit a drugstore but were uncertain of some of their loot. I had a reputation for knowing a lot about pharmaceuticals, as I lived off of scripts for designer drugs and I kept a PDR (Physician's Desk Reference) in my bedroom. This was considered sophisticated in the years before the internet.

He asked me if I could meet him to help out. I found him up in a house in the Topanga Canyon amidst a lot of scary-looking people and found also that he had a tremendous jar of Opiate of Merck that the boss guy - who was full of tattoos and scars with a buck knife openly hanging from his belt – said he did not want opened because it would hurt the resale value. After helping out with identifying that and other sundry pills and capsules, I asked for a cut. The leader, who was so smashed he could hardly walk straight, asked if I did H. I said I sure did, and he reached into his vest pocket and tossed me a folded penny envelope with so much dope in it that I went on a six-day binge of nonstop shooting. I don't think he meant to throw me that much. He had another envelope in his vest pocket that looked smaller.

I also swaggled them out of the Opium suppositories, which I said were probably no good since they should've been kept refrigerated, and now they were warm and melted. "Anyone into putting these up their ass?" I asked, embarrassing everyone and promptly pocketed three boxes.

Somehow I wound up shooting up with somebody I met at this post-robbery split up. We hung out for a couple of days shooting up together, and he made some calls the morning we both ran out of smack and said another drug store hit was planned for that very night.

It was a guy he had met through somebody else, and he would use names and places in a rambling coming-off-of-dope stream of consciousness that I did little to stop. He would talk as if I knew who these people were, peppering his conversation with references to being in the joint, who knew who and the like. I had listened since I was shooting heroin, but didn't really take it in. When I asked if the guy we were going to meet for the drugstore job was in the group I had met before, he lowered his voice:

"No, they kind of dissed him to not have him there, and he was really pissed, and you don't want this guy pissed at you," he adds shaking his head. "Don't worry, he wants you there in case we need you for the books."

"What's my cut? What's my deal?"

"I don't know, but Don will do you right."

That kind of vagueness was unnerving, but I didn't think there was any point in saying more. I would wait for Don, but my withdrawal from running out of heroin was starting to be enormous, and I began to see there was little I wouldn't do to get down. I began to anticipate the Dilaudid, the Percodans, the opiates, and if we got lucky, the exotic extra stuff you never knew or heard much about. The opium suppositories were a good example of that, as they created a body high that crept into your brain producing a mongo opium cloud of blissful delirium. It was a magical place that existed near sleepytown, and the trick was to not get caught napping in sleepytown, cause you could sleep right through the good-times and then wake up worse-than-straight with a raging jones screaming for more. Well, what else was new?

Meeting Don was not a pleasant experience. Neither was it reassuring. He was also coming off heroin, and in addition was a highly offensive, paranoid, ugly, scarred, pock-mocked and tattooed moron. He was unsure of what to do but thin-skinned defensive at even the slightest hint that he didn't know everything there was to know about drugstore hits. When I would ask questions about the alarm, he would act like he was engaging in a vast amount of compassion not to just smash me in the face. He would look at me with pretended kindness *but like, I'm not going to put up with this again.* In other words, he was crazy.

Neil, who I had been shooting dope with for most of these last few days and was also jones-ing really bad, is making faces and using body language to tell me to shut up and not say anything. He sidled up to me at one point when the Hell's Angel was far out of earshot.

"Leave this guy alone."
We had met Don and the kid in a house - part of which was being rebuilt. It turned out nobody was living there while the front room was being built where the porch used to be and the house itself was locked. Whenever a car came down the street, however, we had to duck down because the new construction stood out like a sore thumb and so did we if we were caught in the headlights.

The kid left to do the job. He walked the five minutes to the drugstore, crashed through the window in the back, ransacked for the proscribed two minutes, and disappeared back into the dark streets with a double pillowcase of items, negotiating furtively back to the three of us.

Back at the ranch all three of us withdrew in silence from our addictions and from each other. Within fifteen minutes we hear his rushed footsteps clambering in through the side entrance. He emptied out a pillowcase of disaster. The kid hadn't known what to get and came back with Phenobarb, antibiotics, stool softeners and assorted nonsense that he had grabbed helter-skelter as the loud burglar alarm had driven him into a panic. Prior to the break-in, he had failed to recognize the pertinence of my questions regarding the location of the narcotics cabinet. He had merely nodded curtly, eager to ape Don's dismissive attitude.

> There's little to make him happy
> His vipe is most narly snappy
> His aggravation unearthed now
> He sees you a tempting nerth cow
> He seems to eye you
> in his telescopery.
>
> Your impudence meets absolution
> *"don't do it again"*
> his solution.
> There's nothing worthy in you
> His attitude impugns you
> And he wonders why the others stay away.
>
> His notion is to scold you
> As in *"you see I told you"*
> When one was never given
> the rules to play.
> Yes he's just like a god
> 'an don't you dare annoy him, Todd

cause this Hell's Angel
can bring some hell to pay.
He's a crazy beater booter
A knife he's used
yes, scooter
and he's made some play
neath the insane psychotree.
He's made some pay in ways
you don' wannabee.

He's lookin at you thinkin'
"I'm hungry, Jew"
'n you're shrinkin'
"and you're lookin really,
really soft to me."
And you know it's comin' pain today
And you're wondering just what you'll say
And you're wonderin'
Just how he'll make you pay.

For I insulted the Hells Angel
On this bungled pharmacy foolery,
Had lit him up
a fool for all to see.
My shooting mate six days gone
Could only incredulous face on
As he realized I didn't know
to whom I had said all that to be.
Had I known the rap-sheet behavior
Of this man in such a rage here
I would not have dared
speak't all in his company.

His blood boiling all could feel
My coming beating did have appeal
a true Darwinian happymeal
to be served to all the assembled company.

Alive my pain would serve his pride
I was to be swallowed for a time alive
To suffer now the stronger drive
For his head of pride I had made to hide.

Harsh in disappointed lash-out
I had voiced my disapproving shit out.
As when sending a lad crashing in
two minutes he has to find within:

"Smarter than this
Yes one had to be.
Wise training of the lad
One had to see
to receive the best goodies for you and me.
It's important we avoid not the main thing
To teach the layout clear KA-CHING!
To show what treasures and where they do sit,
So in darkness he finds the correct cabinet;
hence avoiding us all receiving this shit:
cause Phenobarb aint worth dick!
and failure to teach him pure dumbshit!

I rose into the headlights now
Their voices "*get-down!*" grew loud
For as we hid that night
In a porch belonging
to none of us.
Angelic forces took my mindset
within a muted corset
kept my mental apparatus now abeam
and into the lights my legs did stream.
"You can keep my share"
my voice hoped for repair.
As now I footed
outside to that first stair.

Never think about what you think
Not in times like these.
Adrenaline is limited
reaction's intimidid.
And emotional thoughts too near
Can't stop to listen
– the cost's too dear!

My rubber legs pick up the slack
Craning my ears
(they are stretched back)
't the cloved-hooved sounds'
of the monster's attack?
Oh where did I park
home let me be back.
Don't run
o my G-d
Don't run.
But as the parked car got nearer
One thing got much clearer
quicker to the car
Oh, I need to be dearer!

    I couldn't stop the heroin addiction. I couldn't stay in school or keep a job. I was still on SSI (Supplemental Security Income) and only needed a once-a-year check-up to reaffirm the State's decision in that regard. I was in a once-a-week therapy, but being on drugs only tested my shrink's patience.

    The heroin addiction had gotten out-of-control. Nobody in my family would loan me a dime, I was broke and not working, and facing either petty crime or cold turkey, I found a coward's way out with a Methadone clinic.

    Methadone was really a shitty way to go. Maybe that's a good thing. I had heard it 'got you straight.' It certainly did not. It got you from feeling incredibly horrible to simply feeling bad. I was sitting in the methadone clinic on Coldwater near Ventura Blvd. in North Hollywood in order to fill out some weekly paperwork one day when the door opens and two guys walk in. One is a raging queen and the other is raging Hollywood. Very energized, they are totally out-of-place. We make eye contact. In a heartbeat they are next to me and whispering:

    "If you can find us somewhere to cop, we'll give you a freebee." I say I can try. We walk out, and there is Travis Bickle. I am introduced by Raging Hollywood.

    "This is Trav, he just finished "*Angry Roads*," raging informs me. I had vaguely heard of it, but seeing movies is not on my junkie agenda. I start to play the Hollywood type myself, apologizing that I had not seen his movie, but I could immediately see that whatever or wherever his internal place as an artist was, it was so far removed from caring whether or not I had seen or liked his performance that it was a waste of breath to speak further. Cool.

We walk over to the pay phones on Ventura Blvd., and I start dialing. Nobody home, in an era where even an answering machine is considered cutting edge. While I'm trying various people, Travis connects from the pay phone next to mine. Instead of being jettisoned, however, I am invited along, even while I assure him I am broke.

We drive over and arrive at the dealers. Travis gets a huge hug hello, and the other two are nodded at as known and huddle up with the dealer. Travis disappears into another room with the dealer. I am given my shot. It is very weak. Travis comes out smiling and asks how I liked it. I make a face and admit I barely got straight. He shoots a really disapproving look at the raging duo and my suspicions are immediately confirmed: the stuff was really OK, but they took so much of what was supposed to be mine I got shorted. Travis, to his credit, is genuinely annoyed.

He suggests we leave for a movie they were planning to see, and invites me along, waving aside my comment that I am still as broke as I was before. *Godfather* is still playing at the small theatre on Ventura Blvd., even though it's been out for a long time. It is the pre-video era, so movies could hang on in theatres a bit longer, and amidst my psychotic withdrawal anxieties, by the time the evening is over I wonder if the guy sitting next to me doesn't look a hell-of-a-lot like the guy in the coming attractions for Godfather II. Although I am not in the mood to appreciate creative performance, I am impressed with the princely street behavior of Mr. Bickle.

* * *

Giving up on Methadone, I had struck up a heroin friendship with a guy named Bernie. He and I palled around scoring. One time, when we were out of dope and bored, he had whipped out his impressive dick and raised his eyebrow. I declined. Later when his girl-friend was with us, I sensed they were into three-somes with at least one of the other junkies, and that she was actually annoyed that I had turned her boyfriend down. She gave me the creepy feeling like she was about to accuse me of feeling morally superior, or something along those lines. There was definitely a chill in the air. Bernie and I had a falling out over dope and I didn't speak to him for months.

I began using coke. But while trying to score cocaine one night, all I could get from the dealer was heroin, but when I went over the dealer's house to buy it, Bernie and his girl are there. We mutter to each other, and

Bernie asks, after mumbling some half-assed apology, if he and his girl can get off at my place.

Never having learned my lesson from Larry in Brooklyn, I am still willing to die for approval, so I grudgingly say yes. I haven't done heroin in a long time, and this stuff is very strong. I shoot and feel a burn knocking out my "head-lights" as I lose consciousness.

I wake up alone hours later, and stumble out my own door staggering and puking. The next thing I know the cops are there, and I am in jail. I am very sore and sick in my stomach, and the jail doctor sends me up to another doctor, who examines me and sends me to the county hospital. I have internal bleeding from trauma to my midsection. I need surgery to sew up a lacerated liver.

Bernie would later claim they were trying to get me to come to (consciousness), but a doctor gave me the impression he thought their efforts might have had less benevolent motives.

* * *

Soon after crashing and burning at Cal State Northridge, I was just starting my Quaalude roll when I enrolled in Tech School. I noticed her during mid-morning break.

The scene with Elle was truly amazing. A short, delicious blonde with a cute nose and pretty face, her 18 year-old body boasted beautiful breasts, a slim waist and a small, almost non-existent ass. I nodded hello on a Monday at the lunch counter. I talked briefly with her Wednesday as to what courses she was taking, what she thought of the people in her classes and the teachers at the tech school. On Friday I asked her if she got high, and 5 minutes later we were smoking a joint in her car, taking Quaaludes, and making out.

If you took a headshot of her all you would see was a fairly fresh and innocent pretty blonde face. The whole picture, on the other hand, told a different story. The lowcut jeans combined with an sexual easiness that you can only sense.

Our make-out in the parked car started out kind of normal. Kissing, stroking her cheek a little, her neck, her hair behind her ear, then her ear lobe, eventually beginning to squeeze her firm left breast. Still busying ourselves kissing, her hand came up to push my hand away, and as this routine recurred once more, I lifted my right hand up the moment before it was to be pushed away, and quickly clamping it down on the hand that was on its way to push mine away, proceeded to squeeze her breast rather forcefully though her own hand which was now imprisoned between mine and the beautiful bosom. She emitted a desire to yield that was so strong I found myself emitting a low growl from somewhere deep in my throat.

She pulled back with a deep breath and suggested we go back to her parents house as they were both at work.

Elle's sexual hunger can best be compared as that of an infant's desire for the milk-bottle's nipple when he's hungry for it. Sometimes a baby's eyes will roll back in their head with the total relief experienced upon sucking on the nipple of the milk bottle. Elle gave off that same vibration of relief when she got a cock in her mouth. It was a source of succor for her to assuage the tensions inherent in meeting new people, or in most social situations. I suppose symbolically the act was grounded in the logic of *who would want to hurt you if you're sucking their cock*? She was the only girl I ever knew, who – on more than one occasion – would ask me to stop fucking her so she could finish me off with her mouth. And it wasn't that I was a bad lay. Elle simply loved it that way, and she seldom lost a drop. A true nymphomaniac.

After a few weeks of cutting classes to have sex every day, I asked her about her early sexual experiences, and she confided that when she was a young teen she went with four high school boys to a motel room and blew every one of them. I found myself extremely turned on by the picture of it. I couldn't stop eating her, fucking her and coming in her mouth. After a bizarre situation passing muster with her father and stepmother, she asked me to move in with her at their house.

Her Parents

Although I had been carrying on sexually with Elle for a few weeks, I hardly had any contact with her parents. They would be at work while we were playing hooky, and when I did see them in our limited contact I didn't like what I saw. The father had been a cop for many years before he got pissed off at the bureaucracy and quit the force.

"Never work for the government," he'd say with a scowl; "everybody's your god-damn boss." He'd look me up and down, and since I was stoned most of the time, he was always scowling suspiciously. On a deeper level, I saw he had the same spirit of violence that Jim, Ronnie's gangster friend had. They were both comfortable in allowing physical violence against another to dominate a situation for their willful purposes. A mean man with very hard eyes, he scared me. The sense that violence was right under the surface, waiting, willing – perhaps even eager – to explode filled me with a dick-wilting anxiety that always begged for another Quaalude.

One afternoon while doing each other with no one home we hear the front door open and the sound of her dad calling, "Elle, get out here! Is Marty with you? Well, him too!"

I got scared. I was going to be in for a physical confrontation.

We jumped up, pushed the bed in and hurriedly dressed. I make a quick inventory that I have everything I need on me should I have to run out of the house without having to come back, and with a deep breath we walk out of her bedroom and down the hall to the living room. I do a double take, reset and look for a reality check from Chris.

In the living room we find her dad, step-mom and another couple butt-naked with drinks in their hands. Later she would say to me "Yeah, I should've told you about my parents."

"C'mon Marty, get free!" say the ex-policeman. This was an invitation to undress and join the nudists. Nudism in this case needs some explanation.

In Southern California in the early 1970's, nudists could be broken up into two main groups: One group is comprised of people who just like to be nude, and who will simply carry on the normal activities of reading in lawn chairs out in the sun, grilling, walking, swimming and laying around in full view of other nude people. At places like Elysium Fields in Topanga Canyon or in each others' fenced backyards, these were simply your average folk without clothing. As I would soon come to find out, ninety-percent of these people would be far more attractive if they'd put their clothes back on.

The other group within nudism were simply there because they liked sex. Called "swinging," it usually involved a single or couple agreeing to sexually involve themselves with other partners – in groups or privately. Elle said her dad and step-mom "used to be" into swinging, but it was bad for their marriage, so they stopped, and were now simply sunshine folk who enjoyed socializing *au naturale.*

Sometimes these swinging people would appear to be just like the other nudists, but in reality they were always "trolling" for sex partners. How do you get the 'natural-nudist' to become a swinger-nudist? Often with a bridge. Sometimes the "bridge' is that part of the Topanga Canyon Nudist colony that separates those who simply like to be nude, and those across the bridge by the waterfall who are looking to fuck their brains out.

Sometimes the bridge is not physical, merely just enough alcohol, low lights, innuendo and a devilish type of manipulation that would have the most nature-loving nudist transforming herself into an *"I'll try anything once"* pagan. It wasn't a drug, although alcohol flowed freely enough. The change-agent was a massage. The group's "Star" massage to be precise.

Everyone's nude as one person lies on his or her back (the Star) on a bearskin rug in front of the fireplace. The dance of the flames is casting the only light. Soft music plays low. Depending on how many people are there, one person sits behind your head, one on your right side by your shoulders or elbow, one by the left side, another couple by your knees or feet. So maybe 5 people (more is much better I'm told) have their gentle, hopefully experienced hands roaming your naked body. The ultimate aphrodisiac, I lay there as the central figure as all thought floated away into the tactile revelations coursing through every extremity and limb, save the genitals. They were not being touched. The sensations of so many hands roaming, touching, messaging every part of your body takes your breath away. It is absolutely overwhelming in its hypnotic ability to strip away all inhibition within its sensual carnality. Sometimes the genitals (or if a female is in the center, her breasts) are caressed gently; but only in passing. Your thoughts "go out" into the tactile sensations, leaving only a wanton craving for more pleasure.

Then it was Elle's turn. Her beautiful breasts were also hardly touched as she began to slightly undulate under the group's rising enthusiasm. Hands began to give extra sensuality and intimacy as she mewed, whimpered and shuddered under their moving fingers. Her step-mother leaned over her and asked in a low and throaty voice:
"*How ya feelin now?*" Elle, not a first-timer to this, looked into mom's eyes and muttered huskily "*I'm ready for anything.*"

You really couldn't say 'no' to this thing, but that would have been the last word to come out of Elle's mouth at this point, anyway. The male husband was on her immediately, his hands moving hungrily over her body while kissing her on the mouth. He then moved from the kiss to her breasts, and soon had his face between her legs. Like wolves on a downed animal, Elle was being set upon. The man's wife and I kissed her lightly around her face and neck while hands went everywhere.

Some time passed like this, with partnerships beginning to form. Elle's dad was all over this other guy's wife, and Elle was having her lower regions attended to by the woman's husband while I was now one-on-one with Elle's step-mom. Gina was a striking and attractive executive at some Fortune 500 company. Upon first meeting her, I was immediately taken by her good looks and figure, but it was her posture, her carriage which kind of projected an arrogant dismissal that got my lower regions tingling. Her smug look – which she seemed to always have set at semi-snear – erotically amplified her attractive thirty-something face, while allowing her fabulous ass the status of worship.

At first I was too anxious about her husband beating me up to get too hot with her, but watching the ex-cop concentrate on coaxing his three-quarter semi into the wife of this guy who was orally servicing Elle lent confidence and freedom to my lust.

The idea of going down on Miss Smug Thirty-something as a way to stop thinking about Elle filled me enthusiasm. I kissed her and soon was squeezing her breasts and nipples with a hunger that comes easily to those new to each other. I intuited something about her lust, and I put her hand on my head and pulled it in the general direction. She moaned as she pulled my curly haired noggin between her legs and I dove in with a slavish relish. It was just a small thing in itself, but I sensed she'd dig it, and she orgasmed quickly and powerfully. We relaxed for a short while, drinking and smoking a bit while watching the others. I was aching with a fire-down-below, but I knew I was impressing her by feigning(?) control. She put out her cigarette, and as she turned to me I gave her a long kiss.

Elle had intimated to me earlier that there was some problem for her father to come in his wife's mouth. I allowed the pleasure of spurting in her suckling maw a special place in my fantasy-life as mentally became one with Elle watching her go down on the other woman's husband. Coming out of the kiss and embrace, body language told me Gina was ready to return the oral sex, so turning to Gina with a kind of gang-leader sneer, I muttered "...*got somethin' for ya.*" Her eyes widened slightly, her eager smile disappearing into an eager "O" shape as oral service began.

While preparing to unload, I became feverish with the idea of fucking her in her exceptionally attractive ass. Elle refused to allow me in down there, and the thought of having different women under the same roof with different sexual pleasures to be had from each was a sailor's dream, While contemplating this was enough to complete my eager sexuality, the post-orgasmic reality of it all became less than satisfying. Also, I began to worry that after coming in his wife's mouth – and hopefully soon in her perfect ass as well – there would be serious issues between her husband and me regardless of how "free" everybody pretended to be.

But even that became a moot point as the devil's kick in the pants was that, even with a girl like Elle, I could not enjoy the spectacle of watching another man have sex with her, even when another attractive female was there for me to even things out with. I felt protective of this stupid little bitch and didn't like to see another man have her. Even though in fantasy such imaginings always triggered powerful lust-filled orgasms, in the light of reality the limp dick of betrayed loyalty and failure-to-protect always chose to step forward and in one way or another inhibit me. I fought against conscience. I tried to get turned on by the orgy, but I had to make an effort to release in orgasm, I felt somewhat awkward doing it, and irritated and depressed afterwards. Sex should not be this much work.

The fly in this ointment was that the same spirit that made Elle such a wonderful sex toy also filled her with a compulsive disloyalty. Maybe you can't have one without the other. The promiscuity that feels so delightful today puts its fist up your ass tomorrow. I had felt flattered that this beautiful queen of whores had chosen me as a bedmate at her parent's house, but, on reflection, I think I was the fly and she the spider. I was there for a tasty, constant sex meal and to pass-the-time with, but let's get crazy with lots of men was the activity demanding all our attention all too often. When you want the whore you get the Jezebel too.

I mused over the possibility that Elle also represented an opportunity to get into the sex trade with an ad proclaiming *"man and great looking blonde looking for generous threesomes."* I know I would have probably been in jail fairly quick in a drug and/or impassioned gunblaze. Elle was the type of girl certain men would kill for, and she and that kind of man were destined to be mutually attracted to one another. I was fortunate to get out of there in one piece, as I think fate had a *'death coming alive'* T-shirt with my name on it just a little further down the road.

After a few months of this Elle and I drop out of Tech school, and the situation with her parents disintegrates. I move back with my folks for a while. One night, while copping dope with Elle over some dealer's house, we run into Bernie and one of his friends. While I was scoring from the guy behind closed doors I knew they would put the make on her. I knew Elle was an insatiable whore, but *please*, I said to her when we got alone out in the car after I came out; *Not with these guys*. The making it 'prohibited' must have made them twice as sweet to her. Maybe I tried to be like G-d:

Of all the dick in the garden
thou may'st freely suck.
But that dick which hath tried to kill me
of that you may not suck.

Of course she soon hooked up with them. When I found out, I tore up our tickets to Wallapalooza, which to Elle was the smashing of the Holy of Holies. We broke up and she left the state.

* * *

I wasn't doing so much coke then, but fell in with people with doctors getting lots of different kinds of speed. Because I was so loaded with Quaaludes, Valiums and Tuinols, I was valuable as a 'go-to' guy when the speed-freaks were crashing from their binges. I also got turned onto their doctors who continued to dispense speed in these riotous times until the State shut them down. The green triangled Dexedrine and big black Bi-phetamines were almost boring compared to Disoxin and especially

Preludin. I found an especially pernicious sexual apatite could be readily obtained through this latter drug. I had never heard of it before. The pills were pink shell coatings over a softer white inner core. I called them "cream-filled." If you sucked or carefully peeled off the pink coating, and crushed, soaked and shot a couple of these inner "fillings," you – and just about anybody else this side of virginity – would offer free sex to anybody who could get you more, as two exceptionally good-looking Hollywood hookers made clear to me.

It was called (for lack of a better expression), a "mellow" high, in that you weren't into the frantic, nervous running around that is so characteristic of many amphetamine products, but the high level of sexual excitement that it seemed to feed on – particularly the calm-yet-exciting sexual plateau – was becoming legendary. Tactile sensations combined with sexual abandon to the point where you could easily agree that "anything goes." It felt good to be so. Kinky stuff seemed to be an attractive alternative, a libido on steroids running riot.

The level of excitement was so great that it easily created demands of its own, and after more and more of its bondage, you came down into pure, unadulterated hell. In desiring to get more, it was time for you to really prove your commitment to its worship. And then it's always "ratchet-up" to the next level, even if that includes an Oedipal episode and/or potential manslaughter.

I swung into my parent's apartment to pick up some cash. There was a Preludin connection waiting for me (I had already used up my prescription), and all I needed was $50 to pick up ten, which meant probably three days of hedonistic sexual riot. Consequently, when my mother pressed that fifty into my hands, it was with a placebo rush that I received it, and I was still high on the last of my *Preludins* when I arrived at my parent's apartment to get the money. I was so "up" I was in my own way delirious. But 'delirious' in a way my mother might call a "good way." That is, very happy, quick-minded, considerate, intelligent and most-of-all, replete with a 'feeling-no-pain-with-life' good mood.

As I was heading for the door to leave, I walked through the kitchen in which she was busying herself with something on the kitchen counter, and, as I had done all my life, made the brief hesitation for the kiss good-bye. She, also attuned to this, stopped what she was doing, wiped her hands on her apron, and started to turn towards me for the ritual we'd performed all our lives.

Without any thought at all – my mind racing excitedly over the soon-to-be injections and sexual riot I could carry on with all over Hollywood, I swung the female into my arms, my body easily coming alive with her soft flesh in my hands, and kissed her deeply on the mouth, in as erotic a movement as I would have given any woman on a first date. As my tongue started to explore her lips, a hint of reality snapped me back to into what I was doing, but before I stammered and exclaimed loudly, and before her "gasp" could be uttered (as I pulled my own head back open-mouthed as I became aware of what I was doing), I was impressed at the look of absolute closed-eyed bliss that was momentarily upon her face.

"I…I.. I'm s..s…sorry! I…I'm stoned!" I yelled, running out of the door. She kept smiling in astonishment until I saw her mind starting to work to accommodate the voice that must have been demanding to be heard in her head.

Months later I was coming off a long binge of these Preludins and was sleeping over Janice's apartment. This was early in our relationship. I had run out but knew where I could pick up more. The problem was I was broke, Janice was leaving for work, and I already owed her some money. It would have been too un-cool to ask for more. She asked me to pick up some stuff for dinner.

"Surprise me," she said.

"Give me a twenty and I will," I said. She did, and left for work.

I put my small revolver in my sock, shaking and breathing hard. I went down to the supermarket, building myself up into an angry frenzy regarding anyone who would dare get in my way as I went about destroying myself. I stuffed two large T-bones down my pants and headed out the door past the cashiers, a definite bulge visible from under my warm-weather clothing. Just as I approached the exit. I noticed a young bagger eyeing me. I saw myself drawing my gun on him if he made a move to stop me out in the parking lot. We made eye contact. He might have noticed I looked a little insane, and decided to stay where he was. I think my crazed look saved my life.

Chapter 10 – Marriage and the Best Use of Cocaine for Sex

I was approaching thirty, and had just come to a meaningful conclusion: Like Mr. Spock in the Star Trek episode where he has to return to Vulcan to find a mate, I saw that I needed to settle down and get married. My mom thought it was a great idea.

She had pretty eyes... genuinely pretty eyes. I scanned her face as she brought me the drink. I blanked it out and took her in anew with a "refresh" reality view. Sometimes a second look reveals the extra makeup, sexy clothing and smile which beguiled you into thinking she was fantastic looking, but then you see the illusion. You were merely *stunned* by the lingerie suggestion, the pose and innuendo of her feminine smoke and mirrors. But no, there was no doubt about it. This girl was a nine-point something. An exceptional find.

"I gotta go," she said with actress–like remorse, biting her lower lip and making her eyebrows come together full of young-love regret that our flirting was about to end. "My turn to dance," she added, smiling. I gave her a five dollar tip for the drink.

Sure it was all an act, but I sensed there was something different about this girl. The undercurrent of bitter hopelessness or hopeless bitterness normally found in females working these strip-joints appeared to be missing somehow. As I was soon to find out, she was about to be unfettered and released; freed from this prison of cheap feels and dollar bills.

But I'm getting ahead of myself. I had, after all, just won $500 as a mutual-ticket clerk at the racetrack. That is to say, as a Pari-Mutual Betting Teller, I had punched out bets I had no money for and had won. It was the 1970's, and Marge Everett, owner of Hollywood Park, had said "*no*" to the union.

* * *

The pari-mutual clerks – the guys who take your money and give you your betting tickets at the track – had gone out on strike, and since my dad and I had practically lived at the racetrack, I immediately knew what line to get on when the strike hit and the track needed scabs. I was now a pari-mutual clerk, eschewing the $100 a day salary to steal and gamble as much as possible. I was supposed to be straight, with drugs a "thing of the past."

I was in AA, but found working for the racetrack not unlike being a sex-addict working in a whorehouse. Wiser heads in AA told me I should get out, but the money was really good ($100 a day in 1970), and my psychotic mentality kept emphasizing the fact that 'I was making better money at the track than what these wiser-AA-guys-who-were-telling-me-to-quit were making,' and it was like, "*Yeah, I really should get a different job…*" I had grown up with horseracing as religion. I regarded horses like *Spectacular Bid* and *John Henry* as totems to the racing gods. I loved John Henry's peak as a champion horse. So I punched out $10,000 to "Show" on him.

Having only $5 on me with $10,000 in tickets in my pocket proved I was now also a champion. I was in the running as well; in some ways more so than any of the hundred thousand plus people in attendance. I certainly had more to lose than anyone. As John Henry crossed the finish line ahead by five lengths, the jockey slowly waved his whip in return salute to the roar of the adoring crowd. Yes, he was certainly waving it at me, bonding me into it all with his salute in that wonderful moment. With no small amount of moisture wiped from my crazed eyes, I felt the chills shudder off my trembling body. *I had beaten them.* With my gambler's insight and heroic betting, I had created wealth for myself. The momentary sense of excitement and quasi-godlike assumption was instant magic; something beyond sex or drugs.

Because of the incredibly high one-sided betting on the part of the crowd when one of these legendary champions show up, the track gets special help from the Legislature that mandates they don't have to pay the usual minimum of ten cents on the dollar, so a "show" bet will not pay the minimum $2.20 for a two-dollar bet as is the normal case for pari-mutual wagering. When a horse is bet so much that the pool of money is insufficient for the track to pay $.10 for every dollar wagered on a particular heavy favorite, it creates a situation known as a "minus pool." The track is in a position in which it could lose money if the horse comes in first, second or third, as there is not enough money bet on all the horses in the race put together for the track to pay off at a minimum of $.10 on a dollar. The track might have to gamble. The racetrack does not like to gamble. Gambling is for the losers who make the racetrack rich.

Consequently, the state legislature allows the track to escape unscathed financially, and the track is therefore only paying $2.10 to show. Still, $10,000 to show allows me to cash my tickets, take $500 out of my till, and put it in my pocket. I lose $100 in the ninth.

I'm kind of pumped and decide to head back to Eva's after a call home to lie to my wife. It's a shame I have to have this burden to figure out how to keep her out of the immediate situation, but I shoulder this responsibility as a man now does taking on the added tasks of married life.

A man dutifully calls home. After all, I'm married, and what kind of man doesn't call his wife when he's not coming home?

All my previous drug life has centered around psychedelics and then anti-psychotics in experimentally mammoth dosages, and after that, heroin, barbiturates and soporifics like Quaalude, as well as Percodans, Dilaudid, Morphine derivatives, etc. Opiated, mellow and relaxed was what I sought. I did not care for stimulants – or even marijuana – at all. My love affair with Preludins, Disoxin, methamphetamines and bi-phetamines had been relatively short-lived. If I took a Contact cold pill, the stimulation of the medication had me masturbating three times in an hour. In the world of uppers and downers, I was definitely a downer kinda guy.

Nevertheless, I found cocaine intriguing. I bought a gram from Eva and enjoyed folding up the little envelopes again, which I hadn't done since using heroin years before. I made three little packets of cocaine totaling maybe half-a-gram. These would be my special offerings. And so here I am, looking at this most attractive of strippers in the most high-end strip club in the Valley.

* * *

Her "*I don't give-a-shit*" attitude merged with nature's perfect gifts to give her a regal sexuality. Her natural blonde mane fell to her shoulders, leaving the eye to travel from the challenging pout in her dance face to the twin mounds below. Her blue eyes smiled and laughed mischievously, while her perfectly round breasts stood firm and impressive, joining her eyes in daring you to turn away, daring you not to love her. When she caught your eye she riveted this focused vibe right into you, her feline movements suggestively reeling you in with seductive orbs which alternately demanded, begged, and commanded. She could catch you in her tractor-beam, and I returned her look surrendering myself with approval. I sat at a table about twenty feet from the stage. At the stage level, men paid-with-tips to sit close and be tormented by her buttocks of perfection.

She defined the word '*stunning*' as an active verb, and immediately became my top choice. At the close of her act I got up from my table and walked the few feet to the far right side of the stage, waiting for her as she bent down to collect the offerings from the supplicants to my left.

"Why don't you check it out?" I said, looking pointedly at the folded bill leaving my fingertips and being now placed before her; and then let me buy you a drink?" I asked, as she bent down in front of me to pick up the tip. I watched her beautiful eyes take interest as her fingers felt the bump of the coke envelope inside the ten-dollar bill.

She was one of three. Each came over and thanked me. I smiled and told them they were welcome, adding that people didn't understand how hard they worked, and *why shouldn't they relax a little bit too?*

Now shmoozing comfortably as we all now know that I'm not a cop, I bring the conversation around to well, I hope – sincerely – that *you won't be insulted, but I have to ask*," I add - eyeball to eyeball - *would you be interested in some private work… say, $100; a motel room?*

The first gives me a colder "no' than the second, who does the walking in place, *'Oh golly gee, I wish I didn't have to say this'* gum-chew with face turned up at the eyebrows and mouth.

"*I have a boyfriend*," she says somewhat apologetically, the last word valley-girled out so as to imply mine is not a terrible suggestion; but it just ain't gonna' happen anytime soon.

"*I mean, I'm not a nut*," I hear myself saying to the blonde goddess with the tractor beam dance attitude. I barely notice the irony in my come-on. I am, drink in hand, immersed in flight from reality, but floating in total self-entertainment. After an initial uncomfortable silence had greeted my proposition, I notice nothing furthers been said, so obviously she's giving it a second look. My foot's on the accelerator.

"*I know you have to be careful*," I say, placing my hands down on some imaginary foundation.

"*I parked in Valet Parking here. So you can ask the valet guys to get the license number. Normal license plates linked to my home address. See, you can tell your friends*," I say aloud, taking out my wallet to pull out my driver's license, which I hand to her, mimicking as I do her talking to her friends in an imaginary conversation:

"*I'm going out tonight with Marty; here's a copy of his driver's license, his fingerprints, his mother's maiden name, his father's rabbi's name…*" The stunner with the awesome behind laughs for real and after another quick study of my face, says slowly and deliciously: "*OK*."

To me it was as if I had proposed and she had accepted. Let's arrange for the honeymoon suite.

"So sit and have a drink with me." We talk.

With appropriate boyish hesitation and what-I-hope-she'll-interpret-as-sweetness, I stammer a little as I tell her she's head and shoulders above anything else in the room and hope all the bullshit she has to put up with at this place is worth it for her financially. She tells me it's her last week. She's marrying her boyfriend 1000 miles away and she could use the extra hundred for the traveling.

As we got into the where, when and how she begins to get nervous and

I could see her trepidation is genuine. She was no hooker by any means. Now the desire to bed her was volcanic. It was as if I had this treasure in my hand which threatened to slip between my fingers with one wrong word. It was maddening.

She was about to verbalize something I knew I wouldn't like so I quickly said: *"Let me take you to dinner first." I know a nice Chinese restaurant... we'll have a nice little meal, a drink, it'll be fine... and then we'll go..."* watching her eyes, I decide it's better not to add the word "motel." The ice is so thin I can barely breathe until I hear her careful *"OK"* and we both smile. Night after tomorrow, six o'clock. I'll pick her up at her place.

I couldn't stand it. I almost left then. But of course I had to stay to watch her dance one more time. In those days the girls really danced, had some moves, some attitude with some showmanship. They didn't just grind their genitalia into a pole or your embarrassed face. She showed me that attitude and that body talked to me with a language all its own, dominating and submissive, wiggling, whimpering, demanding and begging.

I walked outside limp with lust and dizzy with anticipation. But I soon faced a reality as glaring as that hot LA sun that hits when coming out of a cool, dark club.

Wife. Debts. But paying bills just didn't feel right at all. There was something so inherently wrong with that. I mean here you had money that could feel *so pleasurable* to spend, and instead to choose to put it in an envelope and send it to something as sterile and empty as a utility company or a landlord just seemed so counter-productive to life. I knew the bills had to be paid, but certainly they could wait until next week, couldn't they? I leaned towards the Scarlet O'Hara school of finance: *"I don't want to think about that now. I'll think about that tomorrow."* And Scarlet wound up with that whole plantation! Surely I deserved a little pleasure from this rat-race life?

Two nights later I pick her up in front of a little house in Sherman Oaks. We went for dinner and had a couple of drinks over some nice Schezuan chicken; and as we talk of this and that, there are actually not too many awkward silences. I like her. A lot. Then it was time to go.

We get into the car. She starts to say "maybe this isn't such a good idea," and I answer – trying to sound upbeat although a terrified energy was squeezing my heart at the thought of losing her – "Oh, it'll be *fine*, really. I already bought booze and I put a bottle of champagne on ice in the room."

"You did?" she asks with genuine, pleased surprise.

"I *did*." I responded, smiling with pleasure, as if she's my girlfriend of years.

Wonderfully, all she said was simply "*Oh, OK.*"

I already had the key to the motel room, and it was winning to find the air conditioning already on and the beer and sparkling wine in the ice bucket. She seemed genuinely pleased, and it took the edge off both of us. I spread five-twenties on the dresser.

"I'll take it afterwards" she said.

We both got out of our clothes, I for a moment regretting that I hadn't prepared any music to ask her to strip to. That quickly became a non-issue. Naked, I pulled the covers back and we laid down on the crispy clean sheets.

We embraced clumsily and out of habit I started to kiss, but I learned no lip kissing was allowed, or tongue anyway. It is an ancient tradition of prostitution. Kissing is supposed to be kept for boyfriends and husbands. Sometimes. I relaxed, stroking her face and breasts, kissing her neck and slowly fondling her breasts. Placing my hands on her skin was to merge somehow with her soft, young, ripe perfection. I could hardly dare to lower my hand and caress, stroke and squeeze those perfect buttocks flowing into her wonderfully silky smooth thighs. I could only do it slowly, as if to feed on her beauty longer with each moment. She reached for my growing apparatus and after a few squeezes started to go down on me. I let her for a few seconds, curious to see if she was gifted with any special talent in that area. I felt a pleasant amount of warm wetness surround my head, and after concluding I'd felt enough, gently brought her shoulders back, propping her head on a pillow at the headboard.

That bottom of hers had teased and tantalized me for weeks, and could not now be treated askance. Smiling patiently and gratefully, I paid patient and sincere tribute to her smallish round breasts with soft caresses; first nubbing my lips across the sweet richly pinked nipple, squeezing and licking them till they both stood up hard. My hands brought me to the smooth paradise of her buttocks and thighs. Only then did I allow myself to continue south, the smooth soft skin of her midsection a testament to her perfect youth. I continued on, slowly submerging my face into her lower realms, settling in with my arms coming up around her bottom so her thighs kind of sat on my shoulders while my hands met below her belly button. My two thumbs entwined in the supernatural softness of her small patch, while what was left of my brain marveled at the multifaceted perfection of the slang word "*pussy.*" I was ready for the smorgasbord.

Not only could my forearms and shoulders move this delightful buffet this way and that for my mouth to delve into, but my fingers could so gently push and pull up that extra little bit from her kitten-soft patch area – when and if necessary – to manipulate that precious little ball inside with an extra protrusion, a little extra perch, and from there it could be engulfed more easily into my mouth, where I could stay servicing her pleasure into eternity.

I started to gently kiss and lick the high inside of her thighs where they melted into those perfect round melons. She tasted incredible. The scent of her down there was perfect. She hadn't covered it all up with some astringent douche like some women do. That could make eating a woman seem the same as licking washed meat. Her scent was getting me hard as my brain reeled out of this world. I tantalized myself as long as I could before starting to joyfully eat at that folded entrance.

I think every woman's v-word is unique. No two are the same. I learned my way around her, tasting and tonguing each fold, finding her button first with my tongue's tip, then investigating its centrality by pushing my upper lip into the area just north of it, causing it to come out and play into my mouth below, which was plastered like a suckerfish over her private region, holding this delightful arrangement in place, breathing when possible. With my fingers pushing upwards ever so slightly on the region around her pubic hair, I could tilt my newfound friend to a more accommodating position in my suckling mouth. I soon had a rhythm going licking and sucking on the little thing far into my mouth, my nose pressed deeply into those exquisitely soft hairs. Experimenting going around it, under it, flagging it quickly with the tip, the front and the bottom parts of my tongue, I found that the gentle sucking, occasionally interspersed with rhythmic licking of the little guy was creating spontaneous, loud and candid exclamations of rapture from my young princess.

Confident that I could find the lovely bump whenever I needed to, I could now make the necessary foray south to that one-eyed place that I had thought about since getting it shoved in my face from the stage weeks before. When I finally could get my tongue into, around and across the essence of her bottom, I was delirious with the taste of her; a sense of perfumed, musky fruit, the momentary scent of it hardening what I didn't think could get any harder.

Like most women when they first sense a tongue down there, she tensed up and temporarily alarmed. *But this was too great*! Her gasp and body language alerted me to a most wonderful intuition: I was her first ass-lick. I knew she needed to hear what so many females need to be reminded of in situations like this:

"It's Ok, I *love it* like this," I gasp out from underneath her thighs.

Getting your ass licked takes some getting used to. It is an acquired taste from both ends of the sexual exchange. Often a woman needs to hear that a man is truly enjoying himself while serving her bottom before she can truly let go, allowing herself the luxurious abandon of giving it all up, relaxing and loosening her lower sphincter muscle control as if she were evacuating in a carnal worship to the hedonism.

I felt her sphincter relax as her moans now took on a wanton abandon, and I was reassured to feel the steady ache in my hardened desire. I returned to the natural honey pot. After bringing this back to boiling anew, her cries louder and her fingers tensing, I returned to the bottom, slurping up any juices that had run south on gravity's command, and I could taste its delicious love freely now with a hungering, animal-like mouthing. With her moaning echoing both our desires, I returned to that wonderfully tight and juicy object with dedicated passion. Like a starved carnivore about to eat, my own sucking mouth craved her small and swelling item as the center of my universe. I went out of control in the sucking and licking of it, losing myself totally in her service.

After a crying release of satisfaction, she lay gasping beneath me, her eyes closed, her breasts rising and falling as she caught her breath with an ever-widening smile of joyful satisfaction. Aching in my rock hard state, I was now there: lover, caveman, king; my beauty beneath me. As I rose up to mount her I barely had to use my hand to guide it into her entrance. I started to penetrate her as my weight settled onto her. Her eyes flying open as these lower lips, still pouting from their prior exertions, now part for their rock-hard guest, they settle onto mine doe-like and happy, closing her arms around my neck to bring my mouth down to hers. I continue to slowly enter her moist, hot, tight cave of pleasure, giving her all my love in the kiss, not yielding to the urge to drive in quicker. The lips and growing tongue-love is in concert with the slow progression of me into her. The hot wet easiness bears witness to our compatibility; our love; our joy... I am in love. I smile into her eyes and touch her cheek. At this one moment she is really joy, a young woman in springtime. She has a wonderful look in her eyes that allows me to again lower my lips to hers, and she is slick and tight and steamy as she takes me in to the hilt with a slow suction, enveloping me in a gasping, giving, moaning love.

Such freedom there is in this ride, such glorious uncomplicated pleasure. The first time is always so uncluttered, so free of anything but the giving; releasing it all up in pleasure and freedom from control, analysis or worry. Just the ride of pleasure, the riding of the orgasmic wave, not thinking about it, just riding that tidal experience. The woman reacting with lust and joy to my giving her of my same lust and joy. No emotional hooks, she wants nothing more from me than I want from her, and we are both ecstatic at the arrangement. I find in our climb into wild fucking the love of an agreeable and happy partner, and we wordlessly entwine ourselves in the genetic dance. The orgasm skyrockets and leaves me in an ocean of serenity. We both give a laugh of delight and amazement, soon doing it again with another hour flying by, and we come together beautifully to call it a night a short time after that.

Driving her home in the car, she breaks the silence.

"Y'know, I forgot to ask once we started, but I'm kind of glad you didn't bring any coke. After I snorted the stuff you gave me a few days ago, I got a little antsy, and wanted more. I'd be tempted to spend *this*, she added for emphasis."

"I know what you mean," I answered. We were at a stoplight as I turned to her, gazing at her deeply and at that moment just wanting to kiss her, leave my wife and drive away with her to Mexico or something.

"Tell ya the truth… I don't need drugs when I'm with you," I said sincerely, reaching over and squeezing her hand. She looked down, and even in the reluctant darkness of the streetlight, I could see she was blushing.

I am ecstatic with a sexual satisfaction I hadn't had in months, and feel really loving now towards the whole idea of the wife, family, etc. I mention this to my new friend in the car that I think this has saved my marriage. I had needed this time. She looks at me and says, "I think you're a little confused."

She was right. I soon started shooting cocaine, and the worm would turn… quite a bit.

Chapter 11 – The Worst Use of Cocaine For Sex
One year after starting to inject

I'm walking wounded. It's almost one in the morning and I'm leaving early for the 2 a.m. AA meeting. AA, NA GA[21] – I'm a 3-ring loser for the temptations of alcohol, narcotics and gambling and it doesn't matter tonight what acronym is pasted on the door. It's after midnight and I know I have to go.

I drive on streets that beckon now only sparingly. The glamour and lights have been ordered off and the night around Ventura Boulevard offers only sparse temptation: a loitering couple on the corner, a long and curious look from the vagrant/hustler/drug-addict/killer silently seeking communication from the bus stop bench.

A self-destructive urge nags me to stop, roll down the window and invite him to the meeting. I know I'm not strong enough. Relief rushes over me as I realize my escape in the decision to keep driving. I am now past him and beyond his reach. A glance at the speedometer tells me I'm doing twenty and accelerating. He can't possibly catch me and reverse my decision. My car doors are locked. I've escaped. I feel safe. I'm 6 years old and have staggered onto the shore away from the murderous undertow. I didn't give in to my nauseating vulnerability. I feel better.

These decisions are what pass for life nowadays. I decided not to get killed again. What a good boy I am. And now a father to boot. Well, the wife's leaving me, and I'm impaled a little more on this realization that I now have a whole new role I've failed in.

I park – a hint of pride flashes through my beleaguered mind as I note the very best parking spots are mine for the taking. The reward for the true seeker of sobriety so determined in his path that he leaves home in the middle of the night furthering his commitment. Spiritual pride tries to find soil in which to grow. It seeks a nourishing endorsement from deeper consciousness but fails to find feedback to give it life, instead falling victim to a host of derisive taunts.

Self-hatred, anger and resentment respond energetically and criticize with blistering enthusiasm. Self-pity steps forward, offering it's splayed back and it too is eagerly assaulted as the boo-hoo weenie-man who coulda,' shoulda,' woulda' but ain't, and is eaten alive as the booby-prize; providing nourishment for the monster of self-loathing. I sway under its fiery reverie comparing - via quick hallucination – (or is that simply colorful imagination?) my pathetic existence to the healthy and successful.

---

[21] *Alcoholics Anonymous, Narcotics Anonymous, Gambler's Anonymous*

The mental disarray of fifteen psychotic years of chemical riot weigh heavily as I climb stooped up the tedious stairs for the 2 a.m. meeting.

My shoes creak alone, but the strength that the group provides starts to take hold. They are not here yet, but their consistent success brings their annoying spirit to life. Here among the stale smells and worthless fixtures hope chooses to live. Here amongst these G-d-awful lame and stupid people. How can it be that my journey is so derailed that I need these offensive mechanics? Why must I travel careening into this off-ramp with these droning knuckle-draggers doing the driving? *A shooting star amongst these boring, simple and common lights.*

But success lives here. Hope lives here. If only I could get hold of some ethereal ear and make it listen! Make it understand! Have it my way! I am escapist fantasy or I am the shit under my shoe. I bounce from one to the other and twist in the wind, grit my teeth and take it *"one day at a time."*

Surprise... another person is sitting here. There he sits not twenty feet away. What do you say to another person at 1:30 in the morning on a Friday night in North Hollywood in a shithole like this? The two of us waiting for a 12-step meeting to begin in the middle of the night.

A pathetic energy begins its old patterns, my mother's eager directive reminding me to *smile with my eyes* while manipulative thought-troopers ready themselves within the corridors of social intercourse. I must prepare to proudly inject my "self" into the imminent discourse. Like a disassembled machine project whose parts do not quite fit, disparate elements of my inchoate esteem raise their hands in hope to compulsively blurt something out. My brain short-circuits and the robot autopilots:

"Y'come to this meeting before?

"No," he says, pausing.. "I usually go to the gay meetings on the other side of the hill, but there's none tonight... not at this time anyway."

"Are the gay meetings different? I ask, feeling suddenly sophisticated in handling this subject in such a straightforward and adult manner. We are, after all, all children of the Big Book, or Mr. Bob... or something like that.

He thinks a while before answering. "All I know about gay is sometimes I get an overwhelming desire to suck cock. (long silence) You?"

I froze. *Me? Me what? Familiar with the meeting? Gay? Compulsively desiring to suck cock?* My frazzled brain scans data banks freely associating at withdrawal speed hooked into a fifteen-year psychosis. I'm back at the Adult bookstore I passed driving over here, and back to a time not too long before this, when I drove over to a different place this time of night to visit a different person: a woman from South America.

Big Eva was a Colombian woman in her mid forties; with an unaffected impression of Marlene Dietricht constantly going on. A cocaine wholesaler, she allowed herself to be called *Big Eva* to make sure everyone knew the difference between herself and her daughter, *Little Eva*. *Big Eva* would like to occasionally make the point known that she was a badass, and that people trying to beat her got "beat" in a very final way. She would say that and stare at you with cold black eyes, with a look that said *"y'think I'm kidding with you?"*

She was on such a track this evening, speaking in vague coding to see if I would react to something that had apparently gone wrong in her business life. Looking at me with unsmiling black eyes, I responded that if she found me trying to do her wrong, I only ask one thing: that she promise to torture me a little bit in some kind of kinky way before doing me in.

"Promise me you'll wear those high heels I saw you in the other night, and maybe... a little whip? At least a spanking..." I allowed the words to trail off.

I looked her in the eye and made an effort to keep my face serious. I took her hand and bent before her on one knee. I started to kiss her hand – which, to my pleasant surprise - she did nothing to prevent. I found this tolerance on her part and the on-my-knee-submission to this dominating female immediately stimulating, and, wondering out loud how much more of this I could get, I started to slide my tongue in between her fingers. She yelped and laughed, brushing me off. I knew then I was off her list of possible enemies. Well, at least for tonight. So let's get the gun back and see what she's got in the way of the very best gram.

"$150," she says. Just that, now there's silence. Out of respect I say nothing. I know Eva and the respect game. I also know she's not gonna' change her mind.

"Rock," she adds finally, letting me off the hook. Everybody knows coke is all over the street at $110 a gram.

"Come," she says. We walk to her bedroom and she opens a large jewelry box with a smaller box within it. A small shiny metal case is opened and 4 or 5 good size rocks are there amidst some smaller ones and flake. She wets the tip of a matchstick with her tongue and lets the moist part of the matchstick touch the flake. She offers it to my mouth and I taste the white powder. It is so fierce in its bitterness that I wretch backwards. It is so pure in its offense that I must have it.

I stand and take out the money. $150 for the blow and $175 to buy my gun back. My heart starts revving up a few more rpms. It feels so responsible and adult – even manly - paying out the $325, thereby making good on the commitment I made when she took my gun as collateral for coke weeks before.

"I want to load up here," I tell her.

"No," she says at first. "I don't want you shooting coke here."

"I won't shoot up. I'm just going to fill up the syringes. Then I put the caps back on and put them away."

"What do you mean put them away? Where do you go with them?"

"Sometimes a park, I shoot up and then lay out in the sun. At the ocean, sometimes the strip joint."

"The strip joint?"

"With my big vein I can shoot anywhere. I can be there and drop a dollar bill under the table and get off while it looks like I'm picking something up off the floor. When I bend down to find it - if the place is half empty - I can usually get off right there in just a few seconds."

"Marty, you are too much."

"Yeah," hesitating the necessary beat, I slowly bring my eyes up to hers while I hold her eye. "So are you, Eva," I add with a kindness I know takes her completely by surprise. The sincere, pillow-talk quality of it even took me by surprise. I bring the moment to good completion with a smile and just-enough awkwardness to make it real. She smiles back, and a warm fuzzy is upon us. My credit line just rose in ways impossible to describe. Tough bitch or not, Eva was still a woman feeling some heat. This always comes as second nature to me. "I just need some cotton and water. I have a cap to put the stuff in."

I get up and go into Eva's bathroom and open the cabinet. I had traded her a jar of 1000 10mg Valiums for blow some time back, so I'm at home here with a backstage pass of sorts.

I look for cotton from inside a tablet container, but I have to settle for Q-tip cotton. I take out my bottle cap. I rinse it and then put some water in it, and draw up 1 cc of water from one of my U-100 syringes. It is a one-piece disposable insulin syringe, a thin unit with a very sharp needle affixed. I spill the remaining water out of the cap and I gently shake the entire cocaine rock and the remaining flake into the cap. I drip the water from the U-100 into it, surrounding the rock at its base, but it's not melting right away - only very slowly - and my excitement is stirred even more. There is so little cut.

The odor is so strong it's kicking my head into that strange re-living of the last time I smelled that smell and the cocaine high is suddenly so real I can see what true placebo cures are all about. The mind can recreate it all for you, and does - briefly. My genitals are contracting and my heart is beating faster as my mind anticipates this potency raging through my blood and nervous system. The dissolved cocaine is completely clear save the tiniest of cut at the bottom, and I drop in the cotton, stick the needle into it and draw up 3 even syringes. I point each of the syringes up in turn, flicking the tube with my middle finger to get any bubbles to surface and push the air out. As I do, I a tiny amount of liquid coke is pushed out from the needle's tip. I lick off the liquid and gag at the bitterness. This is gonna' be great, and I fight the urge to jam it into my fat vein right there and then. I replace the orange cap. I am locked and loaded with three to shoot tucked in my athletic sock high above the ankle.

The fact that I control this change in my world, that I can induce this revolution of sensate consciousness within my being, makes the loaded syringe akin to controlling a lightning bolt. To transform myself with this simple act holds me captive with its magic. I want to swim in it, dive in it, and expand myself in it, and wanting to see who'll come to the party tonight allows me to allay the fact that I've been to this chemical mountaintop before and realized its limits, not to mention the hideous withdrawal payment, when there's hell to pay. I'm no longer content to simply shoot up alone, taking the supercharged pleasure-excitement coke-rush to the summit and then come back down.

The cocaine high had a certain sterility to it that I was beginning to identify as lack, and like a sky borne firework floating back to anxious-earth, I am now seeking to fill that sterile mountaintop by introducing a sexual key and see who'll come out the unlocked door. I am determined to lose control and *step out of the way*. I'm going to bring out this masturbation confidant I've been submerging into since puberty. I ready myself for her appearance. There was no turning back; nor did I want to.

"Are you going to the strip show?" Eva asks as I came out of the bathroom.

"Yeah," I lie. "Well, probably," I lie again, in case she wants me to give someone a lift or a ride. There are always a few faces I don't want to know hanging around her front room. We say g'night. Only she can open the door for me to leave. I walk out with that extra sense of paranoia I always have when leaving a dealer's house. *If I can just make it to the car, if I can just get to the car, then it's OK. If I can unlock the car, lock the doors, start and drive away without any headlights following me, I can breath again.*

I think about the strip joint. Last time I did go there first but it's not really enough to shoot and hear the coke-whine and the voices if you can't feel some flesh. Lately the rules have changed in the strip joints and you're not allowed to feel the girls up any more, as the owners now get fined. I just get too horny and frustrated shooting up without any fleshly contact, even though my apparatus contracts into a useless turtle's head anyway. So when I was there last time, I had taken my last filled syringe, left the strip joint and gone instead to the bookstore and while shooting there took a little walk on the wild side. Whatever hunger it had seemed to satisfy had returned tonight with a larger apatite.

This time I would skip the strip joint and go straight to the bookstore. I stop and buy a pint of Tequila and a tall can of beer, placing them in the back seat of my car, parking it in the darkest part of the lot behind the bookstore.

I try to be cool and light a cigarette with the engine off and the window rolled down. I'm going to contemplate what will take place and draw out the anticipation. This lasts about three puffs.

The California night sky slams behind me as I enter the bookstore and recognize the clerk. This seems important to me somehow because I know I'm going to be very paranoid later, and it just seems better if I know the people who work there. I buy $10 worth of tokens. Most people are very uptight in the adult bookstore. Tonight I have a solution for uptight.

I get buzzed into the back room. The new policy is only people who buy tokens are allowed into the backroom where the video booths are. This keeps out the bad element. At the near and far end of the large room are glass cases containing sets of small posters, maybe a dozen graphic boxes advertising the videos available within the booths. There are about ten small rooms lining each side of the room, and an additional corridor stretches to the back wall beyond the rear glass case. Each video is represented by a graphic advertisement, a small description of the plot and the corresponding number of that choice. Should you wish to view that particular video once you were in the booth, you simply pressed the corresponding channel in the coin-operated controller.

The booth was large enough for two people if both were slim; especially if one was on his knees or bent over. It consisted of a bench, a stench – from the sticky tissues dotting the floor and sometimes from their need to be dotting the floor - and a video lens from the back wall above the bench projecting onto the back of the lockable door. When someone was watching a movie, a green light showed *'Movie in Progress'* above the outside door. When the green light was on, and the door still left ajar instead of locked closed, it could only mean one thing: *'man available.'* There were tops and bottoms leaving doors ajar twenty-four-seven all over Los Angeles.

The booth was doubly useful for another reason: the syringe, when spent, could be tossed under the bench, thereby freeing me from having to hide it while my brain was exploding in cocaine trajectory.

As in all bookstore sex, anyone will do. I entered the main video room and approached a guy who had his back to me looking at the selections. He was the only person outside a booth at the time, so this moment spelled o-p-p-o-r-t-u-n-i-t-y. While low, old, fat, ethnic, stupid-looking or ugly would have been just fine – if not preferable - he is tall, young, white, slim, with reasonable good looks. Well, nobody's perfect.

My heart is hammering loudly in my ears while pumping adrenalin in quantities that made my thinking impossible, and I was still totally straight. I auto-pilot up next to him, standing closer than normal. I notice he does not step away. I stand and look at the selections, my eyes falling on one quickly. I'm not sure who or what is in charge of motoring my mouth but it opens and I start hearing my words come out. Lowly and slowly I say,

"*Look at that lucky bitch in number four.*" His eyes move to that graphic to view a picture of an attractive young woman putting her mouth around an enormous penis.

"*If you wanna watch it together, I've got some tokens,*" I add in a low voice.

He half-nods, stunned.

"*Stay here for a few moments till **after** I get in,*" I tell him, and he nods dumbly. I turn quickly to walk down a corridor lined with additional rooms but somewhat separate from the main room. I worry that he might come in right after me as I get into the last booth and close the door.

I immediately jam in a bunch of tokens for movie light against the door, grab a syringe from my sock, bite the orange cap off while at the same time pumping my left fist and holding it against my side. My vein is exceptionally fat and I don't need a belt to tie off. My features in silhouette, my blood billows up through the pornographic light to register in the clear plastic tube of the syringe, and I plunge it all home immediately.

Incredible rush. My heart explodes with exhilaration, and I cannot breathe as indescribable jet-engine whines send lightning strokes of euphoric excitement exploding through my head. My body buckles, crumpling to my knees almost out of control onto the sperm streaked floor. Tossing the syringe into the dark shadow under the bench and pushing down my left sleeve is as much as I can physically accomplish. My own breathing is like a deep, feathery moan. The rush is still driving my consciousness out as I lay collapsed, shocked, paralyzed and unmoving in the ecstatic buzz that is flooding throughout my brain.

Footsteps outside the door are too much for my nerves and consciousness to deal with, but I need not deal with anything, an inner sense calmly assures from within the eye of the storm, as this girl comes alive to take over and is easily here. Languid and impossibly calm, she is doubly satin and eager to please; eager to prove how willing she really is to please. Excitement makes her calm, and her mouth is not dry, even with this mammoth shot of cocaine, it is not dry at all. My legs are being pushed by the door swinging in. My date has arrived.

With my heart beating out of my ears I propel myself between his seated legs with my head still in a roar. I move slowly, hoping my nearly passed out state passes for languid. I rest my lips on the bulge of his denim. He obliges me by unzipping, pulling down and producing a nicely proportioned, cut and clean object of worship. I slowly lower my mouth to enclose it, angling it gently up into the roof till I get used to the general length and breadth of the situation; making sure my teeth are set well behind my lips.

He says something. He is apologizing for not being hard.

Oh, this is love! This was a reason to give without restraint, for I could leave concern behind that he's a hostile nut-job and allow my euphoria to govern. She rules well here, and I am floating free from fear.

I respond without thinking:

"*I like it like this*" and my voice is timbered and echoes pleasantly in my own ears. After all, few behaviors are as positively reinforcing as the hardening of a limp penis through one's oral efforts. The moment when it enters the mouth is like going into a quiet tunnel of escape, a spiritual home in a dark vacation where nothing else exists. A rubbery item is being ministered to, and the reward for your efforts fills you with a mysterious satisfaction unlike the orgasm you're not having, and yet you become mysteriously satisfied somehow not to have. A special moment when this real flesh and blood apparatus – and all that it signifies - comes into your most personal and slavish care. It's the same with an anonymous partner as one whose name you actually know. The scenario has a ritual that smacks of submission and worship, hearkening back to a time before history, in a dimension never described.

It fills the world; this strange flesh that is deep in your mouth, eagerly awaiting your ministrations, a silent communication begins between one who offers "servicing," and the one he needs to "service." An energy aside from the fleshly pleasure builds and communicates in between the submissive humiliation of the degraded and the unseen power alive in the flesh of the one who degrades him while needing him to serve. It is way beyond the physical.

A small voice, however, even within this raging chemical stimulation makes itself known to your consciousness: *"what are you doing this for?"* It is overlooked as I submerge into the wave-like rush of sensual carnality. It is a moment for worshipping energies dark and deep which come alive enriching themselves within and because of my very behavior. I am compulsively driven by the belief that true satisfaction will arrive for me when I – as *'she'* – gets to swallow the reward for these submissive efforts.

A special time in its growth, his length can still be manipulated and pleasured in ways too difficult after the stiffness enlarges it. It slides easily down my throat, my tunnel's own slow and gentle gulping now nurturing, slurping and swallowing his size. Hearing him gasp and moan, she chooses this time to enliven, this time to emerge. I take my date's hand and place it on the back of my head, moaning deep in my throat as he tentatively commands with a little pressure.

I see, feel and am quickly her in my silver-gowned lingerie in my penthouse. My fiancé out-of-town, I protest weakly to the black porter. He comes within inches to place his hand on my perfect soft behind. Bringing me against his hardening body, his thick lips are only inches from my own. I whimper as he pulls me close, his hands taking fuller possession.

"I don't know. I shouldn't have worn this. I didn't mean to tease you. I'm sorry... we shouldn't... my fiancé, you know, I don't really want..."

'*You think I'm going to fuck you... but you'll have to earn that... learn how to suck my cock first, and swallow every drop.*' She moans as I moan, slipping to our knees in the satin garments, taking in this very real, growing, and living one-eyed monster. She enters the task of getting my breathing through my nose in sync with her one-hand pumping, and he immediately moans and enlarges, his thickness reaching emergent proportions. *The spirit within the one speaks to the spirit within the other, and thus the dance is done.*

His moans rise in volume and so does the hardness of his unit; growing now prodigious in size. My slave girl will take-no-prisoners, and doesn't allow for the voice of conscience that even now starts to insist it be heard. Her energy is too high and spirit fueled, reinforced by years of nightly training sessions full of yearning masturbation fantasy. She has trained and strained for this charge since puberty. A wide-eyed supplicant, '*Is this what you like?*' breaks into consciousness, proceeding to hold her breath and take him down to new lengths, the depth of her wet throat holding him completely. A silent call for his essence, my mind reeling, heart beating out of control, I acknowledge the desire. His hardness is very full now, a true life of its own starting to take over this hard tool, expanding thickly to ever-more-impressively stiff dimensions.

"*I'm coming*," he communicates in a gasp; and how perfect. *To actually alert me*! Something within the concern and regret in his voice tells me he has never received a complete blowjob. The fact that he would tell me he's on arrival rather than simply take advantage of an anonymous stranger… Well, this is either caring or fear that I'll freak out if he comes in my mouth. I am eagerly amused to hear his naive assumption that no one would ever *want* to swallow, so of course the proper etiquette is to alert the cock sucker. In either case I am doubly motivated now to receive his delivery, and this commitment allows my breathing to go deeper, holding air longer, taking him completely down my throat; … *I'll show him what a blowjob is all about.* He is becoming louder in his uncontrolled gasps and moans, and we bond in the dark tableau.

He gasps out again the emerging condition of his explosive state. His tool hardens out of control, a separate life with a purpose all its own, beyond wood, the head expanding even greater than what it was. Gasping and moaning loudly, his body shakes and starts to erupt.

I breathe deeply and hold my breath just before I start to taste the hot thick achievement. I take him deep but my throat is awash in its salty fullness immediately and I gag before swallowing the eager fluid, thickly filling my mouth while I hear him snigger-with-scorn at the gagging sound. I see in the mysterious nanosecond database of the moment an image of my own cruel smirk – a Trojan horse somehow – from years before when I sneered in similar fashion to a man gagging on my teenage release.

There's too much and I'm gonna choke now! But not if I worship deeper… *not if I **want** to submit enough by swallowing enough, **desiring** to be used completely enough.* I assure myself that this is true realization.

The disposition of the soul alters the very reality I'm in. I realize the heretofore offensive odor of the sperm on the floor around me is now changed into the fragrance for my ongoing program. No longer an oppressive stench to flee from, my atmospheric bouquet is accepted soulfully as the heady aroma for this scene of adoration and submission. It is no longer assailing but complimenting and reinforcing my senses as well as my deed. So I wallow lowfully in this reward, taking this swickly quickly, and this receiving fills my altered identity with presence and strength. It's part and parcel of this enormous moment. This unique moment of total gasping in giving and taking, this joining of excitement and pleasure in the one being manipulated by the one controlling through submission. I give myself up to mastery in surrender, made all the more exciting by his prodigious size.

By now I am conquered, have conquered, received my reward and am mysteriously fulfilled. My conscience whines objections to the bitch goddess no more. Gentle and slow, soft and wet, I take the half-sized semi down deep, a final effort steeped in obvious request, a sweet treat of obedience, seeking the last drop of his essence. Having swallowed any reward from the last slow pump, I am into the gentle offering of good afterglow.

The cocaine buzz is still felt and I am mildly surprised how easily I remain in this other world. The producer retires into a smaller state still surrounded by my now unmoving wet mouth, and I wait until the owner pulls it out with a plop and a pop, shrunk and disappearing behind his zippered pants amidst a silent goodbye.

Zipped up, tucked in and standing, my date is on his way out, but gives pause to deal with his own post-orgasmic mindset. His demeanor changed, his new attitude is seeking an outlet. As he is about to open the door, he hesitates. I knew he had never come in anyone's mouth before, and either in spite of this - or because of this – seeks to express himself. He says *"thanks"* with a strange sneering intonation that says he has gotten over on me, as if I had been given something that I hadn't wanted, but he alone benefited from. His attitude was as if I had given him change for a hundred-dollar bill when he had only given me a ten.

At that moment I was incapable of guile and proved it easily with a voice full of penetrating sincerity. Honestly and enthusiastically I responded with a grateful *"thank you"* with such straightforward emphasis on the *"you"* that it spoke volumes with its sincerity.

The communication was real enough. His face amazed and crumpled, still-framed and wilting in his own resentment. He himself was now becoming penetrated by the very source of my own satisfaction.

When he realized that the entire act was what I had wanted, hoped and planned for – as my total satisfaction was so very much in evidence – he reacted with a transparent astonishment. I was too lost in the dark, submissive sensuality to feel guilty. If anything, I was happy to be the relaxed, fulfilled city-slut, and he the farm boy who had just satisfied me.

But *his* total satisfaction from getting physical satisfaction was no longer in evidence. He looked used and confused, reflecting an uncomfortable *"I feel dirty"* look. He now understands that I'd be happy to do him again (*well, I'd have to shoot up first*), and it appears he is conflicted unhappily with this realization. He is somehow confused and conflicted by my being pleased and satisfied. His platform of sexual satisfaction rested upon some kind of hostile sexual logic now crumbling on new reality's feet of clay. He had thought the unfriendly nature of the homosexual union was all one-way, and he was getting an education in the world of sexual spirits.

He was using another man for his own pleasure, but never considered **he was being used to give pleasure and satisfaction** by feeding the other man's craving to be used in just this manner. Realizing the other man took pleasure in using *him* has not only betrayed whatever assumptions he had taken into our act, but has now submerged him into some kind of new and dark emotion, birthed and strengthened by the complicit nature of our behavior.

The spirit that was in me is now mysteriously somehow in him as well, holding fast in its new home, feeding within him a new sense of himself through his upset, and gaining spiritual nutrition on and in his sudden and confused state.

From this moment forward he may find himself at odds with his fantasy, or capitulating to new desires he now hears from this new voice in his head. That voice is now living in him as a spiritual sex-child born from our act. Within this mystery he may find himself twisting to avoid the unwelcome identification with a barely conscious counterpart he may seek to deny. His resulting guilt over this new sense of himself sexually will create a need for greater acts of excitement, as only these greater excitements can totally relieve the guilt of his new conflict.

Caverns strange and dark just below the surface of his consciousness are churning with metamorphic activity. This real-world behavior he has just engaged in - fuels and sparks a growing life – a birth, a dynamism – in what was before only subconscious impulse. The persona the young man finds unacceptable, unimaginable and unthinkable today has been given new life from his activity in the world of real behavior, and will demand feeding for its new identity tomorrow. Feeding itself through his soulish worship, it will grow in the young man when he submerges into this new spirit in his own sexual fantasy, whether in masturbation or with another person. Humiliating and humiliated, degrading and degraded, domination and submission all dance, diversify and integrate within the changing world of homoerotic spirits.

A journey has begun for him which may bring him back full circle to these same booths in a different position next time. Next time it could be **him** on his knees saying 'thank *you*' to some stranger for a mouthful of hot goo. Or, holding onto the road of denial, he could become a hostile homophobic, lashing out at anyone making him aware of these repressed energies.

There is an energy present for the master's role within the slave, and part of the slave's role must exist within the very need of the master, for if the master *must have* something, then he is in some sense a slave to that need. My young man has now come to find that out. Consequently, *he* feels dirty and used. The master has become the commodity providing a service. The master – as user – has been had within the mysterious logic of the dark homosexual libido. He stumbles as he leaves.

I sit and think to relax; have a cigarette, maybe go out and have a drink at the bar down the street. But who am I kidding? I still have another two filled syringes. I have never had such a dramatic bookstore experience before, and am steeped in a kind of dreamy satisfaction; albeit for only a few moments.

Soon all my coke is gone. Hell demands payment. Shaky, anxious, paranoid, used up, depressed and strung out, I limply jerk off and feel worse. I walk out quickly with my head down, every breath and step carries with it overwhelming fear and anxiety. Back in the car, I drink from my pint of Tequila, hoping to take the edge off the comedown. Chasing the liquor with beer, I'm hopeful the 30mg of Valium will kick in soon and offer some respite.

But now life's problems rail in my head: I owed money all over, had no more cash and had blown this money which was sorely needed at home. We were a month behind on rent.

G-d, what's my wife gonna say? My wife, Oh my G-d! Real life! What am I doing giving strangers blowjobs in the middle of the night while using up my family's money on drugs? This is beneath contempt. This is inhuman. This is like the guy eating bugs in the early Dracula movies. I have to cut this shit out. I have to stop this. My wife is pregnant! What kind of sick man am I? Maybe I better kill myself now. End it, end it, end it! Where? Where should I do it? Where should I shoot myself? In the car? I do have the gun.

I smoke a cigarette, chase more Tequila with a mouthful of beer. I rationalize:

'*You can **always** kill yourself. You don't have to do it right **now**. Just stop. Stop using drugs. Then you won't have to kill yourself. Clean up. Work. Save. Own a house. A car. A boat. A dog. Don't kill yourself, get rid of the gun before you do.*'

'OK, that's responsible' I think. Yes, here's some hope. The best, most productive and positive thing to do would be to get rid of the gun.

Can't just throw $175 away though, responsibility insists. *I could sell it to Big Eva!* But Eva and I have already agreed it's a crappy weapon. A small, poorly made revolver, I could sell it to someone else. Complicated, that.

A few more swigs of tequila with the beer chaser and this fresh cigarette is actually starting to taste good. I take my first deep breath in over an hour.

Maybe I should trade it back to Big Eva for some more coke. Then **never buy it back!** *HA! She'll be pissed at me, and I wouldn't be able to buy any more coke from her. Then I could be straight!*

What genius! *Yes, the truly responsible thing to do is to end my relationship with Big Eva and cocaine. I'll get rid of the gun and screw up my coke connection at the same time. This act will now put an end to this whole cocaine, perverted sex and suicide track.*

Yes, it's time to get hold of my life and be responsible, and I exhale an 'at last' sigh. *It's a courageous thing to do, a responsible thing to do, and it's the right thing to do.*

I congratulate myself on taking this giant step to give up cocaine and perversion. I gratuitously start to compare myself to everybody I know who's still using drugs but who has not yet taken this courageous step.

Those losers... I'm stopping. It's a done deal. But I reason that there is still a little rain left to fall. Some work left to be done to complete this new sacrifice, for in order to screw up the coke connection I have to trade the gun for some more. It's a dirty job, even a dangerous one, given the current climate over there, but somebody's gotta' do it.

I can't just throw all that coke away. That would be just stupid... thankless. So the good life; puppies, lawns with flowers and children laughing, yes. It's starting now – officially – but I'll have to use up this last score first. It's well, symbolic.

'At least a gram,' an eager bad-cop voice says in my head.

'I don't really care,' good-cop says. '*I'm above such considerations. I may just throw the shit away anyway.*'

'Yeah, right, responds bad cop. *I could shoot half a gram maybe. That would be in-fucking-credible. Hmm... get fucked in the ass while I'm rushing on half-a-gram? After all, it will be my last time...*

This dedication to my new clean life has me looking urgently at my watch in that early morning hour wondering... wondering if it's not too late... not too late to call Eva.

* * *

Sounds are now entering consciousness. We both hear the multiple footsteps as the walking wounded come up the AA stairs; seeking, clawing, scratching, and fighting to stay alive – all a step above the pit – all one step ahead of disaster.

"So how long y'been sober? he asks.

"Almost ninety days now, I fell off twice in the last 3 months before this stretch. I can't go back to it again," I answer with wretched honesty.

I suddenly find my mouth opening, sending more sound through the tedious ether.

"Y'know that definition of gay you mentioned…? He immediately looks a little baleful, readying himself to receive a verbal kick-in-the-ass. "The compulsive desire you talked about?" I continue.

"Yeah," he deadpans.

"I get a little compulsive myself sometimes."

Post AA Sex

After the meeting, he smiled and came over to me. I remained seated, and smiled back. "So you get a little compulsive too," he said as he scooted up next to me, obvious.

"I get to feeling like that sometimes, it's difficult to talk about… like even right now," I said. So we took a drive.

My excitement seemed to diminish rather than increase. Nervousness increased; anxiety increased, but sexual excitement? No. I tried blowing him a little, but it made me sick. I had to stop, but I knew from his reaction that I had something he wanted.

He was hungry, and as the weeks went by, all his early noise about not wanting any relationship somehow transformed into him calling me at my apartment quite a bit with my wife answering the phone more than once.

He bored me. He was so eager to be nice, and to try to turn everything I said into some kind of positive boost for my self-esteem, that it was dick-wilting just to be around him. What I got from it, however, was a phenomenal realization about myself one night.

I had never been sodomized and wanted to try it. After inserting his finger for a while I understood the mechanics of taking it. If you totally relaxed yourself *as if* you were ready for bathroom evacuation, and just relaxed in that same way as if to '*just let it all out*,' it would allow for a complete relaxation of the sphincter. Then there would be a stimulating quality to having someone atop you while his thing pumped in and out of your bottom that was not totally unpleasant – within that '*hurts so good*' masochism. I was hoping it could hit that part that the doctor hits when he examines your prostate and you think your wilted wiener could shoot sperm all over the office if he kept massaging it. This however, the sodomy did not do.

However, if you're fairly psychotic and easily live in a make-believe world anyway, it adds more than stage-prop action to what otherwise might be a purely physical and invasive sexual activity. The whimper in being so used takes you into the fantasy/spirit of the *'bitch-slave;'* a dangerous place to be if activated under the wrong circumstances. I immediately saw how a real dom could easily make you his bitch, and was both somewhat relieved and disappointed to have this eager-to-please-faggot taking charge as the male.

I had absorbed enough of the sodomy mentally, spiritually and physically and no longer could relax, so I called him off me. He immediately stopped, apologizing if he hurt me. Then he left to wash off. Although my bottom hurt a little, this forfeiture of manliness in my allowing the sodomy to at least take-place to some degree allowed for a rising sense of feminine sexuality. While he was washing off in the bathroom, I luxuriated in a stretch, feeling like Cleopatra on a couch. When he returned, I found I could control him with a various languid, coy communications. I found this extremely exciting in the strangest way. It was a female disposition I had never lived in before. I wasn't really hot for him or even more sex, yet I couldn't resist teasing him for it, and then allowing myself to be 'overwhelmed.'

As he quickly came to me, I tried anticipating blowing him as I slid my hands around in foreplay, which added a sensual confidence different than what I had experienced in the past. As he kissed my neck and his hands caressed my ass, I saw myself taking him down my throat.

Although this was a virginal 'coming out' of sorts for me, I was already calculating my partner's deficiencies as a lover. I had to imagine he was more forceful and demanding than he was, and so was responding to yet another fantasy even with his hands on my body. Even though this real-life flesh and blood person was here with me, I was using his flesh as if I was auto-erotic and in a fantasy. Like the "glory-holes' of bathhouses and video stores, in which a hole is cut in the wall and one male hangs his manhood through the hole while another services it without the two ever seeing each other, I fantasized he was someone else. Finally I pushed him onto his back and finished him off.

I was glad it was over. I realized he was not turning me on at all, and having sex with him was sort of *'I'm here; I'm curious; so let's do it,'* but that's about it. He was a live dildo, a living, breathing blowup doll.

He's talking about us and the coming weekend as I'm dressing to leave. The realization of what was taking place in was suddenly shocking and kind of thrilling in a most surprising way. I had never experienced anything like this before in my life – he appeared to be totally in love with me. I found myself in a position I had never known before; the power of the female pleasure-giver realizing she didn't care at all for the man she had just had sex with. My time with him had been, well, a sexual exercise in "unleashing the female within," and I actually had to think twice now to remember his name.

He was floating on air, chatting away concerning his plans for us on the coming weekend. I was looking for my shoes, and I could feel his eyes on me like I was a runway model. As I walked about I noticed that as I mentally re-lived this *'giving it up'* feeling, my body appeared languidly effeminate, and his voice would become excited as he would pause to gaze at me. I was becoming intoxicated to suddenly have this new power, and I stared at my shoelaces lest I bring my face up and give myself away. As my silence spoke volumes, he began to panic. I silently luxuriated in this new position of power-through-silence. By merely saying nothing, I could totally manipulate him. I saw myself as a hot coed in cashmere and satin, a spoiled bitch rolling her eyes at this loser. I had explored a willingness to sexually please another, and now watched fascinated as this person's emotions and self-respect crumbled and spilled out like a gutted fish. He **n-e-e-d-s** me. I'm a shameless cunt, and loving every minute of it.

He began to degrade himself even more, disregarding the rudiments of self-respect as an offering to me, the pleasure-giving sex goddess. I was in charge. He started stuttering apologies for whatever he imagined he was doing that might be upsetting or unpleasant for me, promising to change and do whatever was necessary to please me. As *'this just keeps getting better and better,'* I allowed myself the thrill of being swept up within the power of my sudden pussy. I was being literally exalted; worshipped. He opened up his arms for me to come to him. Inside me something sneered. I did not move towards him. Rather, I put up my hands in a half-surrender, half *'it's-OK-and-let's-not-bother'* gesture regarding his silent invitation to hug, finally answering with words I knew were spearing him.

I found being straightforward surprisingly easy, even though this was my first real experience of this sort. "*You're a nice guy, but I think sexually... well, I'm excited by other... well, things I... uh guess.*"

"*What other things, Marty? Tell me what you like!*" he pleaded with a desperation that utterly disqualified him even more from being able to provide the requisite spirit.

"I like the booths… the video booths," I said, as I stood up to leave, sensing somewhere inside me a teenage slut squealing in delight.

"But Marty," he cried, *"those people… they **don't care about you**!"*

I laughed to myself, closing the door behind me as I stepped outside into the warm LA night. I relaxed and had my first epiphany in years. His words *"they don't care about you!"* echoed in my head. *That's just why I like it*, I realized as a warm thrill rolled through my newly sodomized body. I realized with a smile that now, ten years after the mental hospital, I finally understood something real and true about myself.

"I'm a whore," I said brightly, not displeased to at last to come to grips with my behavior. I slid behind the wheel thinking, *'and now I know what it's like to have sex with a man and then leave him longing wretchedly for me.'* As I put the car in gear, he's dismissed from my thoughts. I knew I wouldn't be seeing him again. There's an unexpected, inexplicable emotional upside to this epiphany. *"**You slut**!"* I shout out to myself with a grin, the tires joining my squeal as I gun the car out of the driveway.

Chapter 12 – To Be or Not To Be

Sex Without Drugs – Epiphany in Sperm

> *"As I have indicated earlier, I think that the whole business of the homosexual entity as an explanation is always to be looked pretty firmly in the face by psychiatrists who attempt to effect any great improvement in the mental health of the patient. One should determine whether this entity is the organization of a definite integrating tendency that satisfies a need or whether it is a complex mental disorder in which the homosexuality is present because it so perfectly fortifies some abnormal mental process, some dynamism of difficulty."*
> *"Clinical Studies in Psychiatry"* (Sullivan) pp163-65

This kind of behavior did not help my sobriety at all and I slip again. Six months of sobriety later, with a new job as a salesman, I am tempted again to believe bringing real-world experience into the world of my fantasy longings will somehow assuage these homoerotic longings; as if by doing so I could bring peace to my demons. After fifteen years of hedonistic riot, my new sober existence seemed grey and lifeless, as if life was hardly worth living. It seemed reasonable to find out what a quick *sober* liaison would be like with an anonymous male. I mentioned this to my shrink and was surprised to sense a real measure of disapproval. I was startled. I thought it was such an adult thing to do. I was being surprised a lot lately as the drugs were coming out of my brain birthing new perspectives every day.

Nevertheless, the voice in my head luring me into my imaginings appeared too attractive to ignore twenty-four seven. In the past it had lured me into narcotics but its voice had been weakened by the light of awareness and my subsequent refusal to follow its siren song of drugs. But the allure of sober homosexual sex appeared to have the voice of a higher-powered lobbyist, appearing alongside my indulgence of sexual fantasies mirroring such behavior, and I believed I should no longer ignore its demands to be served.

I married the idea that a "real" man makes his own choices regarding a spirit of adventure. There was almost a *"poppa would be proud"* kind of motivation to this entire "sexploration," and I determined to go for it; eager for a radical change in consciousness without the use of drugs.

I entered the adult bookstore and could sense a crossroads of higher energies coming together. A sense that something other than sex was approaching… *sumpthin's happenin'*.

Target acquired: a wild-eyed young man in his thirties, powerfully built. We made eye contact. He turned and entered a booth. In a moment the lime-colored letters lit-up above the door showing "*Movie in Progress*," but the door remained ajar in a green light of invitation. I entered the booth, turned and locked the door, and sat down next to him. We watched the porn a few seconds in silence. Part of me screamed "*run out now, go!*"

"Here's a few tokens towards the movies," I said instead, first placing them on the video controller and, taking a trembling breath, placed a hand on his leg. Finding no objection to this obvious behavior, I slid to my knees. There's always something unique and scary about a situation when two male strangers decide without discussion to have sex. It's like we're members of a secret society that accepts things like this, and those mired in the lower echelon of bourgeois normalcy could not understand our boldness to pursue these sexual satisfactions. We were therefore, a superior ilk, free and understanding; far-and-away more in touch with ourselves than those bourgeois goose-steppers.

The almost hyperventilating excitement swept over me, and temporarily removed me from 'self' consciousness. I wait breathless, not unlike a dog meeting another with its head lowered and tail wagging. Submitting myself in a kneeling posture for his approval, I am intoxicated in this, my suddenly realized and rebellious moment. His silent answer unambiguous, he takes out a circumcised firehose of such length and thickness as to leave me temporarily stunned.

Within moments I had everything I could have asked for. A willing partner with impressive equipment, all systems appeared *go,* but after some initial moments, I could find no reason to be here doing what I was doing. I feel decidedly nonsexual and repulsed. It was like I was placing a piece of unpleasantly scented rubber into my mouth for no discernible reason other than to be submissive to this stranger.

A voice in my head was telling me I didn't want to be submissive to this stranger. Singular and quiet, it kept asking me, "*What are you doing this for?*" I had no answer... I could sense a desire to slip away into a submissive fantasy, but no longer had sufficient desire, energy or motivation to do so. Good-cop/bad-cop voices spoke up: *he's not superior to you, so why put his dick in your mouth*? On the other hand, less clear but more muted motives hinted at the excitement and pleasure in submerging into slavish fantasy along with the appropriate behavior to keep such imaginings company.

I soon stopped what I was doing to him. Instead of following the initial impulse to leave upon cessation of my oral service, I knelt to the side, vainly seeking to end my sexual frustration with an orgasm of my own. I tried watching the porn on the back of the locked door, and I began to wish I hadn't even begun to do that, but had left instead.

He likewise started to relieve himself. As I jerked off and started to excite, however, I was overwhelmed with the realization of pleasure within the goals of my sexual fantasy and, at the same time, a sudden sense of desolation and frustration should I just leave and walk back into the street. I suddenly felt life's emptiness swamp me, hopelessly sterile and frustrated compared to the *"life"* the here and now afforded me – and with my searching lust came a renewed urge to take advantage of what was in front of me. My very presence in the booth fed anew not only the increased temptation for my opportunity, but justified it (*you don't go into a whorehouse to play solitaire*). What I was fantasizing of having in my own efforts to obtain relief was, after all, right here, and why not just *get into it*?

There suddenly seemed such a promise to escape my uncomfortable dilemma, to complete a submersion into some *"real life,"* that my own fantasy soon crooned to imagine myself from a feminine perspective and here was a guy to be that way with. Not only to pleasure his huge apparatus, but a compulsion was sweeping over me now to complete the act *all the way* this one time sober. As the excitement of my own manipulation rose up within me, the pendulum continued to swing wantonly, and I commit to just do it all. I left my own jerking ministrations and turned to him.

He was stroking himself as I placed my mouth over his huge rubbery head. He continued to pump his hand into my chin and I surprised myself how gently I placed my right hand over his pumping fingers, causing him to stop as a voice in my head sarcastically commented what a Hallmark bookstore moment this was. He withdrew his hand from his prodigious staff and I took over, sliding my fingers, adjusting my mouth and breathing – my will – into the blowjob.

The moment the large ball of flesh filled up my mouth, the quiet dick-wilting communication of *'what are you doing this for?'* began anew. If I pay attention to this voice I'm out the door and on the sidewalk, and I use what this stranger might think of me to hinder that impulse. The assumption that I owed this man my servicing was by-this-time allowed, and the way to escape anxiety was clear: gain his approval and accelerate into fantasy. As a submarine dives into the ocean depths, I sought out submergence into sexual fantasy as the haven from which to continue my operations.

My dreamstate wasn't currently at a sufficient level of intensity for me to totally submerge into. I needed a greater commitment. I could not continue this activity in my current state of consciousness. I sought to recapture that vision of lust lost within myself, that kind of high-octane energy that sometimes twists your body and makes you cry out loud when you climax by yourself. I was going to have to purpose myself deeper in his service – no, to *its* service – and leave any and all inhibition behind.

I breathe in through my nose and slide the mammoth thickness down my throat, submissively dedicating to providing pleasure, and a complete commitment to swallow every drop of completion that will be offered. A uniting of the will and the behavior, I am holding deeper and deeper breaths in order to allow his huge beast longer time down my throat, I started to forget about technique long enough to merge with that young and beautiful female teenager on her first date, not really sure how she allowed this guy to get her here but wanting her date to be pleased with her. *I guess guys really like this...* This submersion into the imagery allowed my mouth to suddenly salivate to the point where I was giving off slurping sounds which I hadn't remembered ever doing before.

As I submerge into my own expression, I sense him submerge into his spiritual counterpart, and it appears what is being served in him is taking him over with such groans, cries and guttural sounds of pleasure that there is a heightening frenzy in the very air we breath. His moans are intoxicating, and my imagery more continuous in its ability to captivate me. With each slide down my throat, the wet travel itself is increasing the level of intensity in his cries and groans, and as the thick staff turns to wood the head expands with that final life of its own. I am in total submission as his jerking spasms not only begin to pour into my mouth, but his entire body convulses as it enters into the release with gasps and loud cries of pleasure.

As the throat fills with the hot fluid, the tongue senses it as if it's coming from every pore on that bulbous head. The back of the throat is flooded and hesitation is no longer an option. Swallow immediately. It's so hot, salty and sickly thick that I only gag momentarily before completing the sickening act with a *"you wanted this"* from that previous quiet tone in my mind's background. I try to tell myself it's great, but somewhere deep behind the frenzy I'm conflicted to know that's not true *at all*. I did, however, take it all, and this new dedication to service is just in time, for after swallowing the first load, there's a huge second delivery.

I was more into receiving it by then, for once the previous rebellion (urging me to spit it out and run from the booth) had been silenced and overcome, I now remain a more trained novitiate in his stead, and am settling into the silent, unmoving impenitent on his knees with the reality of a shrinking cock in his mouth.

A series of dark rites emerge. Apparently I have earned them. Just as Jesus tells the parable of the man who first refuses his father's request to work in the vineyard, but then goes, and is hence regarded as "*doing the father's will*," so I had at first refused the dark side's entreaty, but had reconsidered and ultimately acquiesced to it. This commitment appears to deserve a reward; a certain baptismal anointing fitting for the occasion.

For as my date slowly withdrew his spent penis, a small pearl drop of fluid appeared off the tip. Swept up by my new and total commitment, I dutifully arched my face up a few inches, extending my slavish tongue to lick it off. Perhaps because of this dark and sudden Eucharist, his stick becomes a baptizing baton, with him wiping it slowly – still glistening wet with his sperm and my saliva – first across one side of my face, and then I, dutifully turning the other cheek, receive its slow return benediction across the other side, completing the accolade. Dutifully thrilling to the silent scream inside my soul ('*something's new here*'), I was now swooning.

In the spirit of the moment, I started to put into words my motivation to meet him the following week for sodomy. I heard the sound of my own voice and I immediately fell into shocked silence.

"*Your wife is so lucky to be able to...*" I heard the sound at the same time I saw what I had expected to see: a facial expression telling me his wife *doesn't act as if she's so lucky*... But I also noted the surprise on his countenance mirroring my own.

When I had first told him of the tokens I had for our use upon entering the booth, I had spoken in my normal voice. Now I had that sing-song high pitched faggy whine of submission in my tone. That twisted vocal that people call *effeminate* for lack of any other term to define it. I had never spoken with this voice before in my life.

I was suddenly in the spirit. I saw a landscape. I was in the landscape. "I" was the landscape. There was no consciousness of anything else. There was *nothing that existed in my reality apart from this landscape*. A territory of life played out in multiple dimensions. There were symbols for various places I would live, careers I would have, and people I would be close to. It had a topographical cross-section quality to it. It was like a baseball diamond in which the viewer could be in the dugout and actually see what was "below" the field and bases. If there was a tree, for example, where second base was, you could see the roots of that tree below the ground as well as the tree above ground. The height, width, depth – as well as present and future – were being presented to me outside of normal space and time.

On the "surface" there were events: future people I would meet as well as future careers and places I would live which were mapped out on the upper plain. Underneath it all, where, for example, one could see roots, were all manner of symbolism for this new and present sexuality. This subconscious world; this "under-foundation" was filled with emotional river-like deposits. I could see these forces generating this new tone of submission within my "new" voice. The tone would always be towards this sexual world, and the individuals I would use in this behavior were just beings to be used in order to satiate these forces. I understood that within the submissive, feminine quality of my voice there was an urge to constantly generate sexual response. Sexual activity would become the center of my life. I saw myself about to enter a universe made up of the constant seeking of sexual contacts, of a kind of sensual vanity as well as mocking and condescension toward all who might disagree with its appropriateness. This would be a life-style centering compulsively around the penis, the anus, felatio, and sodomy, while the amount of kinkiness I would choose to allow myself would complete my individuality.

No matter what my life's accomplishments, the real dynamic sense of life would be felt through this sexual behavior delivered on these rivers of emotion. It was made known to me that if I uttered one more word in the furtherance of a sexual relationship with this man in the booth, I would be committed to this world.

The decision was not made with my thinking mind. It was the soulish disposition of something much deeper. Conflicted and scared, I remained silent on the floor, terrified and stunned, and was never more relieved than when he left.

Was I fearful of societal condemnation or something far more significant? I wouldn't touch a man again for the sixteen-year duration of my marriage. I knew it was time to return to my wife with a new and different perspective.

Was I Just Born That Way?

HS Sullivan, the first man of insight to take Freud's proclamations to new and more useful heights, promulgated a theory of personality growth based on progressive stages of personality. His validation stands in the fact that before the age of anti-psychotic drugs, Sullivan set up a special intake unit for schizophrenic patients and secured an 80% social recovery rate. His insights, lectures and books are all built on this results-driven reality. ***That is why he has credibility.***

His work with newborns, anxiety and his doctrine of empathetic linkage with the mothering one remains a remarkable work never fully explored by the psychological/psychiatric community; even among those adherents who admire his work.

Sullivan had assistants and medical students stationed in maternity wards noting the behavior of newborns with their mothers. If a mother was anxious, the newborn also reacted with anxiety so severe it would refuse the nipple. The inference here, is that a new mother, for example, surrounded in some cases by her own oftentimes critical relations, may feel anxious as to her ability to provide proper "mothering" to her squalling newborn.

Since some mothers would regard this as a "test" of sorts, anxiety within the new mother would occasionally be of such magnitude that the infant, upon crying for milk, would be so effected by the anxiety on the part of the mothering one that it would actually *reject* the nipple. Sullivan termed this an example of *"empathetic linkage,"* and postulated a theory involving the *"good nipple, bad nipple, and useless nipple."* [22]

The dangers of being inured to such early trauma and stress are only too obvious. It is well within reason to consider the empathy and linkage in its dimensional capability to instill within the child not only mere anxiety, but of the same type the mother enveloped, that is, the infant is inspired to receive its first dosage of anxiety in the face of others who are perceived as authorities.

I cannot state with certainty that "I remember" the following, but have re-experienced uncanny and filtered imagery of what I'll call early engrams of it. These are imprints so archaic in the formation of my pre-ego development that they fail any test of definition. It may be of some use, however, for us to venture, however briefly, into a new way of looking at things we are all somewhat familiar with.

My mother was a beautiful woman with an hourglass figure. My father a wimp for mother's approval, sex and gambling. When my mother was pregnant with the author in the late 1940s, the local General Practitioner misdiagnosed her tremendous weight gain as being the result of overeating. Despite my mother's protestations to the contrary, he refused to see it was a tremendous retention of water. So while eating only small amounts of what was healthy and little else, she could still fit into my father's clothes and shoes, who was 6 feet, weighing about 200 lbs.

Consequently, the scenario to which I allude contains the elements that many infants find themselves in. We have to remember that to the infant the parents are 'god-like.' The OEM has programmed us all as infants to look up to parent(s) in this manner.

---

[22] *Interpersonal Theory of Psychiatry;* Sullivan, pp80 Norton and Co., New York

When nursing, the infant is literally "eating its mother" while the sex starved male parent looks down at his wife nursing their newborn with her sudden and tantalizing *new figure*. The female is usually wearing nothing but lingerie over her swollen breasts. A wordless interplay will take place more or less along the following lines: communication involves his expression that he's eager to get "back in the saddle," and his wife, after the long months of pregnancy, is eager to once again demonstrate her power with her full sexuality. Irregardless of whether the man is a wimp or a bully, his need for sex from the woman in order to feel 'like a man' once again is the same. It is undoubtedly picked up by the infant's total submergence in – for lack of a better expression, his or her pre-ego identity-existence.

My impression of this experience deals with my mother making some kind of request of my father, and he disposed for whatever reason to suggest an alternate solution. She then, needing only to shoot off a hint of sexuality with which to yank his leash, spoke with such authority that my father figure; this earthly representative of the Creator, promptly resembled a peasant holding his cap in his hand full of fear and trembling, bowing his head and quickly running off to do her bidding. Consequently, an early sexual vibration definitely communicating who's boss was established while I lay at her breast, my tiny fingers clutching and touching the silky lingerie. A sexual vibration defining who's in charge can often result in a male claiming with complete sincerity that his homosexual disposition was something he was born with, rather than seeing it as the identification with the more powerful parent; in this case the female, and the disappointment such an awareness brings.

What is impossible to determine at this stage is the (dare I say it?) 'resentment' that even an infant can embrace when the heavenly identification of male faith, strength, courage, honor and integrity is replaced by an undeniable yearning for sensuality and carnality. The life in the spirit world experienced by an infant is the least understood – and most ignored – component of raising a child in a world gone mad.

The power of sexuality mixes with the lingerie as life begins and is nurtured with mother's milk. This being the first material most infants touch while being relieved of their firstborn anxieties at the mothers' breast, is it any wonder so many men react with uncontrolled carnality when presented with a female wearing it? The extent to which men are affected by it is seasoned, I believe, by the intensity of the countless variations to the interplay described above.

My father didn't mind groveling before her power. He had evolved with his own 'evilution.' "*She's the boss,*" was the half-serious cultural acceptable reality he kept while pretending this was 'good.' It suited all concerned to make-believe that this grotesque service depicting modern man's self-abasement and concomitant sensuality was "love."

One particular aunt and my mother were very close, and had been ever since they were children. As sisters, they were almost twins in looks, and could still fit in the same clothes. My aunt had married a guy who made millions and it was my mother's favorite thing to haul all of us up to her sibling's million-dollar digs for parties on the occasional weekend or holiday. My father was particularly sensitive of his *less-than* status, and never failed to demonstrate his sense of inferiority by bum-rapping his rich and successful brother-in-law in our middle class digs.

At these parties my mother would dress up in elegant, expensive clothes purchased by her sister from the best stores in the country, put on airs and down martinis served by hostesses and maids. Alcohol was rarely imbibed in our house, so when my mother drank on these occasions, it was not as one knowing how to hold her liquor. The anxiety on the part of my mother in preparation for these events was palpable, my father becoming equally tense in his own way.

It was in this milieu that she flirted with the upper class and wealthy who would normally comprise much of the guest list. Since my mother was good looking, witty, talkative and often quite tipsy as well as sister-to-the-hostess, she didn't lack for attention.

My father – a salesman by trade, and out of his element in terms of economic prestige and accomplishment – would remain quiet, and then when the opportunity arose, would often offer tidbits of conversation to an unsuspecting listener, capture the courteous individual's attention, and having hooked an attentive ear, launch into a most curious communication. The individual, who had merely been content to make conversation following the acceptable courtesies of the culture, might then find himself the recipient of something a great psychiatrist once described as a type of '*substitute process*:' a tale of woe that reflected how all the improbabilities of fate had conspired to make my father a most woefully used and unfortunate character. This "process" substitutes for him having to be aware how unfortunate he sees himself in comparison to these others.

My dad had that totally focused ability to delve into an account of some adventure of his, replete with interesting detail, rhythm, and quick character development – that definitely could catch your interest. Then, just when you would normally expect a successful conclusion to an interesting tale, he would go into what tortuous province of fate had arrived to deal him a hand so dark in malice that surely the listener had to agree that he was the most unfortunate person to walk the face of the earth. He would conclude his story of agonizing loss and failure with a dramatic flourish of word and posture, breathe in deeply through his nose, and with eyes shining, snort an unspoken look that silently shouted "*so there! What do you think of that!*" [23]

He seemed to blink suddenly at the conclusion of his monologue, as if part of him was no longer sure of what he had just done, or what he had actually just said, and where, existentially, he had just gone. He would then slip back into that *lights-on-nobody's home* look, and essentially disappear back into his head from whence he came.

While people blinked a few times at the realization of the point of his account, it was often with no small amount of stupefaction. It runs counter to most people's dignity. Yes, twists of fate do occur in life, but to turn oneself inside out in a dramatic reproduction of ruined dreams and failure with the same gusto normally reserved for success-stories was surprising to say the least. Of course courtesy demanded no one make mention of such a matter, but what anyone not blinded by propriety could see, was the unspoken resulting attitude that said, well, if you want to brag about what a loser you are, '*I'll sit here and look at your beautiful wife a little more. She seems to be poking fun at you too.*'

Under the heady spirits of vodka or gin Martinis, my mother, now loosened with this unfamiliar alcohol, would gently and then not-so-gently put him in his place with subtle – and then not so subtle – humiliation. She flirted enthusiastically with those whose life-stories (real or otherwise) ended on more positive notes. Most of the guests were successful

---

[23] "Substitute activity, in contrast to indirect exploitative attitudes, is not addressed primarily to an audience, instead it is **addressed primarily to avoiding certain conscious clarity about one's own situation,** one's own motivations, and so on. When this is the case, this 'preying on sympathy' actually touches more on ..."*self pity.*' And this preoccupation is actually in the realm of substitutive processes. "...People with massive preoccupation – and this one of the fields of my greatest defeats in therapy – meet almost all interpersonal situations in which they feel inferior to the other person by looking for anything that can be utilized in building up one of these long trains of covert or conversational processes which serve to show what a woebegone and very unhappily used person the speaker is."

"...The element of self pity is within calling distance of a group of substitute activities which I have already mentioned – that enormously popular business of entertaining envy. Envy is perhaps in no sense self-pity, but certainly it is substitutive activity. It is called out in all sorts and kinds of situations where the person with customarily low self-esteem is disturbed. And it saves one from invidious comparisons which would be anything but uplifting to one's self-regard."
"Interpersonal Theory of Psychiatry" (Sullivan) pp353-5

professionals, businessmen and/or politicians. My father would have gladly cut off an arm to be in that group, and in the subtle social interplay of the evening, my mother could mix flattering whomever she was talking to with subtly putting down our own humble circumstances in comparison. So my father, seeking to run from a situation in which he saw himself as inferior (see footnote), was in a kind of existential agony, while my mother teased and talked '*silly,*' flattering some stranger's ability to travel the world or purchase a Winter residence in Florida by comparing it to our own *less-than* circumstances.

I don't believe my mother ever physically cheated on my father. What do you call that kind of behavior which had her teasing and laughing with another man about his success in life, using words my father would yearn to have heard used so flatteringly by her regarding his own life? Could she continue to pretend she didn't know it pained him? Yet her unfaithfulness was bare bones obvious with every laugh at his expense, her non-physical adulteries all out in the open amidst the partied atmosphere for his befuddled mind to deny with a pasted smile on his face; slightly confused but believing he was just being oversensitive. She was right there, after all, to insist such was the case. Wasn't she smiling, when later, after saying his name teasingly in Yiddishkyte, "*my oyvee,*" adding dismissively: "*Oh, I was just kidding!*" She would then convince him that it was he who was crazy. *He was being oversensitive cause he wasn't making as much money as those others*, etc. He could never see the invisible shears she used to cut off his manhood. Neither did my mother consciously understand her own motivations. She was '*having fun,*' '*getting a little tipsy,*' *enjoying herself.*' The wasp on autopilot.

I was barely adolescent, and always extremely uncomfortable around these wealthy relatives, and found myself uneasy around their servants as well. I detested these scenes, often retiring to my own guest bedroom early. They lived on a forty-acre spread in the country, and I had shot a woodchuck while hunting the day before. I was both fascinated and repulsed touching its dead body the next day, hardened by *rigor mortis.*

I found myself in a most unique one-time fantasy that night while taking myself in my fourteen-year-old hand. I saw myself as a female woodchuck struggling vainly to escape the quicker, more powerful male; suddenly being crawled up upon and mounted sexually. The brute had come to have his wild, woolly woodchuck way with me.

I immediately fell asleep and had a most unusual nightmare. It was based on a real event, a swimming contest that I had (in real life) entered into with one of my best friends while swimming at the ocean we had gone to with his folks. His father was the judge. In the real life situation, I was a much better swimmer, and just as in *The Tortoise and the Hare*, I had got maybe ten feet ahead and stopped to tread water, perhaps to poke fun at him while at the same time sentencing myself to lose. As he approached my position, I started to swim again, but a swell took me a little backwards, and I had to suddenly struggle to catch up. I believed I did in time to pull ahead again, but my friend's dad declared him the winner. In the dream, all this took place again, but his father was suddenly saying

"Y'know what I see? I see this!" and it appeared that my pants were down. I wanted to run, but my legs wouldn't move.

Regarding ectoplasmic erotica vis-à-vis the return of my murdered animal, it is perhaps enough to laugh at such silliness, and while receiving rape by a murdered prey in order to make obeisance for the killing might be advanced to no particular purpose, I think instead the slow, 'cowards-die-many-times-before-their-death' agonies my father suffered at the hands of my mother had more to do with it.

Regardless of failing fathers, flailing swimmers or fucking woodchucks, one thing was certain: in the real world it was time to return to a committed new sexual relationship with my beautiful young wife. I had seen the light regarding sex-with-men and was relieved to have been able to escape before homosexuality swallowed me up. I knew I had conjugal duties towards the woman that would not – and could not – be denied. But how to implement these uncomfortable – but still covert – sexual impulses into my life with my wife? That would be the question.

Husbandly Duties and Bedroom Sublimations

Sam was a bookstore clerk I had once blown. He was an older, fascinatingly homely pervert with a lined face that said there wasn't anything he wouldn't do to you given half a chance.

Our relationship started one day when I was on speed or coke, and was looking to take the edge off with some action in the adult bookstore. I approached him.

"Yeah" he consented, with a look that says he's doing me a favor. "I haven't been serviced in a while." He was so low and ugly that the thought of having him cry out in orgasmic release in my mouth made my testes tingle. He took me in the backroom, sat me down and produced an organ of such dimension and color so as to make me believe there was definite mulatto in his genes.

He was so huge I had trouble giving him good head at first, and he became impatient, insisting I just keep still with it deep in my mouth while he pumped it off. In subsequent get-togethers I found myself almost begging him to let me do the stroking manipulation. Then it became time. With enough excitement anything became possible. As the sodomy began, I thought I'd pass out from the pain. No possibility of 'keeping it together,' there's simply no ability to be a tight-ass. The sphincter control is somehow tied to your independence, your masculinity, or ability to be 'separate' somehow. The relaxation of the sphincter - so necessary when evacuating - allows a penetration and sense of violation that brings with it a submergence into the will – or the spirit operating through the will - of the other person. After all, what more violation can one man perform on another than this? So he must be 'given' everything. This is essentially the pimp's control. You're offering the ultimate sacrifice for his pleasure and approval.

"My wife is beautiful," I blurt out while he's gasping towards completion. "I'd love to watch you fuck her." His continued spanking and his hard thrusts into my upturned bottom took pain into a new level of worship. It was as if I was being punished for worshipping these dark forces of treachery and voyeuristic adultery by the very dark forces themselves. Evil doesn't thank you with jelly beans and a blowjob. I moaned in pain as I gave up all I had to him, trying to extract some succor from the trembling excitement that energized me in the realization that I had mortgaged my future home-life to him as well.

"What's your wife like?" he asks later after he comes out of the shower. I am immediately anxious and nervous, feeling a tingling sensation deep in my loins. As I show Sam the wallet photo of my young and beautiful wife, I notice I am breathing hard enough that I have to make an effort to speak normally. His eyes widen at the picture in his hand: she is in a satin nightie, her pretty face holding a sexy pose as she shows off her most excellent figure.

"*I want to meet her*," he says, and I can hear he is also having difficulty in containing the excitement in his voice. Our bonding over this future seduction has me weak with a slave's labor. The energizing desire for him to make me a cuckold fills me with excitement, stimulating my loins with a corresponding tingling.

"She won't just give it up," I say slowly. "But give me a second. Cocaine. Yes, it's definitely possible."

"I don't use it."

"You won't have to... Trust me."

We arrive at the apartment with some good scotch. I have bought two grams of blow. I introduce Sam as a friend. *I have a gram of coke for us*, I add. I shoot up and so does Janice. It's soon all gone and she is immediately wild. The carnal sexuality in the room is obvious to me and I'm about to find out if my wife is picking up on it.

She asks if there's any more.

I make a face. "I don't know. I think it may be possible…"

"What does that mean?"

I nod toward Sam.

"Him? He's got?"

"Let me see what I can do."

Janice makes a "please" expression with a tortured look on her face.

I bend down to Sam's ear.

"She's hungry for your stash." He laughs.

I go out to Janice in the kitchen, whispering to her: "He says he has another gram that he'll share with you…(beat)… if you'll come out in lingerie and sit on his lap," I add with a nervous laugh as I shrug questioningly with a look into her eyes.

Her glance tells me that at some level she knows what I'm thinking. She looks at Sam. He is pure predator without any attempt to look any different. I look back at her with eyes a little wider than usual. Acting oblivious to any implication, she brightly says "*OK*"!

Janice slipped quickly out of the kitchen and into our bedroom at the end of the hall.

"What do you think of her?"

"Man, she is beautiful. Really. What a body, too."

I turn the lights way down, and light two candles by the table where I put out water, cotton and some syringes.

"Ta-ta," sings Janice as she comes out. An exquisite swirl of silver satin kimono flows down to her feet and swirls open briefly, revealing the black chemise underneath.

She bounces onto his lap, the sliding satin giving off its own sensual hiss; the scent of her cologne intoxicating.

He looks at her possessively.

"You look terrific. You did well. Have some."

Can I shoot about a quarter?

"Baby," he said huskily, his hands sliding over her satin thighs, "Do your thing."

"Ooh," she squeals, wiggling off his lap, the satin material swishing with longing as the sharp intake of Sam's breath could be heard going along with it. We all realized how close it all was. Immediately after she shoots up, she makes her decision. She curls into his lap in a collapsed ecstasy.

"I know I *have to* sit on your lap, don't I?" she whispers out between cocaine gasps; uttering her pout with kittenish submission. "Is there anything else you need me to do?" She breathes out deliriously. "Do you want me to leave you alone?"

"Oh, you're not leaving me alone, baby,' Sam says huskily, gently squeezing her ass as he kisses her neck. Janice's body almost spasms as she moans. She is catching her breath as Sam whispers huskily,

"Sittin' on my lap is the least you're going to do for me."

Squealing… "Oh, what else are you… are you going to make me do?" she whimpers in the same helpless, little girl voice, while making the same face.

He whispers into her ear as his hands roam over her thighs and buttocks.

"You devil!" she shrieks with laughter, kissing him on his neck.

"I'm going to show Sam around the apartment, Marty," Janice says, showing me her suddenly in-charge serious eyes I had not seen before. The change from sex-kitten with Sam to this hard-eyed, in-command attitude with me sent chills through my spine. I felt tortured with an anguished pleasure as I watched her lead Sam to the bedroom. Sam stopped her at the bedroom door. He turned to her, and with a glance at me, took her two wrists in his large left hand, pinning them above her head. He kissed her full on the mouth, and placing his hand on her left breast, slowly squeezed it harder and then harder still, while she cried out softly. He looked over at me slowly, making a face like 'how do you like this?' while slowly bringing his huge hand onto her behind. She moaned, undulating against him with a helplessness that left me breathless.

They closed the door but after spending almost a minute wondering whether I should go in or not I hear her call my name. Entering the room, the light was low but clear enough to reveal that my wife and Sam were naked save for Janice's skimpy panties. Sam's impressive equipment lumbered at three-quarter readiness across his thigh. Janice was staring at it breathing hard while Sam leaned over to kiss her on the mouth while squeezing her right breast with his left hand. Janice was on her back, her left hand palm open grasping his thickness, exhaling low exclamations from deep in her throat with every squeeze. Sam whispered something in her ear.

"*Sam wants you to take off my panties, Marty*," she gasped out with a strange cocained voice when she broke free from their kiss. The air in the room was electric with sexual frenzy.

"*Take'm off with your mouth*," Sam said in a remarkably steady voice while glancing at me. Looking back at Janice, his ugly face just inches from her own, he repeated the order: *"Take your wife's panties off for me. With your mouth; now."*

I crawled up onto the bed and gummed the hem of the silky lingerie until I could get my front teeth around it, just a few inches to the left of the honey-vee itself. Once my teeth were on it I dragged them off, with no small degree of difficulty. Janice helped them off with a dismissive kicking of her ankle into my face, causing both her and Sam to laugh. She was now nude revealing her flat stomach and the soft patch of brownish blonde curls.

Sam whispered again into her ear.

"*Eat me,*" she said throatily.

"*Get her ready for me,*" he added, looking into her eyes hungrily.

"*Oh, you are something else!*" Janice shrieked, looking back at him wide-eyed, while I took to my task. Sam responded with a laugh and grabbed her two hands to bring them crossing over her head and, holding them where her wrists crossed with his right hand, he plundered her right breast and nipple with his left. She moaned and cried out loudly, undulating her hips in a writhing supplication. While keeping my mouth glued between her supplicating womanhood, I could hear her laughing as Sam whispered something to her yet again.

I looked up to see her right leg drawing back, the foot placed quickly on my left shoulder, and then suddenly shoving me hard off the bed. As I sprawled onto the floor, I looked up to see Sam with a last look and sneering smile turn to mount my wife, her cries beginning to rise in volume as he plunged forcefully into her yielding, heated pleasure.

Now I'm entering her more fully. I hear her cries as I push open her inviting moist cave with a body turned to rock. I feel her flesh quiver underneath me, as I glance over at the imaginary cuckolded husband now as well, a fantasy '*me* with a '*Sam, bam, thank-you-man*' to the cuckolded mirror of myself. It doesn't matter now, as I'm lost in the convulsive waves outside of thought and fantasy; rocking to the marriage of the primal reproductive force mixed with a pleasure principle buried deep in my dark side. The imaginative scene a booster rocket – there in order to fall away after its purpose is served – allowing the remaining physical remnant to go on by itself – an out-of-control, unself-conscious gasping, spurting male engine emitting loud cries of phantasmagoric release.

My wife explodes in orgasmic cries herself as we both go over the top at the same time, losing ourselves in the vacation from consciousness the sex provides.

I have fallen asleep in the post-coital moment, spooning my satisfied mate. Janice awakes first and, getting out of bed, gazes in reflection at my nude body as it lies in slumber. *"You're all dick,"* she mutters, watching me sleep, deep in dreams within the silent apartment.

Invisible Lovers

I enter your hall
with swollen love,
Thoughts from below
help harden that shove.
Some other male,
z'now my master
- but to rip from this grip
would be potent disaster.

In fantasy I find myself
A prissy for his use.
Please yourself
take some pleasure -
Yes, give me some abuse.

Awash in excitement
Now build up in me great,
and yes of course, humiliate,
else I'd have to see cock's fate
now swollen hard
start to abate.

And I pull it all
right through you,
merging that spirit
right into our screw.

Oh, I almost forgot you're there… Oh honey…
of course I care.
Sure there's a difference
No lie, it's true
between jerkin' my hand
n' puttin' it in you.
A difference clear there is to make
your body's so much better
than my fist in a shake.

You've got breasts to squeeze
and nipples to maul,
an ass that I can grab 'n ball.
Glad we're together
So settle in for the season,
just got Viagra
but love ain't the reason.

Instead this vision
I pull so true
submerging n'it
find life I do.

Chapter 13 – Yearning for Salvation:
The Speaker Meeting

I struggled in AA three more horrible weeks, and then I stopped going to meetings. White-knuckling it, it was like driving with the brakes on. My wife also said I was more fun stoned. I soon slipped back into drugs, and a new round of family meetings was convened to bail me out with rent money and utility bills; with the family now putting me on notice: *"this is it, no more."*

I slip again, and now the wife prepares to leave me with our newborn. My wife leaves to visit her parents, actually preparing the way for her to move out there with our newborn son. She will return once more to LA but it's as a final gather-up-her-stuff-in-order-to-leave effort. I am left alone and un-working in the LA shambles, and am told the truth by my brother-in-law: You only have three things ahead of you if you don't stop: *death, hospital or jail*. I finally 'got it.'

I went back to AA determined like an animal holding onto a piece of meat. Not "one day at a time," but "***five-minutes at a time***." Two meetings a day, three meetings a day, staying after meetings, coming early to meetings. I noticed that in general the guys who said things I could identify with – and with that identification learn something – all had heavy spiritual programs. I heard hard things from hard sponsors: *"If you really cared about that girl, why would you want to inflict someone like yourself on her?"* One talked to me at length and would often say *"this is where I get strength from,"* and point to passages in the bible.

I bought a bible, but didn't hardly open it; becoming a champion at Ms Pac Man instead. This was a coin-operated video game which allowed me something to do while my brain was too frazzled to read a book or watch TV. I was often playing against children at the video machine in convenience stores or other places. I often had the high score, and found it contributed to some rare humor to have twelve year-olds whispering and pointing to me as "the guy to beat" for the high score on the Ms. PacMan machine. It was something to do between meetings.

Two years before, I had spent my wedding day morning lying on a beach in Malibu around 8 a.m., shooting up the greater part of the $500 worth of cocaine I had bought with cash wedding gifts. I would shoot one large dose after another of the high-quality cocaine into my vein, with my humming body lying on the beach blanket, my arm extended towards the surf. The trail from that beach blanket to now was strewn with two years of broken dreams and tortured promises, searing my conscience and frightening my memory.

    I was sitting at the kitchen table in my empty apartment, maybe three weeks sober from my last slip. I was so edgy I could neither carry on a conversation nor watch a TV program. I literally could not stand to be in a drugstore for any reason. The advertisements for the U-100 Insulin syringes on the walls were too much for my mental state to handle. I was defeated and could go no further. I didn't want to go further. I couldn't take it any more. I had finally hit bottom. I opened this book that I had spent all my life cynically despising for its hayseed adherents, and flipped it open to the red print. I started reading again the words of this Jewish guy whose words they print in red.

    "Come unto me all ye who are heavy laden, and I will give you rest."

    That did it. I started to cry. I fell onto floor and proceeded to go deep into the headwaters of the grief. I suddenly saw myself: A terribly ugly, weak, evil creature. I saw there was not a single good thing in me. I was a twisted lie and selfish and small and a failure and a coward. The worst part in seeing through this sudden spiritual eye was that there wasn't a single thing I could do to fundamentally change this creation that I had become. *This is who I was. This is what I am.* Those acidic juices that burn through the skin's surface to erupt in sores were in me by the spiritual bucketful, replenishing themselves through a dynamic, living fountainhead that would not and could not dry up. Any change-for-the-better was simply to be a dollop of egoism dropped into this pool of self-destructive acid.

    I yearned for release, and from deep within my solar plexus wrenched out *"Jesus, help me. If you're alive, I believe you are alive, I pray you are, help me, forgive me, change me. I can't do anything. I can't do anything."* I cried all the more, and as I went into an unashamed delirium of weeping with my face in the carpet in my empty apartment, a light shown briefly at the end of my mind's long dark tunnel. I knew in some way I couldn't explain that I had believed in something real, and had found something real, yet not of this world.

    When I stood up I knew I had hope, and the feeling stayed with me while I blew my nose, wiped my eyes, farted, took a pee, thought of jerking off, turned the TV on and off, had something to eat and ultimately returned to reading the bible right up until the next AA meeting.

* * *

    Almost all AA meetings involve the opportunity for individuals to speak as participants, but there are special "speaker meetings," where (special?) people with something (special?) to say would be asked to speak alone. A speaker meeting was coming that appeared to be a big deal to many of my new-found AA acquaintances. I noticed this speaker seemed to engender respect from these guys, and these guys didn't give respect easily. That much got my attention.

Well, I guess I'll get my ass over to the meeting and see what these bumpkins have to say.

I got there and found, amongst the very large crowd gathered, some faces I recognized. I discovered that the speaker is in everyday life a low-paid service worker. I had kind of expected that the speaker would be someone I could *"look up to."* A degreed individual, a published author, someone in a position with some title or honor. *I mean, he has to have something important and significant to share, doesn't he? I mean, really... Who cares what he thinks if all he can do is sweep floors and not get drunk... Wasn't that obvious?*

To be a worker of low rank, my readiness to shoot him down now took on a disappointed condescension as I pigeonholed him into a cheap suit who drank rotgut in the 50's. *This was like watching grade school children put on a serious play. This guy probably never even did acid or smoked a joint. Probably never even heard of Bob Dylan – not-to-mention any of the prominent post-Freudian theorists. G-d, what am I doing here?*

As he began to speak, I mentally sneered him up and cynically ripped him down, finally condescending to listen. In spite of myself, I found myself reaching out internally to a point he was making, when suddenly... I was gone. **I was in the spirit.** I was at that shoreline shooting coke exactly as I had done on my wedding day morning. My arm lay outstretched towards the water, which came up to about a foot from my hand with the syringe in it. The salt in the ocean has been replaced by cocaine, all the atoms within my world communicated. All I would ever have to do is lower my syringe into the ocean to draw up and I could have all the cocaine injections I wanted into eternity. The disposition of my soul, that inner dimension deeper than thought and ego, responded: *"No, I don't want it anymore."*

I was suddenly back in that uncomfortable AA chair listening to this older soft-spoken man talking about trusting G-d apart from religion. What **was that?**

After the talk, I shook his hand, expecting some voice from heaven to communicate with me personally somehow (*This is my beloved Son, in whom I am well pleased?*), but the speaker appeared to be unaware of the spiritual breakthrough I had had.

Afterwards, I found that when I went into certain 12-step meeting halls that had these old paintings depicting hopeless alcoholics praying in some horrible room with "the light" shining down, I would get goosebumps. Something more than mere sobriety had begun.

Not that my madness was over, it was just that it was no longer chemically colored. I knew it was impossible to deal with life as long as alcohol or chemicals were involved, and somehow my desire to be sober had been energized. I *wanted* to be sober. This was something new and different, and it was interesting to tackle sobriety and move on to something entirely *new*. I sniffed what it was like to be *good*, and found the aroma not entirely unpleasant.

The madness in me, however, was going to take different forms and engage my mind and emotions in different struggles to keep my soul in its dark possession. Religion, for example, was right around the corner. If you want to find G-d, everyone figures church is the only game in town. But sometimes, I found, the game is rigged.

Chapter 14 – Miracle, Religion and Plastic Light

At an AA meeting in Northridge I ran into a guy named Steve. He was very upfront about G-d and Jesus. He was more of a "faith" guy, not shy at all. *"If you will take a step towards G-d, Jesus will not let you fall on your face,"* he said. After the regular meeting, we would sit around and talk. When I told him about my crying and the light, he put his face up to heaven and said right out loud, totally ignoring others nearby:

"I thank you Father, that you have blessed Marty with a sign of your presence, and have blessed him with a faith that many have sought and not found. I pray his faith would grow, Lord, and you would show him the way you have prepared for him, that he might grow in You."

I found these kinds of things impressive, intriguing and comforting. I liked Steve's wild attitude about G-d. Steve lived in an almost bare house, and would take people in; drifters, addicts, people with no place to live, and would let them sleep in this house he was "renting." If people drank, used drugs or played a con on him, they had to leave. If they lied, they had to leave. People came and went. I went to ask questions and sometimes go over bible passages with him.

Some of his previous 'tenants' had apparently put that address as their place of residence, and two city bureaucrats showed up one day demanding to know who Steve was. Did he have a license in rehabilitation, or what?

"The Holy Spirit has given me all the license I have, and that is all the license I need," Steve told the suits in his mellow voice, standing at the door.

"Sir, who pays the rent on this dwelling?" one interrupted in his flat, officious tone.

"G-d does," Steve answered. *"G-d sees that all our needs are met in Christ Jesus."* With that, they walked off mumbling to each other. I was very impressed. Steve was going out to Tallahassee to study at the bible school of a famous "faith" preacher.

I got a job selling cable TV door-to-door and met someone at work who invited me to church. I started going to a large church in the San Fernando Valley. I began to be what some in church-speak call "an alter bum." I would respond to almost every alter call, and I began to believe more and more that this Messiah really did exist, thinking not only of what I had experienced recently in my night-of-the-soul, but remembering what I had seen on LSD in 1968. My mind was far from renewed, however, as I continued scoping on any good looking female with thoughts as carnal as when I ran an Adult bookstore, but followed with more guilt. My dishonesty seemed as real as ever, for example, to give back money when a clerk gave me too much change was like pulling teeth.

I quickly began meeting lots of church people, however, and noticed that occasionally high regard was paid to my Jewish roots. I was drawn to the "faith" crowd who believed in miracles and who believed that a certain free association of vowels and syllables, once allowed to start tumbling out of ones mouth, was "speaking in tongues:" This was seen as a "spiritual gift from G-d" being infused into the "Spirit-filled" believer. I was *there* in a New York second.

This offshoot of the Pentecostal movement also believed G-d wanted you prosperous and healthy, and would pound home the idea that if you *really believed*, neither sickness nor poverty would be at your door. Nevertheless, the cars in the parking lots usually cried out for repair, and people got sick just like anywhere else, but were kind of low key about it, as being sick while believing you were healed by Jesus meant there was a lack of "something" somewhere (I think the often unspoken words were "*secret sin*," spoken so conveniently by those in good health).

The fly-in-the-ointment financially was that scripture could and would often be quoted that "*Prove me, sayeth the Lord if I will not pour out upon thee a bounty so much that you will not have room to receive it*," coupled with "*Tithe unto me (a tenth) and see if I will not multiply ten times, a hundred times, back to you*." This one-two punch was compounded with the knock-out closer that "*If G-d doesn't want you at this church, you should find the one he does want you to go to*," thereby closing the door. Once trapped inside, the logic followed that to follow G-d was tantamount to following the leading of this Church. I went Sunday mornings, Sunday evenings, Wednesday prayer groups, bible-studies at the pastor's house. Tapes of preaching seminars played continuously from the car tape player, and a new bible was purchased with the same excitement the handyman reserves for the new power tool.

So the message from some of the preachers was not unlike some spiritual pyramid scheme in which you gave everything you could to the ministry from which the preacher would trumpet, "I used to be poor like you," but I believed in G-d's word, and now I have prosperity and a this-and-a-that." The one little difference that everyone is *too Christian* to point out is that *sure you're believing in prosperity, it's our money being sent in to you on a one-way street*. Mind games concerning abundance abounded. For example, here's something typically heard when I would be visiting somebody from church at their house.

"What a nice house," I would say.

"G-d just blessed us with it. G-d gave it to us."

Now, to my way of thinking, that means something like this: I'm walking down the street and someone comes up to me and says: "G-d wants me to give you this house." Then I run around saying "G-d gave me this house." But it turns out these people worked hard, saved their money, had good credit, made a bid and it was accepted.

It would be easy to say it's all hokum. All *Elmer Gantry* and foolish bible bumpkins. But then something special happened.

I developed a kidney stone. My sister and brother-in-law had worked hard and became successful. They had bought a house in the San Fernando Valley. She sent me to her expensive Jewish urologist at a high-end medical group on Ventura Blvd. in North Hollywood. They took X-rays and showed me the stone on the black film. If it passed, all would be well, although the pain would be excruciating, according to the doctor. If it didn't pass, I would be a candidate for a rather gruesome surgery.

I was doing pretty good with a new sales job. Although having just started, I was bringing in an above-average flow of sales. I found if I just kept to the script and let my natural enthusiasm for the product flow along, I would get the lay-downs plus a little more. As a salesman, I was not a strong closer.

At work it was let known to me that a new territory was about to be opened up from Louisiana to Florida. I had been talking by phone to Steve at his bible school in Tallahassee and he had been insisting I come out and "*let this Brother heal you.*" I talked to the boss at my company and he said (should I decide to travel there) that I should then meet with the head guy for the new territory. I shared these findings with my wife, and she also thought it was a good idea. So I went.

I got to Tallahassee and was not that impressed with the legendary preacher. He seemed cold and distant, and when he laid hands on me I did go down under the hypnotic suggestion of it all, but I wasn't healed. Later I experienced the painful symptoms again. Steve and I went to my motel room and we prayed and danced and sang into the ceiling until we no longer cared to think before speaking, eschewing Satan's power and all self-consciousness. He and I bound Satan and called upon G-d's power, claiming supremacy and authority, demanding and accepting and thanking G-d for it. We went at it all night, going out for breakfast at first light. Later in the afternoon I met with Mason Rheingold, the new honcho who was making an arrangement with the company to open up these new territories in the Southeast.

He also claimed to be a Christian seeking as of late "a deeper walk with the Lord," and believed immediately that my coming out there was a sign from G-d. I returned to LA with an offer from him to step up and into a managerial situation with his startup territory. When the LA office agreed to pay my moving expenses out there, I was sure I could feel the hand of the Lord in all of this.

After returning to LA, I went to my Urologist. I told everyone there that I had been healed. And lo and behold, the doctor looks at the new X-ray, and asks

"When did it pass?"

"What do you mean?" I puzzle.

"The stone. When did it pass?"

"I don't know anything about it passing. Do people always feel it?" He starts to get visibly annoyed.

"Yes, there's no doubt you would feel that kidney stone passing."

"Well, I didn't feel anything. I went out to Tallahassee to a bible school friend of mine and we prayed for healing. Y'know doc, I'm Jewish too, but I…"

He cut me off and walked out. When they sent me a bill, I returned it with two of those really tacky *Chick* tracts, with the message of the 144,000 Jews at the end times and another of the healing power of the Hebrew Messiah. They sent me another bill and I sent it back with more of the same plus a personalized letter from me to them "witnessing" the changes G-d had made in my life. They stopped billing me.

I moved out to Tallahassee, preparing the way for my wife and son to come out. I would live in this apartment that also doubled as the district office. It was no longer a problem dealing with a lack of drugs. I read and spoke bible scripture as an answer to each tempting thought. If an alluring female image was paralyzing me with a lustful fantasy, I would speak out (when possible) or simply 'think out loud' an appropriate scripture (*To whomever you yield yourself servant to obey, his servant thou art, whether sin unto death, or obedience unto righteousness. Therefore, go Satan, in Jesus name.*) This kind of mental patchwork bridged me across the valley of insanity that heretofore only the drugs – both legal and illegal – had kept me out of for 15 years. I was starting to sense the need – and consequent frustration – of being a failure as far as a provider for my family. Even when I wasn't a failure, my grandiose expectations for myself always made any modest achievements pale in comparison. A consequent bizarre need for approval and love in the workplace always had me sabotaging my position with needless intrigues and self-defeating motivations.

However, I hadn't given into temptation with a female coworker. We had gotten along well as co-workers, complimenting each other on whatever skills we'd notice, and she thought it was really cool that my wife and kid were being moved out to my new territory, and that I didn't go out to bars and all that. We had good vibes. We had been alone working in the office apartment for hours at a stretch on some special deal, having pizza delivered, stopping to eat and then back into the work.

There is something very bonding about teaming with a female coworker on a tough project that can be extremely stimulating. One is overwhelmed by the sense that – by mutual unspoken consent - it wouldn't be a relationship if *it* were to happen, but rather a delicious piece of one-time candy; a naughty substitute for an otherwise healthy diet. I had come to these moments standing next to her when it was all I could do not to take her in my arms and kiss her, with a bed just a few feet away. I refused to allow my mind to submerge into the carnal fantasies, but instead white-knuckled my way through it with prayer and bible verse.

I had done a fairly good job in Tallahassee, and found myself being asked to take on the responsibility to start a new office in Tennessee. I would be sent up there with two salespeople to "check it out" for a week. My salespeople turned out to be two girls. Both in their twenties, one was straight-as-an-arrow, the other a wild and fairly good looking gal with a surprisingly obscene mouth. Apparently a daddy's girl with a steady monthly allowance, she had a brazen confidence that served her well on the job, but was a little "much" in the cramped one-bedroom apartment that was all that the company was providing us as an office.

Problems broke out immediately between the "good" girl and the "bad" girl. Sunday came and I took the "good girl" to a local church. She responded to the alter call. I congratulated her that she was "saved." I congratulated myself on "bringing her to the Lord." There is much to be said about *'pride preceding the fall.'* I found it goes twice as much for spiritual pride, but my lessons were just beginning.

"I won't sleep in the same room with that *bitch*," the *newly saved* whispers to me.

"Don't worry," I heard myself saying. "You sleep out here on the living room couch." Eschewing the fold-out couch in the front room where I had slept previously, I entered the back room that night with a curious sense of knowing I was going to fuck this girl, yet helpless to stop myself.

> *"Stars, hide your fires*
> *Let not light*
> *See my black and deep desires.*
> *The eye wink at the hand;*
> *Yet let that be,*
> *Which the eye fears*
> *When it is done to see."*
>
> Macbeth Act I, Scene IV

With my hand on the bedroom doorknob, I keep thinking: *"how did I get into this situation?"* but I just kept on going right over the cliff.

We had blankets and sleeping bags spread out on the floor, next to one another. I found myself thanking her for something fairly irrelevant and kissing her on the cheek as a result of it. That felt so good, I told her, it deserved a repeat. As I came close to do it again, she looped her arm around my neck, pulling me to her passionately.

It was not very good. She wanted harder and harder thrusts, which is not my style to begin with, and we're doing it on the floor in sleeping bags. Not only wasn't she tight, but she had this awkward way of pulling on my shoulders. I found it too much work, and by the time we were finished, I was probably more sore than she was. As the next day started, it was double embarrassment, as the closeness of our trio easily revealed me as an adulterer to the newly born-again salesgirl, who promptly said she had enough of the situation, and left to return to Tallahassee.

I found however, that my shame and conscience rose up big and bold. I was suddenly mentally incapacitated. I had not cheated on my wife since I had *found the Lord*, and I was paralyzed with an anxiety that had my voice shaking on the phone when trying to do business. The idea of making presentations and sales seemed impossible. Wendy and I stayed in the apartment fucking a few more times, but it didn't get better, only stranger. After the way my loins hurt, it seemed reasonable within my lust to seek a smoother push, and I asked her if she had ever taken it in her rear end. Wendy said she never had, but gave such an uncaring *"why not"* in response that I was taken aback. Any girl I had ever asked that of had *definite* opinions concerning it. Usually it meant much time involving preparatory finger exploration with just one lubricated finger – before actually entering with your prick, and then it's usually many false starts before you can have a woman ready to take it all the way.

This girl just shrugged her shoulders with a, *"yeah, c'mon; let's do it."*

What was with this chick? Had something just *"turned this girl on?"* This just added to the bizarre, unreal, 'un-right' living condition. It was as if she was suddenly(?) possessed with an 'anything goes' mentality which had obviously not existed in her life before. Was she here for a reason not apparent on the surface?

Speak of the devil. During some pillow talk, she explained that her fantasy, running her hand down from my neck to my belly button, was "*a kind of Rocky Horror character.*" My skin goosebumped as my blood chilled. This would be the closest thing to the kind of wild sex I had often fantasized about, but would also undoubtedly end my marriage to my hard working, faithful and (now) betrayed wife.

For what? *To be humiliated, dress up, suck dick and fuck this broad at the same time in threesomes*? It suddenly seemed like a very poor deal indeed. I really didn't want to lose my wife. I was becoming more and more aware that I didn't want this scene here at all anymore. What had appeared exciting and daring, promising pleasure and thrills in a momentary midnight, had become an albatross dragging me into more problems. The sex was quickly becoming simply a physical exercise that lasted a few minutes, and I could sense this would call for something kinkier and different to spice it up. I had stepped in shit with this whole deal and I wished very much that I hadn't.

We went out that night for some drinks. I thought I needed one, as I found it continued to be impossible to apply myself for work. My week's production numbers were abysmal. Sobriety suddenly seemed the least of my problems.

I was 34 years old, had been around alcoholics, drug addicts, whores, raging queens, passing transsexuals, gamblers, con men, criminals, Hells Angels and lunatics from Los Angeles to New York City, but I had never seen any female drink like Wendy. She knocked back Tequila Sunrises and got more spirited as the night wore on. Then double Tequila Sunrises, then a shot of tequila and a double in the drink; then a double shot on the side and a double inside the drink, and only became more energized; more animated. I had never been much of a drinker at all.

An unusual animism began to grow in her: It was spirited, vicious, raw and totally without conscience. That allowed me to grasp – and then gasp – over what was becoming obvious. This was no ordinary girl looking to party who accidentally had stumbled across my path. You could almost see the inner-fangs as she approached some tipsy guy who was ogling her body as she pranced and slinked around to the music drunkenly. She picked him up for a threesome but he didn't understand what was going on and was too naive to figure it out. With him not getting it I wanted no part of it either and so nothing went down. I noticed, however, that when I demurred her invitation to help 'move this guy along' into a *manage-a-*

trois, our roles of manager and salesgirl became switched. It was now she who was criticizing my lack of aggression in carrying out her plan, and it seemed to me she was indicating my reticence was neither approved of, nor was it something that would be allowed to continue. Crossroads time.

The next night I told her I didn't want to go out, that in spirit and in truth I was breaking down – personally and as a manager – and we would be stopping our sexual relationship. I was calm, sincere and trying to be as real and forthright as possible. She began to scream. Foam at the mouth type scream. I tried to go to sleep in the back bedroom, surrendering the better front room fold-out couch, but she shrieked all night in a hideous voice for me to come out, demanding I come to her. I had never been in such a situation before, and shrank frightfully into the corner of the rear bedroom, holding my bible in my lap with both hands, perhaps a picture perfect postcard of the frightened penitent weenie-Christian-loser; perhaps determined to simply hold-on at any cost. Gathering my strength spiritually, I walked to the front room, figuring I had to confront her at some point.

"Wendy, listen. I'm coming apart. *I can't make the calls for the job. I'm failing as manager here. This is not good. This isn't me. It was a mistake.*"

"It's no mistake. *We can open up more territory… just you and me.*" She had become more relaxed, stopping her raging long enough to light a cigarette and take a long swallow from her homemade Tequilla Sunrise. "***You're away from home. Who's to know?***" she bellowed. Her attitude was that of a commander reminding me of what I should have – in her mind - understood. Her tone was neither gentle nor seductive. It was as a captain – a little impatiently – reminding an underling of life's circumstances and his obligations. As she repositioned her pillows on the fold-out couch so she could sit up straight, her skirt hiked up. I saw she was wearing new satin panties. Realizing that she had just gone out and bought them, and that they were specifically the kind I had confessed to liking when the subject had come up, a rush of lust rose up in me, and I had the almost-overpowering urge to rip off her new satin, mouth her until she climaxed, and then sodomize her with a spanking that might bring the cops.

I actually cried out in some kind of moaning howl of "*argghh*" as I jumped up and, walking quickly without looking back, returned to my monkish station in the rear bedroom. Her screams for me to return, commanding and demanding, drove me to the very edge of my will to do what was right. I saw the 'image on the edge of town' fade from a dream state in which those new satin panties were now on me while she directed my acts with other men to the current less exciting but more foundational reality of a man shaking in a corner trying to somehow do the right thing.

I thought I needed to speak to a supportive Christian, and I also knew I needed to get back to my wife. I had recently switched to a new church, and did not know the pastor well. So, I called my boss, Mason. When he heard I had sex with Wendy, his persona of administrative maturity disintegrated. His own level of sexual maturity and worldly experience quickly became apparent.

"*Wow*," he said, barely restraining himself from congratulating me. I realized he was one of those men who, while having made successful inroads into the world of business, had never found in their own personal life the ability to casually pick up women and have sex. While Wendy was sexy and attractive, his own wife was one of the most beautiful women I had ever seen. After I made it clear that I couldn't go on with this adultery and needed to drive home and see my wife, he changed to the thoughtful superior, agreeing it was a good idea. However, his '*golly-gee*' admiration/jealousy/lust persona emerged again: "maybe I'll give Wendy a try. How did you… uhh, how did it happen?" I lectured him on his wife and kids and how much I regretted this whole misstep, adding that I was so upset I was breaking down and couldn't work.

Coincidences From Hell[24]

The next day I was leaving the city, heading for the long drive home. I stopped at a convenience store next to the freeway entrance. As I pulled up I noticed some teenagers walking in. One girl hung back to finish a few puffs on her cigarette. It struck me how unnaturally brazen and sultry the girl appeared. She was maybe eighteen, not beautiful, but she made you look twice. Eighteen going on thirty-eight. When I came out with my sundry supplies for the long car ride home, they were in their car parked

---

[24] *The reference here to "Synchronicity" is again unavoidable. It opens an entire new framework to the exploration of the topic.*
Synchronicity is a word created by the Swiss psychologist Carl Jung to describe the alignment of "universal forces" with the life experiences of an individual. Jung believed that many experiences perceived as coincidences were not merely due to chance, but instead reflected the creation of an event or circumstance by the "co-inciting" or alignment of such forces. The process of becoming intuitively aware and acting in harmony with these forces is what Jung labeled "individuation." Jung said that an individuated person would actually shape events around them through the communication of their consciousness with the collective unconscious.

next to mine. I had not remembered it being there before. As I negotiated the key into my driver's side door-lock, a male voice from their passenger side called out to me:

"Hey mister." I turned. "She'll do ya. She'll do ya for free."

I looked at the girl sitting next to him. It was the brazen, sultry one. Her eyes said she could or would suck my dick and/or slit my throat without giving either behavior too much thought. It took me a tortured two seconds to tear my mind from this suddenly strange new world promising fresh, tight, wet teenage pussy; and to blurt out instead:

"I'm going home to my wife."

The freeway was a block away. I got on the turnpike and didn't stop for a hundred miles. I was terrified. Even in my best-looking days (which were a dozen years behind me), girls didn't stop me on the street asking to fuck me, or have their male friends make the proposition. And this coming right on the heels of what I considered my first adultery. After two hours of driving I pulled over to the side of the road to take a piss. That way I could see if the demon-gang were still following me. It was difficult to negotiate the activity with one hand holding my bible, but I was finally able to.

New events would swiftly bring an end to my relationship with this company, and mark the beginning of the end of my relationship with my wife. Wendy shot down my boss, and his relationship to me soured. After a while I told him we were probably through, and I would move into another territory. Without asking for anything or letting me know he was coming, he showed up at my door with a cop, asking for me to bring him the materials for work that belonged to him. I told the cop they belonged to the home office and then I realized why Ken had the policeman come along. When my "Christian" boss saw my wife, he told her why I could not be employed anymore, even though I had made the decision to leave him.

"He had sex with one of the salesgirls, Janice. That's why I'm firing him."

Chapter 15 – A Born Again Turkey is Still a Turkey

Living now in yet another new city, I had gone to technical school and was into graphic layout and design on computers. I found succor for my fevered consciousness in the infinite forgiveness of the Menu Commands. They never became impatient with me no matter how many times I misused them. I could spend hours getting to know them, totally mishandling and misunderstanding them, and they never copped an attitude. It offered a kind of security.

The idea of placing text and pictures in ever-changing layouts within electronic publishing and the world of motion graphics intrigued me. I would create samples and send them to large companies in the hope of employment, finally succeeding in finding a good job in the 1980's with a Fortune 500 company. I had enrolled in a Tech school as a programmer, and found myself a full-time job even before graduating. *Functioning* never looked better, and although anxiety and religion continued to provide an emotional river which I often drowned in, the time spent 'above-water' lent an optimistic quality to life which was both hopeful and refreshing. My wife gave birth to three more children while I floundered from job to job, strangely unable to get along in the workplace anywhere for very long.

Still active in whatever church "the Lord led me to," I was having some problems with the local body, and chose this Sunday morning to exercise some independent spiritual direction and stay home. It was very difficult not to feel guilty, as the same voices that encourage you to stay in your bathrobe eviscerate you afterwards for not going. *Think how disappointed G-d is, and the pastor, too.*

However, it was becoming obvious that my relationship with the pastor was souring. I had become obsessive about listening to preaching and teaching tapes, read the bible constantly, and occasionally preached to a small men's group. I was suffused in chapter, verse and a theology I understood, and was very well read concerning Israel and Old Testament prophecy. Obsessive reverie on chapter and verse had replaced Fluphenazine Hydrochloride. When my mind raged, scripture gave it a band-aid.

Having traveled and resettled several times, I had immediately set about resettling myself in a new church, and not before too long, in a pastor's weekly bible study. I had observed many people preaching who were less than expert in areas I considered important. Therefore, I was not over-awed by someone merely because they were preaching.

I was fairly conflicted over some serious disappointment I felt in the man. I had begun to see some genuine 'feet of clay' on this local leader within the 'body of Christ.' It had all begun over a moving van.

I had had to move (again), and, having no small amount of experience in such matters, knew that arrangements with U-Haul or similar businesses in these small cities were best made two months in advance with the approach of summer. The pastor and I were talking one day and he mentioned he was also moving at the end of that month.

"Do you have a moving van rented?"

"It's not till July."

"Summer moving is the busiest time, and I found you need to make reservations way in advance for stuff like that."

"We got it covered," he assured me with a slightly condescending tone; made replete with a momentary look he often reserved for matters secular and/or commercial.

As we rolled into June he mentioned in church that he would appreciate any helping hands on his move at the end of the month. I told him after the service that I would be busy with my own moving and said something to the effect that 'I guess you got a van after all.'

"We're getting one this week..."

"For the end of *this month*!? I'll be really surprised if you can find anything."

The umbrage he took to this remark was visible. I could clearly see he was making an effort not to lose patience with me. The pastor had a very high opinion of his own business acumen. I saw nothing in or at his home however, to evidence any of the accomplishments that he continually inferred he had "sacrificed" in order "*to work for the Lord.*" Apparently he felt he could brook no opinions that ran counter to his own regarding anything in the real world.

A week before I'm moving I get a call.

"Yeah Marty. This is Pastor Phil."

"Hey, what's up, Phil?"

In a tone that indicates absolutely no acknowledgement of any of our previous discussions on the subject, he says, "we're having some trouble with this moving van business." Continuing without the slightest embarrassment, he voices enough insinuation in his voice indicating that '*...it's someone else's fault is what it is... if you want something done right, you've got to do it yourself.*' He quickly completes the one-two punch by portraying himself as the forgiving pastor, however. I can't resist pointing out:

"Yeah, like I mentioned to you earlier, when summer begins, the rental situation..."

"Yeah, yeah, yeah..." he cuts me off abruptly with a kind of *'what kind of game are you trying to run here*? insinuation in his tone. *Are you finding fault with me*? His tone is first incredulous, but then immediately forgiving over the idea. He will overlook my aggressive mental shenanigans, since he is a man of G-d.

"Here's the thing," he continues in a tone of voice more suited to a foreman speaking to a confused laborer, "What time are you picking it up?"

"Seven a.m., and I'm supposed to have it back by four in the afternoon."

"Well, how about when you're through with it, I take it and we'll pay any late charges if we can't get it back by four p.m.?"

"Yeah, that works. Sure."

'We have a ton of people volunteering to help us, and maybe we can loan some of them to you, so with them giving you a hand, that would not only help you, but we could get it sooner."

"That'd be great."

An hour later the phone rings again.

"Marty, it's pastor Phil."

"Yeah, Phil."

"This isn't gonna work," he says in his 'take charge' tone. It was as if I had asked *him* for something, and now he is letting me know his decision will probably disappoint me. "I spoke to my wife, and she agrees we need the truck in the morning."

"Yeah, well, I'm sure my wife feels the same way."

"Why? Why would your wife feel the same way?" he asks incredulously. Now I'm really feeling his intimidation, and my discomfort is vibrating from my vocal chords to my toes.

"Well, we just need to get moving and get it out of the way first thing in the morning, that's all."

"Well, y'see Marty, we're planning on having a *prayer meeting* right after moving in, to bless the new house. *Most people* think that's a little *more important*.

"I don't know what to tell ya, Phil," I said in an almost trembling voice. I say nothing more, as I sense hyperventilation on the way, and my knees were turning to water. I fought the urge to give in and end the pressure. It wasn't like me to stand up for myself, but...I did.

When moving day came, a couple of people joined in helping me to move – being sent over by the pastor so he could use the truck as soon as I finished, and I could tell from the vibes that I had been gossiped about as the bad guy. I realized whatever the *spirit of truth* was, it wasn't going to be found around here. Weeks later the entire congregation was invited over the pastor's new house that someone in the congregation had practically given him; with no down payment and a price well below market value. As I wandered around the pastor's new homey three-bedroom, I was having a real problem with jealousy as well as judgment.

* * *

I began to enjoy this Sunday morning freedom and thought perhaps it was a sign from the Lord that it was time to move on to another church. I placed my breakfast on the TV tray, set my bible next to that, and flipped on the Sunday morning TV to watch world renowned Tele-evangelist Jimmy Swaggert do his thing. I had seen him in person, and once sent him money I really couldn't afford to send, but I was "into the Lord," and listened to my thoughts as if hooked up to Him with a dedicated hardwire. Jimmy's ministry had these great singers, and one or both would open his show with truly remarkable talent. Then here comes the man himself, with his unique hypnotic southern cadence, that interesting accent and rhythm, emphasizing certain words that had you leaning out of your seat in emotional rapture.

"I feel a burden on my heart to speak to a matter that has become such a danger to so many Christian families. I am talking about the horrible consequences of this rock music phenomenon. Especially the hero worship, the idolatry that often accompanies the music itself. I received a letter last week from a dear friend. A woman trying to raise her teenage daughter by herself.

She wrote to me, 'Dear Brother Swaggert, I'm at my wit's end. The devil himself has invaded our house. My Jeanne was a good girl (Jimmy would raise his eyes already preparing with mist to the audience), *"and then she started listening to rock music. She became angry. Angry towards me, angry and disrespectful. Last night I found this letter. I fell on my knees and cried out to the Lord. I'm enclosing it to you, Brother Swaggert. Please help me."*

Jimmy looked up at the camera,

"My brothers and sisters, I cried after reading that letter. I wept before the Lord and asked Him what can I do to help this child? What can I do after reading this? It was a letter describing

herself, a young, attractive teenage girl - in detail, and then offering herself...

Yes, I mean she was offering herself to this band, my brothers and sisters. She would become theirs to do with as they wished. She would no longer be Jeanne, a girl committed to her mother, to the church, to Jesus. No, she would be **a tool** for their **pleasure**...

"My brothers and sisters, I had to ask G-d what can we do when this evil spirit enters our very households? We should all be asking the Lord what we can do to help in this fight."

The cameras panned the audience, settling on an attractive teenage girl listening intently. The TV screen showed some people slowly shaking their heads in sympathy, others bowing their heads in prayerful devotion to this cause. But Jimmy isn't through.

*"This girl went on to describe, my brothers and sisters, in detail, every act she would allow them to perform on her, and every behavior she was willing to perform on them; begging them to just allow her to try – let her have the **opportunity** to please them."*

I found I had to move the TV tray in my lap to rearrange some elevation issues which were being raised achingly, especially now as the camera had settled yet again on another attractive teenage girl.

*"She described how she would dance for them. What she would wear. A willing **slave** to do anything they wanted with her for even for a short period of time! My brothers and sisters, this is devil worshi..."*

Unable to take any more *"ministering,"* I was on my feet clicking off the set on my way upstairs. After being preached to in this fashion by Brother Swaggert, I was not all that surprised to hear of his later ministry-ending disaster, caught in liaison with a prostitute from whom he was receiving "special" treatments.

Entering my bedroom carrying my bible, I traded the book for the bottle of lotion sitting on the dresser. It was as if the book, silent and ultimate father-symbol that it was, might effect some observance of my inner and outer explorations, and – should best be kept out of direct sight. It felt good to lie down and just leave self-consciousness behind.

'*Ooh, Cindy girl,*' came the thought as I entered the seminar room for my first "*African-American Studies*" class. '*Someone is beginning to grow as a person here, yes… This is genuinely so much cooler than that lame religious school mom and dad wanted me to go to. Right… like it wasn't enough being in that all-girls school my whole life…*'

I had to stifle my smile, as the words "*grow as a person*" rose up in my mind attaching themselves to some very non-academic images. Memories of my two sexual episodes this past summer added to the previous rush of "filling out" my 35D bra (*and these boys here never seem to stop staring*). It is just so great to be away from mom and dad. This is like *arrival*, I think. Suddenly he took over my world.

"*You are not just a student in this class,*" spoke the commanding black figure at the podium in a stern voice. "*You are here to be part of a universal effort to further racial justice and social equality. This isn't just a resistance to racism we seek to inculcate in this class but a resistance to all forms of social inequality and oppression. The inequality women suffer, not only in the workplace - but universally as sex objects - has got to be torn down and done away with as well.*"

My jaw literally unhinged an inch or two as I found myself staring blankly at this strange, dark man.

"*We know that history is written from the perspective of whites, and that laws and policies benefit whites while putting minorities at an immediate disadvantage. The people who make these laws and policies believe only White Europeans and White Euro-Americans should set the world's agenda and control and distribute the world's resources.*"

'*… the way he sneers...* I thought of my poor father looking up at the professor trying to combat these dominating hammer-like observations. I was immediately lost in my head speaking these same pearls of wisdom to my family over holiday dinners, bending them to these unavoidable newfound truths; speaking these same words; unavoidably dripping with appropriate disdain for all who might disagree. It was suddenly easy – surprisingly easy – to be angry at all who might disagree with these words. Obviously, they are all racists.

"*Whites are like addicts who are unaware of their addiction and how they benefit from - and even depend on - the sufferings of others for their happiness. How can you – if you are psychologically in denial; if you are unaware of your own racism, how can you – be set free?*" he asked, ending the sentence with that surprisingly soft tone that made me feel like I was being stroked somehow. "*That's what we intend to discover in this class. How many of you are ready?*"

'*OhmaG-d! Was I the only one in the class to start sending her hand up in the air?*'

"Many are called," the impressive man added, passing an imperceptible glance over me as he eyed the room dramatically (*did he just look back directly at me?*); "*but few are chosen.*" He concluded his last statement with a voice not only low in tone but tinged with remorse. *No doubt from a life of pain and caring*, I ached. I gazed at him spellbound; the scowl on his face reflecting all the injustice of this dark world.

The bell rang. "*Those who didn't get a chance to sign up for the next special forum, please see me,*" he added in a quick flat tone.

Did he just look at me again? I'd better get down there quickly... probably be a line waiting to talk to him.'

But it was only me. I nervously approached him as he gathered up his notes to put them in his case.

"Uh, excuse me Professor, I, uh, didn't know about the special forum."

"No problem. What's your name again?"

"Cindy Scheiner."

"Cindy, I'm having some of the students over to my house Sunday afternoon around three. We'll talk more about it then. He looked closely at me and said, "See you there. My address is in the syllabus." Without waiting for a response, he picked up his case and walked away from the podium and out the door.

"*Oh my G-d. What have I got myself into? What will I say? Suppose I'm the only white person there? And oh my G-d, what will I wear?*"

Sunday I soaked for over an hour in scented bath oil, slipped on my new (*talk about expensive!*) matching bra and panties, tried on three different outfits and finally settled on a short off-white summer dress. I mean, why get my legs all tan and then cover them up? Besides, my cleavage looks great (*in the new fully-expanded mode!*), and I couldn't resist primping in exaggerated innocence in the mirror while bending low, showing off the natural gifts that men normally only find in centerfolds. I straightened up, and, looking myself over in the full length mirror, concluded, '*The back falls just right, proving further,*' I had to admit, '*that four years and a thousand hours of gym work can get you one bad ass.*'

I touched up my makeup and walked the short distance across campus to the professor's house, arriving five minutes early. Reminding myself that every boy I passed had stared approvingly - if not hungrily - I nonetheless arrived nervous and unsure, standing on the wooden porch of his small house set back off the main walk. It was surrounded by trees and flowers.

He came to the door in his bare feet, wearing jeans and an unbuttoned white shirt. My heart sank.

"Oh," he said, bringing his left hand to his forehead in this how-could-I-forget-gesture, "Cindy, your name is new to the list. I forgot to call you. The meeting's cancelled."

I froze like an idiot, standing there wooden, feeling stupid.

"No, but come on in, this is good, I want to talk to you…please."

Happy not to be left standing on the porch with the door in my face, I also found myself reflecting on his six-pack abbs; and for a man his age…

Within a short time I learned the professor felt the usual rules regarding student and faculty were anachronistic, and insisted on adding wine to the occasion. "*Like they do in Europe*, he said, adding, "*Wine is like a social lubricant among intelligent adults.*"

"*I agree, and thank you, Professor,*" I said, even though I could hardly remember the last time I drank wine, probably two years before at my Sweet Sixteen. I was surprised how pleasant-tasting the alcohol was, and how easily it went down.

"*I thought you seemed a little different than the others,*" he smiled, as a warm glow began to resonate from my midsection.

"*I hope that's good,*" I added with a pretend scared-face and a laugh.

"*I think it is,*" he said seriously, refilling my glass as he hesitated. He was obviously choosing his words carefully.

"*I like to **speak my mind**, but that often gets a man in trouble. Especially,*" he added with soft, patient eyes, "*a **black man**. But I've gotten to a point in my life that I just say 'the hell with it,' and I already sense in you a person I can just speak to as one person to another without all the bullshit rules.*"

I lowered my eyes hoping my spreading smile didn't show. Excitement ran into true realization; *this is a real man!… for the first time, a man who sees the **real me**… A true renaissance man…*

"Most of the class is just middle class white-bread repeating back to me what they think I want to hear. But you strike me as somehow… more… uhmm, real," he added as he lifted his glass, and with a glance urged me to do the same.

Holding my breath listening to his every word, I quickly raised my glass to his.

"*Here's to real,*" he said.

"*To real,*" I added, my face flushing as I began to feel a little dizzy.

We finished that glass and were into one more when the subject of racism arose.

"*We have to see racism in ourselves, Cindy,*" he said quietly. "*It's a personal thing, a very subjective thing. That's where it must be rooted out, and when it's rooted out at its most basic level, that's when true equality begins. As well as true freedom for the person released from their own bigotry.*

"My head nodded up and down as I tried to comprehend what that might mean. "*I...I agree,*" I found myself saying, "*but how...*"

He had stood up and walked to his entertainment center, pushed some buttons and "*Sade*" began to sing. The notes of a beautiful French ballad filled a room that suddenly seemed to go a little dim at the same time the music began. The professor turned from the entertainment center.

"*How, Cindy? As one person interacts with another. As just two people, that's how. You knew that intuitively, I think... didn't you?*" he concluded softly as he reached out his hand to me, his brown eyes softly holding mine.

"*I gue... yes.*" I said, trying to give the right amount of assurance to my answer. As I stood up I was suddenly aware of the wine's effects. My face felt very warm, and my tingling body mindlessly eager to float on the soft chords of the French ballad.

"*Yes, there **is** something very special about you,*" he said warmly, as his arms encircled me, sending my mind into heavenly realms as my eyes closed and I allowed him to lead me in very slow movement. I soon found myself blushing, my face running red and hot. While we were moving slowly, he was holding me really close. While it was easy to flow along in a dreamy sway with his arms guiding me, I could not mistake the persistent large bulge pressing against my stomach through his thin baggy jeans.

Within a few moments, I felt his hand, which had up till that time rested on my lower back, gently caress and squeeze my thousand-hour behind. I jumped. I automatically pushed his hand away.

He didn't react. His voice still soft, inquiring gently,

"Tell me, Cindy, what were you thinking just now when you pushed it away? Ohmagod. Laughing nervously, I stammered: ,"I,' I thought, he's got his hand on my,'uhh,"behind?... I squeaked out the last word, with unsure questioning hanging on it. In reality I had thought , *'on my ass,'* but I didn't want to sound brazen or condescending,",",and I… uh…"

"Go ahead, tell me, Cindy. What exactly went through your mind?"

"Help! ,"Uh, well, uhh, you, your hand?" I added with a nervous squeak and dry laugh.

"But your thoughts, Cindy. The thoughts and pictures coming through your mind,"Wasn't it his black hand? Isn't it that black hand on my behind?… on my pretty silky dress, on my little silky underthings? Isn't it, after all, a black hand that you see, that you're still seeing, Cindy?" he asked so very softly.

I couldn't breath. Oh my G-d, please don't, please don't make me talk about this. I pressed my face against his chest hoping the world would just go away with my heart beating too wildly for me to even think. I was so not going to bring my face up. I'd have to drop his class, leave school and maybe I'll just die when this French woman here stops singing. That would be my way out. Beginning to squeeze my eyes shut in panic, I am realizing that these are my only options.

Then, something wonderful happened: *"Redemption*! I heard my own grateful whimper as I realized the return of his hand. It was actually happening between us just as the professor had said it would. Just between two people on a non-racist plane! It was like a miracle, arriving right on my thousand-hour behind. He had forgiven me. Realization flooded my brain. The relief was palpable. I could breathe again. Face still pressed to his chest, my arms hugging him tighter, I welcomed the return of his hand to its rightful place. Now aware again of the music, my hips began to undulate with a welcoming action all their own. With eyes closed, mind adrift on clouds of sensuality, I moaned with penance as his dark fingers explored with growing boldness under my sundress. With this return to our non-racist plane, I brought my face up to his. He looked at me softly; smoldering:

"Cindy, have you ever kissed a black man?"

"*Not yet*," I heard myself whisper, as a voice inside my head screamed "*slut!*" Half wondering if this meant he was going to have sex with me, I raised my face anyway. Moving my mouth closer to his, I tasted the first of the many interchanges to come, his mouth and thick dark lips providing new territory for my small pink expression to explore.

He immediately began to explore, fondle and caress every part of my backside and thighs with such slow, possessive confidence that I became lightheaded. I heard his moan of satisfaction and felt intoxication wash over me.

I felt his hands on my face, sliding down onto my breasts, to my thighs, under my dress, onto my panties, slowly taking total possession. His hands continued to know every part of me with such slow and deliberate authority that I was having trouble breathing normally. Somehow, a cold, realistic thought overtook me: *'Break free from this and go home.'* So with my mind on fire and my body barely moving to the music, I turned my face up to his to say something like good-bye. The wanton excitement was becoming palpable, and I was encouraged to feel this pleasure was surely bringing further proof that I wasn't a racist.

: *"Professor, I..." "Maybe I should go, I've never just... done it... Y'know, without dating for a while, and stuff..."* He nodded at my words and took my hand.

"We don't have to do *anything,* Cindy." I was astonished to see him looking a little bashful, "*and, to be truthful, I just got carried away... I think I like being with you."*

He looked at me with the softest brown eyes I'd never seen.

"Don't *you like* being here with me?"

"Oh, yes, *of course!*" the words tumbling out of my mouth with such enthusiasm that as he kissed me, I realized that somehow I was, by my enthusiastic response, saying I was staying longer. He smiled, and taking me by both my shoulders looked squarely at me, softly imparting to me his sincerity in a pleasant, nothing-to-worry-about attitude.

"*I don't want you to do anything you don't want to do, OK? You can keep your clothes on.*" Before I could answer, he added with a sweet smile and a long look. "*Most of them, anyway...*" Even as we laughed, I pretended to be angry with a mock attempt to hit him, but I was tingling in places I never tingled in before. He was like no one I had ever met.

He started to lead me towards the bedroom. I saw myself breaking from his hand, running down the hall and out the door. Instead, I continued to note the swirling excitement of my pounding heart. *I don't have to go all the way. I still have my clothes on.* Trembling with excitement, I entered his bedroom.

He kissed me again and somehow the top button of my dress became undone.

"Professor, we, uh, we don't have to... you're not going to..."

"*Of course not,*" he cooed throatily. I thrilled to the Barry White-ness of his voice as the light material of my sundress floated onto the carpet at the same time the alcohol-tinged thought crossed my mind how great I looked in my new bra and panties. As I slowly turned back to him stepping out of my dress, I couldn't help but be drunkenly aware how delighted I was that I spent so much on my underwear. I was stunned to see how quickly he was already nude and under the sheets. As I faced him wearing only my new lingerie, I hesitated for a moment, but was reassured by the notion that (*for today, anyway*) I wasn't going to be taking off any more of my clothes. He slowly lifted up the sheets in an invitation for me to get in. Now that I knew I could trust him I scooted under the covers. As he drew back the sheet for me to slide under, I couldn't help glancing at the strange dark flesh between his legs.

I was now on my back with the soft brown eyes of the professor inches from my face. I craved his full dark lips on mine again, and got my wish. His mouth drew lightly away, kissing my upper lip, my cheek, my neck, as his hands slowly caressed every part of me; his warm, slow fingers grasped and fondled my flesh, making it yield in pleasure wherever he touched me: on my thighs, my buttocks, my breasts, my neck, and back again to my face as he kissed me longer, sending my mind spiraling into euphoric excitement. Always his hand, like an eager child seeking love but being turned away, would return with increasing urgency to my left breast, his thumb pressing down on my nipple, only the thin satin of my bra between his fingers and my flesh.

His kisses literally took me out of my mind while his arms encircled me. I felt his hands circle around my back.

I heard myself moan rather than speak, "*No... you're not going to undo... you promis...*" as his tongue continued to drive my mouth crazy.

"*No, ...don't worry,*" he moaned throatily as he rocked me, and his fingers just grazed the back of my bra and it was undone.

As if by magic, I thought. *I can't take my own bra off myself that easily.* I didn't even feel his fingers on the clasp. By the time I had completed my amazement over '*how did he do that?*' I saw my bra straps sliding down my arms and being tossed to the floor. I couldn't help but delight in hearing his exclamation.

"*Oh, they are **beautiful**,*" he cried, and his mouth proceeded to devour my right nipple while his right hand squeezed my left breast. This new rush of heady delirium had me crying out with all restraint evaporating. Soon he reversed the procedure of mouth and fingers so each of my nipples responded erectly to his squeezing, licking and sucking. He slowly took both my hands, crossing them at my wrists so they were being held there only by his left hand. My arms were stretched over my head. Now he was no longer so gentle, and while kissing and slightly biting and sucking at my neck, he started to squeeze my left breast and nipple with such savagery that I was soon crying out and having to catch my breath. Lightning flashes crazed red behind my tightly closed eyes.

Just when I absolutely couldn't stand the pain any longer he'd switch to the other nipple; while licking, blowing, kissing and sucking the tortured one back to normalcy. While mending the feel-good pain there, the other was then pinched through the same exquisite torment. With lightning rods of pleasurable pain shooting through my brain, I only knew I didn't want him to ever stop. Just when the pain became too agonizing, he would make me take a little more of it before releasing and licking my nipple back to a greater and greater pleasure-filled ache. When he placed his hand between my legs I realized I had never been this like this before. I immediately raised up my hips for his probing fingers to grab and drag the thin garment off me. I felt the small satin *shwish* its way over my knees, the steady demands of the professor allowing me total freedom from my clothing.

He laid down next to me, his fingers taking possession of me between my legs. His lips covered mine as he quickly found my swelling oily button with his right hand. I cried out unashamedly, and found myself beginning to slowly undulate my hips shamelessly as he fingered, grasped and plundered every part of me with such sudden ownership that I was in constant danger of hyperventilating.

What a thoughtful lover he was! He wasn't going to mount me just then, but would allow me more of himself. Locking eyes with mine, he nodded at the prize I hadn't yet explored. Between his legs there was a black baby's arm. A black baby's arm with a purple plum in its fist. I found myself drawn to it hypnotically. I slid down next to it; this engorged black snake I couldn't take my eyes off. He lightly took my little hand to this new discovery, silently encouraging me to know it better. My breath started coming harder and my hand trembled as I reached for the swollen flesh on my own initiative. I gave out a low whimper as I squeezed the hardening pole for the first time. I couldn't stop myself from continuing to squeeze it. By the third squeeze I could no longer get my hand completely around the swollen shaft, and I moaned in protest as his arms started to draw me back up to him. He laughed agreeably; allowing me to stay where I was while he relaxed back on his back.

My fingers grew warm as a proposed recklessness ran through me. The word *anything* began to make a wanton whisper inside my raging consciousness. My small white hand softly stroked up the shiny smoothness of his ever-stiffening black shaft, finally moving slowly and lightly around the velvety hardness of the dark head. I could feel it respond like a separate being with a life all its own. I didn't want to let go, and my mind swirled in alcoholic sensuality with the desire to be ravaged by this very monster.

He was so intuitive he knew before I did what I wanted to do. It was like the professor could read my mind. Placing his hand on the back my head, he gently pushed me in the direction of his lust, adding in a gasping voice:

"*Go ahead, enjoy yourself. Get used to it.*"

I brought myself to it. The amazing velvet-like hardness of the dark, smooth flesh was intoxicating, and, getting close to the mammoth alien, I wetly took what I could of it into my eagerly opening maw. The shock of the bulbous, rubbery smoothness filled my salivating mouth. The thought that if I engaged in this effort long enough I would actually cause the flesh to orgasm into and onto my suckling service added a danger and excitement to the act that made me weak. I felt a slow, warm swoon start to flow through me as I took a deep breath and sucked the giant head down my throat as far as I dared swallow. I saw the gagging coming. I stopped, took it out of my mouth, caught my breath, took a deep holding breath and tried yet again to encircle the headed guest with as much wet, oral devotion as I could muster. Once the head of the beast was inside, I enjoyed trying to slowly circle my tongue around the huge ball without gagging, and as I slowly swirled my tongue underneath and around this strange visitor, I welcomed it down my throat; immediately hearing him gasp and moan. I felt the professor's arms drawing me back up. With my head now resting on the pillow next to him, I whispered:

"*...Sorry I didn't do that very well.*"

"*It takes time,*" he responded in a gasping, strained voice, as he turned and started to mount me, lowering his hand underneath himself to guide in his rock hard staff. I felt the poking, stiff head press briefly against my inner thigh as his weight began to cover me. Out of my mind with lust and excitement, I whispered back in his ear:

"*Can I make it my term project, professor?*"

"*Gawd!*" he cried, as I felt his huge hard wood demand entrance into my barely used womanhood. His hard insistence received more of my surrender. I could feel myself part for his ram, and soon the huge shock gave way to the accepting, all encompassing wet heat that I'd heard about but I'd never really known before. His huge, ever-stiff invasion took over my entire world, and, losing all control, I kept unfolding from a deeper submergence below, slavishly giving more and more of myself to him. His spontaneous cries of pleasure as he experienced my almost virginal architecture drove me over the edge. Normal inner consciousness and reason dissolved as I writhed and moaned, impaled by my own ecstatic submission to this giant live invasion - which plundered with a seeming life of its own. An eager and willing vessel; my yielding rewarded me a volcanic pleasure along with the rising, rippling spasms of a physical and mental intoxication which I had never experienced before. I was soaring up into the orgasmic explosion. Then I realized:

'Holy shit! **This** *is what my girlfriends were talking about!* ***I am finally really getting fucked****!! Oh yes, I'm coming!* **Oh, this is it! This is it!***'* The climax of my orgasm had me losing consciousness, and then into blissful floating...

Now still in the resulting light sleep, I am blissfully unaware of my condition. I can do little except to realize that the sudden and loud knocking on my door is real. *This can't be happening*, I think; *the afterglow will be ruined*!

I knock over the tissue box as I hurriedly dry myself with one quick swipe n'grab a nearby sweatshirt. As I jump into some pants I realize the severe ache from my protesting testes. I get to the door to see a somewhat familiar face.

"Hi, Marty! It's Nick from church. Remember you said if you weren't at church to come and get you? Remember?

"No, I didn't remember," I said, hoping – so badly – that he was mistaken. Why had I gone and told this rather bizarre individual to "come get me" if I'm not in church? I just want to go back to bed. Now I'm also remembering that I have one-foot-in-shit at church since the moving van incident, and realize I have no choice if I am to be taken seriously there at all. Besides, I can't let that pastor bum-rap me as someone wimping out of the witnessing I had promised I'd do.

"Yeah, we're going witnessing at the lake, and we're late. You remember we agreed that I'd come by and pick you up? When we were talking with the pastor?" he repeated.

He was right of course. My head was clearing. "Oh, yeah, I remember. Yeah, yeah, yeah. I spaced it out. I'm sorry. My fault. Gimme a moment to get dressed."

"You're dressed perfect right now," he says, pointing to his own identical Church sweatshirt. I then realized that I had thrown on mine as I made my way to the door.

"Let me get some shoes on and brush my teeth."

"Right, cause we're really late."

Nick has a particular odor that never fails to surround him, even on Sundays. He works in some kind of industrial cleaning capacity and the smell – while not offensive – is not pleasant either. It follows him everywhere.

As we leave my house I notice we're walking towards a brand new minivan.

"*Nick, what's this?*" I ask, remembering the dented bomber I had seen him getting into after church.

"*Another gift from the Lord,*" he said, as if referring to a favorite uncle who was in the habit of handing him these kinds of presents.

"*Woah, very nice. Praise the Lord.*"

"*Marty, last Monday the mechanic told me my old beater had just had it. Needed all new rods 'n stuff; so like forget that. I just asked the Lord, I mean, I didn't know what to do; and then about 5pm, the Lord told me 'Go to Bob's Chevrolet.' I had $15 in my pocket, and I drove out with this…*"

Silence from me.

"*…no money down,*" he adds, his exuberance waning slightly.

He brought it up. I can't resist twisting it in a little, although I make sure my voice remains neutral.

"*Sixteen percent interest?*" I ask innocently.

"*Twenty-one.*"

"*Oh.*"

Feeling guilty for both making him squirm while at the same time jealous of his new ride, I need something to talk about now. I bring up the message I had begun to listen to earlier.

"*Jimmy Swaggert had a message this morning on rock music and it's satanic qualities. I wonder how much of that is actually present in the life of believers, even if we're not listening to the more obvious satanic stuff.*"

Nick had a way of smiling when he felt particularly emboldened. A small upturn of the mouth combined with an imperceptible shaking of the head. I half expected him to say '*Oh ye of little faith, how long must I suffer with you?*'

"*Having to worry about stuff like that is OK for your normal believers, regular churchgoers,*" he said, "*but,*" he added with a facial expression that said *puhleeze*, "*not for a prophet.*" Nick was of a mind that if you didn't agree with him concerning his own spiritual gift, you obviously lacked spiritual insight, but he would of course pray for you to attain the proper level of discernment.

I worried briefly that he really was a prophet and knew of the seditious sexual initiatives that had filled my very recent past. Although this kind of hospital mentality hovered in my consciousness just long enough for me to resent the thought; react to it and make me anxious, it almost never broke out into verbal expression. The latter behavior, as everyone knows, has a category associated with it, called *schizophrenia*.

He turned briefly toward me. "*Did I tell you what the Lord did for me a few days ago?*"

"*No.*"

"*It was a sign from the Lord regarding my spiritual gift. I've felt his leading in this area for a while now. I was driving my cab – y'know, my second job – going down the freeway, and the next thing I know, I'm at the airport! G-d just picked me up and put me down at the airport line for taxis.*"

"*Wow! Praise the Lord!*" I said unsteadily. "*Uhh, I'm not quite sure wh…*"

"*Marty, I was on the freeway on my way out to the airport to get on the taxi line, and G-d just put me there. In a twinkling of an eye.*"

"*Wow, isn't this kind of like Elijah? Did you see anything, like up in the air?*"

"*No. it was almost like suddenly waking up, and snap! There I was… at the airport.*"

My balls are aching terribly at this point, and my energy level is way down as I reluctantly pass on the urge to comment in a way that might contradict the ethereal nature of his experience.

We park and I see two other men from church standing with the assistant pastor. My spirits start to rise as I remember a couple of others from the previous week's meeting who said they would come, and apparently have chosen not to. Gloating with this added rush of self-esteem, I can now look forward to trashing those MIAs who had dedicated themselves to join us in witnessing. I say with innocent curiosity, "*Where's Sam and Ron?*"

"*Not here,*" Nick says with a voice barely able to control his own glee. He too is elated to dump on those who have now been found wanting. The lack of commitment on the part of the no-shows will allow us the opportunity to happily tear them apart within a proper Christian framework in the near future. With proper forethought, a prayerful allusion could be made to the parable of the two sons Jesus speaks of. Each one ordered into the vineyard, 'but only one went' *doncha' know…*

We approach the pastor, assistant pastor, Bill and Robbie, who each offer us a warm smile and a wave.

"*Marty, glad you're here, brother.*"

"*Sorry I'm late. I just… forgot. Forgive me.*"

"*You're here. That's all that matters. Let's pray.*"

Standing off to the side of the parking lot, all six of us hold hands in a circle. People walk by and I feel the natural embarrassment, which I simply attribute to satanic imps.

"*Lord,*" Pastor Phil begins, "*we ask you to bless our time here today, that we might fulfill your word to go out into all the world and make converts of the nations. We realize there are many hurting people here, Lord, who need the saving grace of the Lord Jesus, and we pray that we may bring many into the Kingdom, in Jesus name, amen.*"

The pastor was holding my left hand, and Nick my right. It was at that moment that I realized with increasing irritability that many of the little hairs around my belly-button were trying to break free from their pasted-with-body-fluid state, a result of my hurried one-swipe-dry less than an hour before.

The itch – and the concomitant awareness of it – was becoming almost unbearable, as both my hands were imprisoned in the prayer circle. The assistant pastor was on the Pastor's left, and the prayers started to be spoken one person at a time as each believer had his turn.

"*Satan, we bind you in the name of Jesus.*"

"*Yes, we bind you Satan,*" I chirp in, stamping my foot and swiveling my hip a little in the hope that would break these tiny hairs free from their agonizing semi-imprisonment. They stretched but would not break free of their tormenting state, the pasting tendency of my drying bodily fluid waning *oh too slowly* with every breath I took. I started to feel panic as I obsess over the itch, and it is threatening to overrun my consciousness.

"*You have no place here, devil.*"

"*We count these people saved in Jesus name!*"

"*Hallelujah!*"

"*Glory to G-d.*"

"*Go, in Jesus name,*" Nick adds.

Finally, enduring it no longer an option, I enter into the itch, become its substance, ride its river of calling beyond the flesh into the very spirit of the itch, urging its benefaction on. I ride at the head of an imaginary antennae-like-itch-worm crying out for greater itch even as it buries its tic-like antennae into my skin. I then pull its mammoth head up, increasing the itch beyond any red-line. I stand, riding the largest itch-worm in all of creation, a master of nature – a lesson served in Jedi mind control.

It is now my turn.

"*Father, we know it is your spirit that saves, not our efforts. Nevertheless, help us, Lord, to be clean on the inside, that we would not be like the hypocrites, Scribes and Pharisees, all clean like white-washed sepulchers on the outside, but inside like unto dead men's bones and all corruption. Have mercy on us all, and give grace upon all that we do, that none would be lost because of our own weakness and failing. Help us Lord, in Jesus name.*" Amen.

Divorce

I guess I first started to doubt my religious faith as more and more of my work and business related ideas began to crumble into a continuing pattern of failure. I was sure G-d had his hand on each, and then it would, in the harsh light of day, crumble away under feet of clay. It was cumulative in its effect, making my home life a wreck, my church-life suspect and dark thoughts my constant companion.

Following a voice in my head, I continued to make things worse, losing job after job, moving the family here and there, and finally one day – after sixteen years of mutual torment and failure – my hard working wife (she always *kept* her job) announced she had had enough and took our four children and left for her folks' house. Upon letting me know she was filing for divorce that very week, my wife offered another bit of news: she was through with anything having to do with church and 'all that stuff.'

So here I was, a man in his mid-forties returning to his father's California apartment to live, a total failure from every point of view. I also was through with church. I would fail around for a few more months, getting and losing two different jobs while waiting for the divorce papers to come and two of my four children to arrive who were to live with me in Los Angeles.

* * *

"You have broken what could not *be* broken," Merlin says to Arthur in the movie *Excaliber*. This was not too far from my thoughts as I discovered myself a failure as a father and a husband. I had never thought divorce, failure and a broken family would be my fate, not after having my "conversion" so dramatically lift me out of the world of drugs and perverse sex. I had imagined that repeating scripture from the bible, going to church and believing would be enough. I mean I had heard G-d talking to me, so how could this come to pass? I had prayed and went where I believed the spirit was leading me. I had imagined all the great things I would be doing for the Lord and here I was broke, living with my father with my wife and kids almost two thousand miles away. I had given up drugs for fifteen years – even stopped cigarettes, liquor, pornography and adultery (save for that one time with the salesgirl)– and here I was, unbelievably, in the shithouse.

When things go wrong, it's normal to look for someone to blame. It's not healthy, but it *is* normal. When affixing blame, anger helps you believe in the rightness of your cause. The '*straw that broke the camel's back*' for my wife was our running out of money in the middle of building our house. My inability, however to make a consistent living was always turning the family fortunes into a bottomless pit, that, in reality, no short-term loan would fix. I had a family member who had inferred he would help financially in this latest adventure, but using prudence rather than strict memory, he deferred when asked to contribute this house-saving money.

Since it was easier to blame the relative than myself, I allowed all manner of evil contrivance to surface into my seething brain as I drove down Ventura Blvd. in the San Fernando Valley in Los Angeles one hot afternoon in 1996.

The man on the radio had an English accent. A radio-talk show counselor named Roy Masters was speaking with a caller. I did a double take as I found his words piercing me to the heart.

```
      "When you speak of revenge," he was telling
the caller, "there are a couple of issues.
First, what led you to being tricked in the
first place? Could you have known not to trust
someone so blindly? Should you have known? If
you've been a fool than why not face what a
fool you've been to have believed something
that you later found out to be a lie, rather
than allow anger to ruin your life? But more
often than not, you're being manipulated into
doing something foolish now rather than admit
your own past mistake, and this denial can land
you in jail as you allow the angry voice in
your head to tempt you into doing something
foolish. You, and by "you" I mean everyone,
must understand that the manipulation is not
being done by the person who you think wronged
you, but by spiritual forces you are blind to.
This is allowed to come about in your life
because of your ego's refusal to see where you
were wrong. See the problem?"
```

"The jails are full of people who've found themselves in this situation," he continued. "They find themselves waking up suddenly in prison, as if from a dream. "My G-d, why did I do that?" And they see that they've thrown away their life on that emotional wave of the moment, and that the same spirit that made you feel so right, so true, so manly in your anger now laughs at you, ridiculing you for what you've done, all in an attempt to drive you into further destruction.

We have a huge amount of prisoners we help, and believe me, the prisoners who stay in touch with the Foundation of Human Understanding don't go back to prison…"

"Holy shit! Who is this guy?" I was transfixed. I did something I couldn't remember ever having done before. I parked in order to listen more closely to the radio, and was immediately assailed by thoughts of *what people might think of an older man parked near a park where children were playing; how this guy's accent was English; how I should continue to be doing something productive to help my family; not be sitting in a car listening to the radio*!

When the host mentioned his name and his meditation tape, I thought, "*Oh boy, here comes the con*," but he mentioned it was only $10, and if you didn't have it, call this toll-free number, and he would send it free. Not able to argue with that, I phoned the Foundation of Human Understanding and got this meditation tape by Roy Masters, called "The Classic (Be Still and Know)" free of charge.

I had been around Hare Krishnas in the East Village in the late sixties and had done some mantra/chanting stuff, and had tried some of the positive imagery meditations that one comes across living in Southern California, but this sounded totally different.

* * *

When I wasn't working, I sat around smoking pot and drinking a little, thinking a lot about sex and masturbating.

I picked up a black girl hitchhiking She was all smiles and jive, but she turned out to be a really lousy hooker. We negotiated for $60.00, plus the cost of the room, which I found out afterwards was her room at the motel, which she pretended to go in and pay for. Oh well, a girl's got to make a living, I thought. But when I kidded her about it, instead of copping to it, as I indicated I wasn't going to ask for the extra money back, she just got pissed and piled on more bullshit.

Although she refused to admit it, it was obvious to me she had a drug-habit and as soon as she had the money I could see her urge to cop, and I became merely something in her way. At first I couldn't get hard, and when I finally did she put a bag on me and those things always make it more work, so it ended pretty unsatisfactorily.

I tried a massage girl. She was surprisingly attractive with a terrific body, but she, like the black girl before her, seemed to steal my sexual excitement with her dead eyes and cold smile. I couldn't arrive at a satisfactory conclusion with her either, and figured that I must be gay.

Chapter 16 – The Meditation-Observation Exercise

The tape arrived.[25] After a day or two I found a tape player and listened for about five minutes. *'What kind of shit is this? What nonsense.'* And this *'you are about to embark on the most wonderful experience of your life'* stuff! *This radio counselor simpleton. Probably for somebody like him* (a limey, yet!), *any low-level mental state looks like a wonderful experience, a voice in my head sneered.* His voice on the tape was telling me to sit upright with my arms hanging by my sides, and feel tingling in my fingertips, concentrating on the back of my hand rising to the center of my forehead (which I could either imagine as rising or by allowing the hand to actually rise) and then judging the changing distance between my hand and my forehead. *'Exist in that state for the briefest of moments,'* he said, and life-changing experiences would slowly begin to occur. He also stated repeatedly that thoughts would immediately rise up to prevent my performing or experiencing this mental estimate of this changing distance, and I should be aware of these thoughts. *What is this*???

I couldn't believe this! I was a student of the most brilliant concepts in the fields of psychology. *How could this possibly help*? I asked myself. *What did he mean thoughts would arise to stop this? The hokum people will listen to! Well, what could he know? He was, after all, English. They went into World War II looking ridiculous in short pants and silly-looking helmets. They wouldn't even be here if it wasn't for FDR and LendLease, anyhow, Do they appreciate it? No-o-o. Or was that the French? Remember that class I took in college- European Poly-Sci and that girl I had sex with from that class; wow, was she smart, rubbing shoulders with the UN people; assisting the Full Professor... Her family had money and political connections on the leftist union side and an apartment on Manhattan's West Side. A terrible fuck... Used to hold/grasp me too tight right below my shoulder blades, and kind of drag my upper torso down... reminds me of that great movie 'Election' and the main male character hearing the words "good job" upon completing sex... and...and ...and..."*

I suddenly realized I was no longer in my chair in the bedroom meditating along to the tape, but was now standing in front of the refrigerator while ridiculing his message.

What am I doing in the kitchen? What's going on here?

---

[25] *Free download available at www.trailopen.com and/or www.fhu.com*

Pornographic Epiphany

I remembered something that seemed to have peculiar significance. I had once had a dream I shared with my shrink before I was married. I was in a video parlor – the same one I had shot cocaine in many times, and every door had a 'glory hole' that was cut in the outer portion of the door, and out of each hole hung a penis, all different shapes, sizes and colors. The situation did not appear unattractive. When my shrink suggested the homosexual message here, I became defensive.

He responded with: *"Oh, c'mon!"*

I was unable to get beyond the surface admission that yes, I had engaged in homosexual activities, but somehow the uncanny anxiety had something to do with him, although I had no sexual lust for the shrink. I was still too psychotic with irrational fear to discuss this very thing with him, for I feared how ashamed I was to appear exactly in this light. It appeared to me at some level, that the mere fear that I might have – or think I might have – lust for the shrink, was enough to so paralyze me, so that I was unable to speak of these matters further. It was a matter of me anticipating he would think poorly of me for thinking/sharing such things; that my "standing" in his eyes would be diminished.

It was the phantom at the gate, anxiously turning me away in fear of the uncanny emotion. The same dread, awe and loathing that stands at all our gates. It was enough to keep me from journeying down a path that might shed some light on itself.

I went easily into my thoughts, my mind games, rationalizing that I had, after all, spoken of my homosexual trysts, and therefore, could certainly not be considered guilty of living in denial. I had even tried to brag that I was never interested in hand-holding or kissing a man, and had never had an emotional relationship with another man, to which my shrink countered with something along the lines of *'mores the pity,'* which I very reluctantly – and only after many years - came to see applied (at the very least) to Rick of my youth.

It was easy to tell myself that I was fed up with shrinks, anyway. Also, I couldn't afford one anymore. I hadn't seen one in years. There was a telephone number that I could call, however, to express myself along these lines at a reduced rate.

Press one... Press two if... Press three if you're... Press four if you're a... Press five if you're a man looking to speak to a...

Pressing five, I always wondered if they were really transsexuals. Was there any point in acknowledging these people on the other end were probably not really shemales, but most likely women acting that way when they saw what line you rang in on? I told myself it probably didn't matter... I guess.

The voice was kind of she-male, however; gravelly feminine, cynical, a little nasty.

"Yes?"

"Are you a transsexual?"

"Yes, I am honey, what do you need, baby?"

"I think I need to be kind of... maybe, like... controlled, I guess, like, uhh, well, kinda' maybe directed, dressed to please and made to, uh, serve?"

"What's your name, baby?"

"Elle."

"What are you wearing, Elle?"

"A black peignoir over a silver camisole, with black satin panties and nylons," I lied.

"I'm Alana, and I'm going to tell you what to do. Do you understand?"

"Yes, Alana."

"Do you have a dildo?"

"No."

"Elle, the next time you call me, I want you to have one with you. You should be practicing how to suck my dick and you should be practicing putting it up your cute little ass. Do you understand?"

"Yes...Alana, you're not going to.. to...to punish me for not having one, are you?"

"Oh... you are going to wish you had pleased me when you were supposed to... I'm going to spank you, and I'm going to make you do things for me and my friends that you won't forget for a long time... (beat) Are you on your hands and knees?"

"Uh, no..."

"Get on your knees now, Elle."

"I am now, Yes."

"I'm going to spank you and I want you to spank yourself as I do it."

"Whack!" Sounds come over the phone.

"OK, put your lips, just your lips, up against the bulge in my panties. Don't you dare touch it; I haven't given you permission to touch it yet. Just your lips, you understand?"

"Yes..."

"Yes, who?"

"Yes, Alana."

"You can feel how big I am, can't you?"

"Oh, yes, yes..."

"Take my panties off with your teeth."

"Are you dragging them off?"

"Yes, Alana."

"Come up now. Get on your knees in front of my dick. I've got something big and thick for you to put in your mouth. Place your mouth over the head, just the head. Are you doing that?"

"Oh, Alana, don't make me... do I have to..."

"Oh yes, you *are* going to suck my dick, and after I come in your mouth I'm going to spank you, and then some friends of mine are gonna fuck you so hard you won't walk right for a week. Don't you dare hesitate with me again..."

"Please don't be mad," I whimper. "I... I'll do whatever you want... I'm doing it..."

"Uhhmm, you do that good, Elle, take it down, all the way down your throat. I don't care if you gag or choke when I come in your sweet little mouth Elle, in fact I hope you do. Oh, yeah, little girl, you're going to be chokin' on me, cause you're going to swallow every drop, do you understand me? Just moan deep in your throat to signify you understand."

"Mmmm...Oh yes, you are so big..."

"Elle, I told you just moan! You stopped sucking me to speak! Now you're really gonna pay! Lie down on your bed face down, stretch out your hands, I'm tying your wrists and ankles to the bedposts... and I'm calling in my friends, five big black dudes, and I'm putting a little pillow under you so your little ass is tilted right up for us, and we're going to spank you and fuck you all night long, You understand, you bad little girl?"

"I'm almost there... I'm coming, Oh G-d, I can't believe I'm doing this!!!"

As I frantically shut off the handset to lay in the afterglow, I was swept with realization of the depths I was compulsively seeking in these humiliating, submissive fantasies. Awareness of this realization gave birth to another layer of discovery: Along with the understanding that I was realizing more the full nature of this sexual hunger, I came to see the necessity of believing that there must be all kinds of behaviors in my non-sexual life being thus affected by these tendencies. I sense a 'see-saw' imagery of awareness of sexual fantasies on the one hand, relating to reflections of its motivation in my non-sexual life on the other. The born-loser who always snatched defeat from the jaws of victory in the game of life reflected the fate of one who refused to be aware of the humiliated cuckold born in sexual fantasy.

Perhaps I somehow curtailed awareness of my own fantasies by the way I focused "in" and to the submergence. When "into it," it seemed that on the road to "Big O" delivery, the driver held a scrunched up, squinty-eyed submergence into purely sexual consciousness, but that now, with the sound of my own words still hanging loud in the room, the signposts were not only being seen clearly, but I accepted the responsibility of becoming aware of them. They were out on the bigger stage, as it were.

Call it epiphany, a greater awareness from the meditation, but here for the first time there was a reason not to ignore them. That while in the past I had always hunched into a denial of my devotion to these imaginings, it was now time to confront them. Did my harboring these objects of worship reflect the 'feet-of-clay' inherent in my so-called born again experience?

This sense of *"you can't run from it now"* hadn't existed before. While I thought it must be the shocking experience of hearing my own voice still ringing from the out-loud telephone conversation, I would soon come to see something else was playing a part. But at the time, I was persuaded only that I was free to pursue what I believed I was sexually: I must be gay. For sixteen tormented years I tried to work out as a "normal" husband, using fantasy in order to have heterosexual sex. Obviously, I must be gay.

Lets Talk 2

The current psychiatric myopia seeks to clump all homoerotic urges into one big "*gay*" conundrum. What follows is an important statement *regarding homosexuality* which appears so absolutely necessary to correct this misdiagnosis. This results in the sufferer masking – instead of dissolving - deep emotional problems in therapy.

By playing both the political and sociological "card," this dis-"ease" is somehow explained as a feminine characteristic, despite the fact that no one will be likely to find a female hanging around a male toilet competing with the male homosexual. Ergo, there is no distinction made in modern (pop) psychology between the male who is in an "Ozzie –and-Harriet" gay relationship, and the compulsive seeker of anonymous flesh in the bathhouses and back rooms toilets of gay bars. The innocuous "glory hole," with its anonymous technology, should be a warning sign for emotionally damage, not a qualification for the sufferer to raid our adoption agencies. When no relationship exists, but one compulsively seeks humiliating submissive postures on the one hand, or dominating, abusive roles on the other, the only thing going on here is mental dis-"ease."

The following is written by *Harry Stack Sullivan*, a man who (most likely) had a monogamous, life-long same-sex partnership with a male companion. While no doubt a man of turbulent emotions himself, we have not seen his like amongst any other psychiatric professional, and IMHO, that includes gentlemen from Vienna as well. He points out brilliantly that the man who is compulsively driven to lurk hungrily around the public toilets, or who finds himself in places where sexual liaison is accomplished vis-à-vis a 'glory hole,' is not in quite the same "situation" as modern psychiatry seems to place him.

"As I have indicated earlier, I think that the whole business of the homosexual entity as an explanation is always to be looked pretty firmly in the face by psychiatrists who attempt to effect any great improvement in the mental health of the patient. One should determine whether this entity is the organization of a definite integrating tendency that satisfies a need or whether it is a complex mental disorder in which the homosexuality is present because it so perfectly fortifies some abnormal mental process, some dynamism of difficulty. Where a person has felt that life is eminently worth living only in the preadolescent stage, when he did enjoy great intimacy with another person of the same sex, irrespective of whether that

great intimacy was what may be described as on the non-genital or the genital level, I am quite willing to deal with that person on the basis that he is engaged in actual direct pursuit of satisfaction from members of his own sex, or as in homosexuality, as it may be easily called."

"But where such experience is missing from a person's life, then I think one is doing a great violence to the therapeutic principle to accept the notion that that person has anything like a simple drive to secure genital satisfaction by any type of behavior with members of the same sex."

To work on this assumption, and to deal with this patient's "homosexuality,' is, to my way of thinking, one of the most vicious miscarriages of the therapeutic situation. It takes out of the culture a group of terms, which, in referring to behavior, carry all the culture's evaluations of that behavior." (queer, faggot, etc.)

"You see, if the patient has not found great warmth and satisfaction in intimacy with a member of his own sex, but later on is told by a psychiatrist that such intimacy is what he is after – or has, by his own paranoid processes, come to feel that that is what he is after, and the psychiatrist agrees with him – then he and the psychiatrist are talking about something that is, in its ultimate essence, merely a revolting difference between him and good people. That is all."

"It has no meaning in terms of something that he has experienced, that he has undergone, and that therefore is a part of him. But it does have meaning as a particular type of horribly derogatory formulation. Thus, to attack a paranoid state, for example, on the basis of an attempt to understand the patient's homosexuality is an atrocious miscarriage of the therapeutic process. This is a very nifty way to make it beyond the most perchance that any intimacy will be established with that patient."

"... So it is quite important indeed to discriminate between, first the isophilic (same-sex) phase of personality development and the satisfactions that can be acquired then, and second, the innumerable unhappy caricatures of living to which the term "homosexuality" (or in modern parlance ""gay") is sometimes applied."

The people who have gotten well into the preadolescent phase of personality development before possibilities of further growth failed, and come to us with their life problems formulated in terms of homosexual concepts, are still somewhat near reality.

But people who have not gotten as far as the preadolescent phase of personality development, and who come to us with their life problems formulated in terms of homosexuality, are showing a very much more complex distortion of interpersonal relations <u>and offer a much more treacherous basis</u> for therapeutic relationships because they are that much less mature. Thus this discrimination has prognostic significance.

*It is a discrimination between what is a sort of frantic exploration on the base of what is verbal prescriptions by the patient, as compared with regressive retreats from hopelessly difficult situations to a time in the past that was actually satisfactory, with new collisions perhaps with the culture in the process (being called 'queer,' etc.). Naturally the latter is much the simpler to attack, and the prognosis–the outcome–is much more apt to become favorable. But if, on the other hand, you combine these two into some doctrine of homosexuality as applied to factors in schizophrenia, paranoid states or what have you, **then you have missed the whole point of interpersonal psychiatry**, and your results will be sufficiently mongrel so that you will never be able to feel very secure about what is what. But, on the other hand, you will never have any convincing demonstration of being completely wrong."*[26]

---

[26] *Clinical Studies in Psychiatry;* Sullivan HS. (Norton) pp 160-163
PLEASE NOTE Sullivan's 'writings' are almost always his recorded lectures put to print after his death.

Chapter 17 – Meditation-Exercise Reintegration

I continued to try to get through the first side of the meditation tape. I tried it again. *Oh, this is stupid.* But wait, my thoughts are repeating the words I'm hearing, but if I make an effort to be aware of even *these* repeating thoughts, they disappear as well, and…then there is a flash of something new. A literal spark of *"expansion of consciousness."*

'Wait a minute. What is this? Insistent thoughts are in my head trying to get me to do something else. Anything else. Stand up and leave the room again! In other words, *words were coming into my head telling me to do things just like he was warning me about on the tape message*! How can that be? He's not here! How can he know what's going on in my head?'

Ten minutes later found me on my way to the kitchen again wondering what I was doing. The suggestion was made in my mind that I should stand in front of the refrigerator looking for something to eat. Later, while trying to meditate again, I was reminded that there might be dirty dishes in the sink*; as if I ever cared about that*! I had been sitting upstairs trying to meditate a few moments ago. *How can this be? I'm the mental giant here.* What's going on? Feeling strangely – and suddenly – brave, I returned to the cassette. I sat down, pushed play, and made it about thirty seconds before my mind took off just like he said it would, and then in five more minutes I found myself starting to get up to look for my shoes, again a victim of another one of my own mind games; this time a reminder of some groceries I "needed" to buy. **What the hell is going on here**!?! The "*not me*" of HS Sullivan was starting to get the light of awareness brought to it through the simple decision to be "*aware.*"

Words, emotions and imagination all carry with them the ego's power to entangle you. You cannot possibly improve your overall situation using thoughts in your head. It is not unlike a swamp with quicksand, in which the more you dip your toe in to study the terrain, the greater the likelihood you will be pulled down into it. If you try to think about your own sexuality you will often find yourself pulled right into its atmosphere of temptation and lust.

When you meditate, the concentration of "judging the distance," brings the light of consciousness to bear on these words, emotions and imaginations which arise in your mind. You can observe this while creating an objectivity which is of a higher consciousness and of a different quality. Judging, or estimating the changing distance between the back of your hand and the center of the forehead brings a dimensionality *other* than that of the Jungian shadow – or personal unconscious – or '*not-*

me' (which is comprised of imaginings, words and emotions outside your normal consciousness), and the shadow elements not only are exposed to the light of your objectivity, but, upon exposure, cease to have that amount of strength over you that they had before the experience. A higher power will meet you here, allowing your consciousness more light over these previously dark provinces. Sullivan points out (while healing schizophrenics without anti-psychotic meds), that it is this 'special' opportunity to reintegrate what was beforehand omitted from awareness that is so important.

Eventually, you may experience a contortion of your facial and/or body features as "something" ultimately leaves you[27] and that which plagued and troubled you all your life is no longer present, or at least not to the degree that it was before. Draw what conclusions you may, but that power is the power of the true faith that religion has not only seldom known, but actively prevents you from finding due to its own ignorance. These are the real exorcisms that may take place by yourself through your own commitment to G-d. I believe you will get to a point where you see things about yourself rising up before your objective consciousness that will be too much for your conscience to deal with. It is an intensely painful and private moment, and its consummation demands faith in a power higher than your own.

Your thoughts will not give you up easily. You are in for a fight. A fight whether you're a university professor or the janitor who cleans the classroom. Beggar or billionaire, this is your time. There is no place to run. Whether you acknowledge it or not, it *is*. He is the creator, and we are the created. This is the bag we are all in. Life is all there is, and He is all there is eternally. It is really the only game in town, and we play by His rules whether we believe we do or not.

But unlike the mystified repairman trying to get something broken to run right and is therefore suddenly happy to find out what's wrong with the darn thing, we run from finding out what's wrong with ourselves. We want to remain a god unto ourselves: a god who craps.

---

[27] *Trailopen link for exorcism video_www.trailopen.com/index-2*

Change "inside" needs time to change one's "outside." I was still set in a kind of autopilot headed in whatever direction my dick pointed. I went to *The Queen Mary*, a transvestite bar in North Hollywood. A few of the drag queens looked like truck drivers in dresses and wigs, but after a little while I see a totally passing tall bronze beauty at the bar. She's talking with people but when they walk off I move to the seat next to her.

Bartender comes over,
"What'll ya have?"
"Coors on tap if ya have, and, turning to speak softly to her back, say *"excuse me, dear…?"*
She turns,
"Yes?" Comes the deeply affected voice with a South American accent.

A soft, stoned confidence fills my voice. *"I'm wondering if I could be…"* looking into her eyes, *"so fortunate as to have someone, as beautiful* as yourself (beat, allowing our stoned eyes to share my lucky-to-be-in-her-presence vulnerability), *allow me to, perhaps, buy her a drink?"*

"Honey, you can buy me anything you want."

After the drinks, name exchange, and some yada-yada-yada, I move to a crucial point.

"Y'know, before my business disintegrated and the wife took everything I had, I would've seen if there was any way I could help a goddess like yourself with her rent, or something like that, but I'm afraid all I can do in my current condition is offer you another drink, so if that puts me out-of-the-ballpark, it's all right, hon… I'll buy you the drink anyway… and I won't bother you anymore. I understand greener pastures..."

"Baby, that is so sweet of you."

"Sweet is *so much* my middle name," I smile, looking into those deep stoned eyes.

"It is? Uhhmmm," she says full of innuendo and a roll of her slim shoulders beneath a clinging satin dress. Spaghetti straps hold up good-looking silicone; and her hips and legs are feminine enough to easily pass on the street.

We both laugh and I notice the music is beginning a rare slow number.
"Dance?" I say.
"Sure."

We move with the occasional grind around the floor, and kiss at the end. She invites me back to her place. She says she'll meet me outside and I can follow her back to her apartment but I find myself sitting in the car for over twenty minutes twisting in excruciating doubt, waiting. There's always that female sense of control in consenting to any sexual encounter, but it seems to me the transvestite is more at home using it, and enjoys torturing you with it even more. Color me crazed and horny as she drives up next to my parked car, and with a smile and a signal, I follow in excited relief.

I enjoy the night, but after kissing and sucking and stroking and touching, I fail to get any more excited, and, while not getting frustrated, it is also true neither one of us has an orgasm. I awake first and see her satin dress at arm's length on the floor next to the bed. I pick it up with a déjà vu to that time as a young man fondling my girlfriend's silky top that had so enamored me prior to our quick coupling. Again, it suddenly just seemed like material, and I wonder at the magic it had over me when it was worn. Here again I find myself uncomfortable with the calm thought running through my head *"what the fuck are you doing here? This is just a young man from South America, pretending to be a woman."*

I saw my boy-girl with doctored tits once again a few weeks later but there was little passion, but a lot more money flowed out of my pocket for some outrageously expensive perfume which she had talked about pointedly.

I decided I must be more mainstream gay. I find a middle aged gay guy. He is very well acquainted with the LA scene. As seems to be a pattern with my meeting gay men, he starts off very cool and distant over our first meeting for coffee. *"Maybe I'll call you later in the week, but I'm really so busy right now,"* he intones with an obvious allusion to the brush-off, but then within two weeks he's calling my apartment twice a day. He's not effeminate in public, and appears outwardly normal. I meet his ex-wife, and when they are talking and discussing family things they could be a husband and wife from anywhere.

It is only in his personality that he's totally femme, and consequently, upon our having sex, I realize he is also looking for a 'take-charge' kind of guy to be submissive to. Our one and only sex episode immediately turns into a 'let's get-it-over-with' affair for me, as we are both of the same proclivity. We are like two positive electrical charges, each of us looking to get 'turned on' by our opposites. I share my thoughts on this with him, and – this being my first time in these waters – apparently communicate surprisingly well, and even though he's been gay for years, he seems to find my ability to define our sexual roles refreshing. We hang out together, but we don't have sex with each other. He occasionally likes to touch me, putting his hand on my leg when I drive, or by placing his arm around me, but that creeps me out and I tell him it makes me uncomfortable. He knows a lot of people, and my weekends become filled with gay types from different bars to raging queen millionaires to cruising Hollywood bathhouses.

I am beginning to listen to the meditation tape almost every day and get all the way to the end. I even make it to Side Two. It is beginning to grow on me, as its concepts are being reflected by both my deepest fears and my deepest understandings.

We go to gay bars. Every time we wind up going back to strange apartments with guys we meet I can't get into it. I find myself making excuses later to my gay buddy: *I didn't like this. I didn't like that. This one's personality, another one's breath, something about this one's cock, that one's sense of humor...* bottom line, I fantasize, but in the real world it turns me off.

I start smoking a lot of pot. I confide to my gay friend my paranoid thoughts concerning my psychosis in subjective example. He alerts me to the fact my logic is based on the equivalent of having hostile space aliens camping out in my ears. I find this – coupled with my daily meditations - extremely reassuring, and think, *'why didn't I realize that before?'*

I continue to meditate although the pot is now actually getting in the way of the conscious expansion a good deal of the time, as I find myself imagining myself in heroic postures for a good part of the meditation. When I'm not doing that – or if I'm not smoking pot - I find a clarity to the meditation that is unlike anything I had ever experienced. Also, females are beginning to get all my attention.

As we hopped gaily all around LA, we ran into someone my friend was close with who had his 15 year-old daughter staying with him for a week. She was a physically attractive, spoiled brat with a big mouth, and apparently pissed off at everyone. Everyone except me. For some reason she found my words interesting and comforting, and although we only visited three times, on the third visit the girl lit up when she saw me, and by this time I was totally hot for her. I couldn't stop thinking about her in a sexual manner throughout these past few days, and became aware of extreme testosterone flowing in her direction within my masturbation fantasies.

We came over late on the last night she was going to be in LA, and she came out of her bedroom in an almost see-through floor length gauzy nightgown over her knee-length satin sleeping lingerie. So while there was almost no skin – save her bare arms – showing, she was nonetheless breathtaking, sensual and mysterious. I was stunned, and assumed she was sending me a signal and immediately entered an 'all-lights-are-green' sexual mindset. There was slow music playing and I simply walked over to her as she started to talk to me and swept her up into a dance. I knew I could go to jail for actually doing what I wanted to do, but probably would not have been able to help myself had she been so inclined.

Fortunately, once the girl felt my outrageous excitement press against her during our slow dance, she snapped out of her teenage-tease mode and disappeared from my life. But what did happen was that I realized I was ten times more turned on by this girl at that moment than I had been by all the gay scenes that I was trying to get into cruising all over LA for the past few weeks. Methinks maybe I'm not gay. I alluded to this with my gay friend, who said, "I'm going to take you somewhere you won't forget."

The Bathhouse

It was quite a large establishment. We paid the minimum for a locker and a towel. Things had changed since I last visited one of these places in the pre-AIDS day. There's a much more "we know what we want" quality about the scenes inside, although there is that same sense of tense hunger which always permeates these homosexual gatherings. When a man walks by with a firehose swinging large from his crotch the faces that follow mix lust and desperation with such hungry hope that I've yet to see a portrayal in any media do it justice. Sheer greed for the flesh shows ugly and urgent on the faces of the hopeful as they move quickly to catch up with the well endowed. Hoping for the privilege of submission to the large monster, many risk their lives giving into the compulsion to swallow their thick, slick reward for a job well-done; often blowing themselves to death with a gag and a swallow.

Rather than reflecting any shame or embarrassment, a certain kind of pre-eminence holds sway in the general consciousness. An arrogance of superiority lavishes the atmosphere of all concerned, as if it were an officer's club in the army of independent thinkers compared to the enlisted men in their farmer-Jones missionary positions with their female cows. It is the mindset of the elite who see beyond the conventional morality.

All the private rooms had been rented earlier in the evening. These were about twelve foot by eight, held a bed, a dim light with a mirrored wall or ceiling, and a shelf with a can of Crisco. Two extra towels came with the room.

We decided to keep our shorts on with a wrapped towel, and locked our valuables and clothes in the lockers. Leaving the locker room, my friend ran into someone he knew who had brought in a backpack full of airline-size liquor bottles, and after procuring a few, we decided to relax and finish them. We bought a couple cans of pop, filled some paper cups with ice and kicked back with our mixed drinks. We found a place to hunker down in one of the cavernous rooms amidst fairly loud music while the parade of naked, half-naked with-towels-around-waist, and fully dressed males cruised by. The walls generally portray giant murals of male genitalia. The aggressive and sensual music all tended to sound just as Matt Damon's character portrayed it as sounding in *"Good Will Hunting."*

The little alcove where my friend and I are slumming while sipping our drinks overlooks a most peculiar area right off the main thoroughfare made up of aisles leading to various areas within the bathhouse. There is a depression – much like a sunken living room – in the floor right at the intersection of these aisles so as to give this "pit" a certain centrality. It is a round depression perhaps three feet deep and about twenty feet in diameter. There's a thin railing to prevent people from accidentally falling in (the lights are low), and three young men prowl about within the pit not unlike caged beasts, although they can climb out easily.

Its purpose soon becomes apparent as an older flamboyant gay approaches and halts near the railing while continuing to carry on in a raging queen voice to his more subdued friend:

"Well, Randy is just so out of control now you can't believe it, sweetie."

"Well, he's the guy you said just found out he's uh, *positive*, right?" the friend asks with some hesitation, lowering his voice at the word *"positive."*

"Puhleeze, that tramp knew he had it for months. He just didn't want to stop going bare with strangers. The problem – if you can believe it – is, the little slut still does."

"Wait a minute. How does he continue to… when he's positive?"

"Honey, he is just *out of control*. Completely. I said to him, like…"

He suddenly raises his hand to his friend as to offer a different take: "OK, he's with this guy, who's like, is just coming out. Like this john is still living at home with his wife,"

"Woah."

"I know, can you can believe it?

"Wait, *Randy* is…"

"No, puhleeze, quiet before you *hurt yourself*... Randy has a thing for guys who're coming out; y'know, like are in hetero wife-girlfriend type scenes but are finally realizing they're gay… so Randy likes scoping on these guys, picking them up… these guys who are like, not totally hip… if you know what I.."

"They're naïve."

".. so *trusting*. They think Randy cares for them… buys them drinks, insists on picking up the dinner bill, is just so in *love* with them."

On goes the raging queen: "So they're screwing around for a while, and Randy says to me:

"I told him, 'if you really *trust me*, you'd let me do you bare." I mean, he tells me this…"I just wanted to see if they really mean it when they say they trust me and they love me…," but then *I* said to him, *"bullshit'! cause then you go in bare*! And he says (raging queen laughing), *they shouldn't be having sex without protection*! (laughing loudly)… and screw those little whores they're with, too! I told him 'you are r-e-a-l-l-y b-a-d!' I tell him he's going to get killed, literally homo-cided by one of these guys someday…"

"Or their wives. I got two words for that: *in-sane*…" says the friend.

"…and he tells me this, and he's acting so cute when he says this; this is where he's kissing them off. After fucking them bare for a while, **he** calls **them** up: (mimicking the call) *'you two-timing bitch! You lied to me. I just went in for a test, and I'm positive! And I've only been with you! Only with you! I trusted you!'* And y'know what he told me?

"What?" Says the other guy, stupefied.

He says that while he was reading this poor shmuck the riot act, he's calling the guy *Richard, you betrayed me*, and on-and-on, and the guy says back in a weak voice, 'my name is Stuart', and the guy's wife in the background is going "Stu, Stu who is that?"

His friend is having a problem smiling through all of this, but is managing, albeit glumly.

"Man, how does he do that?"

"Well," the raging queen says, shrugging, "kind of like this." He moves up to the railing and the three men in the pit react as dogs about to be fed. Raging queen points to one, and, then curling the pointing index finger, beckons him over. The other two turn away, not without a little embarrassment in being rejected. The winner is a slim, fairly good looking blonde boy in his early twenties. His eyes say he's completely out of it.

The extroverted gay man whips off his towel, revealing an uncircumcised pudge of flesh enmeshed in pubic hair. His skinny rear end shows the unattractive signs of age as it sags and puckers in a way that makes you avert your eyes as soon as the light hits it.

The young man has walked up to the railing and his face aligns neatly at the other man's crotch. He pulls on the uncircumcised foreskin, licking off what the educated elite call "the cheese" that accumulates in the unwashed folds of the uncircumcised penis.

"That's a good puppy, now… lick it clean. Now take it in honey," the older man croons as the young boy starts to suck on the small penis while placing a few fingers on the staff while pumping it in place. In what seemed like less than a minute the older man started to gasp heavily as the boy, never letting up, began sucking and jerking him faster. The old man's hideous behind begins to tense into small muscles as people walking by stop to watch the climax. People stop talking and when a person would start to comment others would shush him, as the full moment of the ceremony might be lost .

"C'mon, take it bitch! Suck it off, honey! That's right!" the old man gasped it out as the young man gagged horribly and swallowed with an unpleasant look on his face. I suddenly had an urge to puke as I identified. One or two of the onlookers clapped, as the two bodies seemed to slump in such a strange way. It reminded me strangely of the anime "*Ghost in a Shell*" when a humanoid robot was disconnected from its power-supply. Through serving the spirit that had so animated them, they slumped lifelessly, as if the spiritual forces using them had vanished back into the dark caverns themselves.

The guy who had come continued to breathe hard with his face down, while his friend looked a little concerned, and in a voice too low for me to hear, asked him something. He nodded, and they walked off slowly. The boy also walked slowly to the rear of the pit, where there was no foot traffic, while the other two walking the pit looked up with a gleam in their eyes as if to say 'that's our advertisement; anyone interested in our service?'

I was not a drinker, and put my nausea down to the two ounces of vodka mixed with the 7-Up. My friend said he wanted to show me the place. To the left of the pit was a rising walkway that allowed you to look over what appeared as a series of booths below. Some were see-through plexiglass, and some were made out of thin wood. The "roof" or ceiling of the booths were removed so you could watch what took place down within them. These all had the "glory-hole" technology. That is, a hole a few inches in diameter was cut in the divider between the booths. One man could place his penis through the hole, while the other would service it orally. If the erection was sufficient, and the partners so inclined (with mutual heights permitting), sodomy could also ensue. Where the booths were made of wood, the individuals never saw each other at all.

You could stand above and watch it going on, while my guide told me the idea of being watched while giving head really turned him on. I really never could understand the purpose of the plexi-glass booths, however. Perhaps it was just the 'look but don't touch' factor that some enjoyed. In fact, in most of the sexual contact that I both witnessed and experienced in places like this or in the adult bookstore, a peculiar statement seemed to be made regarding such intimacy. For example, placing a penis in someone else's mouth was frequently done while exchanging names was *seldom* done. Often the man on his knees swallowing the other man's sperm was tentative in his efforts to touch the other man's behind or legs, similar in form to having heterosexual sex with a prostitute whom you can't kiss, as that kind of intimacy is reserved for someone she cares for. Hence the popularity of these 'glory-holes.' They were common fixtures in all the video booths in the adult bookstores throughout the country in the pre-AIDS era.

Cocksucking without communication, the jagged holes cut in the cheap paneling remain a silent testimony to the animal nature of the modern male. Perhaps it was just the pot mixed with alcohol, but I couldn't help but picture (once the law is changed) to allow animals, a scene in which you could back up a lamb to one side of the glory hole, and give new meaning to the phrase *"bringing in the sheep."*

We went to a large orgy-type room, which had various bed make-ups. There were bunk beds for twosomes, and large mattresses lashed together for many. I couldn't get into anything. I walked off by myself to a nice, quiet part of the place; secluded with tall plants and benches. I was smoking a joint, and a very nice looking, well dressed young man in his mid-twenties came over to me. I assumed he wanted some smoke, but when I offered, he demurred. He wanted me, and he was a genuine "find" in the overall sense that I was twice his age and he was young, fit and good looking.

I suddenly found that I had no energy within me to move the moment any further along. I had no desire at all. I realized fully at that moment that I had that same empty sense I had encountered some twenty years before in the sober video booth. I wished him well, leaving him with a surprised look on his face. I went looking for my friend in order to leave. In my search I came upon the S&M and B&D rooms, which for me were way too scary to even walk near, and avoiding eye contact, I gave that area a wide berth. Had I seen someone getting a fist shoved up his ass, I think I would've broken into a run.

I found my friend on his knees trying to do a man who was not getting hard.

The man appeared quite frustrated, and sounded as ugly as he looked.

"C'mon little doggie, lick it. Eat it, you little faggot! C'mon bitch, take it down, take it all way down… aahh," he spat the words out, whipping his large dick out of my friend's mouth, walking away without finishing.

My friend did not look like a happy camper. He suddenly looked much older than his forty-something years, and I could see why old homosexuals often choose the "heroic" stature of getting AIDS through dangerous, unprotected sex rather than living longer but frustrated. Being a heroic AIDS sufferer and being surrounded with people who will care for you doesn't sound too bad compared to a lonely life with an older body with kinkier needs that no one was interested in fulfilling. His usual smug self-assurance was nowhere to be seen, and he looked sad and pathetic.

"*Fuck that asshole,*" I told him in a strong voice. "*He's just a shmuck. You're better off he didn't come.*" I tried to assure him and we both chuckled a bit as I helped him up. He struggled unsteadily to his feet. We both knew, however, in words that we would never share, that in the dark world of cock-sucking, it was just this type of guy that would have given my friend great satisfaction were he to have unloaded.

"I've had enough," I said. Not ready to verbalize any further, I added "the booze has got me pretty headachy and a little nauseous."

"You've got to see this one room!" He gushes, suddenly excited. "Just this one, just go in it, and *feel the vibe* in there, it is *so* wild. You've never felt anything like it. I went in just for a little while myself. Just try it!"

Relieved that I wouldn't have to deal with any more emotional fallout from the pitiful scene he had just emerged from, I quickly agreed. Besides, this sounded so bizarre that it seemed easier to just go in and see what he was talking about rather than ask all the questions his words were raising.

The Dark Room

There's a heavy theatre curtain that you enter through on the left side, only to find it springing back into place behind you, leaving you facing another heavy curtain that you have to walk a few feet to the right side to pull back. There is a 5 watt blue bulb that allows you to see the arrow showing you where to pull the second curtain back, and when you enter the room the curtain springs back so you are in the deepest, inkiest darkness imaginable save for a 5 watt red bulb above the curtain entrance where you now stand. Two steps away from the bulb and you cannot see your hand in front of your face.

Immediately I became aware that I was in touch with something not of this world. To stay in this room demanded some unwritten rules; some quiet understandings: There's no place in consciousness for anything other than excitement giving way to silent communication between the giver and the taker, and within the fantasy which exists in the imaginations of each. An ethereal co-existence and communication within the spiritual handshake, the essence of the spirits being served are touched and called upon.

I could sense them here. What my naive gay friend had called 'a vibe' was a spiritual presence so powerful it was easily palpable. I'd lived with them before under the influence of LSD, and to a certain degree had flirted with their more lightweight cousins in that video booth years before. They were palpable here. The air was thick with their presence.

They traveled within and around and through the writhing mass of bodies, the low squeals, the savage gasps and the mournful cries of those who never thought it would hurt so much but are too imprisoned now in their ethereal submission to break and run. They had come in out of curiosity only to find that what starts as a finger in your bottom becomes now a fist up your ass going up to the elbow. You sense many of the men surrounding those thus tormented are turned on by their brothers' audible sufferings, and the moans, grunts, harsh whispers and pants rise and fall with the occasional cry of someone coming in a loud groan.

But what was more apparent, and more chillingly impressive was the riveting worship demanded by the spirit itself. It demanded your attention if you wanted to stay, and it demanded your servitude. A writhing, palpable sense of sexuality that no conscience could stand up to while physically remaining in the room held court with its overwhelming intensity and presence. It tempted me to prove its power.

I could sense that should I submerge myself into a fantasy (as it was tempting me to do), immediately someone would emerge from this shadowy ink-black writhing mass and come to me unspoken to fulfill it. A voice said *"aw, that couldn't happen."* Another voice said *"there's only one way to find out. Prove me, says the dark lord..."* Someone would find me out in the inky blackness for whatever specific purpose I imagined, and there would be no talking, no request line. The spirit in me that reflected the dark purpose would silently call out to another spirit inhabiting some body, and in this milieu my death would be discovered.

The Power of a Dark Room
There's no requests for condoms here
no light to see who's fucking you dear
Are you surprised they'll get AIDS for sure
you don't understand death's dark allure.

Yes, come and take my sweet death juice
It's just my lifestyle; don't be obtuse.
I'm just a girl who wound up with a penis
Sent here from Mars
When it should've been Venus.

It's just the female in me
G-d was wrong,
don't you agree?
I'm sure you know lots of women
Doin' strange men just for semen.
No need to get to know'm
'da girl in me just wants to blow'm.
Is that what makes me female?
A sudden slave for a male,
'n a piece of tail?
Not even caring to know his name
Just happy to swallow
'n so glad you came?

I had all I could do not to cry out as I quickened my gasping escape through the curtains. I could sense a dark presence inches from my shoulder as I turned to flee. I was like a kid running home from a fright on Halloween night as I emerged into the sperm-scented air of the bathhouse, and seeing my friend, said *"I've had enough."*

Escaping into the Hollywood night, I breathed deep; happy I hadn't had sex. It was approaching midnight, and the line of men waiting to get in was over a block long. I felt like I had just been sprung from jail.

Even though as a "meditator," I'm not supposed to get lost in thought, it was almost impossible not to do so for a large portion of the time. As my marijuana use decreased, the depth of my meditation increased, and a strange thing happened. At that time, I was smoking a pack a day of cigarettes. After a few weeks of meditating, I was still listening to his tape on meditation, not having yet graduated to doing it on my own, and I had one cigarette left in my box of Marlboros, and immediately thought *'I better go down to the 7-11 and get a pack,'* when a deeper, more unspoken message radiated up in me: *'what do I want that for?'*

I was immediately re-united with a vision I had had in the late 60's coming off an acid trip. It was a hallucinatory/spiritual representation which showed the bits and pieces of vegetable refuse in the New York gutter often found near fruit and vegetable stores after they spray off the sidewalk. In the vision I took a piece of old newspaper and swept the bits of vegetative garbage into the newspaper, wrapped it into a funnel and lit the giant stogie on fire, with my mouth and nose leaning close to it to breathe in the smoke. It was the spiritual representation of smoking tobacco.

Now, thirty years later, the *impression*, with an *unsounded voice* added to it – which had clearly inferred, "w*hat do I need this for?*" had kicked up that old image into my consciousness. I suddenly felt brave and free, and not a little bit daring. For added panache, I decided to refuse the one left in the pack as well, turning on the faucet and running water into the box to ruin the last stick. I burned my bridge and crossed the Rubicon. I never went back.

Being more than a little familiar with addiction, and having quit cigarettes eight years before that after a three-pack-a-day habit spanning twenty years, I was amazed at the power of the meditation to make the temptation to smoke nothing but a small discomfort. The ability to see the temptation ("*the need for a smoke*") as a need to "*escape the current thought*" allowed the meditation to kind of "*zap*" the craving. I could see the urge for a cigarette and with the meditation be aware of the emotional element demanding smoke in order to override my consciousness, demanding it (my consciousness) be shielded from the awareness of whatever it was that was within me prompting the '*need for a smoke.*' I saw it was a lie, this '*need to escape-with-nicotine.*' I became aware in a more fully realized way that I did not have to give in to it. I was pleased and satisfied to be a '*clean-air breather.*' I was very fortified with the sense of this success. It was an independent success. I was becoming free of the oppressive crutch of the nicotine, and I had surmounted the challenge in an independent, manner. Nobody else in my life even knew I was doing this. This was no ego/head trip. This was a very real accomplishment as I knew better than anyone my weakness to addiction. This inner weakness to *give-in* had crippled me my entire life. Here it was just slipping away almost effortlessly. I had taken the demon of nicotine and bitch-slapped it. No patches, shrinks, groups, programs, books, chants or sayings. Just this meditation. And I wasn't 'puffing up.' There had never been anything quite like this before. I was becoming **self-motivated**.

Within this new dimension in my life, the observation-meditation itself became "deeper." When the hand approached my forehead, and I tried to concentrate on it, judging the distance from the center of my forehead, I began to see an image in my mind's eye of the hand emerging *through* my head, not just *to* my head. As I concentrated with ever lessening effort, the 'concentration' itself became a soulish commitment, not an act full of effort. The hand actually becomes the head in a certain inexplicable way. I had also learned that by opening one's eyes occasionally during the meditation, I could quickly see that my mind's eye "image" of the hand was far from where it was actually, and these differences were made aware to me in almost inexplicable ways. Images – SCARY images – made themselves known, but after a while I intuited a great truth: they're scariest as they are leaving – or losing – their vitality. Ergo, the spirit of fear that you are dealing with at various levels will always seem most fearful when its power is being diminished or disintegrated.

Holy Ectoplasm, Batman!

It was not long after the *battle for Nicotine* was concluded that an experience I can only describe as *inexplicable* occurred. I was meditating in my bedroom and was at a point where I was able to sense that "stillness" that is a result of a sincere (and oftentimes frightening) effort at awareness, when I began to smell this rather bad odor coming from somewhere close by. It was as if a cigarette filter was smoldering in an ashtray, but it was not exactly that odor. I was concerned for fire, and after sniffing myself all over, spent several minutes looking under the bed, in closets, etc. for the source of this offensive smell.

In truth, I received a 'sense' of what it was at the time, but figured that was *too far out* and then forgot about it as the smell simply disappeared. Years later I was listening to a tape of Roy Masters with a group at the FHU (his *Foundation of Human Understanding*) ranch in Oregon when somebody in the audience asked a question concerning this same phenomenon. It is very common, he said. Many of the people in his audience there at the time also acknowledged experiencing it.

What can I say? It happened. It does happen. It could happen to you, too. I wouldn't have believed it either, and at any other time in my life would have led the charge as the captain of the skepticism team regarding this very phenomenon, so I won't say any more about it except this: in the words of Russell Crowe's *Master and Commander*, "*not everything is written in books.*"

Tim Leary Revisited

I had heard that Tim Leary was going to be at the Electronic Café in Santa Monica. I had been helping someone with their computer needs, and it turned out they were friends with someone who was helping Leary as a kind of personal assistant. He was in declining health and needed someone around all the time. I had read the *The Psychedelic Experience* – based on *Tibetan Book of the Dead* on numerous occasions beginning in the sixties, and although Ram Dass (Dr. Richard Alpert) and Dr. Ralph Metzner were also listed as authors, Leary's name was the one most associated with the book, which I felt represented a major effort at helping people get the most 'spiritual experience' possible from a psychedelic drug. Ram Dass had gone on to write "*Be Here Now*," which was fascinating in its own right, and Dr. Metzner continued to be a force in spiritual discovery as an author within the world of chemicals and ethno-biologic compounds.

I had unwittingly associated the glorious experience of LSD heights with Leary in a very subjective personal way[28], and thus had unconsciously put him on a pedestal of astral-plane proportions. My original shrink had practically introduced me to him, and when I entered a state of ego-loss I had "assumed" this was somewhat synonymous with Leary's state, which was an absurd proposition. Consequently, I greeted the feedback I was now receiving from my 'mole' concerning my hero with some concern. While I imagined a mellow, transcendental spiritual guide, I was being made aware of the fact that Leary wouldn't even speak to someone unless they plunked down eight thousand dollars for the privilege. I was also the recipient of insider doings on just how intensely impatient, vain and egotistical he was.

Leary had been featured in a national news magazine after going into a classroom somewhere in the US and speaking with a "*Cee-You-Cee-Me*" digital camera with a computer link-up to a classroom in Japan.

While this technology *was relatively new*, it was not regarded as all that fantastic by true geeks in cutting-edge computer technology. But because Leary had done it, the spin in the magazine was that *he* was the pacesetter of this 'new' technology. What was disappointing to me was that this was a role that Tim appeared to relish rather than correct, and he spoke as if he indeed was the pioneer who would bring off these unique global communications. Where was the true humility we were all encouraged to seek? It struck me that night that the *Tibetan Book of the Dead* featured authorship by him in bold print, with the names of co-authors Alpert and Metzner in smaller plain text as secondary authors. That this might also be a tweaking of the genuine contributions of the latter participants to that effort began to appear a genuine possibility.

The note being struck tonight was that Leary would be speaking through this astounding new medium again. This time he was to be in contact with some people up in San Francisco at the MacWorld Computer convention. Having been a Mac owner since 1986 and a part-time Tech

---

[28] In Sullivanian terminology, a "*parataxic distortion.*" If you were raped as a child by someone with a red beard, you will have some type of "*parataxic distortion*" (even as an adult) upon meeting people with red beards. Leary was similarly akin to the 'height of the expanded-consciousness'-experience' itself in my mind. More than priest and shaman, he was unconsciously assumed to be more than merely human.

school instructor in Electronic Publishing, I knew what he was doing but was unsure why, but that didn't stop the stars from coming out.

I got down to the Electronic Café early, with a half-ounce of some excellent seedless I had picked up from Humboldt County contacts. The Electronic Café had mounted several extra computer screens to be viewed by all the people seated on temporary fold-out chairs placed for that purpose. I located Tim, introduced myself as an old tripper from the East Village, took a picture or two and offered a smoke. He was tense and didn't look good. A film crew from one of the national media outlets was there. Two pretty, hard-looking, hard-driving gals from a media outfit were going over notes with a cameraman, tensely detailing instructions, directions and all the things that they were hoping would help make their story a success.

Limos arrived, delivering all kinds of people, including some who wanted to put AA on the internet, and also Brett Leonard showed up, the director of *Lawnmower Man*, which still (in my humble opinion) boasted some of the greatest quasi-psychedelic effects. When we smoked some dope, I wondered briefly if whatever Leary had could be contagious over the pipe we shared, but I quickly forgot about that as I watched the old man totally transform before my eyes. The hottie from the magazine came over to coo and (kind of) pat him on the head, reminding him of something on the schedule of events. His eyes glazed over from her sudden and temporary warm smile. He was instantly and completely twitterpated (see Disney's *Bambi*).

What was neglected in all the tumult, info technology and self-inflation was the understanding that one-hand clapping does not a story make. As the Standing-Room-Only crowd here in Santa Monica glued their eyes to the multiple telescreens, with Leary standing on the stage ready to pontificate his vision of this new world, the cameras and computers started to roll. Only there was nobody around in San Francisco.

For Leary, it was a meltdown at his media showdown. The spirit of corporate greed and material egotism that he had once insisted the 'new expanded consciousness' would replace, had now come full-circle to bite him in the ass. He himself now became a victim of the same hypocrisy he once said the psychedelic adventure would put a stop to. He just crumbled muttering before my eyes, physically dying a short time later.

TIM LEARY IS DEAD; YES, YES, YES
He brought that karmic death
upon himself
in full view of all of us that day,
although it was evening really
at the cybernet cafe.

All Santa Monica did arrive that night
the limos, they were white
newsweek gals and info-babes
a camera with a mike.

Oh Tim, they cooed
as we did smoke
and i don't mean a 'rette
Oh Tim Oh Tim
you're looking good
just be like that and set.

They cooed to this new money- man
for it was true they say
you couldn't get near to old tim's ear
without that eight thousand to pay.

And the young
the tough
and the restless
their lights and mike in tow
came to almost stroke his hair
and got his soul's control.

She allowed the old man a moment
- a warm vibe to be precise -
to re-live what it's like to matter
to a woman as hot as ice.
That flow of her body exotic
worked well as the intoxicotic
but then it was gone
but in that sweet song
the sugar accomplished its narcotic.

His head 'n neck crooned up off the ground
as the cat does in cartoon
when its master comes by
with godlike sigh
and puts the stroke on you.

It was said a kidney ailment
was indeed his inner assailant
but a look at the torment apparent
said the A-train was running the gamut.

The camera's now on
the audience is keyed
Hollwood's new age
looks on eagerly.
It's the digital future
we'll line up to score
it's a tim leary special
its gotta be more -
for the masses…
seated asses..
for the many
that be in store.

The macworld expo up in north francisco
will video-communicate you see;
This is important to all it must be;
Obviously, so obviously…
well… it's history and too much for me
to commune to someone this late
either you're hip to the scene
or you ain't.

the macworld expo up in north francisco
will video-communicate you see.
to us in santa monica
to the king of LSD.
To what end this effort be
to what end this magic account
charming the stoned elite to alight
to this place to this time
to this point here tonight?

*"Yes, crooned the owner
of the Electronic Cafe
it is us, and guess who we
have in the way?"*

"What say you? Who are you? Say what?"
came reply.
*"It is "I" the Electronic Cafe we did say!
We have Tim Leary waiting in the way!*

*"It's the cyber cafe in old Santa Monica
Is someone there
to accept our sweet moniker?"*

There appeared on our screens at that moment
to a crowd all straining to see
a new voice and one who would tell us
where our *who's-in-charge* would be.
A visage of red skin and pimples
did appear was all we could see.
"What say you? Who are you? Say what?"
he did say,
and squirming as one
we did all in dismay.

The people in San Fran had dropped the ball
had not shown up - *no* - for the call.
As the MC was spinning he tried to keep winning
the brains of the nerds at this port o call

*"It's the cyber cafe in Santa Monica!
We have here a name known to any commoner
Yes, you must know it's true
seeing you're hip like you do
and i've the guru right here for you too!"*

And all the nerd would say was *"WHO?"*

The audience all shocked unbelieving
the MC's brains were a'silent 'n screaming.
Old Tim stood there standing
not gloating
for the worst had arrived...
he wasn't floating.

"Yes i've heard his name"
came the tech's reply
but you're in my server:
"c-u-cee-me-live."

*"I guess u wanted some other
but to my tasks now
I must take some bother.
I guess who you wanted isn't here
maybe he missed your schedule there.
Sorry to leave you so short of fine,
but i guess we'll see you some other time."*

Tim stood there silently shrieking
his soul enmeshed in his weeping
he knew not at all what to say
his visage was oh-so-Dorian Grey.
Where was the flow
that Tim must've know'd
is the key to survive
for every good soul?

Lost in the maya
now into its fusion
old Tim just stood there
in freeze-frame delusion

The old guru had lost his touch
(perhaps he never had it, Dutch)
He glowed and gloated when he could
but had he ever really understood?

If you think your thoughts are you dear
Pride will really screw you here.
Now you're alive but on fire
With pride tormenting your pyre.

Laughter's good medicine
and priced at a pittance
But pride's cost you its inheritance.
Clint Eastwood its said
gave a wise piece of bread
with which Tim did not choose to be fed:
'Keep the work on the highest most serious
yet of yourself be not so imperious'
were words wise and true
but Tim chose not to
live by them
soon dieing
un-mysterious.

Chapter 18 – A Pornographic Epiphany
Reintegration in Las Vegas

Most of the jobs I got fired from were while working for printing companies in the field of pre-press in what was known as electronic publishing. This entailed photo retouching and taking files from ad agencies, corporations, artists and the like and getting these files ready for actual printing off of the huge presses inside the plant. I knew the field very well, and had taught the technology on a part-time basis in the evenings to adult ed. students. I just couldn't work long without being fired. I was still too psychotic to do a good job on a consistent basis for any length of time. My need for approval and 'love' made me so anxious that although I mentally understood all the technological procedures, my emotions always sabotaged my efforts.

I gave great interview, however, and was able to cover my tracks well enough to land yet another job with an outfit that printed a great deal of pornography. Mainly the video box covers that the VHS / DVD porn tapes would slide into.

I met a guy who had the right computer equipment and had an actual customer who needed his video box designed and laid out, and wanted to do it cheaper than having the printing place do it. The guy who had the equipment had tried, but didn't know the ropes from a technological point of view, so after getting fired yet again, I looked him up and we became partners.

After actually completing a project for this one customer, I was shocked to actually get paid quite handsomely for what had amounted to a couple of days work. My partner and I soon had a falling out and I ordered some better equipment for myself, found places that would let me use their more expensive, specialized equipment for cheap if I needed to, and decided to go out on my own. By this time two of my kids were living with me, and my ex-wife had remarried.

My two youngest children were still living with her and I had had a very emotional phone call with my boys regarding our estrangement. I called every Sunday, but found that one can't have meaningful phone conversations every time you dial, and although both kids were always respectful and loving, their attention was really more on the new Simpson's episode on TV than on re-hashing an uneventful week with a far-away father after the usual *"I'm-fine, school's-OK, how-are-you?* talk. Then it's, *"I guess I'll talk to you next week. I-love-you-son; I-love-you-dad."* Click.

The CES (Computer & Electronics Show) in Las Vegas is one of the biggest electronics and computer events of the year, and strange as it may sound, the porn industry has its own presence at the show. It went by the name of the AVN (Adult Video News) Expo. It is, of course, given its own pavilion, a separate hotel in Vegas where in the convention center of that hotel all the main porno production houses have their booths. Many were quite flamboyant affairs, as the boon in porn had made multimillionaires out of people who just a few years before had been merely pimps with cameras trying to keep one step ahead of the vice squad. I had learned that many had made huge fortunes, as their profit-margin was enormous. Girls in Eastern Europe would do everything that was asked all day long for $20. Even most of the top girls in the US were only paid $500 a film.

I drove to Las Vegas from LA with a briefcase full of my newly printed business cards, flyers, prices and catchy slogans. The porn business was centered in a small community of production companies centrally located in the San Fernando Valley and a few other parts of LA. Now that I had done a few video box covers and proven my credibility, I could continue to get business by undercutting the normal pricing as I had no overhead compared to the normal printing companies. I could do the layout (with electronic publishing software) and all that was necessary on my computer working off my dining room table.

I paid my $50 entrance fee and began to make the rounds. Since being able to save money is high on everyone's list, I immediately began racking up appointments to meet back in LA. I was riding high after a few hours and began to believe I had really found a niche.

It's hard not to think about sex on a personal level when you're surrounded by so much advertising on the subject, and I noticed that almost without exception, the girls (representing the vendors they were under contract with) had 'doll's eyes,' that is, blank, unfeeling orbs which pretended to smile as their faces creased in the reflexive activity normally associated with such activity.

After having touched base with everybody, I was preparing to leave for LA when I struck up a conversation with a porn vendor from New York. As a fellow Brooklynite, we bonded over the 'good old neighborhoods' and, finally feeling comfortable enough to broach a possibly sensitive subject, I asked him what general rules there were regarding getting together with one of these girls. Since most were being paid only $500 to screw a few different guys five different ways, I wondered what they might charge for a relatively tame encounter with someone like myself.

He said getting together with a porn actress depended on the girls' relationship with the vendor. If she was under contract to one house, you might have to ask the production house people. When I mentioned that the girls looked so burned out, he nodded in agreement, saying his house had a girl that was new. "*She's still fresh,*" he added.

A few minutes later, as I'm preparing to say goodbye to my Brooklyn friend and leave the hotel for the drive back to LA, a pretty girl in her early twenties comes walking out from between some curtains behind his booth, and he turns to me saying:

"*...and here she is! We were just talking about you,*" he says to her with a smile, and she comes over to receive a kiss on the cheek while he puts an arm around her waist. He proceeds to introduce me to this surprisingly pretty girl, who along with her impressive young figure was able to do something none of the other girls I saw there could: *actually smile with her eyes*. They danced attractively with a touch of mischief and amusement. I was instantly struck, and strangely horrified to see the definition of "*still fresh*" playing out before my eyes.

As I drove back to LA, I mentally started to calculate how much money I could start making within a relatively short period of time. I imagined having enough money to have squired off with that very attractive New York girl. I thought of the young New York girl becoming available through a Los Angeles version of herself. As I imagined hooking up with a carefree female replete with mischievous sex, I started to get extremely depressed. I was about an hour out of Vegas when I pulled off into a Rest Stop. I was being filled with a strange melancholy. I lit a joint and sat atop a picnic table to watch the sun set.

I tried to think of the success I had coming as a result of my trip down here, and immediately thought of my two kids living with my ex-wife and her new husband a thousand miles away. I realized I would not be able to make my Sunday evening phone call in time tonight. It was equally depressing to realize that my kids probably wouldn't notice much difference if I called tomorrow, and by attrition would one day not notice if weeks went by. I was not only losing my family, but the more success I achieved here in Los Angeles, the more I would be bonded into staying in this place.

That brought back to mind the porn queens and having sex (which I hadn't had in quite a while) with someone like the New York girl, and suddenly I had this picture in my head along with silent, ungrammatical wording running along with it: "*Yeah, you can pay to rub your old body against hers and help her eyes to become as dead as the others...*"

I suddenly found myself leading an inner revolution, muttering, "*fuck this shit*" out loud. Looking at those cold desert mountains fading into the ugly Nevada sunset, I suddenly got a glimpse of my own mortality. Where did that come from? How insignificant my one death would be here amongst the wilderness surrounding me. Nature itself would remain as unmoved and immutable concerning my death as it would by a leaf blowing off a tree.

I found myself realizing, in a way for the first time: "*I can say NO to these temptations. It's OK to be good. It's OK to do the right thing.*" Suddenly willing – and apparently able – to follow this totally new path, I realized what I was going to do. I would find a job out where my kids lived with my ex-wife and move there with my two sons who were now living with me. An adventure was in the process of being launched without destructive and/or sexual elements involved.

I was reintegrating my improved ability to deal with people successfully with a new ability to deal with life successfully.[29] Oh my G-d. It sounds like Jesus. I don't think of it with that noun. I am no longer religious. If I was to label my new "sense" at all, it would probably be with words like "hope" and/or "faith." The drive back to LA went much better.

* * *

Within the month I went out to Carvel, Pennsylvania to find a job. I met my ex-wife's new husband. After hugging and kissing my kids, I kicked back and watched my ex-wife browbeat her new husband in much the same impatient, belittling manner that I had experienced so often. I began to smile. I got a motel room, and within three days landed a decent paying job from the three interviews I had set-up long distance weeks before.

---

[29] "*In general, important aspects of personality existing in dissociation are not reintegrated except under extremely fortunate circumstances. One of these fortunate circumstances is when the need for intimacy can lead to very considerable improvement of the partition of energy between the not-me component and the other components of the personality. And at the same time this newly integrating tendency is being called out by maturation, certain eventualities are likely to occur which may have favorable influence in reintegrating a dissociated tendency system. Interpersonal Theory of Psychiatry* (HS Sullivan) pp322

I drove back to LA to collect my kids, pack up a few belongings, and moved back. Now that I could be close to all the kids and they can be close to each other, I felt burdens I didn't even know I had start to lift off my shoulders. For the first time, quiet excitement was running in a high-spirited romp without something shameful waiting at the finish line. I was getting deeper into the meditation and starting to listen to this guy Roy Masters on other related subjects at www.fhu.com.

Returning to my two previously estranged sons with their other brothers in tow was pretty cool, and being able to get an apartment in the same complex where my ex was living was also a coup. I was able to institute a modicum of respect with heart-to-heart talks with my young ones: telling them I left them once, but I never would again.

Having managed to get some credit, I borrowed $4000 to help my ex-wife leave her new partner, who was turning into something rather unattractive. They had purchased a house together and the $4,000 was to buy him out of his share of the house. This would also allow her to call that suburban home they had purchased her own. I paid for her lawyer.

One day my youngest son mentioned that in his class at school the subject of "heroes and role models" had arisen. He said simply that for him there was no debate: it was his dad. Twenty-five years after leaving the hospital, the worm was definitely starting to turn.

A Hero Goes Swimming

I had been meditating regularly during all this, and found myself in the unusual situation of being propositioned by my ex-wife's girlfriend. This middle aged lady, not unattractive and certainly not shy, was one of those people that my wife called "a friend," but who was only too happy to take verbal potshots at my ex while trying to fuck every male that came in the vicinity, including, it was rumored, my ex-wife's new husband. As things became clearer to me what she wanted, I said I didn't think that would be fair to my ex, showing up from out of town and then sleeping with her friend. She responded "Then I guess we'll have to sneak around." I demurred. Although I spent more than a few lonely moments alone in bed at night kicking myself, I not only *knew* I did the right thing, but *I was pleased with myself for doing the right thing*. I was not even puffed up about it, although I saw in meditation that I was tempted to be.

Except for some occasional marijuana use, I was, for the first time in twenty-five years, out of the hospital, out of drugs and out of religion. I didn't feel I was out of G-d, though. The inexplicable results I was receiving from the meditation tapes along with a very 'hands-off' type of guidance from Roy Masters was bringing me into a spiritual walk totally devoid of religion. It was filling that tremendous gap I observed between spiritual heights and everyday reality, and it was filling that unmentioned emptiness in religion that intimates that belief in the Messiah is good insurance for when you die, but as for the here and now a good psychologist can better help you understand what was happening between your ears. I never could get totally behind that way of thinking, although up until now I had no alternative. Basically religion ceded the area of psychological understanding (read: *'everyday life'*) to secular reasoning, with the afterlife heavily tilted in favor of what is commonly called 'faith." I found that religion, in its blindness, was ceding the very battleground salvation is built on.

In reality, such faith (in oneself) is universal, in that we all think, "well, I'll see G-d, and he'll see I'm *basically* a good person." Everyone, deep down, can hear a voice telling them *'I'm a good person.'* Hitler and Stalin also heard that voice. The suicide-bomber too. You're not believing in G-d when you believe that, you're really just believing in yourself and its intellectual ability to define some dogma you attach the concept of "faith" to. This is the same "self" Adam chose in the garden.

Yes, one could pay lip service in religion's defense that we are encouraged by Judeo-Christianity to 'be good people,' and to follow one's conscience. We are even exhorted, for example, to study the bible to counter the more obvious temptations toward the sins of everyday life.

However, the repressed urge to hate one's parent(s) or other family members, that idiot driver on the freeway, your boss or spouse; your inability to stop behavior that your conscience reacts against vigorously; the pride, anger, covetousness, envy, gluttony, sexual lust, drugs, alcohol and the myriad temptations of injustice within both the personal microcosm and the global macrocosm of our society overwhelms religion's pithy sayings as a flood does a sandbox.

I had been functioning as a plastic-person; robotically in tune to speak and react from a database of acceptable responses. *Hi how'r you*? *I'm fine*; comment *weather*, how bout those (name of) *sports team*? Acceptable indignation and resignation towards politics, self-deprecating humor towards finances and social life, smile and easy-going-guy-it for all things threatening. Inside my skull, however, the psychotic persecutory thinking process still reacted energetically, although the immediate connection to my vocal chords had been cut.

I had found small periods of stillness during the meditation exercise. Light waves of awareness were battering dark castles of twisted fearful egotism. They were melting psychological complexes built on psychotic anxiety-creating mechanisms. In the security operations of my dark side, it was as if spirits in dark caverns were running around in a panic, always trying to get me **not** to meditate. It was as if meditation produced a giant spaceship with a million lux lighting system that was about to shine down on them, and the light spelled doom the way sunlight takes the stink out of manure. I saw the same thoughts, but in not reacting to them, the emotional components started to separate and the psychological complexes disintegrate. But as Roy said on one of his tapes, "*Your thoughts don't give you up easily.*"

Indeed. They were doing everything to stop that light from going off and then, after more tries at the meditation from an understanding that it was only me and spirit within me; that progress was based on a true faith of forgiveness and being forgiven, that then faith in the risen messiah began to grow. I was able to give of myself totally for a split-second – all while sitting still in a chair in my room alone. In a deeper and more courageous way, I was able to get out of my own way, silence my chattering ego by simply being aware of its noise without comment or reaction, without agreement or disagreement to its shrill reasonings or subtle insinuations, and for the briefest of moments, I could understand what the Hebrew messiah meant when He said *"of myself I can do nothing; it is the Father in me, he does the work."*

I was out of my ego-self-consciousness for maybe half-a-second, the pure light of awareness struck through my darkness, and my life continued to change dramatically. I experienced what would be the first of many energies momentarily contorting my facial features as they dissipated out of me. This first one was slight but the follow-ups rather dramatic.[30] I understood the parable of the prodigal son more keenly than I ever had. I could sense as I battled to be effortless within the stillness that there were forces trying to keep me from achieving that objective state, and that the Lord was seeing me coming, I was still yet some distance from Him, but the blessings were already being poured out.

I could begin to sense something that would grow more and more in my understanding concerning the mechanism of the meditation. I had seen on several occasions back in the LSD/DOM madness when I slipped into my pre-hospital psychosis that energies relevant to my personal ego nature 'projected" out of my skull, out of my forehead. I began to sense that these energies were literally my ***projections*** onto people and reality in general. I had began to grow vegetables as a hobby, and I realized how tense I would become verbalizing anything to them, imagining how critical they were of me, and the epiphany lit me up that if I am scared of my plants, imagine how much fear (Sullivan's parataxic distortions) I'm projecting all over people before they even say or do anything!

Now, when I brought my hand towards the forehead, these forces were made vulnerable to this still, conscious awareness, and the light of this awareness began to break the power of these projections, and literally expand my consciousness. It's like one 'takes over' that territory that was once lost to the unconsciousness projection. I can state in faith that this is especially true if the light of awareness has found forgiveness for its own dark nature in the special miracle only the true seeker finds, often in the quiet and lonely space meditators know about. A place of tears from deep within but only between you and Him.

I believe Dr, Jung was correct to call 'projections' the 'shadow dark side' which seeks to stay hidden, but after forty years of wandering, I was finding a light to shine into this darkness. What was most wonderful about this, was while I was using Roy Masters as a guide, it was *my* meditation, *my* light, *my* darkness, *my* salvation. I wasn't following another human

---

[30] *Video of "exorcism" of the author through advanced meditation available on www.trailopen.com*

being. I was using his guidance to be able to follow this growing spirit within myself.

In a daring follow-up maneuver, I stuck the meditation tape into a small portable tape player with headphones, and set off in my bathing suit for the apartment house swimming pool, armed only with a bath towel and a bottle of water. I hadn't done anything this social in years.

I entered a different world. **I was instantly being made aware that thoughts were trying to assume that anxiety-filled persecutory state** in which the words between a mother and her small son seated near the pool were meant to have something to do with me. A part of me I hadn't known since 1969 just looked at that proposition as a grown man might a yapping puppy. As I just WATCHED THE THOUGHTS they did not become my identity. Kind of like *"get out of here, they're not relating about me, or in any way that concerns me."* I glimpsed something that I had been blind to before: that all my assumptions – *those thoughts I reacted to* – and by reacting to them, gave them credibility and a part of "me," were *purely persecutory* in nature. In other words, the assumption that people were saying things that related to things in my head was in and of itself persecutory by definition. While it doesn't take a genius to say *"duh"* here, for some reason I had always been blind to this most obvious fact. You could say, if you were in a Sullivanian state of mind, that I had been "selectively inattending" to this. More simply put, "nuts."

For the first time in twenty-five years I began to separate mentally from the world around me. I then placed the headphones on and as I listened. I both luxuriated in – and experienced some fear – by my separateness, and for the first time since my breakdown I dared to allow thought processes freedom to roam upwards out of pre-consciousness uninhibited by a fearful reaction which I would EMBRACE (we always embrace that which corrupts us).

As I lay on the lounge chair by the pool, I smiled as thought processes dared to come to consciousness as timid children who – having been in hiding – were now coming out into sunlight. Looking at an obese woman walking by me, thought springs up in my mind unchallenged: *'Look at this fat chick wearing a bathing suit like that. I guess you don't give a shit. You're cool, or maybe you're an asshole. I can be aware of either; never knowing, that being aware of this choice of 'good-cop'-bad-cop' without choosing means I can think anything I want without anxiety! Decent and indecent, courageous or cowardly, I just wanted to be able to think these things without imagining the world reacting to me and my thoughts. Hee hee hee. This is great!'*

This ability to recognize as my own thoughts what previously were reacted to as unacceptable "*not-me*" components of fear or anger was now the benefit of an expanded consciousness that "reintegrated" conscious critical observations of others into my own "self." I was able to be aware of thought without reacting to the thought. Merely observing it. By doing so a great amount of delusion disintegrated further. My "*self*" was not growing because of the quality of my thoughts concerning "*the other*," but by my willingness to be aware of thought without reacting to it. Critical thinking concerning someone's interaction with their child merged with hearing "my own" lust-filled monologue in-my-head concerning the attraction of teen age buttocks in a bikini. Yes, I realized, it was possible to actually look at jail-bait, think frank jail-bait thoughts, and still be just as human as I was before the unreal excursion into sexual dalliance.

If I believe that in a bit of overheard conversation, for example, between a child and her mother saying: "*You should try to stay warmer*," I see the initial reference process seeking my own situation vis-à-vis my body temperature, but then is compounded by autochthonous and autistic impression that she is referring to my attitude which needs to "thaw out."

Are these part of the "early reference processes" of which Sullivan speaks when he refers to processes "*most of us have left behind when we were three years old?*" This is the infant reaching his arms up to the full moon in an effort to touch the luminous orb. He is in the process of absorbing the differences between 'inner' and 'outer.'[31] I saw that contrary to my fears that being aware of antagonistic or sexual thoughts would make them stronger and myself more conducive to obsession, it was the exact opposite that was the case. It was as if I could look at some inane, emotional reasoning, and it would fly out of my mind after stepping back to allow the light of awareness to shine on it. Overcome with victory-day energies, I decided to throw inhibitions to the wind and dive into the pool. Diving with great energy off the short side I careened fairly rapidly underwater with my arms stuck limply in front of me enjoying the cool rush of the invigorating water right up into the other side of the pool, which I struck mightily with my head. Not missing a beat, I jumped out of

---

[31] "*Apparently, if one is sufficiently uncertain about life, one loses the cognitive assets which serve us in DISTINGUISHING PRODUCTS OF AUTISTIC OR PURELY SUBJECTIVE REVERIE FROM PRODUCTS WHICH INCLUDE IMPORTANT FACTORS RESIDING IN SO-CALLED EXTERNAL REALITY; and when one has lost this ability to distinguish between such reveries and such objects having more external points of reference, one begins to sink into mental processes significantly like those we experience when we are asleep.*"
Schizophrenia as a Human Process, Sullivan. pp221; (Norton, New York)

the pool hoping I wasn't bleeding. I managed to walk back to my chair, even more inspired to see that although I was embarrassed, I was aware of thoughts cascading around me concerning what a fool I had just made of myself. I was able to shrug it off.

I wasn't humiliated into believing the situation to be any more of a major calamity than it actually was. I congratulated myself on my ability to take the pain, and reminded myself that while I used to be a powerful diver, I was now stronger in a new and different way. I didn't have to be perfect, and by indwelling such an understanding, I had a subtle sense that perhaps I no longer had to fixate on the imperfections of others. I began to sense that if I needed to speak to someone, I had all I needed right between my ears. In beginning to accept others, I began to respect myself.

I sat back down in the lounge chair. After starting to get into the meditation experience simply by closing my eyes, I was inundated by scary images. Being aware of them was enough to dispel their reality, but that ushered in additional frightening new realities. If I was suddenly "apart" from these people, that is, not vulnerable to their perceptions regarding what I was thinking and seeing in my mind's eye, then it was equally true that this newly realized separateness carried with it a sense of "aloneness" that was likewise difficult to totally accept in one sitting. It was scary.

I was peeling off layers of the onion rather than throwing a toggle switch. This was the beginning of spirituality through faith, not religion; seeing the spirit delivering me out of the murkiness of sin, delusion, fear and obsession in the most personal of ways. If it was going to work at all, I had to get out of the way. To be most productive, I had to stop trying. In fact, it was impossible for it to work – for me to make progress – if the "*I*" of my ego was involved. I would be my forsaking over-controlling-ego for spirit. I was learning, but oh, so very slowly.

Four Years Before The Mast

For the next four years I labored to make the American dream my reality, only to find a growing impression – reinforced with imaginative imagery every working morning – that I was entering a prison. I had never worked so long anywhere; before or after leaving the hospital, and much to my surprise, found that even working six-hundred hours overtime one year did little to change my circumstances.

I found myself just walking away from my desk quite a bit, ostensibly on my way to the candy machine, but in reality just walking away from my work. This became so obvious that management was soon asking me to stay at my desk more often.

My life became full of a dreariness punctuated by the anxiety of shrill management with whom I still psychotically tried to endear myself. Looking for love in all the wrong places, I craved approval and escaped into office intrigues, filling my waking hours with anxiety and disappointment. I began to fantasize myself as a hero in the workplace, but also dream of putting some of my cutting edge multimedia ideas into a reality that would take me far away from the nine-to-five life. I found more and more my paycheck resembled the old lie inherent in the strip joint and the pornographic magazine: Looks like sex. Sounds like sex. It ain't sex. It looked like a lot of money, and it seemed like a lot of money, but it wasn't a lot of money.

There would be no trips to Disneyworld for me and the kids, no fishing boat to tow behind a non-existent SUV. What I saw was a future of nickel-and-diming, which would in and of itself present not so terrible a circumstance were it not for the mind-numbing fatigue that followed me home after work. Creative ideas seemed to bubble to the surface of my mind effortlessly. My fatigue, however, was so complete that I couldn't begin to create any of the home-business projects that danced imaginatively through my head. I often found myself overcome with exhaustion and trying to nap sitting on the toilet seat in the workplace bathroom.

I had become something of a hero to buy out my ex-wife's no-goodnik second husband, thereby giving her 100% legal ownership of a pleasant little house in the suburbs after her divorce. I even paid for her divorce lawyer.

I was welcomed back into her bed. This was especially nice the first time, sexually very straightforward loving, but my ex-wife was so pleasing in bed that I soon found my sex-drive hungry for things my middle-aged body could no longer deliver on a consistent basis. I talked to my doctor about Viagra. He asked if I awoke in the morning with an erection. I answered in the affirmative. He responded that Viagra probably wouldn't help, as my loss of potency was not physical. My doctor was wrong. After getting Viagra, I found I had so much tiger in my tank that I could have satisfied three women. My sexual imagination began to take over again. I once had a spat with my ex just as we were getting into bed. I returned to my own basement bedroom, called on my demons, and had no problem masturbating three times in less than an hour. I was fifty.

I knew the path for my life lay outside of that job. Timing? Well, that's *another* story. I decided I was going to leave my middle-income job, cash out my 401(k) and start my own business. When to leave the nine-to-five nest? Not an easy decision, and one fraught with peril. With life-numbing overtime I had made almost $60,000 in one year. In considering whether or not – or when – to cut the secure income, only the most sober thought could be admitted into the halls of decision, only the most prudent logic need apply to service such a task. Departure from my job consequently ensued based on a co-worker's behind.

The Sign

The girl was barely pretty. But she had two things going for her: A kind of vapid lack of intelligence that always adds an extra edge to any male's sex drive, and an absolute *ten* in the ass department. There is something about the dim-witted face – the seeming lack of awareness – in a girl who is still undeniably attractive that inspires the primal in a male. It's not conscious. It's not something thought out. It is the modern day equivalent to the caveman simply picking a female up and throwing her down on the caveman bed. Maybe it's the sense that a green light for sex is just a manipulative sentence away, and therefore the possibility exists with higher probability given the right place at the right time.

Perhaps the exquisite guilt that as a male you know you don't care for her at all – may even own a vague dislike – and the impetus to escape from this guilt creates the urge to have her all the more. In my case this is all academic, as I am middle aged, unattractive, and the girl in question is in her early twenties.

She and the assistant manager of the department were an item. It was obvious they were sleeping together, as they would always come in together in the morning, laughing, exchanging looks and touching. She would sit on the edge of his desk and stare into his eyes. In *Bambi* terminology, they were clearly twitterpated.

There is a certain confidence that a young woman exudes when she is getting a lot of bedroom attention from a lover and doesn't care who knows it. I don't know if it's strengthened when her lover is also a coworker, but a definite brazen quality emanated from her walk and talk, and making eye-contact was sometimes an almost harrowing experience. If you remember the look that Gwenyth Paltrow's character gives her co-actor after her assignation with *Shakespeare* (*in Love*), you get some idea. Only our heroine in this case was not quite as classy.

Since I was almost thirty years her senior with nothing about me remotely attracting her, I consigned myself to regard her as a challenge to my spiritual life. '*I will not enter into lustful imaginings,*' I told myself, and was successful to a large degree, determined to remain polite and professional whenever we had to communicate on a project. But this meditation goal and its application were still in the learning stage, and I apparently needed more testing.

Like all women she undoubtedly knew the effect she had on males, but like many women didn't care at all about those males about whom she didn't care at all. Most men run into these situations, especially as we get older. I found this to be an even more damaging blow than the slow realization that you have become invisible to women you pass on the street. When I was young and single my *wanna have sex?* smile and eye-contact was at least noted by the opposite sex (occasionally earning me a return smile). My life as a divorced forty-something however, offered only something inert and neutered. I was below their radar. I no longer existed. I had become invisible. Consequently, when a woman wears the most outrageous come-get-me outfit, and then glares at you when you look at her, she is telling you that *you* are not part of the male species she had in mind when she was putting on those clothes.

A female in the workplace may titter and laugh at obscene comments by one guy, girlishly using her body language to show off the positive effect of the attention, and then glare in hostility should another male try to use a fraction of the same familiarity. While the same principle exists in the animal kingdom, the lions, dogs or horses so treated seldom live in fear of sexual harassment charges.

While I was never in danger of such claims, her sexual signature as a female-in-heat was nonetheless difficult to ignore, and I found myself tested severely one afternoon. Anyone familiar with the black-and-white movies of years ago may recognize the concept of the black-and-white semicircles which were made to spin concentrically so as to create the visual impression of a hypnotic effect or dreaming.

She was wearing very thin skintight pants with a black and (not-completely opaque) white striped zebra design. You could see no underwear. The black stripes were curved in a shape similar to that of curved daggers, the points of the black stripes arching across her upper thighs and splendid backside only to disappear into the holy of holies. Every male in the office stared, and when finding another with whom he could bond on such an issue, shared a silent but wide eyed "*can you believe this?*" Her ass in those pants would undoubtedly be the most whispered about subject all day long. The unusual office space in this particular department necessitated climbing a steep flight of stairs. On this particular day, I entered the secluded staircase to find her hypnotic hips ascending upwards barely five steps ahead of me. Too weak to obey the silent voice urging me to look elsewhere, I entered into the silent seduction, a willing animal being led into the black and white slaughter.

Allowing my eyes to hypnotically feast on the slight quiver in her most exquisite cantaloupes, I knew she was teasing me with a little extra hesitation and hip movement, but it mattered not. My annoyance at her for doing so only added to the sensual stimulation as I found myself suddenly lost shamelessly in her perfect rear. I allowed the soft quivering stripes to hypnotize me – with a simple walk up the stairs – into a lustful heat that would overwhelm my consciousness for almost two weeks afterwards.

Perhaps I saw this as a symbolic crossroad into my going out on my own. A descent into cheap thrills, the meaning of my life could prove itself by victory over such mental depravity, but by doing that and little more. This not-so meager accomplishment alone would become my mark in life. A fight not to become a dirty old man as I got to be simply an old man, worn out trying to make ends meet a little above 'getting by' as my dreams of creativity became thoughts of 'coulda been.' So I quit.

After cashing in my 401(k), paying the taxes and associated loans, I saw my $14,000 dwindling to less than $4,000. Nevertheless, I bought my ex-wife an $800 walking exercise machine to celebrate my freedom. Exhilarated by not having to enter my prison the next morning, I was sure financial success loomed right-around-the-corner.

With this type of budgetary restraint, I of course failed. My effort to gain financial independence with my web animation ideas fell apart although it was undeniable that I had good ideas. Suddenly I couldn't find work anywhere. Even for a lot less money than I had been making. I was broke and unable to supply my side of the monthly finances. My wife's daily lacerations in front of my sons became my daily humiliation, as my offspring stood watching their father failing and flailing in pathetic response to their mother's taunts and criticisms.

I had taken them all around me in a circle, and said I was leaving the safety of middle-class America to follow my dreams for ALL of us, and instead of trumpets triumphant, and the happy affirmations that "*Dad did it!*" here I was crashing and burning.

Now living in a basement bedroom that we had created by throwing up cheap paneling on the bare two-by-fours, bugs would fall out of the ceiling on my face during certain climactic conditions. The Box-Elderbugs appeared impervious to the usual extermination sprays. This combined with smoking a daily regimen of Canabian (Canadian-grown award winning cannabis) with THC counts in the twenties had me contemplating bugs on my face and arms even when there weren't any on my face and arms. It was time for a new crossroads.

There can be something especially frightening about the return of failure. Like the horror movie in which the hero vanquishes the monster only to find it reemerging in unexpected strength, so I found myself failing and broke, mere months after quitting my $20 an hour job to start my own home business. I had come up short, failing again.

Chapter 19 – Use the Force, Luke! Miracles...

Although I had come up with money to help my ex-wife get out of a bad situation, that was then and this was now. My car needed a repair that I had no money for. I prayed. I was still smoking pot, but I prayed a lot. I went to open the mail one day and noticed a government refund check for overpayment of some real estate tax or some such thing in there for my (ex) wife. Somehow I just felt the "right thing" to do would be to use it, intending, of course, to pay it back real soon. I had no other way out. Without a car, I was nowhere. Maybe I knew what would happen, and needed to get out on my own, and this act would facilitate that. I rationalized that I hadn't asked for anything in return for the $4,000 I had given her.

Consequently, when she found out, I was "out." I looked for "Room for Rent" in the newspaper and visited a few. For about $400 a month there was a room in a beautiful luxurious home nearby which was owned by this one single guy.

I met with him. He seemed a bit hard with a hollow smile, but as we talked about life's ups and downs, he alluded to the fact that he had experienced problems of a chemical nature. I confessed that twenty years prior I had also been involved in drugs (I didn't consider marijuana a drug), at which point he also confessed that at one time cocaine had been a problem for him as well.

I scraped together every penny I could lay my hands on and moved in.

While moving my old bed in, a piece of carpet, perhaps a quarter-inch in length and width, got snagged by a spring popping out of my box spring in my bedroom. A piece of the shag now stood up like a piece of unruly hair in a morning rise.

The first night he wasn't home until late, and I walked around the beautiful home feeling like I was truly blessed to escape my ex-wife's harping shrillness, as well as relieved to no longer feel so worthless and debased in front of my children. The excruciating humiliation I had been receiving at the hands of my ex-wife had to be relieved, and I looked at my taking of her few hundred dollar check as a necessary act in order to *'move me off the pot'* so to speak. Otherwise, I might have stayed there playing the hapless animal in her "kick the dog" scenario until I blew my brains out.

Over the next 72 hours, I began to actually "feel good" about life and myself, once laughing out loud in bed about how one minute I was laying in a downstairs bedroom with bugs occasionally visiting me from out of the ceiling, unable to fend off the slings and arrows of my ex-wife, and now I was free from her onslaughts while living in a gorgeous house.

In the evening I heard Jeff come in and after about a half hour decided to go upstairs and make a cup of tea and to see my "roommate." As I walked up I noticed it seemed rather dark. I got to the top of the stairs and I saw the belt first. It was on the table still looped in junkie fashion, and then my eyes came up to see a man whose visage resembled more a Halloween mask of evil than a human being.

"*What do you need, Marty*!?!" he half-screamed, half hissed in a lunatic voice so cold and hostile my blood chilled. I retreated downstairs, full of dread and wonder as to what I had suddenly got myself into.

The next day he appeared much more normal although very nervous. He half-apologized, mumbling that he had had some personal problems the night before. Apparently his cocaine addiction of "the past," meant he had been straight only a matter of a few weeks. Last night he had returned to the evil, and it was obvious over the next few days that he had some extreme emotional issues. I recognized some from my own psychosis, but the high level of intense hostility that he so easily exhibited was something new to my experience.

If I came upstairs while he was watching TV, he would visibly tense, and he would concentrate on what was on the TV to the point where you could see the veins in his neck stand out. The TV experience was for him a constant test of his own critical taste and/or creative abilities. It was easy to see that a voice in his head was so hyper-critical of all that was being said on TV and its reflection on him, that he would channel surf making excuses for what was on the channel he was leaving, as if I was blaming him for the poor programming or knocking him for watching an apparently sub-par show.

When I said I didn't watch much TV, he took it as a personal slam that he did, and when I declined to watch a particular show he would mention, he reacted as if personally slighted. After watching *Wall Street* (which I had seen at least twice on VHS) on cable with him, I mentioned that I found the ending improbable and nowadays simply working in a company that is about to do something that will dramatically alter profits for better or worse, prompting you to either buy or sell stock based on that knowledge equates to insider trading. He practically flew into a rage. He would later implore me to watch something, and sometimes I would. After the show was over and I was leaving the room, he would say something to the effect that *'it was about time I left him alone.*" It was a constant "damned if you do, damned if you don't scenario. I once had to drive him to his heroin program's methadone clinic (he was addicted to that as well), and had to listen to his criticism of my driving all the way there and back.

He would talk about getting some escorts over, maybe us both doing one without them charging us extra. This I did not want at all, but knew if I said "I'm not into that," he would go off on another psychotic rant as he would perceive that as a 'holier than thou' slam, and so I said I wasn't into anybody else's seconds, and someday when I could afford it, I would pay for my own, adding that it wasn't a priority for me.

I was eating mostly Raman Noodles with sliced turkey or roast beef in order to save money. He went into a rant one day saying that I probably didn't think he knew anything about food since he didn't eat Raman noodles.

My car developed a very rare problem that required almost a thousand dollars to repair, and I still had payments to make, had no more credit, and had lost my job, which was probably the twentieth or thirtieth job I had lost since the hospital. When I told him my car was gone and money almost nonexistent, he became surprisingly calm. I found a car for $300 and Jeff advanced me the money. I got a job the same day delivering pizzas.

Jeff asked me to come with him to buy another car himself. He leased a fashionable auto, and insisted I accompany him to an upper class "Gentleman's Club" to celebrate his continued upswing in mood.

Instead of saying that I had no interest in the temptation of this stripper fantasy I had so thoroughly explored years before, I again lacked the courage to be forthright; being aware it would sound like a putdown to him. In essence, the ancient Hebrew proverb, *"The borrower is servant to the lender"* sounded loud and clear. I was under real obligation to him for the $300 car loan and was behind on rent. I told him repeatedly I had no money for such a thing, and then he volunteered effusively to give me – not a loan, but give me – a hundred dollars to spend, adding the drinks and entrance fee were also all on him. Since I had been using the *"I'd like to go with you but I have no money"* excuse, I was snookered.

Jeff would go on about how one of the girl's there really liked him, etc., and since I couldn't resist bringing up the fact that that was how they made more money, he insisted that this was different, and also confessed that this place was good "therapy" for him. He alluded to the fact that it was a major psychological breakthrough for him to be able to sit there and have a girl pet him. He kept insisting that there was something 'special' between him and this one girl, and then become angry at my interpretation from hours before. He would bring up things I said in the past as if they were responses to notions going through his head in the present. It was not unlike the commandant's character in *Schindler's List* talking to the maid thinking he was in a dialogue that was really a monologue.

Before leaving for the Gentleman's Club, Jeff downs a triple bourbon right before leaving the house, placing another double in the cup holder on the driver's side. On the way to the freeway he honks at a young girl stopped in front of us at a Stop Sign, urging her to go even though it wouldn't be safe for her to do so. I look down in embarrassment.

The club is a very upscale joint. There was valet parking, a door man in elaborate uniform, a coat check girl and they charged twenty bucks just to get in. Jeff was a regular, and had some kind of discounted entrance passes. The accent was on lap dancing – not stage dancing - and the $150 private rooms for "better" lap dancing was there to really take the bigger spenders. Jeff told me with no small amount of pride that "his" girl would take him in the back without him having to pay the $150... most of the time. '*It must be love,*' I reason sarcastically to myself, but say nothing.

To me this was old hat. Jeff was very nervous and surprisingly hostile with the girls. When the drink gal came over for our order, she asked for my order and his, and when she asked if he'd like to put it on his credit card and run a tab, he tossed the credit card on her tray in an obnoxious manner. When she asked if she should keep it running for both of us, he snarled at her "*of course, what the fuck do you think?*" It was embarrassing, and I made a face to the girl which said, '*I don't understand this asshole either.*' I was surprised at the quality of the girls. Some were exceptionally good-looking: high eights to low nines.

I would go into the men's room stall, take a huge hit out of my proto-pipe (which had a cover that could be slid over the pipe's bowl so at to eliminate the tell-tale marijuana smoke, and then hold my breath till I got outside the bathroom, slowly exhaling the high grade pot through my nose as I walked back to the table. I hadn't drunk alcohol in over a year, and I was drinking beer after beer and soon partying hardy.

There are many misconceptions about these places. The girls are rarely paid as employees. They are independent contractors who – in 2000 anyway – were paying about $140 a shift to the club. The girls simply keep the tips and the clubs make great money on drinks and low overhead. Some people think all the girls are whores who can be bought. This is not true. Other people think none of the girls are whores who can be bought.

This is also not true. In any one of these places, only a very small percentage of girls will go down unequivocally for cash at the drop of a hat. A certain percentage will however, as circumstances permit, a certain amount of pay-for-sex in the "Private" areas but always within certain limits, which are determined by management. A club in small-town America will have different (*de facto*) rules than a club in Las Vegas, although on paper they may appear identical. In all places, however, there'll be girls who'll agree to meet with a customer outside of the workplace, where all manner of arrangements may – or may not – be made. Almost all the girls at the clubs are stoned. This often creates a situation wherein Girl A says *no* to giving a customer a handjob in the Private Room at 8pm, but by midnight she's so drunk or coked out that she's blowing someone in the Champagne Room for half the money she turned down earlier. By 1 a.m. she is repentant and tells all the men willing to pay that she doesn't do that anymore. The quintessential moving target, strippers can be just as quixotic as any other girls can be. After all, girls will be girls. Girl A might be in the mood and/or need cash, and Girl B simply does not give sex at any time. If a guy starts to unbuckle his pants in the "Private Room," she'll tell him she doesn't do that, but may offer to get another girl for him who she knows does do that. Girl C is that other girl.

A stripper can make $1000 - $3000 a week in these places without prostituting herself if she's got the goods and knows how to work a man. It's all fantasy, and with enough smiling, stripping, cooing, whimpering, squeezing and kissing some girls can find well-healed players who will drop $5000-$10,000 a night just to get high with his favorite stripper(s), oftentimes with his buddies. Consequently, the aim of his evening here is not to try to squirt off some furtive fluid in a Private Room, but rather indulge a sense of hedonistic riot. Amply fortified by drugs and booze, a man could "forget himself" amidst beautiful, smiling, scantily-clad girls dancing and stroking him, well, wherever... The girl – also fortified with chemicals and alcohol – may rationalize that allowing a strange man to squeeze her behind a few times a small price to pay for untaxed thousands.

As to meetings after hours, a lot of the girls are curious if the stakes are attractive enough. The girl has to be sure you're not a cop and also reasonably assured you're not crazy. Once she determines that you're safe, a lunch or dinner (sometimes for a fee) can be a starting point for all kinds of negotiations. What the girl does with the guy from there is all about the individual girl's situation, morals and taste. One girl thinks a guy is cute while another girl thinks the same guy is a dork. One girl may consider sleeping with a guy when she needs help with the rent while another would never; but most girls enjoy the presents and the nice restaurants. It often becomes like dating. Then it sometimes becomes dating.

    Jeff was sitting next to me and was getting more uptight the more he drank. Apparently the girl he was in love with wasn't working after she had told him she would be that night, and he acted as if he had been stood up. He regarded any other girl who came over as a usurper of his love interest who didn't quite measure up, and was extremely rude. However, the beer combined with my inhalation therapy had me feeling no pain.
    A buy one-get one free lap dance was announced. A real cutie– I'd say between and an eight and a nine – came over and sure, let's do a dance.
    "I'm Doris," she says.
    "I'm Marty, " I respond in a friendly tone.
    Hello, Marty," she replies seductively. I had tossed on some Feragammo with a touch of CK1. I'm almost bald on top, with my few thin strands of hair there so thin I paste them down with a glue-like hair gel. When the girl sits on my lap, she inhales deeply and croons: "*oooh, that smell! What are you wearing? I love it!*"
    I notice Jeff's eyes grow wide upon hearing this and he looks like he's about to lose control of himself. I'm not sure whether it was because he was paying for this – having given me a hundred – but he seems overcome with what-looked-like jealousy.
    She felt it too, and looking over at Jeff, who's sitting one seat away, says, "*how you doin' honey? You want me to get a friend for you?*"
    "*Fuck off,*" says Jeff.
    "Woah! That's enough of that! Come on Doris," I say, and, taking her by the hand, we move to another couch and table a short distance away.
    She starts to caress the back of my head and neck. When I feel her fingers on my plastered down hair, I say, "it's like plastic, I know."
    She responds with a low moan implying plastic hair on bald guys is what really turns her on. I laugh appreciatively. She was *really* good.
    "I've got a problem," I say.
    "What's your problem, baby?"
    "I keep looking for a woman who'll love me for my money."
    She whips off her little shift with a body expression and groan that says '*at last that's gone!*' All the girls give lap dances bare-breasted. She gives this great feline growl sound, and starts nibbling on the side of my neck while gyrating to the music. When she comes up for air her naked breasts are about a half-inch from my face. I am wearing a shirt with the top few buttons open and her hand enters into my chest hairs and I respond with my own little growl of encouragement along with a snap of a twenty

into her other hand which elicits an *"oh, Marteee"* from her which was so pornographic I couldn't help grinning and engorging at the same time.

"*You're terrific,*" I say, and we're in love. We are actually. I would have, if I could, at that very moment, mortgaged my house and taken her to a tropical resort. I think that's the love 90% of our culture believes in. The "it feels so good to be with you love." She reaches back into my shirt and starts to squeeze my nipple while she's still nibbling on my neck.

"Hmm, is this silk? she coos almost innocently, as if oblivious to my gasps. I was 'gone' in one intensified gasp after another, interspersed with low moans. While I silently reveled in being under her control, she continued to torture my chest expertly while kissing my neck lovingly. I closed my eyes to see red-hot lightning flashes going off through the darkness behind my lids. Her fingers create a celestial torment that sends me outside myself as I blend into the pain to a level I would not have imagined possible. I literally didn't care if bled as I finally hit a kind of plateau, a relief which seemed like something orgasmic without a literal release but leveling me with satisfaction nonetheless.

She immediately realized it as well, and we both calmed down. I needed a bathroom break from the beer, and gently indicated that she and I were done. I continued the fantasy in a different vein by mentioning that once in a while I fly out to Vegas or New York to see a championship boxing match. *Maybe we could hook up for a dinner to discuss if she'd like to come along?* Dropping the sexy pout, she gets real and, looking me straight in the eye, said it had possibilities. She then whispered close to my ear to come back and talk to her about it, and ended our relationship by kissing me on the cheek. Since the customer is not allowed to touch, my slow full handed squeeze on her delicious behind was all the more thrilling since it was not only not allowed, but earned a smile from my new love interest. Throwing me a mischievous look, she bounced away like a little girl, returning like a fish into her sea of feels and dollars. Happy to be in love, I ambled off to the men's room, hoping my erection would soon die down so I could pee.

Upon relieving myself, I realized as I talked to myself out loud that I was really drunk. I only talk to myself in that voice when I am really drunk. No longer exuberant, I realized that not even the large hit of high potency marijuana was going to change the direction the alcohol was taking me in. I returned to the table to listen to Jeff rant on about what a great body his missing girlfriend had, and by way of description mentioned she had small tits.

"Some people think big tits are everything," he snarled. He became extremely hostile and belligerent regarding all 'those' people who thought large breasts were everything, and had a look on his face that said he was ready to fight about it. When I mentioned something about different tastes, he looked at me like I was a traitor. I was rapidly losing patience with this guy and simply kept the mantra going in my head that I was moving out as soon as possible.

A girl with a great body but an even greater presence came over. When I said OK for a dance and paid the fifteen bucks, she struck a pose like a stage actress, head up, shoulders back, arms at her side, posture perfect, and dropped her gown revealing a beautiful body and above-average breasts. All she had on was a thong and high heels.

"You're a goddess," I said.

"And what would you like?" she asked.

"Well, I'd like this," I said, falling to my knees before her. As she sat I handed her up an additional twenty, proceeded to remove her shoe, take her foot gently in my hand, started to message it, then gently started licking in between her toes, and then started to suck on her large toe as her delighted and delightful laughter started another reign of lust raging through my body.

The rules in these places are all the same. The girls can touch you. You can't touch the girls. But the bouncers and workers normally on the lookout for any hanky-panky that can get the owners in trouble could not easily see what was going on with our particular table because I was literally below the radar. The gal was a fun loving dame probably stoned out of her head and seemed to be enjoying it as well. Then I feel somebody tapping my shoulder in an effort to get my attention. It's my psychotic landlord, who, after driving us to this place doing 80 mph with a large glass of bourbon in the cup holder, is now trying to advise me on what the rules are. I simply straight-armed him away from me without looking up or taking the girl's toe out of my mouth.

We soon retire to the normal lap dance position where her fingers lightly run wild. Even though I was driving a jalopy and delivering pizza for $9 hour, it seemed reasonable to offer her an opportunity to be considered for my coming trips to Las Vegas or New York City that I make for the big prizefights. Perhaps she'd be interested in a kind of "business" relationship? I convey the word *'business'* in the softest of tones direct from my lesbian center. She moans and squeezes my arm.

It's great fun, and she volunteers that I should take her number. I don't have a pen, and she adds that the management frowns on seeing customers writing down the girls' numbers anyway, and so suggests placing her number in the cell phone Jeff has out on the table. She reaches for it and

Jeff flips out, cursing and berating the girl. It turned out later that he didn't know how to add a number to his cell phone.

I immediately come to the girl's defense, calling him an asshole along with some other alcohol-inspired insults which really did cross the line. While looking at Jeff with the girl standing next to me, I hand the girl my last twenty and (slowly and illegally) squeeze her luscious fanny while telling her I'll see her again. I alcoholically relate the moment to Cyrano de Bergerac tossing his month's wages to the owner of the theatre in that great old movie. I realize I am now completely broke, but the moment was too special to ignore. It helped to complete this ridiculous fantasy with the girl, while in a strange and illogical way piss off Jeff. I couldn't resist the temptation to give in to it. So what else is new? She gives me a kiss and takes off.

Now broke, I hope to G-d I have a twenty left in my bank account for an ATM withdrawal so I can take a cab home. When it does indeed slide out of the magic metal box, I am relieved in ways words cannot express.

As I'm preparing to leave, I realize I have to return to my table for a pair of prescription sunglasses. As I approach, I see my psychotic landlord standing in an aisle berating some poor innocent sitting a few feet away. In the dark club, Jeff thinks this guy is me, and is snarling my name and cursing the poor fellow, who sits confused and frightened looking straight ahead.

As I approach the table he sees me, and with my back to him I reach for my sunglasses and I feel Jeff pushing me on my shoulder. I freak out and start screaming at him "don't you *ever* touch me. *Ever!*" I now cross the Rubicon with Jeff. I indicate to him that in my thirty years of partying he is the lamest individual I have ever had the displeasure to be brought down with. When I told him I was leaving without him, he looked like I slapped him upside the head, making the twenty it cost me for the cab-fare home the best money I spent all night.

Getting home I swallow four aspirin to help with the morning hangover to come, and I'm in bed battling alcoholic non-sleep when I hear him enter the house yelling to himself. Just loud exclamations. I hear him slam something. I put a hammer and a knife next to me under the covers. Home sweet home.

In the morning he comes to the bathroom door while I'm preparing to shower. He stammers that he might have been 'out of line' the night before. Keeping the mantra running through my head that soon I will be gone from here, I respond that everyone makes mistakes, especially in that heightened atmosphere of the club. I add I know he was disappointed that his girl wasn't there. *Just let me get out of here in one piece*, I think. *The borrower is servant to the lender.*

I want so badly to get out of this house my demeanor is a constant act. He is pleased by my willingness to overlook his abusive behavior and adds as if an afterthought while walking away from the closed bathroom door that if I'm interested in a guy relationship, he is open. Then it hits me. A neighbor had informed me that he seems to go through an inordinate amount of tenants. I do not get turned on, but spend an inordinate amount of time making sure a weapon of some sort is near me at all times.

My son comes to visit me, knocking on the same garage door that Jeff had insisted we use when moving in. Jeff later goes on about why he didn't use the front door, and seeing my discomfort at his criticism of my son, presses the issue to the point of later calling his actions stupid. I leave the room. Incidents start to intensify: I buy a quart of ice cream only to later find it half gone. Jeff informs me my choice of an inferior brand is unacceptable, reminding me that I owe him for the car, rent is now due and he has decided to replace the entire rug which holds the quarter-inch of ruined shag. This will also be placed to my account to the tune of $400. While doing the laundry I am not there immediately to move my wet wash to the dryer, and arrive in the laundry room only to find my wet clothes on the floor with the washer going. I lift the lid to see two pieces of Jeff's clothing being washed. He lectures me on how I just can't take advantage of his good nature by hoarding the laundry. I better get it together, he intones. He announces I owe him over a thousand dollars and he wants it. He also adds the hundred he gave me for the strip club, insisting he would never had given me the money without expecting me to pay it back.

I react by losing my Pizza delivery job, but get an assistant manager position at a local bagel shop. My car needs a new radiator and a water pump, neither of which I can afford. I have no credit, my checks won't pass muster on the little check machines, and I have to add nine plastic milk cartons of water every time I want to drive my car. I see the danger of incarceration as a natural progression as my poverty looms up in my consciousness as economic helplessness meets the needs of basic living.

I am meditating and praying constantly. One night I wake up about three in the morning I go into the bathroom and am overwhelmed by an urge to pray. I start to vision and see my life ruined with drugs and insanity. I weep. I was about to be tested. There are words spoken by the Hebrew prophets of old in which it is intoned that G-d will not allow you to be tempted beyond what you are able to withstand.

Jeff soon comes to my bedroom door. I stand about a foot inside my room; he's at the doorjamb. He is in one of his highly demonic possessed states. In these conditions, there is a very high degree of empathetic linkage to voice inflection as well as facial tension. The snarling anger and rude inflections are like knives, and the resulting intimidation can be overwhelming. It is like every nuance in the voice or unspoken language of the face and body seeks a deeper weakness or higher resentment as its target. All energies are ratcheted up. Armor is being probed. It is designed to be provoking and offensive; a physical confrontation being its goal.

"I want my money," he says.

"I will get you your money as soon as possible."

"When will that be? he asks belligerently, moving a step towards me threateningly.

The words of a tape by Roy Masters came into my head. *Don't sink into your thoughts. Just leave it to G-d, even though you don't know what to say or do. It's OK to be scared, your knees may shake, but just continue to leave it to G-d.*

I knew in a less than a second what would take place if I gave in at that moment to my rising anger. I would start to say angry things, and would want to smash him, to beat him, to hurt him badly. I also knew that this would lead to an assault charge, the police coming, my being either arrested or at the very least evicted, and assuming I didn't kill him in the fight which could start at any moment, he would take my computer, which was all I had going for me. I also realized, in less than a moment's time, that this would so enrage me that I would come back and kill him, and then my life would be over. I am thinking in my head, "*help me Jesus, Puhleeeze, help me. I am helpless without you…*" while standing in the doorway less than a foot away from this psychopath.

"*You will get everything you have coming to you,*" I hear myself saying (**where did that come from?**). I notice he is totally taken back by this, for he has to consider whether I'm being sarcastic or not regarding the words '*you'll get everything you have coming to you.*'

"When?"

"I am starting a second job next week. That'll allow me to pay you out of the first paycheck,"

"How much will that be?"

"Five hundred." Yes, that's true, I think to myself.

"That's not enough."

"I'm looking for a second job's paycheck as well and there is my security deposit you have," I hear myself say and am pleasantly amazed at the emergence of some kind of quiet faith in my voice.

"*To hold a security deposit as rent is against the law, Marty!,*" says the cocaine using, psychotic heroin addict, now snarling ugly six inches from my face. "*I want that money, Marty*, and I'm gonna get it," he intones as if he's considering all manner of evil against me.

"*I know you do*," I say again with the perfect mix of flatness and sincerity, "*and you'll get all you have coming to you.*" I notice his face working on this last statement again trying to see if he can react to my words as if they're a threat. He can and he can't, and again I see he is becoming unsure of himself over it.

"This can't go on," he adds with a smirk and a little laugh.

"Well, I'll move out," I say with an apologetic tone, not able to keep the relief out of my voice at even just the thought.

"*OH NO YOU WON'T*" he screams, getting closer to my face. "*YOU OWE ME OVER A THOUSAND DOLLARS AND YOU'RE NOT GOING ANYWHERE UNTIL YOU PAY! I KNOW WHERE YOUR KIDS LIVE. I FOLLOWED YOU HOME TO YOUR EX-WIFE'S HOUSE ONE DAY!*"

I wanted to hurt him. I wanted to beat his head with the hammer that was just a few feet from my hand. Ignoring the implied threat to my children, I responded.

"OK, Jeff... *You're going to get what you have coming to you*," I repeated in an even calmer voice. I had said it slow enough that he started nodding energetically at the idea of him getting, and again he had to hesitate and think over the meaning of "*what you have coming to you*," but since I had not added any belligerent or sarcastic intonation to my words, he couldn't react aggressively to it. He became unsure of himself again, and the word "unhorsed" shot through my head. I felt the entire burden slip off me then. I knew I would escape out, as the Lord had taken over and had answered my prayer.

I had been so full of frozen anxiety that I could hardly think, and it was just that small amount of faith and guiding spirit that had stayed with me that kept me from ruining my life. One punch, one sarcastic challenge that would have had him attacking me, and then calling the cops and blaming me would have changed my life. I would have ruined my life and might be writing this from jail.

When I thought things couldn't get any worse, they did. I was driving away from the house one evening at dusk, and I didn't recognize Jeff's car as it came towards me with the headlights on in the fading light, but I saw what looked like the ending of a half-wave from the driver as we passed each other. I knew this signaled a psychotic opportunity for the demons to run wild in the demented man's head, as he had actually waved to me and I knew – that in his mind – I had ignored him. About an hour later, I'm back at the house, and he comes up to me in the kitchen.

"I got to talk to you, Marty. We got a problem," he said.

"What's up?" I ask.
"Well, you know those Pyrex bowls I had in the cabinets?"
"No."
"You don't remember seeing those Pyrex bowls I had down there?" he says, pointing to some cabinets I can't remember ever opening.
"No."
"Well, they were a wedding gift I kept from the divorce, and they're gone."
"You think I took your *Pyrex bowls*?" I couldn't keep the ludicrous nature of the charge out of my voice.
"Well, I didn't take them, Marty, and it's just us two living here, isn't it? If anything like this happens again, I'll have to call the police."

Miracles in Doses

There was a small gas station on the corner midway between my new and former digs. It had been in the quiet neighborhood forever and had been grandfathered into the zoning regulations. Two old bays for car repair, two old dogs roaming about, full service gas that had no computer readout inside the station telling how much you pumped.

A sense of neighborhood loyalty stemming from my experiences growing up in Brooklyn made me a steady customer. The owner proved to be an honest mechanic and I found myself going out of my way to bring him my business. Perhaps it was for another reason not made clear to me at the time.

When getting gas or auto repairs done, I found myself in conversation with Melvin. He was an interesting character. We bonded on national as well as local politics, the racial situation, crime, the hideous cruelty of our divorced wives, alimony, our kids and child support. I also liked the fact that he was completely dead-pan with his sense of humor. Occasionally I had him hold a post-dated check to accomplish a repair. Over the course of time we had done this a number of times and I had always paid on the promised date.

I was complaining to him on how I had to move out of my current situation, which had looked so good at first but had become a nightmare. He mentioned he was trying to sell his trailer without much success, as he had just moved out of it and into a house. I asked if he would be interested in renting it, and within a week, with no deposit and barely enough money for the first month's rent, I moved out while Jeff was at the gentleman's club. I was tempted to fuck up his house, tempted to poison his dog, tempted to urinate in his methadone. I did none of those things. I had something else in mind.

Jeff had confided in me weeks before that he was in a legal tussle with a customer who was taking him to court. After getting screwed by him as the contractor, the people wanted their money back, or were refusing to pay what he insisted they owed. He then went on their property without being invited, and they were trying to get a restraining order against him. He was very concerned about the restraining order, as he apparently already had one issued against him by somebody else, and these tended to *"make you look bad,"* as he put it.

I feigned interest in the situation, as he had copies of the legal action they were taking in his hand. He said *"here, you can see for yourself,"* and then went upstairs. I scanned all the documents into my computer, and after moving out got in touch with these people in order to help them in any way I could against this maniac.

Right before I was able to make my getaway, Jeff had gotten a DWI, and was unable to legally drive for the thirty days following the citation.

I had moved out, and stayed in touch with these people who were bringing Jeff to court, and drove over to meet them at a coffee shop. I soon gained their trust, and learned a lot about restraining orders.

Synchronicity – A Miracle in Time

After leaving my noon meeting with these new acquaintances, I was possessed by an impression to drive to where I knew Jeff bought liquor, although I had no knowledge of when – or if – he might show up there at all. I was just impressed to do this, with a kind of unspoken 'knowing.' After waiting ten minutes across the street, I see him drive in.[32] I call 911 on my cell phone, relating that someone I knew who just got a DWI was driving when his license was suspended and he was buying liquor. I didn't feel bad about it at all. On the contrary, for the first time in my life it felt good to aggressively wear the white hat.

The cops get him just as gets near his house. I am so pumped to see the action that I park a block away and walk across someone's private

---

[32] *Synchronicity is a word created by the Swiss psychologist Carl Jung to describe the alignment of "universal forces" with the life experiences of an individual. Jung believed that many experiences perceived as coincidences were not merely due to chance, but instead reflected the creation of an event or circumstance by the "co-inciting" or alignment of such forces. The process of becoming intuitively aware and acting in harmony with these forces is what Jung labeled "individuation." Jung said that an individuated person would actually shape events around them through the communication of their consciousness with the collective unconscious.*

property to stop and stare, peeking at the action from behind a bush. The people who own the home are suspicious of me kind of hiding, so they call the cops on me, and I give my identification to an officer. My name then comes across the cops' radio with Jeff sitting in the back seat and he recognizes my name.

An hour later he calls me on my cell phone. At first my blood runs cold as he says "what'ya gonna do Marty, follow me around?"

"Follow you around?" I found myself responding in a surprisingly aggressive manner. "I may just park outside your house and when I see you leave for work bust your ass again!" He starts to stammer. There was something empowering about making that speech at that moment. The living Spirit had entered me and I was never the same.

A different Jeff started speaking. He started to whine, asking me to please see things from his point of view, then asking in a little boy voice: "Marty, why did you move out?" I answered with two words:

"Bye, Jeff."

The people I was helping make a case against Jeff advised me to file a restraining order as well, which I did. They won their case for a restraining order against him and I knew he was freaking out at that plus the prospect of mine coming up had to be keeping him up at night.

When we went before the judge it didn't look all that good for me until Jeff bit into the same spiritual territory that got him nabbed. He tells the judge that I was stalking him and called the cops on him saying he was drunk. He goes on to say that the cops pulled him over in front of his house, embarrassing him in front of his neighbors.

"Were you drunk?" the judge asks.

"No sir," he says.

"They didn't cite you for being intoxicated?" the judge queries.

"No, I wasn't drunk at all," he answers, making me appear like the asshole, and the judge kind of frowned at me.

The judge almost doesn't let me respond, but I talk over his honor, loudly proclaiming:

"I didn't call the cops on him cause he was drunk, I called the cops on him because he had received a DWI a week before, and **wasn't allowed** to drive! Let alone to a liquor store."

"Is that true?" asks the judge with renewed interest.

"Well yeah," says Jeff and the *'well, fuck you, then'* is right there on the face of the judge. I win the restraining order. I found it spiritually fascinating that the same spiritual 'property' which had me finding him driving illegally was being used again to hang himself with in front of the judge. That incident should have been the last thing Jeff should have brought up. This is the Spirit working.

The universe "opened" in a dimension outside the normal extensions of time and space common to all our normal life experience the moment Jeff's car showed up at the liquor store. Then another "deliverance:"

I had kept a small home business alive insofar as I had a post office box for it. I opened a letter addressed to a name very similar to my business name which had been placed in my box. It was my exact address though. Apparently a very large company had mistakenly got my address mixed up with a vendor of theirs with a similar name and had sent me/them a check for over $3,000. I got rid of the nine containers of water and the car they stayed in and bought a dependable car for $1400 and paid off bills that had to be paid. The thought of buying a hooker or returning to the Gentleman's Club wasn't even taken seriously, and I simply and literally thanked G-d for the money. The company didn't press charges.

'Oh, that must be coincidence' says the voice in my head. Somehow I think not.

Consequently, I was able to get a dependable car and pay my rent in a trailer park that one had to be an owner to live in, and in order to rent, the owner had to be living in the trailer with the renter. Since the manager of the park had been fired and a new one was coming in the day after I moved in, I slipped in through the cracks. I found myself, therefore, a surreptitious renter looking "up" socially and economically to the slanderous term *'trailer trash.'* Blessed and entering the promised land, I couldn't have been happier.

Reintegration and The Observation Exercise: Standing on Sullivan's Shoulders

"In general, important aspects of personality existing in dissociation are not reintegrated except under extremely fortunate circumstances. One of these fortunate circumstances is when... "there is ... considerable improvement of the partition of energy between the not-me component and the other components of the personality. And at the same time this newly integrating tendency is being called out by maturation, certain eventualities are likely to occur which may have favorable influence in reintegrating a dissociated tendency system."

Interpersonal Theory of Psychiatry _ Possibility of Reintegration of Dissociated Systems (Sullivan) pp322 -

Ghost Riding In The Trailer

It had been thirty some-odd years since I had done any psychedelic drugs, but the closeness I was sensing to the spirit world (the escape from Jeff's and the heroic nature of my righteous revenge) made me believe it was time to try navigating within these other dimensions once more. Not long after moving in to the trailer, two of my sons arrived excitedly at my door with something called *Salvia Divinorum*. It was legal in our state, which naturally raises the question, *how powerful can it be if it's legal*? I had been smoking hashish dipped in hash oil on this particular night, and was enraptured with the stirring sounds of Handel's *Messiah* when they came *a'knocking at my door.*

I soon got my answer. Apparently the drug manages to stay legal because of the strange way it is absorbed into the body. If you just smoked the leaves in the same manner you would a cigarette or cannabis joint, not much would happen. The smoke from Salvia does not enter the bloodstream through the lungs in the same manner as pot or nicotine.

A small waterpipe was produced – as the smoke can be quite harsh – and the bowl was filled to the brim with a 40x mixture purchased at the local head shop.[33] One of my sons lit it while I was encouraged to take as big a hit as I could, and hold it as long as I could. When I exhaled, I was exhorted not to breath in any air, but suck in another huge hit, and repeat that process again, also without the benefit of a separate breath of air. By the time I was inhaling the third hit, I could feel changes, and after exhaling the third breath I knew internal systems normally reserved for waking consciousness were shutting down. I knew not to pay attention to the pipe in my hand, and yet I had to in order to lay it down on the kitchen table. Once free of that annoying duty, my consciousness was able to release itself as I had been training myself with thousands of hours in meditation, and immediately the normally black, gray and white dots of "stuff" that normally make up the 'movie screen' that we view the inside of our skulls with when our eyes are closed began to resonate with color. First light orange and redish hues, then growing increasingly rich and immediately deep in texture and complexity. I began to "trip out." I laughed out loud in the freedom of my release from the consciousness of this earth-bound ego system. I had only one thought, which was *"don't think."* Immediately following that came another thought to give this same advice to my sons, and I opened my eyes. Immediately the shock of light-

---

[33] *I will attempt to keep active links alive on www.trailopen.com for sources of good and verifiable information concerning Salvia Divinorum.*

bulb-in-kitchen-on-fleshly-faces- of-my-sons had me teetering on the edge of this newly arrived state.

With the world stopped on the edge of that universe, I sought to remember "something." "What was I supposed to say?" "Wha…?" I saw my children looking at me, and suddenly I felt very vulnerable, inferior… as an ego, as failing to bring some character, and faltering in some significant way. I heard one of my sons speaking in midstream to the other son "…*how much you need*?" I misinterpreted it with the psychotic mindgame that comes so easily when coming out of the state I was in. It's based on the premise that *'everyone-around-me-is-cool-and-unconflicted-and-knows-exactly-what's-going-on*. The fact that I am no longer free from the gravity of ego and worry accuses me of 'needing' too much emotionally in order to enjoy my 'self.' It's the autistic interpretation of their words within the bent of "*how much* (emotionally) *does he need*?" as a criticism. The delusional assumption being bought is that they can "see" exactly what is going on in my inner consciousness, and are even now commenting on it. Only problem is "*I don't see, I don't understand*," and I'm falling psychotically into that '*how much do you need*' statement with the misinterpretation that the statement refers to the amount of love, or self-confidence that I need in order to maintain my equilibrium in this trip. The voice in my head "proves" to me it's right when it finds me guilty of falling from heaven, as it brings its own horrible imagery to prove its point. I am now paranoid and react, and by my emotional reaction, bond to the fright. We always embrace that which corrupts us; on any level.

Now I am falling with the fear of being so vulnerable, with the guilt that in falling I am also guilty in spirit and in truth as lacking in faith; apparently not having "their" (my sons) ability to stay on that (prior) plain of paradisiacal colors, and I am the only one falling. I am the only lame who couldn't keep it together. I start to fall into the bad trip and realize the small amount of consciousness I had before is being eaten away, and there is no room for even the slightest thought within my mind, which is now being squeezed like a vice in an incredibly horrible pressurized hellish nightmare (in trying to return to the ego state too soon). As my consciousness totally gets taken over by this, I gasp out with my last breath of sanity, "*how long does this last?*"

The son - who possesses the most hostility towards me - answers with a small laugh: "*About two weeks.*"

I realize in less time than it takes the reader to read this I will lose my job and be thrown out of the trailer. I can neither think, speak nor stand. *Two weeks of this*? Fortunately, I come later to see that my son's interpretation of what "*this*" experience *is*, and what *it is* for me are two very different things. However, at the time I assumed he was experiencing the same effects I was. Immediately hostility rises up within me towards them for giving me this stuff and depriving me of home and livelihood, and it is all I can do to propel my legs to carry me to the overstuffed chair in the living room a few feet from the kitchen. My legs collapse under me just as I take my second step. I lay there burning alive. I'm an *Alex Gray* painting called *"Holy Fire Panel 3"*.[34] It is no doubt an archetypal state of some dimensional reality.

After about another five minutes of this it's over, and a steady return to normal consciousness ensues. I see it takes several Salvia experiences to understand its unique nature. I also find out that some people simply do not *'get off'* with the Salvia experience. Both my sons, apparently – are included in this latter population. My imaginative appraisal of the situation; that they were tripping along with me and could "see" my "internal state" when I had first opened my eyes way back when, to hear them say *"how much do you need?"* was just that, my imagination colored by my unconscious assumption of massive inferiority spoken of by those magnified sounds: *"what would the neighbors think of a boy who can't stay in ego-less paradise?"*

My sons, upon inhaling the same quantities of smoke I had, had immediately gone into the comedown, which is, by and large, a rather unpleasant experience. It is NOT a party drug by any stretch of the imagination. Nobody familiar with the drug's powerful potential would ever casually say, *"Hey, guys, let's smoke some Salvia."* The "high" and the insanity into which you may enter is not fun at all. It is painful insight or just plain painful. It is a spiritual tiger-by-the-tail. It is the spiritual equivalent of getting knocked down by a large wave and being thrown around and torn-about underwater and there's nothing you can do about it. With *Salvia Divinorum*, when you try to do something about it by trying to gain control of your mind, you get a hellish experience. This understanding may be built upon, however, to further a spiritual journey with its use, but it is definitely not for the faint of heart nor the spiritually myopic.

I had to dissect my experience. There was a kind of blending of responsibility as to where I ended and others began. I saw as an infant I had stretched up my hands to the moon with the same expectation I had when I stretched them out to a rattle on top of my crib. Where I began and ended physically was a matter of daily education. Psychologically fleeing disapproval and anxiety, I reacted to all older humans as 'authorities."

---

[34] *http://www.alexgrey.com/cards/35.html*

Psychologically I was subordinate and vulnerable to everyone. I was 'finding my limits' now psychologically as I had done physically as a toddler. I had muddled my emotional reactions to people at age three with the demands of modern adult life at fifty-three. It was this endless cycle of reaction, this Gordian knot that no amount of intellectual understanding was going to unravel, that the meditation was now simply disintegrating. It needed something supernatural, and that was what I was finding on a daily basis with my reaching for the objective state and transformation.

Salvia is capable of conscious expansion, but the people who take them mostly are not. The drug (like all conscious-expanding substances) is not like a sedative that has a measurable effect. For example, if you factor in a certain ratio of body-weight to sedative dose, you can put the subject to sleep. Or with a certain amount of a pain-killer, one can reasonably assume certain pain thresholds are being dealt with by using a certain dose. But a conscious-expanding drug is not like that. It is more like one of those space-shuttle-jets that can take off from a normal airbase and has the potential (based on the subject's mindset) to soar outside the earth's atmosphere. 90% of all the concert-going, hippy-type, gen-X whatevers who take these mind-expanding drugs are like boob-pilots merely driving their planes up and down the runway yelling, "*wow, this baby is doing 100mph! I'm really trippin'!*"

Mostly teenybopper-mindsets on ego trips, these people all think they are experienced in this field, and hence poor information abounds all over the web as well as on news shows. A conscious-expanding experience should always be done alone, except perhaps for the first time, when the tripper may benefit from a "guide" to help orient the novice through this new psychic territory.[35] Otherwise you are really just mentally masturbating, and all these supposed "insights" wind up little more than fortune-cookie sayings pinned up on the refrigerator.

* * *

Summer arrived. We rented canoes and went camping. My four sons and I set off for three days in the wilderness, and it was pretty cool, or – it could have been pretty cool – I'm not sure which. There were no bathroom facilities, grills or other people. That was the good part.

---

[35] *I normally shy away from the popular Buddhist associations relating to the 'psychedelic experience.' Based on the Tibetan Book of the Dead, however, I've found The Psychedelic Experience" by Leary, Alpert and Metzner to be the closest thing I have ever read to mirror that actual spiritual journey within the "experience." I disregard the religious piffle they include with it, however."*

One son was experimenting with a psychedelic drug called "*2ci*" and had such an open hostility toward me (and to a certain extent, his brothers as well) that it made the entire time a trying and annoying affair, as he continually managed to sabotage every opportunity for any joy or creativity amongst the group. It was the typical 'Debbie-Downer' "high" of the sarcastic stoner making sure all around him was aware of his aggressive cynicism on hand to immediately stifle creativity, dampen spirits and kill innocence. Two of my sons were at the teen's age of combining aloofness with coolness, so they had a good time on their own which made me feel all-was-not-in-vain, and my other son and I got long well.

Upon returning to my nine-to-five, I told everyone how wonderful it was to have been away. The more I told the half-truth, the more I found myself imagining being away at this idyllic spot on my own.

Britmania

In the meantime, I had come across a young sensation by the name of Britney Spears. I was still watching a bit of TV in those days, and I found myself transfixed.

After the celestial rescue from the psychopathic landlord, the daring do of the liquor store Holy Spirit/Synchronicity and the transformation from scared mouse into growling cat, I emerged as a bit more of a real person into the world of trailer life, crowning this 'next-level' move with my win in receiving the Restraining Order.

How then, did Britney Spears figure in all this?

When an old(er) man eyes a young woman dancing, it earns an eye-rolling "*ahem*" – a euphemism for '*a-dirty-old-man*' thing. Yet, I was struck by my own lack of sexual arousal as much as by the fascination I found watching her performance. I was not involving myself in the imagery for prurient purposes. I became so fascinated by this phenomena that I continued to not only watch her commercials and videos, but purchased her "*Live From Las Vegas*" DVD.

I, as the reader has no doubt concluded by now, am not one to abstain from admitting to the weakness of the flesh, and yet, I find myself in no way ogling the girl with puerile motives. I found myself blinking, transfixed at the myriad of energies that appeared to radiate from the totally unique performing art of Ms. Spears.

It seemed to be a repertoire of the female spirit performed with such a lack of self-consciousness that the viewer was transformed by her genius. Her performance appeared to reflect sexual invitation in a series of lurid dance moves replete with facial come-ons that would have made any temple prostitute green with envy, only to be suddenly interspersed with a bright high school cheerleader smile that says *"I'm only kiddin' ya,"* and then she'd do it all over again. I had never seen anyone like her.

In a daring move of self-love, I took off three more days from work to go camping by myself up to this same spot we had found. It sat astride a mountain stream flowing down into the river. I found myself actually giggling upon canoeing up to the place. I was able to pitch my tent about an hour before the warm summer rain started.

I had fasted from both food and cannabis products for three days prior to my trip, and having procured ample amounts of the aforementioned 2-ci[36] plus psilocybin mushrooms, I had added to these the "backup" substances of hash, hash oil and hi-quality bud. I was well-fortified with helpful supplements with which to venture into both the known and the unknown.

I lit the Tiki Torches in front of the tent in the midst of the evening rain, ignoring the shrill voices in my head criticizing such imprudence. Inside the tent, I set out my recorder, notebook, cannabis products and broke the fast with psychedelics; ushering in major dry heaves. Once past that, I realized I had failed to take an adequate dose, and I've always found that simply adding more at this juncture seldom equates to the same effect as having taken an adequate dose to begin with. Nevertheless, playing catch-up appeared a better alternative than not playing at all.

Soon I was face-to-face with that 'GIVE-IT-UP' voice that I know I have to float downstream with, and the more I fight - the less my trip will be. That's just the way it is in that 'hyperpersonal typography.' Afterwards, it's almost impossible to totally get the mind around this extra dimensional environment in any way other than to use thought-word-stuff like *'just let go,'* and *'all you need is love,'* etc.

I found myself in a setting – which doesn't lend itself easily to explainable communication within our three-dimensional world of consensual validations. It was "like" a StarWars bar scene, but only a "hint" of that really. A being *like* a cosmic hyperbeing wiping a barglass was looking up as I *"came in"* and said clearly to an audience greater than just the two of us: *"Marty is back!"* It was with a very real sense that I had been *there* before in the 1960s. There seemed to be kind of murmurings like *"hey, cool"* as if you're entering a place where everyone knows your name and is glad you're there. It was a very pleasant and welcoming

---

[36] ***PIHKAL, A Chemical Love Story*** *('Phenethylamines I Have Known and Loved")Transform Press 1991. pp539*

sound and a general sense of good-hearted welcome permeated the room, and I received welcoming beams from several other *beings of light* that were there. I sensed them communicating to me that they lived in a world or universe above the ego, and well, here we all are.

Of course I freaked out. I couldn't handle it long at all. I think we were like 'flashing" our lights at one another and regarding how beautiful we all were and there was floating out into such generations of beauty – as if one could imagine the most glorious jewelry one-thousand times more beautiful than the most radiant combinations from the best New York stores – and I got caught up in it and stopped flowing and started describing and characterizing it to myself and kept reaching out to my reason to explain it and became "self" conscious.

I also started seeing archetypes of beautiful women. At first their visages were made out of these jewel-like creations, ethereal with their cheeks made out of the galactic elements and earthly jeweled textures, outside of anything in this real world, but as I hungered for more, my mind created more "real" apparitions wearing these fantastic creations, woven with architectures that have never been seen in this world being strutted and flouted by supermodel type beings who I imagined were my consorts.

The look from the women gave rise to the idea that these were courtesans of mine who were delighted and proud to be having all this 'good stuff' which *I* was giving them, as I was becoming a sort of extra-terrestrial sugar-daddy, and of course I got a glimpse of my mother as a beautiful woman, and that got me feeling and thinking (a most dangerous thing to do here), and then reacting to my own thinking, and of course by this time the heavy gravity of the ego entered in, and I start reacting to negative thought hallucinations that I should *now be concerned* (QUICK! QUICK!) they (*eek! the creatures of light!*) were reading into my mind like hackers reading another's hard drive. What would they think of me (ever hear that before?)? They were seeing my shame-filled contents relating to mother, sexuality, and now homoerotic fantasy!

This wondering if they could read my mind, soul and complete personal history either pissed them off – or *I imagined* it pissed them off – which, in my rising guilt, imagined that *my imagining they were pissed off actually then did* piss them off. They let me know how easily they could read my mind – but also with an annoyed sense that *"what do we want to look at your garbage for?"*

I got so embarrassed at my own anxieties that the added fear was enough to end the trip. Once down I realized what I had done. I also realized I hadn't had sex in three years, and was not only being a wee bit hard on myself, but that the entire experience was an interesting symbolism of my entire personal unconscious. I laughed and prayed in silent thought as well as some out loud, and immediately smoked a huge amount of hashish.

Closing my eyes, I lay back into my sleeping bag, the night's warm summer rain continuing to fall with a delicious dreamy patter onto my tent. Then, coming toward me from over the horizon, into and through the no-mans-land of my closed-eye consciousness, was none other than *Britney Spears*.

First Visitation

What was Britney Spears doing here? Surprising. Her costume was as non-sexual as any she wore in her *Live From Las Vegas* show. Her outfit was the patchwork-quilt below-the-knee skirt from her performance in her "*Anticipation*" number. I didn't know the words very well, but at the time I thought I heard her singing them as follows:

"I'll be anticipating
This is our song they're playing
I wanna to rock with you
You're feelin this right,
Let's do this tonite...[37]

Her arms were outstretched exactly as she had extended them to the audience of largely young teenage girls in the Vegas show in order to create the sing-along. I felt this was like an invitation to something very innocent and light. That this was a manifestation from the land in which the *beings-of-light* call home. The manifestation of what the father of the North American psilocybin mushroom movement (Terrance McKenna) called "the other." A Mescalito Castenadian moment. The Holy Spirit of the Living G-d.

Who can say? I am only one voice. And yet, here was the single undeniable truth: I capitulated my consciousness to trust the spirit of the message... to flow without desire, certainly without the desire to 'have-for-myself' (which is, I suppose, the definition of lust), and was immediately transported back to yet another face-to-face encounter with a lord of light. The *'being of light,'* the same who had welcomed me back, was there to greet me, apparently not holding any grudge over my prior freak-out, ministered to me in some unknown way, and then directed me to get some feedback on my hash smoking.

---

[37] *"Anticipating"by Britney Spears (Jive Records)*

He spoke to me directly. *"Marty is over there, smoking hash."* I turned to see myself smoking like in a 60's poster with a big hookah and the smoke was forming the letters "H-A-S-H" which floated and stayed up in the air like permanent smoke rings. Within the rings I could see something that reminded me of a forest setting out of Bambi or some similar animated movie.

Now *in* it rather than looking *at* it, there came about a scene from the four rivers within this magical, archetypical simple-yet-magnificent garden scenery. The rivers converged into a single headwater at the top of a small rise, from which they all flowed out and down to the rest of the earth. As the barest hint of my questioning consciousness rose into being, the waters receded into a single stream. The stream was not unlike a graphic from a Disney movie, flowing deep blue amidst a forest-garden. There were flying insects over the water, however, which became the distinctive feature I was suddenly aware of, and being made aware of, and understood was not to be missed. They were flies, mosquitoes, dragonflies and bees which were buzzing around the water's surface, becoming louder the closer I came to the water, and it was revealed this is the buzzing nature of thoughts trying to get me to react; and the dross from reacting to thought; and then it was gone and I was back in the tent.

Resigning myself to the fact that my astral plane experiences were done for the night, I settled into some reflection. Cerebral Marty started to explain things: *'You didn't eat for three days, you took some serious psychedelics, and you saw an image of Britney Spears.* **Big deal.** *You could've just as easily seen Joe Stalin swishing around in a bikini.'*

This was not a mere hallucination. There was a 'ferryman-gatekeeper' essence to this whole Britanic emergence. Even though the *Paltrownian Synchronocity* was still months away, there appeared to me (even then) to be a depth to this phenomena that was more than what meets the eye.

I found that using the meditation exercise and Roy's tapes as a way of returning to normal consciousness after a conscious-expanding experience was **extremely powerful** in **ridding my consciousness of psychotic assumptions**. I found myself existing without that uncanny, inexplicable fear that had always been part of my existence. I found within this new reality not only a desire not to hate, but that irrational fear was simply disintegrating. I couldn't wrap my mind around it, but spiritually, I knew beyond doubt I was changing fundamentally.

Chapter 20 – First Talk With Roy Masters
Ending Schizophrenic Processes

I had returned from my spiritual and psychedelic experience more convinced than ever to explore my situation firsthand with Roy Masters. I had developed a multimedia software and was sure great wealth was imminent. The visions of females draped in jewels had not been entirely forgotten, nor their significance completely diminished since my return to the nine-to-five. I was concerned that once my ability to make money was realized, women would soon surface in my life, it might be better to stay celibate. After all, the idea of "beautiful women" also carried with it the notion of *young* beautiful women, and I was passed fifty.

I had been listening to Roy Masters' tapes. I had bought many of his books. I listened to his Sunday morning shows – which were more like group therapies – on the internet. I didn't get his radio program live but could call in and listen at www.fhu.com. Finally, I called into his show.

The *Foundation of Human Understanding* Advice Line Live Tape Numbers 2052/2053/2054 July 8th and 9th 2003

Roy: In Minneapolis, Minnesota. Hello Marty.

Me: Hi, This call I've been holding off making for about a year, but I figured this is it. I've been meditating for about 7 years, and I was up to the ranch once[38].
And just to go briefly what I need to explain, when I was seven years old I was sexually abused by two other boys, and when puberty hit I found something that was to remain with me my whole life, and that was – I'm attracted to women, the idea of kissing a woman or something has my feet floating off the ground – but I was very sexually active and what happened was, in the midst of the sexual act I would find my

---

[38] The "ranch" is a base of operations that Roy Masters uses at the Foundation for Human Understanding in Oregon

Roy: ...with boys...

Me: physical excitement would only be perpetuated by almost a transformation to...

Roy: ...with boys...

Me: where I would become the woman. I wound up becoming a drug addict for many years – twenty years ago – I found that I would have compulsive desires for men, not handholding or kissing, or anything like that – but... the act.
I found your meditation, I had a marriage whereas you put it in one of your tapes, I would draw the fantasy, like through the woman, to fulfill the sexual hunger, and then with your meditation – I was divorced after 16 years, but with the meditation I've been celibate for about 5 years and I cut off TV, and church and synagogue and friends – who were not really friends – and I dedicated myself to insight and to a relationship with G-d and although I'm Jewish I believe the carpenter from Galilee has defeated death, but I don't want to get too far off the subject.

Roy: (laughter) Hold the line. We'll be right back, look we'll right back with Marty. A really intelligent caller, we'll be right back.

(returning after the station break) Now Marty, we've got about seven minutes left and I'll give you all this time, we've got

	people waiting, but this is a very intelligent inquiry.
Me:	Thank you.
Roy:	If we can't finish it, will you call me first thing tomorrow, and we'll go all over it again? I can give you all the time necessary.
Me:	I look forward to that.
Roy:	All right, let's start then with you being molested by two boys. Let me tell you what this tells me. This tells me, that you didn't have the influence of a good father.
Me:	Absolutely right.
Roy:	Right on the money. And that you were terribly needful of love, that you mostly identified with your mother, and so therefore tended towards homosexual; tended towards any kind of affection that would be showered upon you sensuously; because when you have a lot of anger toward a father or parent, you reject one and become the other, and the sensuous feminine side awakens and wants attention, and kids from broken homes, abusive kids, will sense that, and you'll attract them. So you attract that kind of thing. It doesn't just happen by itself as a rule.
Me:	Yes.
Roy:	And so, you basically have, you know, a feminine nature, that is, you're woman-centered, but you never had, your mother

never had, the correcting love of a man, and you've never had the correcting love of a man, but you're trying to be a man so much… remember, how can I say, you still have the image of the woman inside you that draws you – because even a spider - male spider will crawl up the TV if it sees a television picture of a female spider. It recognizes its opposite sex and is awakened by that deep imprinting deep in the psyche. You follow that, don't you?

Me: When I'm by myself, sexually, that's where the battle is.

Roy: That's right, this is where the trouble is:
You have so much guilt, and so much loss of identity in that the only way to be an individual or person is get into – I'm trying to find the right words – is to be more of that which is more of what you identified with as a child. In other words, you rejected your father, and you got your mother's identity and the only way you know how to be a person - whole person, a complete person, is to be more deeply into what had you in the first place. You follow that?

Me: This is what I'm trying to get away from.

Roy: So trying to be a man, which is the sexual act... how can I say this, it's not easy to say but if I falter a little bit you'll forgive me. And you may be able to piece it together – but the thing is you're identifying with women, and most men have a woman center, and they don't have a G-d center, they don't love what's right, they haven't found the Father within, because they never had a father without – the father they can see – If you love the father you can see, you love the Father you can't see, and then you become a man. But if you don't love the father you can see, you hate him; you reject the masculine aspect and can only be drawn to become more complete in the feminine aspect. You follow that?

Me: yes, I tried that…

Roy: But you are followed by the conscience of the heavenly Father, you're followed by a pain, and so this pain you don't understand, and the only way you know how to be, is in the sexual act, you have to get more excited more than you normally would be, in order to excite a sense of completion.

Me: To maintain the physical ability to have completion.

Roy: That's correct, so what you need to learn to do; I'm going to be a little rude here, a little crude. When you have sex, you have to avoid getting into… more than is in it.

Me: That's what I've been trying to do this last year, but with just by myself.

Roy: By yourself. Meaning you're having sex with yourself, but you still have an image of a woman, and you are arousing yourself by that image, because when there isn't one around, the one implanted in your brain will do. Follow that? And that's a spirit. That's a dangerous spirit.

Me: I'm a little confused, so I'm going to ask. Because this image of the woman, there's a dichotomy here, because there is the image of the woman like in a playboy centerfold where I'm the red blooded male, than there is the image of the woman which, kind of parallels your expression, you croon for Satan to come in;

Roy: you croon sweetly for his presence in, and it arises as if you croon sweetly for his presence.

Me: Then my body responds

Roy: They're one and the same. The image of the woman behind the image of the woman is that which you just mentioned… the dark Eve, the dark evil Eve, that lurks in the image, you don't see it, but as you get into the image of the woman with its excessive excitement which it offers, then the spirit of Eve gets into you through the experience, and makes you more addicted, and makes you more effeminate…

Me: Well, I gotta talk to you tomorrow. Cause this a real… I'm getting chills all over.

That's just what I've come to the last 72 hours; that I see there's like no difference. There's no difference between fantasizing I'm the macho male or I'm the female a macho male is coming to ravage.

Part II of First Talk with Roy Masters:
Tapes 2052/2053/2054 July 8th, 9th, 2003

2053 – JULY 9, 2003

Roy: Well, now we're going to go to Marty in Minneapolis

Me: Hi Roy. Thanks for taking my call.

Roy: This conversation we had yesterday, we're going to do this on the air, and we're going to spend time with you. What I am going to explain to you this will release you. It's already done you some good, hasn't it?

Me: Yes

Roy: We need to go into it a littler deeper. What we're going to go into on the air should really be done in secret, this info I'm going to give you shouldn't be spread abroad, cause the people of America are not ready for this.

Me: Obviously. Cause you should be bigger than Pat Robertson and Billy Graham put together, and you probably have the same percentage that Jesus has that really believe in Him, but go ahead.

Roy: This is painful. What I am going to tell you is very very painful. Cause what is wrong with you is what wrong with everybody, but in you it's much more advanced. You see what I mean?

Me: Yes I do see what you mean, and have an instinctive belief that you're right. But, when I try to talk with, like, peers, like when I used to be involved in Church groups, everybody just gives a blank look, as if, they would never touch themselves, or have a fantasy or anything.

Roy: Well know what, the clergy and the educated elite they only know what they're taught. They don't know anything else. They don't even have the common sense to know if what they're taught is right or not.

Me: You would think that when a man is alone, with thoughts especially sexual thoughts, one would have a level of awareness that you would want to bring to his spiritual lord.

(Crackling)

Roy: By the way, do you have a crackling on your phone?

Me: Yes, I can hear it.

Roy: Will you hang up and call back?
Me: Yes.

Roy: This caller yesterday, kind of shocked, he kind of put the fear of G-d into everybody, so I'm not expecting many calls. So I'm going to be talking with Marty.

Roy: We're going to go to Marty now.
Hello Marty. I hope that was an interesting explanation for you.
Me: Yes, yesterday we touched on some things, that today, kind of reaffirming it with the love of evil. I know that sounds kind of classical, but
Roy: No, it's true
Me: When I was just 14 years old, I was a voracious reader about WWII, and found myself emotionally backing or rooting for the Germans and the Japanese, and I'm Jewish living in a household that didn't allow German products in the house. I was totally bewildered by my own reactions to that…
Roy: That's not difficult to understand. It only represents a loathing towards your own father and religion.
Me: Yes, this is absolutely true; I'd like to turn our attention to matters of sexuality

Roy: Of course… That loathing opened you to be molested by boys. Cause you see the loathing towards… Was it your father…

Me: Yes, my father was a… (sigh) It took me many years to see – to see my own contempt and hatred and come to grips with it. The meditation allowed that to come to the fore, and before he passed away, I did have at least a couple of minutes where I spoke to him asking him to forgive me for my resentment of him because he allowed my mother to really take the stronger hand.

Roy: You resented his weakness

Me: Yes

Roy: When you resented your father's weakness you rejected your father and could only accept your mother's identity, because a real father's love, if there was a real father was in that body, a real president in that office of fatherhood, he would have loved you in such a way as to save you from your identification with women.

Me: And that accounts for the fact that I have a real difficult time when I am in the presence who is strong, and right, I can feel my emotions flip-flopping but I think that might have been years ago. And at this point I'm still trying to deal with…well, a feminine identification during the act of love. It starts out, I feel real red blooded, and, uh, manly.

Roy: Well, you're trying to be a man, but you have a feminine nature which is embarrassing to you

Me: OK

Roy: Your identity should be an "it" identity, in other words, a G-d nature in you, a godly nature; you lack the link to your creator that makes you a man, even as your father did, do you see that?

Me: Let me give you an instance

Roy: and you're bonded to a woman, but you don't know have to overcome this bond, you only know how to run away from this truth of your femininity trying to be a man by virtue of getting high on sex and apparently getting the upper hand in your own mind, you get high on sex, and forgetfulness… Can finish the thought here…

When a man like you tries to be a man which you're not – and the whole idea of manliness being derived from the best sex you ever had, the best performance, the most excitement you can get, that really defeats the whole purpose. The whole purpose, most men get their sense of identity from successful relationship with women: The best sex, the most excitement, the most pleasure.

There's nothing unusual about what you do, it's the same mistake every man that ever lived makes: he always tries to give himself the idea that he is something- a man - but he is a bigger beast at the very best, or a big wimp, for sex - at the very worst. But they're both bad, don't get me wrong. But the idea that you can become more of a man by having better sex, more exciting sex is only a distraction from the truth: that what is really happening is you're becoming more of a woman.

Me: This was made clear to me about 5-6 years ago. I without trying to bore your audience, and without trying to make myself sound heroic, I left that life, lifestyle, and yes its true I always tried to get to the peaks of delirium with sex. Well, what's given me a hope, that I had achieved growth, and am wondering whether I should pursue it is I had returned to my ex-wife as a little bit of a hero. She had remarried a no-goodnik, and I had cleaned up my act to return so I could be with where all my kids were - all of us together - I helped bail her out of this bad second marriage, I paid the second husband off as far as his interest in the house purchased together.

And at that moment when we were together and we - I'll use the expression, made love - and I didn't sink into - nor did I lose my potency nor did I have to resort to these fantasies in order to gain pleasure and physical excitement to complete the act.

Roy: Well, that's very important…

Me: Then two days later, or later, when I'm sittin' around the living room, a thought comes into my head "Boy, that was kinda' nice, we should do that again"

Roy: You had better watch for those thoughts…

Can u hold the line? I apologize. Can you hold for a minute?

Me: Yeah

Roy: Every once in a while, my callers become like guests on the program, even though they're kind of patients. Such a person in Marty, and we're going to continue.

What were you saying before we made that break, Marty?

Me: The amount of submergence that I allow my mind to submerge into fantasy

Roy: Escape, escape…

Me: The more pleasure I crave then I'm going down into the pit… into the toilet

Roy: All men must realize that, and women, too…

Me: The same way that smoking fell away when I first started your meditation tape. The same kind of "letting it go" happened when I'm praying a lot and I'm meditating two-three times a day, I found that I could go weeks without, uh, 'taking myself in hand,' so to speak to relieve sexual tension.

Roy: That's very clear.

Me: I had to give up television, and I found that if I don't submerge into the fantasy then I'm able to walk clearer and more spiritual.

Roy: That's correct..

Me: However, the whole question that has been on my mind is "Can I look forward to a life; should I try to find a female to have companionship for this next few years. Or would I be doing her a disservice and myself getting into..

Roy: I think that you in your lust and your confusion contributed to her misery and suffering. Whereby you weren't really a man. She went off looking for a man the way women do when they are disgusted and angry, they usually end up with one that worse. The relationship of marriage is sacred, and if at all (possible) that you can be the father towards the children and the husband to your wife, as you appear to be moving towards, that is very very essential to your recovery.

Me: The children I'm still actively trying to – I've screwed them up.

Roy: But you've become the father in you in the manner of speaking, you've done the same thing your father wasn't there for you and you won't be there for your kids. And all you're gonna do is let the women imprint them with her nature

Me: She has already. They're fifteen to twenty-three years old…

Roy: I know but that's why we have feminine men in our society. Beasts. Beast men. We have lusty beast-men like yourself – beasties, and weak, feeble men, "yes dear" weak for sex, weak, feeble men, subject to dominating witch women, who will give up their life to the women as long as they'll sexually mother them.

Me: That was my father 100% and that was me, till I feel I spiritually changed. Maybe in a carnal physical nature I might as well say "Hey, I had ten times more sex than any normal man and I'm just gonna let it go and stay celibate for the rest of my life; or would I be a jerk for taking that road and…

Roy: My advice to you is this: Go back to your wife, and if there is never any sex between you at all, be a husband; be the father you never were, for every man is looking for the mother he's always known, and every woman is looking for the father she's never known. Try to be that father to her. Women need a spiritual quality that is like a good father in her husband, and that good quality in you transcends your wicked, selfish need for sex, and you can transcend that wicked need for sex, if are a very secure person and you love your wife. Love the hell out of her, so to speak. But you love her and you're true to her. No matter what if she's cantankerous, and she's manipulative, whatever it is. You're patient and you endure her and you provide for her and protect her and you cherish her. There is a quality about that which tames the sexual impulse. It helps to tame it. It helps to order it, so it's not an abuse for your own glory and sexual pleasure, follow that?

Me: Yes

Roy: Cause you're feeding the beast every time, and you're becoming less and less of a human and less and less of a man, more and more of a beast and more and more in the extreme a wimp, and a stench in the nostrils of every woman.

   Follow that?

Me: Yes I do.

Roy: Remember what I told you about fantasy. Even if you don't have the woman, but you get disgusted and you find yourself affected by them too much, and you run away from them, because they're dangerous then, cause you've made them dangerous. When you conjure up that image so you can awaken your sexual feeling and lose yourself in it in your room you're getting into the image and you get excited but what is behind the

image will get into you, and it will kill your soul.
Me: Absolutely.[39]

---

[39] www.fhu.com Roy Masters_ Foundation of Human Understanding

Second Visitation

I came away from that call invigorated spiritually; reaffirmed in my belief that I was *on the path*. For the next sixteen months, I would look closer at my sexual fantasy through spiritual eyes. I would no longer regard myself as engaging in something so horrible that it was better to just not think about, but instead a pilgrim – a prodigal son – yearning for absolution. *He who the Lord loves, He chastises.* My 'hand-on-my-penis was no longer my-hand-against-G-d,' but an opportunity to learn about the carnal forces triggering erotic reactions within the deepest recesses of my personal conscious and unconscious.

Things began to change in small ways seemingly unrelated to the great truths I was seeking. For the first time in my life, I no longer sought unfair advantage. If I was overpaid by a clerk making change, I returned the overage without puffing up and congratulating myself. I began to be patient in traffic. I began to make allowances for mistakes on the part of other drivers on the road as well as annoying shoppers in stores. I no longer took offense so easily in the workplace. I could speak to women – and note the temptation – without submerging into sexual lust. I began to do things – good and right – that people never even knew about, and I wasn't getting a swelled head over it. *'Two steps forward, one step-back'* began to deliver me into a progressive march of self-improvement.

In John 15, the Hebrew Messiah said: *"Every branch in me that bears not fruit He takes away; and every branch that bears fruit, He prunes, that it may bring forth more fruit."*

I was bearing fruit. But as my bed burned with sexual hunger, my fantasies offered newer, more pleasurable and more dramatic story lines as their essential content became more clear, yet seemingly more demonic.

I found myself becoming aware of the true nature of excitement. This 'emotion' reigns supreme in the heights of cocaine intoxication. When I was shooting up hundreds of dollars worth, and could inject any amount I wanted, I saw that even at the very height, there really was a cosmic sterility, an emptiness that was simply raw excitement. That was all. Excitement is not even true euphoria. It is not even a total release from anxiety; it offers a temporary exhilarating substitute. It is not nirvana. It is saccharine sweetness instead of milk and honey; the air conditioning of Las Vegas compared to the mountain air of the Rockies. It was drinking salt water to quench a thirst that would always return.

I had rediscovered the books of Carlos Castaneda. I found that to *'live like a warrior,'* by reducing my wants to nothing dovetailed perfectly with my realizing a Samadhi consciousness through the meditation ("*A man has four natural enemies: Fear, clarity, power and old age.*"[40]) Yes, clarity (aka awareness) does appear (falsely) as an enemy.

I did not read every page in his books, or seek to force his spiritual philosophy into my life. I allowed certain of his ideas to take root and support others I had already given light and attention to. The idea of being a spiritual "warrior" fit well with my daily regimen of meditation and prayer. The same warrior voice speaks in non-grammatical urgings when I'm writing at 4 am on a wintry morning.

'*Let's go for a walk; gear up for a four-mile walk along the frozen river on icy paths at zero degrees. It's 4 am so bring the cell phone. T-shirt, turtleneck, sweater, flannel-lined shirt, sweatshirt-with-hood, heavy coat, gloves. Don't forget matches for the joint.*'

"Oh no..." another voice responds without grammar. "*It's freezing out... got half-a-cold already.... back hurts.... all this walking could make things worse.*" Prudent middle-class-momma spirits eagerly engage lazy energies to form an alliance celebrating inertia.

Sarge: *We're going. Sneakers or boots*?

Rest-of-Marty says "*OK*," a little less grudging each time. And I start to walk daily along the river and through the forest. Five miles. Ten miles. Repeatedly. Life begins to change. "*Yeah, let's take a walk!*"

I would be in the second day of a fast and in a checkout line. The candy right next to me beckons with a sudden supernatural delicious attraction, an exploding mix of sweet chocolate coursing almost-tasted through my tongue's memory pipes. The warrior within, already strengthened by the fast, speaks in a sergeant's tone:

'*Oh, does the little bitch-boy need a piece of candy? Is that what you need*, (sarcastically) '*I want my candy?!*' *Are you gonna' whine like a little girl, now*?' I shrug and don't give it another thought. I begin to feel a humble yet spiritual swagger.

While Roy Masters would have been the first to object to such far eastern categorization of his meditation techniques as well as the mind-expanding substances co-existing within the meditation, I was nevertheless aware that my consciousness was becoming on par with many of these eastern definitions.

Castaneda's acknowledgement of the "*beings of light*," along with that of '*The Mescalito*' fit nicely with my own experience. Also, his definitions

---

[40] *The Wheel of Time, Carlos Castenada; Washington Sqaure, 2001 p21*

concerning the power of a man's decisions, detachment, will, patience and long-suffering were also dovetailing nicely with my growing use of meditation, prayer, and fasting. In addition, other changes were going on of a totally self-motivated nature. Often it simply seemed like a natural outgrowth of living.

One such case was red meat. I had always looked at the expensive steak as a special treat. Now I found myself afterwards feeling so sluggish and logy that the steak was no joy at all. Looking at the animal's remains on my plate, I sensed something vaguely offensive about the heavy piece of dead meat. I found chicken and fish more palatable, often eating no meat at all for extended periods of time. There is a spiritual leanness to disciplining the food intake, and this is the last great battle of the flesh. This began to become apparent after about five years of meditation, and for the last eight years I had kept no alcohol in the house, and never drank spirits. I would drink a little wine or sometimes a few beers, and a couple of pitchers with the once-a-year-dancing-till-the-band-closed at the local summer festival. Sometimes a year would pass without drinking any alcohol at all. Very soon after starting the Observation Exercise/ Meditation, I found myself giving up refined sugar, nicotine and television reception. If I was told there was an outstanding TV series, I would simply buy or rent the series on DVD. I added – sometimes spacing the imbibing between periods of months or years– the prudent, occasional use of the *psilocybin mushroom*, a *phenethylamine*[41] and/or *Salvia Divinorum*.

I tried the *Salvia Divinorum* experience again. It was powerful, dramatic and completely terrifying. What was totally mind-blowing was while researching the plant's effects prior to taking it, I was impressed with the fact that when a group of gringo psychiatrists had gone out into the Mexican desert to take *Salvia Divinorum* with the local *cuaranderos (shamans, healers)*, they had been made to repeat words of acknowledgement that what they were about to experience would be met with great respect. I came across the following pronouncement by the eldest *cuarandero* (translated here):

> **"Salvia Divinorum is primarily used in situations where the cuarandero (sorcerer, shaman, medicine man) feels it is necessary to travel into the supernatural world in order to discover the true cause of the (patient's) trouble."** [42]

---

[41] *PIHKAL ('Phenethylamines I Have Known and Loved" Transform Press 1991*
[42] www.sagewisdom.org; *or www.trailopen.com*

This experience offered something different than the "*other*" of McKenna's Psilocybin mushroom, and/or the *Mescalito* of Carlos Casteneda. But another '*space of life*' was in even greater presence within the Salvia experience. As always, when thought returns to the consciousness, the total confusion has one scrambling for mental control of one's own mind. You want to bring to consciousness 'thought, control and understanding.' **Rushing into this is a BIG MISTAKE**. I wailed in my own hell.

After a complete after-death-experience of complete hell and terror, I started praying in a babbling sweat of tears with snot running out of my nose. After going to hell and praying to G-d after returning from the effects of one particularly hellacious Salvia experience (my next-to-last one), I had started to meditate, and literally saw a neon type of halo surrounding an image of my body. There was a golden glowing smoothness and a graceful flowing, except where my upper left ear and shoulder area was concerned. There it appeared grossly jagged, just like a police-chalk-outline. I realized what the Mexican Indians had said about it was exactly portrayed as the trauma of my childhood:

> **Salvia Divinorum is primarily used in situations where the cuarandero sorcerer, shaman, medicine man) feels it is necessary to travel into the supernatural world in order to discover the true cause of the patient's trouble**.

After great preparation, I ordered a bunch of *Salvia Divinorum* in "tea-leaf tincture" form, imbibing a little at a time. Although to my frightened mind I was waking a hibernating bear up 'a little at a time,' I had to find my "*governing dynamic*," to quote the great John Nash.[43]

Revelation came: I was able to see barriers fall away that had previously existed regarding this early childhood trauma. I had assumed when talking with Roy Masters in my July 2003 phone call that my trauma was initially one of being sexually molested by the two boys in Brooklyn, as if that was the first major traumatic experience. Now, after the *Salvia Divinorum*, I saw it was the situation of being slapped by my mother on my upper left side that I was reacting to (hence the sharp police-chalk-outline). I realized (within epiphany) that the humiliating scissoring of my pants – coupled with the physical abuse by my mother – held within it a certain dynamism that helped to create a behavior by which I could position myself before those abusive boys. The true post-traumatic-stress-

---

[43] "*a Beautiful Mind,*" (*Nasar*) Simon & Shuster 1994. Oscar-worthy performance by Russell Crowe in the movie.

disorder created the urge to send me down that block to be abused that night by that Brooklyn gang. I was already the vampire's apprentice looking to get bitten. I was still – half-a-lifetime later – infected with it. It was still within my journey to rid myself of it.

*In other words, it wasn't what my mother or father did that was crucial. It was **my reaction to it** that created the trauma*, and my continued reaction to it within my mental experience that was crucial. My parents were both dead. It was ***my*** hatred, my anger, my resentment which festered beneath consciousness that caused the problems of my life. This emotional volcano caused me to enter into more wrong behavior which caused more need for dissociative "not-me" activity until I broke under the weight of the denial.

I had also been given a glimpse of something even further back in my life, an event experienced while nursing at my mother's breast that also prepared the ground for a feminine nature within my male psyche.

I needed to look further into my hyper-personal sexuality. With the exception of Roy Masters, there was no one I knew of who really had a clue how to overcome the beast. I had to talk to Roy. But first, something else was nagging at me, and even then wouldn't let me go.

Chapter 21 – The Paltrownian Synchronicity
"Britney Spears' 114th Dream"[44]

Over the course of the next two weeks, I found consistent energies returning to direct my consciousness – both in and out of meditation – to watch a particular videotape. Finally, I obliged the notion by taking from my closet a tape of Gwyneth Paltrow's interview with James Lipton from "*In the Actor's Studio.*"

Why – I asked myself – am I watching this? I had watched most of it when I taped it when it originally aired, then watched it completely when I had had the time. Now this urging to watch the interview a third time. There just seemed to be a continual, nagging leading… I determined to complete the investigation and sat down for yet another ministration under the spell of the peerless Ms. Paltrow, but the experience was not unlike dragging a complaining little boy into a work of serious theatre.

The show started and then – as if I had never heard it before, I hear her say, "*We work out our conflicts through our art.*"

B-O-O-M — *That's it!*"

This same source was now speaking to my consciousness. There was a releasing of all kinds of understanding which spoke to my brain. It was an *erupting*: '*This is what you're supposed to be doing! This is why you've been dragging around these notebooks full of ideas for nine years.*' I realized with no small addition to my mounting individuation that I had been *led* to this moment, by forces both within me and without me. I had entered another state of Synchronicity.[45]

---

[44] Skeleton outline of the screenplay at www.trailopen.com/index-3.html

[45] *Synchronicity is a word created by the Swiss psychologist Carl Jung to describe the alignment of "universal forces" with the life experiences of an individual. Jung believed that many experiences perceived as coincidences were not merely due to chance, but instead reflected the creation of an event or circumstance by the "co-inciting" or alignment of such forces. The process of becoming intuitively aware and acting in harmony with these forces is what Jung labeled "individuation." Jung said that an individuated person would actually shape events around them through the communication of their consciousness with the collective unconscious.*

I had entered a state of understanding: *The same force that motivated my desire to watch the tape was energizing this realization in me.*

The existential proof could be explained as that sudden realization one has when finally remembering a name when you're trying hard to remember it… it's on the tip-of-your-tongue, and then suddenly it comes to mind and ***that's it***. You just *know* that that's the right name. I just *knew* it. It was elevating and humbling at the same time. It was definitely not an ego trip. It was energizing without the stimulating side-effect of excitement or self-inflation. It was something new I was to journey into...

I started to write. Sexual themes of a more and more bizarre nature began to rise up. I didn't dare stop to contemplate them; I simply had to translate them onto the page. When the demons came to tempt me, I received at least part of the answer concerning what was different about the present situation. I wasn't capitulating into submergence into the subject matter. I couldn't write about sex before because I became too enthralled by the lust of it to continue objectively to write. Writing about anger suffered the same fate. I couldn't write concerning resentment of parents as long as the resentment itself bested me to submerge myself in its emotional imaginings.

After months of writing prodigious swarms of impotent beginnings along with raging, sputtering, off-track musings, I awoke in the middle of one very special night. Pressing and prescient, a consciousness was so upon me and pressing so heavily that if the muzzle of a gun barrel was being pressed to my head along with the words *"don't move,"* my attention could not have been captured more completely.

I dare not knock it off its prescient seat by thinking. I knew in a way other than words can describe I was not to think where my glasses were in the dark next to my bed, or even consider text-entry by waiting for the hard drive to un-sleep, no, no, no…I was directed by a sense rather than a voice – and if it must be called a '*voice*,' than an ungrammatical one which the sound of a distant cricket could overpower. It directed me out into the kitchen where a nightlight would provide all that was necessary to start writing on a large white envelope of junk mail this same spirit reminded me (in the same non-grammatical preconscious) that had a dull pencil sitting next to it. I walked toward my writing elements bent over in the same position I had gotten out of bed in, lest the straightening up of my body cause an uninvited consciousness to be entertained.

Thus would begin the fabric of a play written in a dream about a dream. Sputtering like water in a pipe that's been shut off for a long time and is now turned back on, ideas, concepts and relationships shot out onto that junk-mail envelope. As the story content entered a sensual plane never before explored, I was tempted to submerge into thinking about this sexuality that was around me and within me. The demons' temptation of me became their undoing, for I simply became aware of them, and looked at them without reaction of any kind. Immediately, these demons of sexual temptation, appearing like foxes and hounds of hell together, were beneath me and harnessed like Alaskan Huskies on a sled. I, standing in another dimension within this ethereal landscape, stood poised within this spiritual steppe on this sled, and directed these demon-dogs; bleeding their ink onto the page. Phrases and ideas bubbled up one after another. Spirits were everywhere as my character became separated into "good" and "bad" halves. Poems, jokes, characters, amusing quips and bizarre dream-sequences all started flowing out in archaic and seemingly chaotic formulations, only to reset and reorganize within a creative mentality pulling the pieces together into a complex coherency that was unseen when I began to write it. *You can't discover new oceans unless you have the courage to lose sight of the shore.* Thus was the musical video screenplay *"Britney Spears 114th Dream"* born.

When C.G. Jung said the anima is a female oriented archetype in the collective unconscious of males, he was speaking of a spiritual entity. While we know the world is eager to swallow the sludge of pop psychology, there is no bigger misunderstanding of *anima* than to think it has anything to do with the sensual or even worse, homosexuality.

There is a "gatekeeper' or 'ferryperson' quality concerning the anima concept that has been neglected by those who claim to study such matters. It remains to be seen, however, if those who "draw maps" and those who "make the journey" agree on things so esoteric. What else but the anima can speak of temptation in the manner provided in the later acts of *Britney Spears 114th Dream*?

There was perhaps – due to my traumatized makeup – a time when I needed the excitements of the world and the flesh in order to grow. *When I was a child, I did childish things. Now it is time to put these things away*, says the apostle. In the search for salvation, the path will always lead inside to Him. Thus we see this struggle most acutely in the later acts.

"You can't discover new oceans unless you have the courage to lose sight of the shore."

The Paltrownian Synchronicity, in conjunction with *Homage to the Anima Productions,* is pleased to bring to you

Britney Spears' 114th Dream©[46]

A Three-Act Musical/Music-Video/Screenplay

1st Britney - In the Time of Chaos

2nd Britney - Going for the Gusto, But The Gusto Gets You (Bad Britney vs. Good Britney)

3rd Britney - Into The Light

Mitch Abramson
PO Box 165
Chaska MN 55318
mitchpod@gmail.com
WGA #1005253
"I will use the foolish things of the world to confound the wise" (1Cor:1:27)

---

[46] *Outline/skeleton of the screenplay available for free download* www.trailopen.com *- Light for Britney*

Chapter 22 – Jacob Angel

With the completion of *Britney's Dream*, I assumed all Britannic activity was taken care of in *"Wonderland"* and *"Alice"* was behind me. I determined to fast, pray and continue to work at my humble, low-paying job while finishing my undergraduate degree online. I had started physically thirty-five years before in uptown New York, and was now completing it on a PC. After that, I would determine if I could stomach any more of this sham known as "education." If I could I would go on to obtain a Masters Degree courtesy of 100% loans from Uncle Sam. I didn't want to show up at age seventy at my kids' door broke, and I was only a lost paycheck away from living in a cardboard box.

I could already hear the manager of the homeless shelter: *"Golly, you're such a smart guy! How'd you wind up here?"* Images of my now-deceased father proclaiming proudly *"The head administrator for all the homeless centers for the entire East Coast said my son was **the** smartest guy ever to be in a homeless shelter!"* I had found a job as a security guard on the graveyard shift making three-quarters of what I had in my hi-tech-cubby-slave-job but it gave me lots of time to meditate, read and write while going paycheck-to-paycheck. I had everything I needed.

Jacob Angel **on line one!**

Who was he? Where did he come from? These things were never spoken of. No one dared. Obviously the reader, however, has a right to ask. He had to be connected through the arrangements of *Salvia Divinorum* as well as through the Castenadian *Mescalito*. I knew the *Beings of Light* were definitely no strangers to his cosmic handshake. Something of the *Order of Melchizedek* hung vaguely about his ancient resume; the sound of a page rustling within a fourth dimensional whisper. You can't play games with *time*. There's certainly no place to hide. You wouldn't dare. You've come too far, for He who judges all knows just how much you know of Him, and holds you to this account. He is judge of all things at all moments at and for all time. Break open your heart now and cry-to-death in His arms. He will bring you back to a new life.

My heart yearns to be servant to the Hebrew messiah. There is a temptation to be a coward and a traitor, but there is always temptation. Only the closer you get to *"truth,"* the more subtle the satanic mental operations are at mixing a growing desire to please G-d with spiritual pride in order to convince you that the critical voice in your head *is* G-d's.

The enemy is a liar and mocks ever so devilishly, but being free from sin I also know with grace I am a son of the King. I am also a son of

Abraham. Now I have to represent my "self." For me, meeting Jacob always means placing myself in the same mental state I would be in if Mr. Spock were to place his hands on my head in preparation for a Vulcan mind-meld. A space alien from *The Simpsons* sits perched inside each ear, monitoring my obedience to the command not to submerge into *thought*.

"Yes, Jacob."

"Need to see you. Important. A "can" [47] has just surfaced in Burbank. I'll meet you at *Winkies*.

The scene at *Winkies* (from David Lynch's *Mulholland Drive*) offered a sense of relevancy only Jacob provides. I arrive to find him sitting at the same table as in the movie, of course. He is in the *agent-friend's* role (the witness-helper to the dreaming guy who went looking to find something he wasn't ready to find). He is eating, and looks at me as I eye my full plate, very aware of the assumed roles from the movie. I eat with confidence however, and refuse the intimidation. Jacob smiles, and I drop my eyes as I realize he is pleased at what he must consider my pluck.

"I brought my appetite," I proffer with a sense of the upbeat.

"Better eat now then. You *may* lose it."

I take heart in that he used the word "may" and hope my smile doesn't give too much away. *Let patience have its perfect work…* I gulp and focus on the blood creating a tingling sensation in my right pinky, then ring finger, in my mind's eye… *Innermost being is calmly sending out energy to its outermost limits…* I'm seeing and judging the distance from the back of my imaginary hand emerging to and through the center of my fore...

"Here it is," he says suddenly, freezing my thought as he spins a laptop around towards me. My movie is playing. It's near the end of the *114th Dream*; the Britannic "*last supper*" is followed by Britney's "*I have a dream*" speech, but something new was happening here. Instead of the fadeout and credits, the screen pulled back to reveal the two *Britnii* watching from their seats in the movie theatre, sharing a tub of popcorn held in *Good Britney's* (GB's) lap.

As the credits role, they get up to leave as do others in the theatre. *Bad Britney* (BB) murmurs a little drowsily, as they start to rise and move toward the aisle: "*Uhmm, cutie at 3 o'clock.*" They both flick their eyes to the right to scope on a good-looking young man walking up the aisle leaving the theatre.

GB shrugs, and, turning to face BB, directs her attention to the screen with a raised eyebrow. "*Well?*"

---

[47] *A film can from a professional film production*

BB considers a moment. "*Pretty heavy, all that good and **evil** stuff,*" making a body-language caricature exaggerating the word '*evil.*'

"*Good and evil? That's what it's all about. Not this craziness,*" GB answers impatiently as she starts to build up steam. "*Where'ya gonna be in ten years? Handcuffing yourself naked to a parking meter in front of some Compton strip-joint?*"

BB is taken aback, blinking. "*Wha? Wha whazzat? What do I handcuff myself to...? that sounds kinda....*"

GB laughs, shaking her head in spite of herself.

"*Where?*" BB asks in a low tone (putting her arm through GB's and laying her head against GB's shoulder as they continue to slowly walk up the aisle. "*Where should I go?*" she asks in a soft whisper.

"*You should go home. Come home... and... we'll take care of ourselves... ourselves.*"

They walk in silence, camera from behind shows BB tentatively putting her arm around GB's waist.

BB slowly sighs "*...come in on it with me?*"

GB puts her arm around BB, as the latter rests her head on GB's shoulder.

"*I still have love for us; although the flesh does war against the spirit... (sighs)... life's a journey, ya big stoop,*" whispers GB, placing her arm around BB's waist.

They walk out, the backs of their blouses demonstrating a logo of two different horns on the same goat.

Jacob clicks the laptop off.

I exhale. "This is what you got, huh?"

"It's enough," Jacob responds.

"What do ya' mean, its enough?"

"This invalidates your whole program. This is the leaven leavening the whole loaf. Good and Bad Britney merging in some kind of sex-abation? This takes all your credibility and shreds you like lettuce on a cheap sandwich. This is worse than a sellout. You know what this is? This is *Swaggert*. You ain't got dick anymore."

"I have more than dick. I will stand, Jacob, for what is coming. I am not in denial here. G-d is inherently accepting regarding our growth... although admittedly I hope I don't die too soon," I add, suddenly frowning in concern. "He who the Father *loves*, he *chastises*. The word *chastises* would not be in there *to begin with* if we were all perfectly deserving of his love. It shows we can be saved even while we're still wrestling with our flesh, but I know G-d's not a chump I can play. I am trying to play it *straight*. I'm not trying to hide anything. He sees my heart wrestling. Part of my flesh is my sexuality. This has been created by the forces of this world since I was five years old. A five-year old is not responsible for the evil in this world. I have been effected by the trauma and the evil in this world, and when I have to release my pent-up seed I need to visit the sexualized energies stemming from that trauma. If I can be "objective" to my fantasy, if I can stay "detached" while I slip a moment into neutral gear and receive wisdom rather than submergent pornographic consciousness, I better understand what excitement and pleasure means to me in relation to that very experience. I continue to be effected by it. Resentment and repressed anger over the unjust and cruel forces thrust upon us since childhood produce these imaginary sexual seas I swim to satisfaction in. This is all an *inside job* anyway," I turn to Jacob, whom I catch looking not displeased.

"I refuse to believe I'm still a whoremonger. I'm not manipulating my lust into the lives of others, but releasing the sexual tension in the dream of self-release. I'm not "*repressing*" but dealing with the deepest of my sexual energies in the healthiest way possible. I'm not blinking. This is my age and my time. There is a psychological purpose for dreams. You know. In some cases it blows off psychological steam; literally with nocturnal emissions for some people."

Jacob nods that he understands this elemental intellectual foundation. "Also, it is the natural wholeness of light and dark; yin and yang. Mother Theresa might have dreamt she was kickin' the crap out of a crippled beggar. What is inadmissible to our consciousness by day we see in our dreams at night. Certain of the chosen who are still lost and burning still only see safety and security in their sleep; to awaken is to live in the anxious hell of their consciousness. Or if in **those very special cases** where anger dominates our living, we may find peace (only) in dreams and also hate to wake up. Obviously, if it is only in dreams that one is secure and free from anxiety, then you could be living dangerously close to the "mirage" of schizophrenia. That is their yin and yang in the twisted agony of the tormented. Such are many who the Father is calling.

"So be it for all eternity, that they who yearn shall be filled; in the name of He who was raised from death," intoned Jacob.

"Amen," say I, and plow on. "However, let's look at these fantasies as messages from the unconscious to our "conscious" selves. In addition to their role as psychological geysers which alleviate unconscious pressure, they "live" in order that you become aware of your conflict, your duality. For it is with awareness of these dynamisms that the destructive force of them is lessened. Yet part of the dynamism's effort to "stay alive-in-you" is to deny that it is there. It does this by keeping us busy with attention elsewhere. It does this by calling them infrahuman and inferring G-d would fall off his throne if He were to see them. The more we can enter into a consciousness that is still and quiet awareness the less power it has over us."

"Consequently, my esteemed friend, let me say with all the humility received from He with whom I have to do, that I am entering that which is normally the *'not-me'* of sexual dreams in order to create a more perfect "me," not a more pornographic "me."
Jacob is dismissive.
"This doesn't look straight. Do we engage in sin that grace should abound?"

"Is it sin if I do it by myself? The prophet says Moses "had moisture" till he was over one-hundred. What did *he* do with his? I am still fighting the good fight...." I offer with a stutter.

"But that's just what you have here! Where's the *good fight*? GB has let evil back in, and now must bow to it at some level."

"Let evil back in at some level. At some level…" Now, that is an interesting statement, Jacob. How can one discern the depth of the sexual twisting of the childhood trauma without sorting it out – putting it up on the stage of consciousness; in slow-mo as it were – in sexual behavior – masturbatory or otherwise? You cannot be a psychic explorer without making the journey; if you investigate quicksand you're gonna stick your foot in. Else you're a doctorate on the wall, a virgin holding forth as a sex-pert. The Lord of all spoke of the Father seeing the Prodigal Son coming from "*a long way off*." Am I further away than '*a long way off*? I think not."

To answer that question then of "*where's the good fight?*" it is not a matter of content or levels of submergence into 'bad' or 'good.' It is a matter of awareness. Spreading every nuance of the fantasy open for conscious dissection is part of an awareness that brings understanding. It might even be within calling distance of something called '*wisdom*.' I'm not sure," I add quickly, noting his look go aghast. I plunge on.

"The mental observation of spreading expanding consciousness via the exercising of awareness from the "*innermost being to the outermost limits*," takes the sexual awareness and sends your exposed inner censor/demon running out of the room. I learned they're most scary when they are leaving. It helps for me to remember that rather than react to them as they leave. Cause reacting allows them to stay longer.

"There is another dimension here, Jacob: Are we into 'works' that I should run into heaven kneeling in my mind to proclaim "*See, see! I never* touch my pecker or think sexually active thoughts? Never think proud thoughts? Never imagine myself in heroic, powerful positions rescuing those around me in order to receive their adoration? Do I get more "points" in heaven for seeing myself a big shot giving to charity as opposed to a sexually charged horndog? We know there is one who judges. Someday I will stand before Him and know."

Jacob looks away, rolling his eyes a little while shaking his head. Yet I did not imagine it; *I caught the hint of a smile*!

I pressed. "Yearning for right standing with Him with whom we have to do, while the flesh demands its due from a prodigal son staggering home. Is that sin? Is that what you mean 'GB has allowed BB back in *at some level*?' Should we shake the sexual tension from our bodies in PG-13 only? Shall we repent as sinners when seeking bodily relief by ourselves? Where does the sky meet the sea? Where does the soul accept the responsibility for sin, and when is it merely the temptation of fantasy we are aware of within the dynamism generated by our human experience? I am believing that at this point in my life, I need to – both physically and psychically – rid my body of this sexual tension."

"Let me question here what the *'thorn in Paul's flesh'* could have meant. The prophet says that was something that would keep him from being too proud of himself. Well, one look into my sex fantasies accomplishes that. Something else, too. The Apostle Paul and all the Prophets didn't have to walk in malls where teenage girls sashay saucily in front of them wearing short-shorts with the word "**J U I C Y**" stenciled on their bottoms."

Jacob, now genuinely reflective: "Let me help you. I'll pose the question: Is this merely bodily relief or taking opportunity to worship in Satan's playground? Yet it is not linear, for as you say, the prodigal son is seen afar off. The Lord of Hosts judges all things."

I plunge forward. "I will seek that difference with Him with whom I have to do, for I am not in denial. Didn't the Apostle Paul say it is better for a man to marry than his body burn? So there is acknowledgement that the body burns with its own physical needs… even in the saint?" I speak these last words trying to make it sound like a statement of conviction, but the lack of surety belies my confidence. Perhaps faith grows most in these areas of doubt, where our yearning to do right merges with our conscience surrounded by the accusing taunts of the enemy of our souls pretending it's the voice of G-d. And the closer you get to G-d the more subtle the enemy is. I take everything I have or might ever have and wager it on one roll of pitch and toss:

"*I refuse to believe my hand on my penis is my hand against G-d.*"

Jacob appeared so still that I had to blink and refocus. Although he didn't move at all, a reorientation suddenly seemed necessary for me to be able to continue looking at him. He appeared so perfectly still that I allowed my own awareness to transcend the urge to think and categorize what I was seeing. His hair started to flow as if affected by some soft wind. His chest area to his waist appeared transformed into a jeweled hill with sun and sky, scarves of floating color. Metaphysical flowers representing the *fruits of the spirit* filled the changing ether around him.

But in each case I couldn't help trying to focus and describe and categorize the phenomenon to myself, even as it disappeared as a dust mite does when you try to focus on it. I was trying to imbibe, rather than just be aware. Suddenly he was back: looking normal in the little booth.

"He will see you," he said quietly.

I started to choke up and my eyes misted. He rose to leave. I hastened to my feet, standing opposite him, unashamed in my willingness to show reverence and respect. Unabashed, I bowed slightly without affectation. As I lifted my eyes back up, he no longer appeared to them.

Chapter 23 – Sexual Showdown

From whence comes pleasure? A seeming silly question to pose to a man laying in bed with his hand on his *Johnson*. Let's go to the point at hand: You're alone in bed trying to sleep. Your mind is overwhelmed by sexual reverie and you decide to rid yourself of the tension by committing to engage the physical behavior necessary for relief. You decide to "*do it,*" and make the necessary arrangements to deal with the matter. Again, '*from whence comes pleasure?*'

'*You manipulate it, and you get pleasure, stupid,*' a scoffing thought answers.

'*Oh, really?*' counters the new good-cop. '*I believe I could manipulate this tool and all I'd get was sore without fantasy,*' adds the spirit of understanding.

'*What do you mean?*' says bad-cop.

'*I mean I could lay here pullin' till the cows come home, but without a fantasy to stir into the mix, nothing's comin.*'

So reader, what happens next? Do we *decide* to "*think about something?*" No, we release from normal "self" consciousness, and croon sweetly in effortless indulgence for another consciousness; another spirit; a somewhat eager, alien dynamism with which to enter, submerge and replace our normal 'self' consciousness with. We croon for something to come up into us to release us from our conscious cultural proscriptions. (In coitus, the male may all too often draw up this "something" **through** the female. Some men, yes; some men, no. Some women may understand this more than others).

But even in autoerotic behavior, excitement joins pleasure as we silently gasp and moan, losing ourselves in the current reflection of our hungers. Normally '*not-me*' cultural aberrations flood consciousness. Unconscionable role-playing reflects expressive dynamisms, and excitement and pleasure unite with the urge-to-submerge into it deeper. Losing ourselves in the energy submerged into, we worship it as it envelops our lost consciousness, and we moan as the hungry getting fed.

We are swept into worlds we refuse to call our own. Dark and exciting, these vacations into unacceptable, seemingly infrahuman behaviors are unconsciously kept secret even from ourselves. The increased symbolic representations too much for most of us to acknowledge, we toss the awareness of our 'pleasure-center' right along with the moist evidence of its reality.

This new energy we drown in is beyond male or female; it is archetypal.[48] We swoon as its spirit floods into us; and we submit ourselves to its direction. Now we are *in it*, and we *are* it; commanding and commanded; degrading and degraded; humiliating and humiliated. Titillated, enticed and teased, we may titillate, entice and tease in our turn. Bonding ourselves within its passions, we lose ourselves within our roles, merging the moment of physical release to drown soulishly in our private and special "sub" mergence. A complete worship of orgasmic proportion, night after night, year after year, the "dynamism" longs to convince us its features need real-life expression, and we may begin to believe the voice of "*it*" is "*my voice* – or simply put, *'me.*' The more we refuse to become aware, the more possibility exists for the non-sexual expression to occur as "fate" in our lives.

Consequently, the business partner symbolically sodomizes you, but your poorly placed trust is metaphorical, not sexual. You let him push over your earlier objections, his more powerful personality overcame your tepid resistance, and now he has your money, or your wife, or your business, or whatever.

Your personality may seek to 'cover-up' and hide from this truth, conveniently – but actually being further emasculated – as you fall into personality substitutions that have you crying the blues over how badly this evil world has treated the innocent "you."

Perhaps it is the fantasy itself that needs its presence ministered to, its spirit worshipped, more than our bodies. Obviously there's more to the spirit of submission and humiliation than sexual release.

'*What's the point, genius?*' bad-cop says.

'Perhaps what we have here is the parallel that when we're hungry we think of food, but we can also just think of food and *get* hungry. So then

---

[48] *CG Jung's concept of a collective unconscious includes "archetypes." These are archaic, primordial and universal images that exist within the "collective unconscious" of all mankind. Any posture within man's consciousness or personal unconscious can and will be reflected by these emanations: for example, the Wise Old man, the Great Mother, the Trickster, the Loyal Knight, the Traitor, etc. Think on the shocked and disturbed four year-old who meanders into his divorced parent's bedroom to find a stranger in bed with his parent. The child will become upset. Why? No one told the child rules about matrimony and adultery, but at a totally unconscious level the toddler is deeply upset. Archetypes are part of our spirit world, a world not limited to the traditional concepts of angels and demons, but far richer in its diversity. ("The Archtypes of the Collective Unconscious"_Bolingen Series 1959_ CG Jung)*

we're hungry whether we were hungry or not when we began to think of food. Now the hunger for food (in this example) is not a natural result of living, but an emotional stimulant seeking satisfaction apart from the natural role. Just like constantly imagining sex. In this case it is not the physical sex urge that is making the cyclical demand for relief, but the spirit within the fantasy which is using the body to gain ascendancy (and worship for itself) through the physical manipulation of the creature-in-its-service. Is there not some nameless dynamism *behind* the fantasy? A motivator seeking such activity within us demanding behavior from us?

So even though you just had sex a relatively short time ago, you start thinking about it and now you're hungry for it again because you started thinking about it. You didn't start thinking about it because of the body's natural desire to procreate and release its pent-up tensions, but rather by an ignition of fertile imagination in order that the orgasm be made available for this spiritual, sexual and sensual imagining. The pleasure and excitement of the physical act the mere 'transport-mechanism' or 'requirement' by which the spirit comes alive and has its being.

The more one partner uses the other in such a manner, the more opportunity for enslavement, as sex becomes weapon and reward. The adoration of the female during sex, the knowledge within her how she is turning the man on all combine to create a man who loves the hell *in* the female, but doesn't love the hell *out of her*. Yet how can one avoid thinking about sex – and hence creating more bodily fluid needing more frequent release – when one is surrounded by the suggestive imagery of our culture 24/7?

Let's imagine a tribe where almost all the men have been decimated. The few males left spend all their time impregnating women, who, in this example, would be lined up outside his tent waiting their turn. Three to five women a day, ten pregnancies a week, 500 a year, twenty years equals 10,000 children. If a woman has ten kids, it's shocking. The male can shoot a lot of pollen.

Conclusion: The DNA within the male creates a being that sees a woman's sexual potential whether she's eight or eighty. The gentleman does not lust after his neighbor's wife, the under-aged or the elderly, but he does note their status. It is part of the DNA that allows him the capability to fertilize 10,000 women. In the Colonial 1700s a visiting male guest who was to sleep overnight in a household with young women in it was tied into a *'binding bag'* (see Heath Ledger's role in *"The Patriot"*). Perhaps they were more upfront in acknowledging a man's urges – and a female's lack of ability to resist – than we are today.

Our new-millennium culture has no precedent in human history regarding the total abandonment of clothing norms and sexual attitudes that had defined Western culture and couture for the last two thousand years. For almost 2000 years – from 'Day One' to about 1900 – women covered themselves from ankle to wrist. The paintings of the renaissance notwithstanding, for a woman to show her ankle, even in the 1800s, was considered scandalous.

As a teenager, I frequented New York City brothels in the mid-1960s. Some of the girls stood outside the doors looking more-or-less sultry and sexy. Their outfits can't compare to what many high school girls wear today. Now, fifty years later, it seems every female – even the church-going teen virgin – has at least one '*prostitot*' outfit in their closet (it's called *sexy*).

The effects on (increasingly younger) males – in their quasi-pathological urge to prove their virility in the light of this culture – can be seen in the amount of prescribed medications to subdue the emotional wreckage of the culture's worship of sensuality.

The epidemic of heightened sexuality gives rise to men who NEED sex to reinforce their conviction that they are indeed "men." Their sexual activity is "life" for them, and all else pales in significance. Consequently, this gives the woman tremendous power, as a critical female may decide to deny her male "life" that night. Consequently, the children hear a lot of "*Yes dear*," and "*Kids, listen to your mother*," which often reflects the man kneeling at the approval-seeking trough right along with the kids. He seeks mom's approval trying to protect his self-esteem. This is obvious to even the very youngest child in the family. Again, Sullivan saw the dangers even in the 1940s:

"In our type of society, that sort of organization to which the analyst refers to as the "Oedipus" complex is prone to develop. Instead of an attitude towards the father resembling adult awe or fear or respect or reverence, there grows an attitude of more or less concealed jealousy and hatred. "... even more destructive is the situation in which the woman is the (culturally acceptable) "boss." In such homes, any possible good which might derive from a benign matriarchy is utterly swamped in the child's reaction to the woman's effort to be a man, yet conform to society, and the man's effort to protect his self-esteem. When the father is a fanatic, from paranoid feelings (to protect his self esteem) or what-not... the matter of wretched adjustment of one to another parent, and of one or both to the conventional pattern to which they strive to conform, grows more

and more important as we try to understand the coming of subsequent disaster to the offspring.

All too generally, these factors effect a castration on the boy, sometimes by frank fear of penal amputation, more usually by placing in him the fiction of fictions – that system of symbols to which we may refer as the notion of Sexual Sin. Well before the occurrence of puberty, when such generic notions might have a real referent, the youth has come to a clear "appreciation" of the black wickedness of all things sexual. He is then loaded with dogma completely divorced from his biological necessities, taught more or less clearly that his hand on his penis is his hand against G-d. He is also filled with the most fanciful notions about feminine goodness, and warned against "wild" girls."[49]

If a man gets on his knees and prays to his deity, we can – without too much fear of contradiction - call that worshipping, and can point to the fact that the man chose to *give of himself* – his physical presence – to this spiritual entity. Whether prostrating himself, kneeling or whatever, he makes his body a part of this worship, the container of soulish effort by which he engages the world of the spirit. Where his *head is at* is another story, and, impossible for an outsider to tell.

Does it not also follow that if a man (or woman) submerges into a sexual fantasy and then offers up his or her body in the service of that fantasy (in this case into orgasm), isn't that also a form of worship?

If the river of imagination is necessary – and it does appear to be so – in order that the release of excess sexuality in (even) the lone individual might be accomplished, it is the level of awareness of the aforementioned fantasies, spirits or emotional complexes that matters. The courage to 'see oneself' reflects one's desire to live free from uncontrollable unconscious forces within. **It is the total *awareness* of the fantasy that is required, not the altering, diminishing or ending the fantasy's content**. It is the flesh, or one might say, the spirit of the flesh that one must become aware of. As the 'light of awareness' shines upon this energy within the factors inherent in the Observation Exercise, the forces "seen" pale in their ability to control the observer.

The relationship of being physically abused and humiliated within my childhood trauma to the essential motif of the fantasy is obvious. What is much more subtle is an inner voice that I have come to call my own. A

---

[49] *"Schizophrenia as a Human Process" (Sullivan) pp94-95*

sense of reverie that speaks to me in ungrammatical pre-grammatical communicative thought; and makes me think it's "me" thinking – and we all think it's "me" speaking to ourselves in our own ego mind. I can also get tripped up just as easily REACTING to what I'm thinking, as this is a device of the same spirit. Remember, we were told this "ego tree" is the **Knowledge** of Good and Evil." So it's not just evil we need to avoid, but the cloak, pretense or assumption that *"this is right;"* or *"we are good"* is to be feared as well. The spirit of being *"a good Christian,"* *"a good Jew,"* *"a good Buddhist"* – is a CULTURAL reflection; and as such is really part of the spirit world that replaced the image of G-d (which we were originally created with) when we got traumatized. Culture is the world. You see, a "good preacher" may announce he is a *"good man"* because he opposes abortion. Another preacher stands up and says he's a *"good man"* for helping women find abortions. This is the Tree of Knowledge trap we all fall into, forgetting that good and bad are two horns on the same goat.

This spirit whispers in us (as if it's the *'first-person-singular'*), encouraging us not only to create more and more (in this case, sexual) excitement within ourselves, but aids us in making bad decisions in every other area of our lives, having us seek emotional stimulation within an entire range of activities which are rooted in a source designed to bring further calamity upon us. It does this first and foremost by keeping us blind to our blindness. The rationalization that "I'm OK" is just so tempting to believe. Problems are the faults of others. We'll even go to religious institutions that help to support us in our weakness.

I was overwhelmed by anxieties, worries and temptations as I experienced my journey through life. I had a boat going through life's river bumping into "landings" of family, friends, work and romance but this emotional river kept coming into my boat, threatening to get me to go overboard, and I was spending all my mental life bailing water out of the hole in the boat and trying not to drown in further reaction to it.

Why not fix the hole in the boat? I was being "taught" to see these things in myself by listening to these tapes (other than the Meditation) from Roy Masters at fhu.com.[50]

---

[50] *One truly feels for those laboring under the added weight and confusion of prescribed pharmaceuticals. While helping the patient avoid destructive and harmful behavior at the outset, it appears to nonetheless dull the mentality necessary to motivate complete awareness and health. "Mental Health Professionals" use the meds as a fig leaf-of-sorts, rescuing the 'doctor' from exposure of his or her incompetence to engage in actual therapy. Shamelessly creating a convenient fog into which both patient and doctor can*

Anybody who has ever repaired anything that wasn't working correctly prior to their efforts knows how pleased they were to discover what's wrong. Aha! *That's why it didn't work. Now that I see that, I can go about repairing the problem.* Why don't we feel good about seeing the problems in ourselves? The "me" that doesn't want to see the truth is in *conflict* with truth. It is the spirit that entered us at the time of our trauma.

The deepest root source is "resentment," – almost always to the parental (or authoritarian) figure. While it is an emotion closely associated with hatred, it's ability to be regurgitated, and maintained as a cow chews its cud – gives it a unique dynamic quality. It spreads as the dust of the streets, affecting everything. The nature of the traumatized spirit will be served by reflecting the trauma. My reflection involved submissive humiliation (caused by the sudden physical abuse and scissoring of my long pants) energized by my hate of the one that caused me to suffer. That hate cannot be dealt with at five years of age, and oftentimes not at fifty-five either.

Consequently, to take away the anxieties stemming from my hate-filled reactions, thoughts and emotions, I've created a 'self-system' that lives to avoid this anxiety. We all seek the avoidance of anxiety. The culture craves approval, sex, music, movies, television, drugs, alcohol, sports or celebrity hero worship, church worship, intellectualism, materialism, obsessive goals, etc. as refuge centers to lose ourselves in. We make excuses for it. We defend it.

Excitement equals fun equals good. You go for the gusto but the gusto gets you. Each group of devotees – the 'gangs' that collect about these above mentioned cultural properties or social geographies – suck you in to make you feel good about yourself by mimicking their corruption.

You seek the approval of the pastor/teacher/shrink/parent-figure and you get patted on the head. You seek the approval of the drug dealer/gang-leader thinking you're a rebel.

The drug dealer/gang-leader/parent-figure is now your pal, and your pastor/priest/ teacher/shrink/ parent-figure is your enemy. The young girl, sleeping with all the band members, is quite sure of herself when she says *"I'm nothing like my mother. She goes to church all the time, and bakes cookies for the church leaders. I am totally devoted to the band, sex and drugs. See, I'm nothing like my mother."* But both roads put the individual in compulsive bondage to please others who are seen as authorities.

---

hide, these 'guidance-counselors-with-prescription pads' make sure the doctor's prestige and sense of esteem is taken care of first. Anything left over goes to the patient of course.

We embrace what corrupts us. This activity may tend to let us feel good in a way, but we slide further from ourselves, and from truth. Our new inner masters tend to make promises they can't keep, but we keep trying to win their approval anyway. Meanwhile, the soul stays in darkness, feeding on this junk food, growing older, growing deader. The conscience bothers us, but we may find priests, pastors, rabbis and shrinks who get between us and our conscience and convince us to ignore it. They are swimming in the same stew, you see.

We are programmed – listening in and to – our new wasp-impregnated identity. There is a voice in ourselves that subtly assumes in its logical perception of our reality that there's nothing greater than itself. *"It's the way I feel. It's what I believe. This is what I think about you, them, it, or anyone else who thinks differently."* It is lower-case *g*: *"**I am a god who craps**,"* says lower-case *g*.

It is most impressive in its ability to blame others for problems. *So why not do what feels good?* What feels good certainly seems *"right,"* and what doesn't feel good certainly seems *"wrong."*

It feels so *"good"* to be angry, and when one is angry one always feels *"right."* When we acknowledge this understanding in ourselves, we have arrived at a point of (at least some) clarity, and it is usually accompanied with the agony and conflict that a life lived in this corruption will bring. Yearning to end this is a good sign. It usually comes about only after years of the most intense pain. *"Come unto me, all ye who are heavy laden, and I will give you rest."*

But remember, *"many are called, but few are chosen…"* Do you *yearn* to be chosen? Are you like the merchant in search of fine pearls, who, upon finding that one pearl, sells all to obtain it? Or do you shove your bones into a religious service thinking G-d will see you and 'punch-your-ticket' that you're sitting in this religious observation and hence you'll be saved? The pastor, priest and rabbi can go to hell too, you know. Many have.

Sexual Awareness

When we get to the point in our lives where we begin to get that first hint of our own mortality, we are only aware that one day we're gonna' be gone. We begin to accept this end-of-life future as having definable features as we mature. Our eyes see the top of the escalator. We feel decidedly 'less-than.' Shameless or shamed, we (as men, anyway) push such thoughts out of our minds, replacing such reverie with fantasies of glory, honor and power; dispensing wisdom in decisions noble and wise – often near-royal in fashion - to the adoration of significant others; this group may include adoring, beautiful women, at least one dancing girl, and/or find us basking in mature accomplishments while receiving respect from those who would presently treat us askance.

Men (at least as we get older), often find ourselves seeking self-satisfaction imaginatively reliving sexual episodes of days-gone-by. This is the *'based-on-a-true-story'* sex fantasy. We find ourselves conveniently altering past events to make them a bit more juicy – somewhat more bold and satisfying then what they actually were. In our fantasy, it's as if we're chasing some promise of *real* life, that gusto that so eludes us now in our normal waking consciousness. We submerge into that imaginary excursion for a few moments of intense excitement and release. The nature that defines us in this sexuality needs nurturing. It demands to be worshipped, fed and compensated in this manner at least, resulting in a feeling of being intensely alive – albeit in a highly emotional and momentary state.

It takes time to see these wheels turning. Many of us just can't see the mechanism at work. Carl Jung said the search for one's soul may take half-a-lifetime. Take a moment to see what you're becoming in your own mind's eye at that moment of supreme sexual release – then tell me I'm wrong.[51]

Many men, sliding blindly into their dieing stage, often simply repeat (with slight variations) their few selected historical fantasies, peppering them with new and ever-more-revealing sexual twists and imaginings, then flushing them from consciousness, much the same as the moist evidence. *I shoulda' done it that way*! The ache of frustration is as if one's whole life would've suddenly been different... Oh, such satisfaction, pleasure, peace... *I would be **so contented if only** I would have* (everyone makes their own list here): *taken that girl back to my place that night, fucked her sister, his daughter, her mother, his brother, her*

---

[51] *Come to www.trailopen.com for the module on Sexuality.*

girlfriend; did her in the ass, made her swallow, made that Rocky Horror freak scene, did that threesome with so-and-so, ad infinitum.

We worship in our jerking ministrations right up into the death rattle. You sit at work or in your car with a *"based on a true story"* fantasy raging. You know the kind: it brings that ache that only comes when your head and your raging wood become attached in a most frustrating symbiosis. A circumstance comes to be achingly real: if you're not submerging into this sexual fantasy, the pain of 'not submerging' is a frustration painful and somewhat frightening in its sudden amoral nature.

It nags you for release as soon as you can get the opportunity. It's difficult to observe the sexual quicksand without falling into it, isn't it? Besides, it not only feels good and necessary, but the truth is, *we can't do anything about the urge to do it, can we?* If you're still reading, walk with me a little further.

We have to be aware of the spiritual dimensions of these sexual representations. These energetic ties bind us to earlier disturbances – their emotional births – in our lives through trauma. It needn't be dramatic trauma. My own was comparatively panty-waist compared to the whippings, burnings and rapes so many of my brothers and sisters have experienced within their traumatized childhoods. It doesn't matter. The effect of trauma is the effect of trauma. Period.

It is only through heightened awareness – in my own experience using the Meditation/ Observation Exercise, for example, – that something "other" than cognitive efforts are engaged in bringing into being (from unconscious into preconscious into awareness) of a new realization over what was heretofore dissociated components only coming alive in sexual imagery. These have arisen as a result of trauma, and your reaction to it.

Of greater importance to the spiritual journeyman is the sudden understanding through awareness of its representation in our reality as "fate" in our non-sexual lives.[52] We see our behavior in previously inexplicable personality quirks, failures and misunderstandings between ourselves and significant others. It's as if we see our behavior mirroring an ego-identification, which may, in the very unfortunate (traumatized), contain too much the unsung aspects of our sexual unconscious.

---

[52] *Jung adds the following: "The psychological rule says, "when an inner situation is not made conscious, it happens outside, as fate. That is, when the individual remains undivided, and does not become conscious of his inner contradictions, the world must perforce act out the conflict and be torn into opposite halves." See my two website videos (trailopen.com) including Jungian Baroness Von der Heydt on the video link ("Jung-Himself-Archetype-Freud").*

In order to understand this spiritual warfare I'm taking you into, the reader needs a quick lesson in understanding this particular battle as well as the battlefield it takes place in. So in this unique illustration, I shall give you the actual history of the events by which memorable basics are drawn from, as well as the changes made in order to feed more the fundamental nature of the beast. Within the spiritual warfare of our sexuality, we are re-inventing the stimulating memory while taking lots of liberties, as the following will endeavor to show.

The Street Hustler

I submerged into the *actual* memory concerning a street person/hustler I had picked up thirty years earlier right at the end of what would become known as the "pre-AIDS era." This slight, blonde, attractively submissive young man wasn't looking for much. I told him I had no money, but he was welcome to come up to my apartment if he still cared to.

"I think I have some beer," I said at the market where we started to talk. It's that strange talk of the existentially hungry; often the stoned and penniless; the drifters, the druggies, the almost-homeless. Your mouths move in somewhat innocuous conversation communicating more in subtle changes of voice and innuendo, in body language hints while your eyes feast hungrily over each other for surer signs of availability, pleasure, lust, excitement and who knows what? It's not what's being said as much as the continuing, somewhat dangerous excitement in the creation of this hook-up. Soon up in my apartment looking at the four cans in the frig, I told him, with my hand on his shoulder, "you can have them all." Apparently that was enough.

Three cans later, he was looking into the refrigerator as he stood holding the last can.

His fey persona was becoming much more noticeable now and it was having its intended effect. It had been very subtle at the market, but I had read it even before I drew full focus on his physical stature. His female-within-a-male persona was in much greater evidence now within our alcohol-fueled privacy. Men can often be more seductive than women when they get this way. Their tempting *'don't you want to use me for your pleasure?'* energy is wrapped in a slightly-annoying-teasing-come-get-me submissive posture. It is 'in your face' with its availability, and slightly annoying in an attitude that somehow teases you into wanting to put him in a position where you can both demean and use him for your sexual pleasure at the same time. So now it's time to accept it or reject it.

I certainly had no thoughts of rejecting this eager-to-be-used vibe emanating from this submissive young man. I had a stimulating eagerness to take him, use him, and my lust was evidenced physically by my own growing engorgement.

Standing slightly behind him at the refrigerator, I touched his shoulder with my left hand while my right slid down the right side of his chest to his belt buckle, which I tugged on briefly, pulling him around to face me straighter. I let my hand slide down to his upper thigh, slowly pressing my palm against him as I slid it up slowly up over the bulge of his crotch and onto his belt buckle.

"*Don't come in me*," was all he said. Walking to the couch, we tore off our clothes. He sat on the couch while I stood in front of him, bringing my bulging excitement to his face.

"*I have something for you*," I found myself whispering.

I slowly rode my hand along the back of his head as my brain and body reacted to the initial shock of receiving the oral sex. The sense of domination in bringing this stranger's head onto my unit to receive the initial jolt of pleasure caused my knees to go weak. I groaned and squeezed my three-quarter semi from within its own muscle to lend a more personal communication to our growing relationship. He received my body language with a whimpering moan from somewhere deep in his throat as his saliva became even more hotly abundant. I enjoyed my swagger and the bully in me grew.

"Let your tongue slide around just the head, sweetie, in your mouth, always in your mouth…" I ordered him softly, eager to enjoy his soft, wet tongue bathing my most-sensitive extremity a few inches inside his stuffed mouth. He moaned, and I couldn't help releasing some pre-cum into his suckling cavity. He moaned in higher octaves now, and I heard his slight gag as he swallowed my partial delivery. I could feel his tongue licking and sucking for more.

"*Take a deep breath through your nose and hold it… take me deep now honey, give me your throat, baby, Ahhh*,' I groaned in delight, overwhelmed with the sudden pleasure of his deepest throat. When he came back up for air, he was mewing and moaning in slavish delight, and I realized a tremendous urge to sodomize him. "*I have to fuck you now*!" I gasped out. I was rock hard and filled with a demanding necessity to sodomize him. I had no lotion to ease the otherwise painful entrance. As for using saliva, I certainly wasn't going down there with my mouth. He looked up at me willingly.

"*Try to get it real wet*," I said.

"*Just don't come in me*," he panted again as he carefully spit a bit of saliva on the head of my proud staff. Licking around the top he spread the spit all over the head. He turned and bent over the couch, and I let my left hand slowly squeeze his left nipple while my right hand spanked his right buttock, which was as soft and firm a teenage globe as one could hope to find. I felt an urge grow that sensed I could spank him without stopping. I maneuvered his youthful bottom low before me, taking a hand to guide myself into the entrance. The growing pleasure was effecting my speech:

"Uhmm, something's nice here. Ooooh, just relax baby... give it up... give it up for me, now honey... Give it up to for me, baby."

"Y..Y..Yess" he whimpers, the sound barely audible.

"Oh, yeah, you don't have to answer, if you don't want," as I began to enjoy spanking him again as I entered into him deeper.

"If you don't choose to," I add, elongating the words "choose to" as I ground into him deeper. His hot, tight slickness is a moaning honeypot of greasy pleasure servicing my new-found butch posturings.

He groans deeply.

"Oh, what sweet pussy... You just need to be my little bottom for a while..."

I reached around and squeezed a hard little nipple harder, sending his body gently undulating a bit more, his moans becoming more alarming as I began to squeeze without mercy. Starting to slap his buttock feverishly,

"Don't you? Don't you need to be?

"Yeesss," he moans in masochistic delight.

"Yeah, cause I got more for you. Oh yeah, get used to it, cause I am going to be fucking you all afternoon," I gasp out, driving in as deep as I possibly could, holding it at that depth till he stopped gasping and could adjust his sphincter relaxation to accommodate the total entrance. As he started to moan with that *'hurts so good'* ache, I knew this would bring me over the top very soon.

Even as I was coming, I was really looking forward to fucking him again all the more all day long. His ass was an incredible pleasure offering. For extra spice I added now how good it was going to feel coming inside him. I added this verbally cause he had asked me twice not to release into him.

He, upon hearing my intention to deliver my lust inside his rear, cried "*no!*" and twisted out of our physical entanglement. I groaned with the sudden frustration, sitting back to hear him go on about some disease he imagined he might be getting. He had heard on the street that there was some strange new "*thing*" going around, and fluid-in-the-rear seemed to spread it. *I* knew nothing about such a "*thing*," and therefore didn't think it was of any consequence; staggering achingly now to the bathroom and washing myself off.

Returning to him, I quickly figured it was time for us to part. In a round-about-way, I started to verbalize my desire to be alone by ticking off the reasons why our afternoon should be considered too inert to continue, "Well, you don't want me to come; I can't come, you can't come…"

"*I can come*," he said.

Suddenly a whole new thing was on me.

"Yeah?" I asked shyly. "*Y'want to let me…? Uhh, give you a little…?*" It was almost as if I half-expected him to shriek insults at me for even daring to think of such a horrible thing, proving that not much had changed inside my head since the "not-me" traumatized mentality of age five (*what would the neighbors think?*). But *surprise*! Instead of him being angry at the audacity of my suggestion, he laid back and pulled down his pants, which he had pulled back up minutes before.

I laid next to him on the couch, my face near his waist, overwhelmed by excitement and a little unsure of exactly what I wanted to do and how far I wanted to go in doing it.

"*Go ahead*," he said.

I touched it, holding the small circumcised instrument, and then kissed the tip, blowing on it.

"*I guess that's my blow job*," I said hesitantly.

"*It's ok, go on*," he said, placing his hand on the back of my head and pushing it gently towards his growing unit. "*Put it in your mouth*."

I did, and the more I accepted the rubbery flesh into my deep dark swallows the more I didn't want to stop. The more I wanted to commit, the more I wouldn't stop. He was small enough that it was quite easy to take it all the way down my throat without choking. The harder he grew, the louder came his cries of pleasure and ecstasy; along with the spasmodic tensioning within his body, as my brain rode like a magic carpet helped along by emotional octane released through his ecstatic approvals. I was making him moan, my submissive sexuality was having its intended effect: he *needed* me. I was his sudden drug, I was fueling his pleasure as a syringe pushing liquid into a vein. I was playing the female role, submerged into my own twisted version of it.

His cries were excitingly real, and my brain was in sensory overload at the realization of what I wanted, and what I wanted to do to get it. My mind filled with a head-trip of sexual relief as I rode on his wave of orgasmic ascent. I became him somehow in an inexplicable dark spiritual moment as he swelled and came spurting down my throat amidst physical spasms, gasps, cries and moans. His delivery was minimal, hot, thick, slick, salty and actually didn't taste too bad.

The astonishing upshot was I felt rather satisfied. I, who minutes before had been frustrated at not being able to complete my own orgasm, was now feeling content. The hustler, speaking very little, soon left.

I was amazed at this remarkable turn of events. A few days later he came knocking at my door. Although not turned-on by his arrival, I let him in, and he quickly got down to business. He had taken out his thing, which unlike before, sprung erect from his underwear once freed of the imprisoning cloth. *Golly, he remembered me.* We did it all again, but I had a greater reticence for the whole thing. Whether it was my being orally submissive, or allowing him to sodomize me, I had to fight the urge both times to simply stop the behavior and tell him to leave. I simply found myself not wanting to do it. Like a mule bawking to go forward, I felt repulsed and offended by the same sex that had seemed so satisfying and exciting the time before. The *"I'll do anything once"* fascination which accompanied the erotic, sinful and sensual realization of my *eyes-wide-shut* first experience was gone, and I found an off-putting fleshly atmosphere of *'been-there-done-that-and-I-don't-want-to-do-that-again'* overpowering my own attempts to *get into it*.

He returned a third time soon afterwards. His unit, however, now appeared to have a red dot on the tip that I didn't remember it having before, and even though to a normal person this would be reason enough to consider not having sex, I found myself simply using it as an excuse. The truth was I didn't care a whit about the red dot. I simply had no libido at all to engage in sex with him any more. If I hadn't noticed the red dot I would have found some other excuse. He left and returned once more. That's when I told him I just wasn't into it anymore. I never saw him again. **The above is history**.

* * *

In addition to this main historical unit, there is an adjunct historical event. It might appear a small, seemingly minor source of inspiration to the larger picture. However, you will see in retrospect how it helps spice up the overall situation as an eager side-dish.

When I was barely adolescent, I was playing around naked with a boyhood chum. We were holding and touching each other's thing – more out of curious, tentative lust than a determined effort to actually achieve anything. We took turns laying on top of one another. Neither of us inserted ourselves so as to sodomize the other, but found that if we placed our erect pole between the legs of the boy lying on his stomach, the head then being pushed up against that area (the *'taint'*) between the butt and the balls, the enclosed soft thighs of our youth offered soft, ample friction for the "top" to pleasure himself with. My friend got so into it with me underneath that he humped until releasing himself within that area of which I just made note. I pretended to be angry at the time, but in truth felt the episode to be intensely stimulating.

So these are the historical facts upon which the fantasy is built within the spiritual battle to follow.

As I lay down, preparing to come to grips with the familiar ache in my loins, I seek a way to find release but refuse to mentally hide from G-d. I then commit to the giving over of myself to that behavior conducive to relieving sexual tension by myself. We shut off self-consciousness in order to allow this new consciousness to enter. '*We croon sweetly for its presence.*' I am immediately aware of a pleasure that grows in direct relationship to the humiliating, imaginative scenario.

There is also a related and immediate acceleration in the flow of imagery, exciting emotion concomitant with the promise of physical release. I also notice there is a "hunching over" retentive quality to (the holding in one's mind of) this mental abstraction. It's as if one becomes a paranoid miser, selfishly holding his bag of valuables, mistrustful of all who might wish to look into it. If conscious "expansion" allows consciousness to flow out from the innermost being to one's outermost limits, this mindset now in sexual fantasy gives the impression of a squirrel hunching over a nut he's trying to eat, nervously intent on not losing any of it.

By compartmentalizing it in this manner, there remains a guarding of the amount of awareness we allow to be accorded to the imagery. By keeping a "lid on it" in this manner, it makes it all the easier to put it away in the '*not-me*'[53] drawer after submerging oneself in it. I allow my mind to simply be aware of this sexual direction without submerging further into it and instead expand outwards using the mental power I'd developed through the Observation / Exercise: as in meditation. "*From my innermost being to my outermost limits…*"

I found a help in the following CEV (closed eye visual): There's a ballroom being prepared with many tables all covered with white linen tablecloths. Each table represented a different fantasy, some with just enough variation to them to warrant its own 'table.' Slight variations are accorded by the "chairs" surrounding the table. I found that by taking a step-back (into awareness) fantasies began to bubble up with even more depth of content regarding intense traumatic attributes. So I could expand

---

[53] "*The Interpersonal Theory of Psychiatry*" *(Sullivan) pp 145, 152, 161-64, 168, 201, 267, 314-16, 361-63, 371n*

my awareness with an *"I'm familiar with this"* sense on my part, rather than what had existed in the past, which was more like:

> *"I don't dare make a conscious effort to observe this. It's too terrible, too infrahuman, it has a quality that causes too much anxiety for my ego to be content with. It brings with it the 'not-me' mental symptoms of awe, dread, horror and loathing. It flies in the face of acknowledged cultural norms. I would suffer the most intense anxiety should anyone I currently respect, hold in high regard, or whose approval I desire(G-d) know of these things.'*[54]

Complying to my imaginary partner's pressure while playing the feminine homoerotic role, humiliating and submissive story lines flow up easily into my waking dreamstate. The *'Spirit wars against the flesh,'* but as long as we are sons of Adam and Eve, we have this flesh. Sexual imagery is part of it. G-d knows this, but we don't know His will concerning it. *Is my hand on my penis my hand against G-d?* And if my hand in my mind is on another man's penis, *is that pissing G-d off more than my hand imaginatively on a female?* We know we are to procreate, and we're set up that way inside and out, yet we sense something unnaturally sinful about this sexual fantasy life, and the sexual apatite(s) it creates, demands and frustrates us with. I ask G-d with sincerity in my mind and seeking in my soul, and in less than a second I receive understanding: I open my mind to Him to help me with this.

I immediately find myself in imagery of a thread from the trauma of my emasculation in childhood at age five (See Chapter 1) to my fantasy now of me lying in bed in lingerie with this same street hustler. Instead of sending him away – as I did in reality – I am eager to have sex with him. In some cases in my fantasy I have won money at the track, purchased cocaine and lingerie, and allow him to spank my satin-covered ass while removing a twenty-dollar bill I place in the elastic hem as a gift to my "man;" my pimp-to-be. I'm whispering in his ear, kissing his neck while squeezing his swollen shaft. He starts to squeeze my body, the lingerie giving his hand a smooth slippery quality over my skin. I moan under the pleasure of his stroking hand and gasp this out:

---

[54] *This anxiety is, of course, also the dynamism entrenched within the "Transference" mechanism; that keeps the patient from sharing effectively with the psychiatrist.*

"When I was fourteen, my friend got on top of me while I laid on my stomach and put his thing between my legs. Not inside me, of course. I thought maybe you might like to try... something like that..."

At this point he flips me on my stomach and starts spanking me sporadically as he climbs on top. I feel his hot weight pinning me down as he begins to enter me from behind. I am as surprised as I am vulnerable, exclaiming weakly in my *I'm-being-overwhelmed* protest that this was supposed to be him doing only what my fourteen year-old friend did!

"Oh... no... you're really **doing it** to me!" I exclaim in shocked helplessness. A sharp spank from his right hand interrupts my whimpering stammer. I moan in surrender, allowing no tension to exist in my sphincter as I open my body and soul to serve him. It's his lust, taking its pleasure using me that is so pleasurable and exciting for me to realize. My worship to his satisfaction, this euphoria I seek appears linked not only to being used in the physical sodomy but in being humiliated by it as well. Thus my physical submission can then be added to dignity's surrender.

Back on planet earth, I refuse the emotional temptation to submerge into the fantasy to completion. In doing that, in committing to self-improvement while denying the "flesh," I experienced the first of many entrances" into the rewards of such journeying. They are multidimensional and hence unspeakable, the way a dream encapsulates so many different strands of ones life in a momentary symbol that would take hours to explain to the bored listener. Nonetheless, "grace" was a concept beginning to be understood. Son-ship was a concept beginning to be understood, wisdom was a concept beginning to be understood.

In refusing the emotional riptide by simply "stepping back" and observing it, a small amount of understanding became more foundational within my awareness. By simply becoming aware of these urges – explicit and unblinking – into a total and waking consciousness – in the same way one would examine one's own clothing or getting a new car – the submission and humiliation scenarios gave me an appreciation that this doesn't occur in a vacuum. There is more to this than simply a realization of pleasure at the idea of being used sexually.

I am immediately given understanding. The dynamic energy that has created the tempting excitement and pleasure for this scene of being used sexually for another's pleasure is born - derives its essence from - my resentment of my mother's abuse that day of emasculation so many years ago, and the embrace I gave to my corruption.[55] (See Chapter 1) The **resentment** is the energy – the **power** – the **dynamism** seared into my

---

[55] *www.fhu.com See Roy Master's audio on "Embracing Our Corruptor"*

being through that sudden childhood abuse. It is my hatred which causes these essential elements of the trauma currently redirected into forming my present sexual realities.

In less than a heartbeat I flash on the non-sexual elements in my life, and an instant parade of slides appear detailing my dealings in reality which reflect this eagerness to give in and agree to another's pressure; and in many cases… become the one taken advantage of. It showed me what I thought was clever was really a substitute process sub-personality exactly as demonstrated in my Britneyzian Prophecies.[56] I would seek approval from others in order to service my own continued disadvantage. I had to embrace my corruptor and serve him like G-d in order to avoid seeing what I was doing.

Resentment and anger over the childhood emasculation/trauma coupled with my refusal to admit it was the repressed dynamism insisting to be heard. It had insisted all my life that *"it"* be regarded as the legitimate source of reason, the interpreter of life - and above all, to be reacted to as if it was *"my own"* thought; that it was indeed *"me."* But through the meditation, objectivity had now brought the light of awareness to – or upon - this spirit. [57]

I realized at that moment (even with my hand on my now-wilting *Johnson*) more fully than ever that my mother didn't know any better. She wasn't aware of the forces that caused her to scissor my pants in front of the whole neighborhood and strike and traumatize me. Forgiveness was necessary, and by forgiving her, be relieved of these imprisoning compulsions. My mother's mother's mother as well as my father's father's father all the way back to our shared antiquity of Adam and Eve had been doing the unconscious ego-trauma-slam in one form or another to their progeny from then till now.

---

[56] *Please see "The Britneyzian Prophecies"* (www.trailopen.com/index-3.html).
[57] "In general, important aspects of personality existing in dissociation are not reintegrated except under extremely fortunate circumstances. One of these fortunate circumstances is when the need for intimacy can lead to very considerable improvement of the partition of energy between the not-me component and the other components of the personality. And at the same time this newly integrating tendency is being called out by maturation, certain eventualities are likely to occur which may have favorable influence in reintegrating a dissociated tendency system. *Interpersonal Theory of Psychiatry (*HS Sullivan) pp322

The connection between the traumatic abusive humiliation and my sexual arousal reflected this identification kept alive by this anger and resentment. Forgiving them while still discerning their emotional illness was setting me free (little by little) from this unconscious urge to lose in life. The next stage would take awareness a step further.

Seeking to forgive her in this new unemotional way – and realizing on a more meaningful level that she didn't know what she was doing – was taking me deep into the spirit; deep into the place known as the collective unconscious. I saw the spirit of submission and humiliation that had made itself so clear to me in that LSD experience[58] almost forty years ago come out of me. I saw it clearly rise apart from me. It rose before my awareness opaque and multi-dimensional within this fourth dimension. I looked at it. It screamed and fled. I did not react. I was surprised but not scared. I was suddenly just laying there, small and shrunken with eyes wide open.

I brought them back, like dogs pulling a sexual sled; like mice in a science experiment; to use… to show me who they were, for I was no longer fearful to be aware of the imagery or the temptation. Sex would still be part of my life. I had to understand all I could about it.

I saw the symbolic future within my sexual imaginings: I brought them back by re-engaging these energies. I would have the street hustler bring in his friends, with him coaxing me into serving them sexually so they could pay the hustler for my sexual favors.

I saw the hustler sodomizing me from behind while one of his companions had me service him orally at the same time, and, upon completion, with my head pulled back up by the hair, my available throat would be offered. I could see the *fantasy excitement remaining unchanged* as I objectively observed the death I was purchasing. This is what I was doing in reality (symbolically) by giving my life to this spirit. **I was death coming alive**. Awareness now allowed me to see the one sodomizing me take the knife and slit my throat from behind as he poured himself into my rear for his own pleasure. As I was victimized, I could stay aware and observant enough to see – with my hand continuing to urge my completion – that I was experiencing *no diminishment in the level of excitement*.

I could sense something dark crying out to G-d while pointing at me:
> "*this is what I've done with the creation made in your image, and he came to me willingly of his own accord.*"

I again saw this hermaphrodite spirit (of which I spoke in my 1967 experience) jump out of my cut-open chest (that had been slashed open as well), and leave somehow, by entering the dark belly of a larger,

---

[58] *See Chapter 6 on LSD*

incredibly merciless and consummately hateful spirit, which it served. That larger spirit had the most intense hatred imaginable. For the briefest moment, I was able to not react to it, and became simply aware of it. I just watched it for a moment and it fled. *It was made known to* me (from that same Spirit that guided me before) *that this demon spirit had to flee. It cannot stand an objective gaze from a soul not under its command.*

I inquired as to the dark side's motivation; the answer was delivered at the speed of light, the words of *Melville* from *Moby Dick* rising up immediately in my mind:

"... *to the last I grapple with thee;*
from hell's heart I stab at thee;
for hate's sake
I spit my last breath at thee."

As the momentum for my physical release was no longer flowing towards completion, I allowed myself to dip into a different aspect of sexual imagining – which was like skimming briefly over a hundred different scenes without submerging into any one of them. It was not unlike those very short clips promoting a movie studio by showing two seconds of each movie they've made in a quick-changing slide show format. Just enough to catch your interest, stimulate a memory, an association reverie, and then the next one is there to do the same. Each glimpse was an awareness of a sexual symbol, which, when explored, would be the basis for a more excitingly detailed, more emotionally specific fantasy, but was now simply a symbolized spur to my passion. When enough momentum was assured that I would 'deliver' into port, I became aware of myself watching my hand manipulating my body, bringing to release my seed amongst the pre-conscious sexual symbolisms skirting across my mind. It was a sexual exercise not too far removed from any other healthy physical exercise. I was pleased to see my body able to rid itself of the excess fluid and the excess tension, and it was extremely pleasurable in a physical way. As far as an anatomical function, it was sexual, of course, but it appeared more like a physical exertion with psycho/sexual/spiritual understanding rather than some dark and shameful voyage. Being aware of these lusts was subtly but significantly different than submerging into them.

I began to see masturbation now as something vaguely along the lines of an excretory operation. Over time, my journey in these spiritual provinces would always revolve around the degree of *submergence* and *awareness*. It is neither the sexual urge nor the imagination that one can – or seeks to – change or prevent. But the *submergence into the imagination* ceased to be a source of denial. As I opened myself up to the conscience within, this new spirit would allow many areas of my non-sexual life to become clearer. As I calmly, unemotionally and objectively became able to observe and identify the sources of sexual excitement in fantasy, my anxieties – and consequent difficulties they created in my non-sexual reality – diminished dramatically. With this diminished anxiety came diminished vulnerability. I was becoming somewhat reintegrated; two steps-forward, one-step back was working as I followed The Lord's Prayer' running through my mind like it was breath itself. I found beating myself up too much for lack-of-perfection / failure can be pride as well. By hiding nothing within consciousness from this conscience, I become more secure in His love.

"Unwanted or unnecessary thoughts may be disintegrated in this manner." These words are on the audio section of the Classic Meditation. It is true, and the lifting of the Mirage of schizophrenia began.[59]

I wanted to share these dramatic changes with the only person I knew who not only could understand them, but give me feedback I could use to stay on course. He was the only person I had ever heard speak who really could.

I often had trouble speaking of the matters alluded to above. My mind often seemed enclosed in a thick blanketed fog. Cannabis smoke would throw open the barn doors, but thought would come pouring out like wild horses from within. There was only one person in the world who could throw a rope around these undomesticated notions and respond intelligently to them, and that was my new friend at the Foundation of Human Understanding. Roy Masters' radio show was not picked up in Carvel, so I was on the phone and on web radio to www.fhu.com.[60]

Second Call to Roy Masters – www.fhu.com – Nov 29, 2004
Tape # 3518

The *empathetic handshake* (during my first call) between myself and Roy Masters concerning my vision of the spirit of submissive sexuality had cemented in me the understanding that I was on a true journey. The meaning, relevance and reality of the meditation to the soul were all providing similar ingredients to the 'missing link' between my two never-to-be-forgotten conscious

---

[59] *http://www.trailopen.com/Roy1.html*
[60] *www.fhu.com; #3518 Nov 29, 2004.*

expanding psychedelic experiences of the late sixties and the current state of my searching no-longer-schizophrenic-soul. The blazing cross I had seen as a naïve, atheistic Jew approaching the throne of G-d was now, almost forty years later, about to take on a new and living relevance.

Tape # 3518 (www.fhu.com) – Nov 29, 2004

Roy: All right, we're going to go to Marty.
Me: Hi Roy Good to speak w/you again.
About six months ago (*Author's note: actually it was sixteen months*), I spoke with you and you ended that conversation by saying "you're a woman." (*Author's note: A Freudian slip here, as the phrase Roy actually used was "woman centered."*) I would like to just briefly take thirty seconds to pick up where I was and pick up what happened since that phone call.
Roy: Yes, sure.
Me: I had a world-class approval-seeking people pleasing mother very weak father only into gambling and having sex with my mother and looking for her approval. I found myself even though I was in a Jewish household which didn't allow any German products into the house because of relatives killed in the holocaust…
I found myself emotionally drawn and supporting Germans in these WWII books I was reading, I had a tremendous hatred for my father
Roy: Fascinating.
Me: When my adolescence came along, I found that sexually I would start off being excited thinking of a woman in the normal sense of a

playboy centerfold, but as my fantasies progressed, I found in order to maintain the high level of excitement or gain more pleasure I found myself becoming female or submissive or humiliated and this brought me into all kinds of horrible situations in most of my life and I found I was able to keep heterosexual relations in a complimentary fashion, because in a way I sold my soul to the devil by going in further and further in these submissive feminine fantasies I would have while in a heterosexual relationship.

Roy: I understand that…

Me: I also had homosexual relationships going on, and I always had this pangs of conscience, and I didn't quite know what to make of it; know what to do until I found your tape about seven years ago and I called in and said I had no money and got it for free and that was a long time ago and since then I've been to the ranch, etc.

Basically, when you said that to me, "you're a women," I thought to myself, well, I know and I'm sure Roy agrees that homosexuality is not the way, I've been celibate for 3 or 4 years now. What's happened since you said that, is while I've been meditating I was able to relive when I was 5 years old to a new suburbs in my first pair of my long pants. Just come out from Brooklyn in lakes and weeds and had my first pair. We called them dungarees in those days… They're Jeans for everyone else

Roy: I know what they are.. .

Me: I developed holes..

Roy: You've got two minutes left. Can you finish up, in two minutes?

Me: OK, My mother wanted to cut them into shorts, I said "no," and she cut them into shorts in front of the whole neighborhood, so I felt that that kind of humiliation, I was able to experience and my resentment and hatred for her and also towards my father and that that caused the pleasure experience to come alive in the submissive sexual position.

Roy: Sure, are you ok?

Me: I can't hardly hear you

Roy: Are you getting better?

Me: Yes, but when I meditate now, I feel like a snap, crackle and pop in my head – or something like that in my head, and I feel energies moving around in my head.

Roy: Oh yeah. I tell you what. Would you like to talk to me a little more about this? This is interesting, and I think I can give you some input, which will be more than useful. Would you like to hold on for a few minutes?

Me: Yes, I certainly will.

Roy: Well, hold the line now. Because this is… I'm not available so much during the daytime, I just couldn't handle all the phone calls, so I have to do it on my radio show. That's why I do two hours, and sometimes I waste that time just by pontificating, and I'm always glad for a call like yours because it gives me an opportunity to be useful, and provide a service that you might not otherwise have. So hold the line...

Roy: I'm going to suspend some of my commercials so I can talk to my friend Marty.

Let's see where were we, now? can I just give you a heads up on something here? Are you there, Marty?

Me: Yes, the connection's much better.

Roy: What awakens sexual feelings is hostility, excitement, any form of excitement, undo excitement which transfers – and I'm going to say this very slowly, and you can fit your own scenario in there, any form of excitement like anger towards anybody or anything, I mean resentment – the word is resentment – and anger, hate, hostility all that is built on little bits of resentment – as the example you gave about your mother humiliating you by cutting up your dungarees, And there's a whole multitude of those, the resentment towards parents, or resentment towards anything as a child awakens sexual feelings very early.

I once saw, I discovered this, I was in New York forty years ago, and there was a traffic jam, the driver got so frustrated,

Me: he got out in the middle of the street and opened his pants and you know what he did.
Me: Yes.
Roy: Just to relieve the frustration. Anger and sex are connected. Women can frustrate men, upset them one minute, awaken the sexual feeling, and complete the act, go to bed, relieve their pain and get them addicted, to angry (lust). Anger awakens the lust for them, they gratify the lust and they are a slave of it, and now the only way you can have sex at all is for being upset, so you have to think of something in a disturbing way in order for her to have it. Your disturbing way is rebellious, like thinking about – having an affinity for Nazis, because you hated your Jewish parents.
Me: If I just might comment on what you…
Roy: Sure. That's just a rough outline.
Me: This may seem alike an aside but there may be other people in the same boat- I had a terribly difficult time making strides to create my own home business. Every time I was about to make some sort of little breakthrough, I would become very sexually aroused and wind up taking care of that, and falling into a nap.
Roy: Frustrated, That's what it's called: frustrated. The frustration is the resentment I'm alluding to.
Me: I understand. It's also been lately in my life – and I won't say coincidentally – I'm

sure it's connected, that lately I've been enjoying myself at a low-paying, humble job… and doing much more than I need to, without telling anyone about it…

Roy: This was a very short break, I'll have more time with you after the break. Do you mind holding on now?

Me: No, not at all, cause I have something I want to share that's…

Roy: Hold on, I'm listening, I'm listening… cause it's very valuable. I have other callers, if these callers would please be patient… We'll dispense with this gentleman and give him the help he needs, and we'll give you the help those of you who will be patient enough to hold on.

(Commercial message for Advice Line)

Female voice: I had a dream I was being molested. That's how I feel about sex with my husband."

Male voice: I just want to talk about my error-making decisions, and the fear I have about going to the gym by myself.

Roy: The lady says she has a dream of being molested. That's how she feels towards her husband. Actually, her husband is molesting her, because she's yielding on demand rather than out of love. Remember that's the point I was making. Do you do the right thing

because you love it? Do you buy Christmas presents because you're under compulsion? That's like being violated. Being made to do the right thing but it's out of somebody else's pressure to suit somebody's needs and purpose. And not your own. It's not out of you. Could be she was molested as a kid, and projecting onto her husband. There are lots of combinations, you need to call me about these things.

Roy: Meanwhile I will be talking to Marty about his problem and I hope you've been following and you need to pick up some of the gist of this if you've just tuned in.
 Finish up, I'm sorry about these commercials. We have more time now.

Me: No, I feel privileged to have the conversation, and let me now, take it… go up a notch. Because I am so angry... I was… much more angry than I am now, and I was a world class alcoholic, drug addict, gambler, no-goodnik. I found myself, overwhelmed, in spite of my prayers, in spite of my meditating with anger, and hence, I would be overwhelmed when I came home from work or late at night with sexual fantasies I felt I had to relieve. And what happened, as a result of being able to understand my resentment towards my mother as an etymology of my pleasure seeking to twist this, I got to a point whereby… and I'll try to be discrete, whereby when taking myself in hand, I needed the fantasy to complete the objective.

Roy: Exactly. I think everybody understood that.

Me: I found however, that I didn't have to merge with the fantasy to get all the way into port. There was a certain momentum built up, where the completion of act could happen without the fantasy, and in that time, I... I opened my mind as I would in meditation, to G-d…

Roy: Exactly.

Me: … and I came face to face with an image, I mean the spirit of the humiliation and the submissiveness…

It was like in a kid's movie called "*Monster's Inc*." where the monster looks at the kid and they each scream and run the other way.

Roy: (laughter) I never saw it but I can see it.

Me: OK, and I thought: I saw that! and then over the course of time, I was able to see that **same pleasure principle**, that I was seeking in my fantasies, could take me to being tied down on a table and murdered by these sadistic serial killers, and that same spirit would jump out of my cut-open chest – I had a vision of this – and go into a bigger spirit that he's serving, the so-called principalities and powers.

Roy: Actually, what you are observing is spiritually accurate.

Me: Yes, I know.

Roy: It's not something everybody gets a glimpse of. You're talking to me and I understand every word you said.

Me: Oh, this is very meaningful to me, and uh…

Roy: This is not imagination any more. There's an imagination factor. Let me just reiterate some of the things you say so I can show you I understand you.

Me: I know you do.

Roy: When you said you were angry, my first observation was anger is a sin, and all sin is sensual. I never said that to you before quite that way, but every time you contemplate sin, or actually do the sin, and one of the seven deadly sins is anger, right? Resentment.

Me: OK.

Roy: So all sin awakens the sensual, because it separates you from the motivation of the sensible. Is that clear?

Me: Yes.

Roy: The "sensible" meaning your conscience. Moving and having your being as a noble being. The sin awakens the mortal self. The base nature, there's an appeal to the base nature. Something stimulates you, upsets you, degrades you, makes you hateful; especially that hate, which is the most subtle of all, which you don't recognize it as hate until it's too late, called resentment; many little resentment-izzes. They separate you from the sensible, and you die. Literally, is a sentence of death. Anger is a sentence of death; a very slow death; where the sensual displaces the sensible. But it awakens death coming alive, meaning; the first duty of an animal, the most important love that an animal can have is to reproduce itself; to replace its dying self. That's the most urgent call, follow that?

Me: Yes.

Roy: When a human being dies, spiritually and becomes egotistical; puffed up in judgment and anger, it separates from G-d, and becomes egotistical, or ego-testical in your case. Do you see what I mean?

Me: (laughter) Yes.

Roy: And so, therefore, the urgency to reproduce a dieing self, as if it was the most glorious thing, because women do make that glorious, don't they? Hollywood makes things like that glorious, they put it all to music, don't they? They call it romance. And so you start to fantasy the source of your new existence; while reproducing yourself endlessly, even uselessly. Follow that?

Me: Yes.. after..

Roy: Just one more point, and then you can take over the show.

So, you know that when you're hungry you think of food. But… and then you're satisfied with the food. But you can do it the other way around. You can just think of food and get hungry. You discovered that once the corrupt nature starts to awaken in you; the sexual nature, the sexual impulse.. or the sexual beast or sexual spirit gets into you it's ego, it knows how to keep on.. it creates a dissatisfaction, it creates a wider gulf between you and your creator and a greater emptiness and a greater meaninglessness a greater inferiority and a guilt. A remembrance of what gave you pleasure, and so even if the woman isn't there, especially because you're afraid of women; because you know what women do to you, you know what your mother was able to do to you. But you can conjure them up like a centerfold. You know, a Playboy centerfold in your mind, indulge them, get into the pleasure, relieve yourself, and then get exhausted… but the point is, the more you do that it's like giving your life to the spirit of that image. You understand there's a spirit behind that image. Anytime you sin, anytime you overreact to something, there's an energy.. you become disconnected from your true self, and the motivation to move and have your being comes from the outside, but with that comes thoughts and ideas, and a spirit, and this indwelling spirit with it, and this indwelling spirit lives in your subconscious. You can never see it, it's always there. When it thinks you think it's you that's thinking. You actually think it's you that's thinking. But it's thinking through you, and you're caught up in it, and you can't see otherwise. And it will show you how to have pleasure, how to have life, how to get rid of the pain of conscience, cause it's conscience's enemy, follow that?

Me: Yes.

Roy: So, therefore, when you were able to detach from the image, sort of relieve yourself without the glory of escaping, because what is happening is when you fantasize with a sexual act you're actually experiencing a glorious feeling, aren't you?

Me: Worship.

Roy: A relief of pain of conscience, but at that moment you're getting worse. You're becoming more depleted, more possessed by that spirit, that lives within the phantom of the opera, so to speak, the phantom that's hidden there in all the fanfare and beauty and music and glory and excitement, follow?

Me: Yes.

Roy: And so when you separated from that, and just did the act by itself, like dispensed with the excess, if you'll pardon the expression,

Me: No, I understand.

Roy: ...you began to be separated from that, you began to be free. It was just sex, stupid, you see...

Me: It was a quantum leap. It was a giant leap of freedom, and it took a tremendous amount of the bondage out... and just so I don't sound like a know-it-all, my pride came in, after about thirty or forty days without taking myself in hand, and I began to feel really cocky about myself, and then began to think, 'wouldn't it be nice to spend my last few days with a woman..

Roy: You'd be back in the saddle again, wouldn't you?

Me: I...I went flying, I went flying back worse than I was before for about two days, I actually looked up pornography on the internet, and then I said "I can't do this," and I went on a.. I'm on the third day of a fast, but, I'm working and it doesn't affect my life. I fast a lot.

Roy: Young man, you see; the fact that you were becoming a woman means the woman was your center. When your mother became the center of your being because your father who was weak. You weren't delivered over to a strong father who represented, G-d's bureaucrat, because when you are handed over to a strong father who's noble, then you have your G-d identity. You love the good in him as a roundabout way of loving the good in yourself and your mother supporting the love of the good in your father would also be a good woman, but this was a divided house, where your mother, was a control-freak.

Me: May I just say one thing…

Roy: And you became feminine. You took on the woman's nature. The woman's spirit.

Me: I want to put an accent on that, because when I was about twelve I was a coward being pushed around by a bully (in the neighborhood). Had a cousin come in (to visit) and the two of us were walking to the candy store and the bully came over my cousin just stood there. Like a rock. Didn't make faces back at him, just wouldn't let him push him around, and the bully backed off.

    Within a year, I went to my cousin's house; something came over me. I walked upstairs, it was his birthday, he had just been given a single-barreled shotgun as a present. I took the shotgun, put a shell in it, snapped the barrel up, brought it to my shoulder, pulled back the hammer, and… it was as if something in me was wordlessly saying 'just go ahead, it'll be all right if you just take this next step.' And my cousin, G-d bless him, just had the courage to just say my name, with a little bit of a laugh, like "don't," and it snapped me out of it. That's how nuts I was.

Roy: You know why you picked your cousin for this?

Me: He had courage, and integrity and honor...
Roy: In other words, the evil in you hated him.
Me: Yes.
Roy: And you understand why they want to kill President Reagan and President Bush and why they glorify Al Quaida and Sadaam Hussein and people like that? You see the affinity is for evil and the hatred is toward good. Look, all I want to know..

    I have to let you go now, as the calls are coming in. All you have to do now is learn to endure the cruelty like your cousin, learn to become like him in learning to deal with cruel things, deal with imperfect people, mean people, demoralizing people, degrading people like your mother with dignity, patience and calmness. If you just do that, all your illnesses will go away. I promise you. They are going away right now, G-d bless you.
Me: Then it would be possible in my later years to meet a woman, maybe one that goes up to the ranch...
Roy: Yes, one day. You're not quite ready. You need a woman to practice on. To learn to... You need a woman not to lust, but to love. See the difference? That may involve sex. But in the beginning your relationship must begin with her, you must court her for a year or two, I don't care how old you are, you must love her for herself, before you have any other relationship. There must be a

love and therefore she will respect you, and not rise to the occasion as a girl of your dreams, the nightmare of schemes, the one who caters to all of your weaknesses. Follow that? And turns you into a weak father. Got it?

Me: Thank you Roy. G-d bless you.

<u>I Hang up</u>.

Roy: (To radio audience) Now those kinds of conversations you won't find on any other program on earth, so please, would you please consider supporting it with your tax deductible donations?

* * *

Like going to a shrink, sometimes one visit isn't enough. I re-called Roy Masters three weeks later.

Third Call to Roy Masters – www.fhu.com – Dec. 17th, 2004 Call#3 Tape #3545

Me: I know what the objective state is, and when falling from your thoughts kind of grabbing from the tree of knowledge…

Roy: Yeah, that's very well said.

Me: Thank you. Got it all from you, I got your books and tapes, and am well-versed.

To put that aside, your books are the only books, outside of the "Big B" that I can pick up, leaf through a page or two, and say "Oh, there's me," and put the book down. As far as a scripture as you started off the program with, I came up with this as I was sitting here:

"Whomever you yield your self servant to obey his servant you are

whether sin unto death

or obedience unto righteousness."

Roy: Right, that's correct.

Me: I think I have something to offer. I don't know but I guess I'll find out with this call, concerning my own experiences regarding fantasy taken into action regarding the world of homosexual perversion and also what I was able to see there, but before I do, if I may, because something's been rising up in me that I need to deal with. When I started out saying I know what the objective state is. Ideally, you come down into being a man, who has an experience in life that goes all the way down and is foundational in Jesus Christ, and things like that. But if you come out of the objective state and you find yourself described as you described me as a woman – not a homosexual – but a woman, I wanted to ask some things about what you think regarding my kind of conclusions about my life.

At five years old I suffered this trauma where, my mother cut off my long pants into shorts in front of the whole neighborhood because they had holes in them and she was an incredible people-pleaser, and I said to her

"I hate you." I was five years old. My Jewish mother hit me, which was probably as far away from her mind as expecting to do as anything, and I think I yelled - or I thought - "I hope you die," and she began to go into this psychotic chant, as if Satan was telling her, say this: And she would repeat over and over "What would the neighbors think if they saw you with holes in your knees? *What would the neighbors think*? So I had this trauma, but I also have this terrible fear that if I don't pay attention to what everyone thinks about me, I'll re-experience this kind of trauma.

Roy: Fascinating, fascinating… go ahead.

Me: On the other hand, my resentment towards my mother…

Roy: It's what caused … it's what allowed it to get in you.

Me: Yes, and the pleasure that I sought in becoming a submissive, sexual object to usually anonymous men, had me in a denial that I was becoming a woman, that I was becoming a homosexual. I actually had - and a paranormal experience that led to this - a month-long love relationship when I was eighteen in 1968, and I kinda somehow in a denial phase, posturing somehow that I was the man, rather than just a homosexual, uh, and I made such a good impression on my shrink at the time, that he said to me - 1968 - 'we're having a special speaker at the Brooklyn Psychoanalytic association this year, if you wanna come – I said 'who's the speaker? He said "Tim Leary."

So I got into this whole conscious expansion thing looking at Jungian collective unconscious, but what I found was that there was a continual denial about what I was doing sexually, cause I was terrified about the so-called Freudian super-ego and what people would think of me, if I prance around in women's clothes, even though that was my fantasy. I am therefore, right now, when you say I'm a woman, I know I come out of the objective state,

Roy: Can I hold you there. It's all very simple. It's a wonderful story, well, I won't say wonderful, I'll say it's a fascinating story, and it's very typical and it can be typically cured in the snap of a finger…

Me: Snap it!

Roy: (laughter) I know, you're almost there. I hear you, I hear you…

Me: I believe that, Roy.

Roy: What it is, is when you're a child, let's see if I can take this story from something ordinary. For instance, you had to learn to pick up a fork and knife. And at first it was awkward, and you had to give consciousness to it in order to do it. You had to agree with what you were being taught. How to pick up a fork and knife. It was innocuous, and so you agreed to it. It wasn't so bad unless you were rebelling of course. But after giving consciousness to it, and allowing it to set as a behavior, natural effortless behavior, there's ten thousand billion other things that go through the same process... Being conscious of it, learning how to surf, and liking it, and using your consciousness allowing your behavior to be installed like software. You know what I mean?

Me: Yes.

Roy: So because you can't be conscious of everything all your life, as if you're doing it for the first time. You'd go cookoo. Your body has a marvelous learning curve. You just have to allow for it.

But when you're under pressure, and your parents have no tolerance for your consciousness. For which reason, because they're crazy, or because they're willful, they won't allow you to have this consciousness which is of G-d. That it knows what to allow good behavior; what is good behavior, useful behavior and what isn't. They won't allow you to be true to yourself. They want you to be true to them. And if you don't please them, they terrify you into submission, and your weakness here, as a child, couldn't help it, five years old, what can you expect? Your weakness is to get resentful, and that is the key. Anytime anyone wants to control you, they can:

"a," intimidate you like your mother, or similar. All they have to do is scan your being for your weakness, like scanning your armor, for a chink in it. They know exactly, the sociopath, the manipulator, knows exactly… you're giving off the signal anyway, they know where to hit you; and then they reinforce that behavior, or they create new ones, because you're so sensitive to being upset and resentful and programmed; the resentment is the programming emotion. All you have to learn to do now is to unlearn everything you've ever done, but you don't have to go back into the past with Freudian psychoanalysis and all the other junk.

All you have to do is let the tree of programming die. If you lived on a desert island, and you didn't have anyone to speak to for ten years you probably couldn't speak when they discover you; like Robinson Caruso. It would be a hard time coming back. You would forget language. You would forget everything. You'd probably go native.

What I'm saying to you is bad habits *not only will die*, but *this is what makes the transformation through being objective so remarkable*, but the minute you realize the truth that resentment is judgment. It's hatred towards your parent, and your parent couldn't help herself. She didn't have a proper Dad, or husband. She had a problem with your father. I mean she was a willful witch, excuse the expression. Willful people, whether they enjoy being willful, or can't help being willful, because they have no way of escaping what was done to them, and they grow up as parents doing it to their own children, it doesn't matter.

You are special in the sense that you have a grace that allows you to retrieve your consciousness from the bond of being lost in emotionally based thinking. It's called being saved, in religious parlance. That state, is the state of consciousness they took away, your mother took away, and others, when you were a child, and *installed this kind of behavior*, and up with that emotional reaction *came her identity*. And so every time you become upset about something, *the nature that took shape in you is hungry for that upset* because *you're no longer you anymore*, because the anger separated you from your own good unfolding, *and put a parasitical substitute nature in you that was like your mother. It was the image of your mother, not the image of G-d that you were building.*

And so you were addicted to being upset. You're addicted to fantasy so if a person isn't there you'll fantasize with them, in order to get into the memory, into the thought, into the feelings. You awaken those feelings, like when you are hungry, you think of food, but if food is the basis of your being, you think about food in order to make yourself artificially hungry so you can get into the food and whatever the nature of the food is gets into you and it completes itself. You complete yourself to food, you complete yourself to your mother. You complete yourself to women. You complete yourself to the drug pusher and the spirit of the drug pusher. It's always the spirit that grows inside you that cries out for the very violator of your childhood.

Me: I had an experience with this spirit of violation. May I speak of these matters?

Roy: Is this making sense to you?

Me: Yes! Very much so. I have, actually been forgiving… not some kind of religious words…

Roy: That's right

Me: It's coming from inside, I've seen an image of her…

Roy: Patience. Be patient with her. As I open the Bible, you talk about being patient, look forward to little problems in the future, so when your mother's there, and she starts her monkey business – she probably hasn't changed – and so, as a man, instead of reacting like a child, you react in a brand, new way. You don't react at all, you're patient. You endure her naughtiness. What would have traumatized you and messed you up, serves to give you strong character, to love her, to return and overcome evil with good. See? Hold the line a minute. Don't go way.

Me: All right.

Roy: Y'know, I'm spending a lot of time with you, and I've got a lot of people waiting, but I just love talking to you, cause you're a very intelligent gentleman, and not a woman, any more. I see man in you.

Me: Thank you Roy, finding your meditation technique seven or eight years ago, which in my pride I refused to pay for, I listened to it for 15 seconds, threw it in a drawer. Two days later I listened to it for 30 seconds, and it has transformed my life once I saw the stillness - as the goal. I let network television out of my life. I've never seen a reality show, never seen "Friends," I don't go to churches, I don't have fiend friends, cigarettes fell away, I don't drink, and this has brought me so much closer to G-d that I feel… and I hope; I know you'll be honest with me, if I now discuss my crossroads experience with homosexuality it's worth talking about.

Roy: Well, the thing is, you're not any more, I assume?

Me: No. You're absolutely correct. That has been out of my life for ten years, and...

Roy: So it isn't an issue

Me: I know, I…I thought perhaps it might be worth something…

Roy: No, I got the cross-dressing thing you mentioned. You're taking on the shell, you're taking on the identity. When you have the identity of your mother, and not the good quality of your father that should have saved you from your mother but he couldn't save himself if you know what I mean, then that identity tends to try to complete itself with fantasy and that kind of thing..

Me: The thing about completing itself. I saw, in the spirit, I had made a decision after fifteen years of shooting heroin, cocaine and every pill in the world, I was sober for three months. I'm going back twenty-five years now...

Roy: Yes.

Me: I decided I'd go into a video store, an adult bookstore, which is the same in the pre-AIDS days as Sodom and Gomorrah. You just go in there and find an anonymous individual. And at first I thought, well, I don't want to do this anymore, but you had mentioned last time, that you feel this sense of loss, desolation, like you're... Satan just says *"you're empty now, you need this... Just this once"* so I turned and I started to service this anonymous individual, and; and because I first thought, 'I don't want this any more,' and lost all my lust, when I made that decision to get that lust back, it's almost like I had to walk into Satan's courtyard and worship him in order to enter that image deeper, this time, and go deeper in its *service*, and when I had finished, and had completely given myself, I started to talk, and my voice was not my own.

Roy: Yes…

Me: It was… what the British word for a cigarette is.

Roy: I do hope you… That was a long time ago, wasn't it?

Me: Yes, and I saw, if I said one more word, I saw my whole life would be like that. Sexuality would become my life, and the loss of... what I can see now would have been the loss of my soul, and I'm certainly not saying anyone who is trapped by that is beyond redemption. But I saw that, when you keep giving yourself to the wrong choice, *"To whom you yield yourself servant to obey..."* you are going to wind up going into a hell, you hope you don't wind up on that rotisserie….

Roy: Marty, I've got about one minute to get out of this segment. But I think you're a very eloquent gentleman, and I wish you a happy forever… Happy Christmas, and I know you are on the way to salvation if you are not already there.

Me: Well, G-d bless you, Roy. You are the only one in the world that has this message. I don't care if people have read CG Jung and HS Sullivan and all the great… You have answers, but as you say, they're not your answers for people to line up and bow to you, but you let people find them in themselves. And May you live forever! We can't make it without ya.

You better hang on, buddy. Be well, G-d bless you and yours.

Roy: Thank you. G-d bless… Make yourself known to me one day.

Me: I'd like to come up there again. Can I send you a letter?

Roy: I'd like to shake your hand.

Me: I'd like that very much. G-d willing. Bye bye.

(Hanging up)

Roy: G-d bless you.

Yes, that's a nice thing. I don't usually let people talk that much, but that man had something to say. He had something to share. He's been through what you may be going through. I do suspect not quite the same, but similar. All right, so there is a good and evil, isn't there? And there is a choice, but you didn't make the choice to be wrong. You were born that way. You have to be saved from it. That's why you need a savior. It's so simple.

Chapter 24 – Patience: Reintegration 101

I was able for the first time – albeit tentatively at first – to exist free from the persecutory delusion(s). A layer of resentment and reaction had been stripped away by my becoming aware of these dissociated tendencies. A veil had lifted and awareness stayed to see my sexual fantasies as an extension of my fleshly creation. This "awareness" dissipated the 'dynamism-of-difficulty'[61] which was "me" creating my real-world fate and destiny. I saw that my life had been reflecting my submissive and humiliating dynamisms by consistently finding ways to overreact, get angry and fail.

I saw my hatred; my angers; jealousies of such childish nature that if any girl went home with any guy (other than me), I was bothered. The depths of temptation - to release myself into sexual imaginary positioning - began to be 'observed,' instead of being submerged into. The release from anxiety in performing the sex act became illuminated: *"I'm free of anxiety that people will harm me unless I'm doing some sort of obeisance. What more security can a paranoid individual find in life than to lose oneself in sexual service to another?"*

This was clearly my 'dynamism of difficulty." A paranoid behavioral adjustment to uncanny anxiety, it created more submissive homosexual behavior; including a continual need for a more dominating and humiliating life experience. This is not a healthy seeking of "gay" intimacy with a male partner in an Ozzie and Harriet monogamy, but rather, in Sullivan's words, creating something that is *"merely a behavior which separates the sufferer from decent people.*[62]*"* In bathhouses and (in the pre-AIDS days the back rooms of Adult Bookstores' video booths), one finds the ubiquitous "glory hole." This was a hole cut in the wall between the booths, enabling one man to hang his manhood through "sight-unseen" for another to service. This was – and probably still is – an enormously popular homoerotic behavior. How then, can one fail to recognize the complete divorcement from intimacy, and not come face-to-face with Sullivan's dictum, which my own life's experience validates?

Now I was becoming more aware of these tendencies and imaginings. Now things had changed. I just took my hands off the rudder, and allowed the *"Father in me"* to do the works.[63] I had the sense that my "boat," was

---

[61] *"Clinical Studies in Psychiatry" Norton & Co., New York (1956) (Sullivan) p5*
[62] *"Clinical Studies in Psychiatry" (Sullivan) p163*
[63] *John 15*

now being directed more by inner knowing than my decisions, mostly indistinguishable in the past from conniving, and was indeed now cutting through the water. I was going through life's obstacles more successfully and with less care. They were no longer piercing me. Obstacles were no longer penetrating my conveyance and causing me to flee into defensive anxiety, anger or agreement (the animal reaction of flight or fight). There is a shame in not being able to stand one's ground in the infinite permutations of the self-system's security we attribute to ourselves and thus reflect in our personal culture. I found "not-hating" to be the basis for confidence. Not-hating is loving. It is the true love, not the *let-me-lick-your-face* love. It is the logical understanding of life as it is developing in the communication with "the other." It is "Mr. Spock" laying down his life for his friends in *Star Trek*. The word "confidence" is from the Latin "with fidelity."

I began to take a different view of the concept of "sin." It always used to conjure up an angry image of some preacher with a big black bible metaphorically hitting someone over the head with condemnation. Consider instead a narrow road with the word "*signpost*." The Hebrew word for '*commandment*' was actually translated "*signpost*." "*I will write these on their hearts*," says the prophet concerning the Messiah's mission.

The words of the Messiah, the rabbinic master from Galilee who defeated death, are full of references to "*missing the mark*" as a definition for the word "*sin*." Metaphors of an arrow flying towards its target, a path made straight and narrow are all used to mark our journey in life.

Consequently, I see my journey, this walk down the road, as an arrow making its flight, a commitment to walk within these signposts, but these '*signposts*' are written on my heart.

Temptation in the "new" and the "now"

It had been years since I had had sex. I was parked in front of a pawn shop and was preparing to leave the strip mall when a very attractive girl in her mid-twenties drove up to the pawnshop. I saw the large TV in her backseat, and put my car into Park and shut off the engine. Soon a clerk was helping her bring the large TV inside, and soon enough he was returning it to her car. Her pretty face was contorted in her predicament. (In a great performance, Sienna Miller's character says in her movie "*The Interview*" "*men see a woman in fishnet stockings and high heels. The net reminds them of a fish, and the high-heels a vulnerable one, falling into the net.*")

A sexual opportunity; floundering helplessly in financial vulnerability. I fantasized having her and reached for my door handle, a predator on the hunt. I straightened up, made eye contact, and started to brave the energy all around me pushing me back into the car, making it seem like I was spiritually walking into a 100 mph wind.

Nodding toward the TV in her backseat, I schmoozed sympathetically. *"Couldn't get enough for it, uhh?"* She stood hesitating by her driver's side, reacting with enough self-pity to at least prolong the conversation. Without thinking, I went right for it. *"Have any other ideas… I mean* **options** *how to get …"* I stopped in mid-sentence. The word *"options"* had been spoken by my mouth but the spirit of licentiousness had given it just the right amount of innuendo. Innuendo that was pulling back the cool crispy sheets in the cold motel room. The awareness of my conscience caught up to my awareness of my lust – now laid open for me by hearing my own words), and I started eating shame. It was impossible to go further in my quest without forcefully demanding sin and flouting/abandoning/denying G-d's will – and my fealty to that will – in my life. I had done that all my life. I didn't want to do it anymore. I shut my mouth, looked down, and wished her luck. I started up and drove off refusing to look back.

I didn't need to call my priest, pastor or rabbi. I know in my heart I'm heading off the road tempting that girl to have sex with me, I have a spiritual life living inside me, and when I react in OBEDIENCE to that urging, I am strengthened for the next trial, but am also buoyed up in a quiet joy. I'm glad I didn't degrade that girl and myself. I don't need to call somebody in a costume. I know in my heart I'm missing the mark here, and that pains me more than the frustration of lost sex.

I found, however, that the Hebrew Messiah had saved me from "missing it" by providing a love of Himself as a way of me living in Him, and I started walking without "missing it" – generally. The *Father in me, he does all the work…* I didn't think of it at the time, but I was being saved from (missing it) sin.

The signs of supernatural presence were there: the '*synchronicity*' within the crossroads experience at the rented room, the responding to that leading of the spirit to trap that abusive landlord, his admission into that same psychic territory before the judge in order that I be granted the Restraining Order; thousands of dollars showing up in my mailbox; my following the inner leading to create the multimedia software (which had been purchased by several high schools); my return to on-line university to complete a Bachelor's degree and start a graduate program. I was becoming more patient and forgiving with my sons, co-workers, supermarket shoppers and even those other drivers on the road. I found my attitude towards other drivers on the road a particularly keen barometer of my new life's contentment. Another behavioral change was my commitment to simply do the best job I could. This humble, low-paying job gave me ample opportunity to see my humility juxtaposed to my pride.

I was making consistent moral decisions freeing my life from humiliation, worry and regret. Within the two-steps forward, one-step back behavior, I went online and downloaded some porn after being free from it for months. After a few minutes, I found I just **couldn't submerge** into identification with it. I felt low, uncomfortable and abruptly tossed it all, thinking "*I can't do this any more.*" I found my own fantasies to be far more brilliant anyway.

As in a nightmare, what was filling me with emotion a moment before in sleep is – after awakening – now referred to simply as "thought-stuff." "*Oh, that,*" I think, as I bring to consciousness a scenario in the nightmare. Then, upon awakening, I can refer to that emotionally charged moment objectively with a few words in my mind. In the same way, I think of a pornographic video action, or imaginings with the 'pawn-shop girl,' and I think "*Oh, that,*" rather than having to mentally dive into it. It's *power over me* was diminished to the point that I began to gain confidence in my ability to ignore it. The 'master-slave' relationship had turned around as a result of simple – but continual – awareness from with this Observation-Meditation Exercise.

* * *

If the... eruption of abhorrent cravings, are followed by experience which is able to terminate the association of a major part of the particular motivational system with these uncanny emotions, and associate it with the main trends of personality development, then we would have achieved the integration of a previously dissociated motivational system with the rest of the personality, and there would be none of this dreadful spectacle of the schizophrenic way of life, with its exceedingly ominous probable outcomes. --- **Dr. HS Sullivan Interpersonal Theory pp327-8**

At the end of the first round in his first fight against *Mike Tyson* – *Holyfield's* manager looks him in the eye when *Evander* returns to his corner. *Holyfield* sits with his stone-faced expression, raising his eyes to his lifelong trainer, who yells into his face:
"*Just stay calm, and it's you! You see everything...*
You're the bully in here. He ain't the bully!"

In "*Return of the Jedi*," there's a scene at the battle for the bunker that harbors the shield protecting the *Death Star*. An *Imperial Walker* comes up to the heroes at the bunker door, and everybody is momentarily alarmed, but the hatch pops open and *Chewey* comes out. That makes all the difference, doesn't it? It's very important in life to know who's in charge of your *Imperial Walker*. Those who seek truth sense **a yearning** within us whispering without sound that dares to want "*The Force*" to win; the loud, selfish 'other' carries the insistent and strident voice of "*The Dark Side*" being the cooler, more obvious choice. As you approach behavior conducive to disintegrating your "*Dark Side*," you've got to know who you *want* to be in charge, because the voices become louder, more unreasonable. Your sickness doesn't want you finding the medicine that will end its own existence in you. The darkness does not want you to find the light. The biggest problem with schizophrenia is this difficulty in the sufferer understanding that the voice(s) that speak(s) in his head as "I" have the *Dark Side* as their master. The *Bard* deals with this same kind of issue when he says:

> *But tis strange, and oftentimes,*
> *to win us to our harm,*
> *The instruments of darkness tell us truths,*
> *Win us with honest trifles,*
> *To betray us in deepest consequence.*

It's no accident that Shakespeare has the noble *Banquo* asking:

> *Were such things here as we do speak about?*
> *Or have we eaten on the insane root,*
> *That takes the reason prisoner?*[64]

The Meditation/Observation Exercise gives new birth to an ever-increasing strength in this *Imperial Walker's* silent commander. The epiphany I had experienced in the Las Vegas desert had become deeper, more "a part of me" (I sniffed what it was like to be "good," and found the aroma not entirely unpleasant). The production mechanisms of tension and anxiety were having their fuel-energy lines disturbed. The "stillness" is allowing an opportunity for my soul to be charged. The thoughts turn emotionally complex, and become emotional "complexes" which are like atoms combining into molecules; and then into complex molecules, all

---

[64] *William Shakespeare, Macbeth Act 1 Scene 3*

part of the same "tree-like-branching' design[65] in order to cause one to become 'lost in thought.'

You don't have to go too far down this road before realizing that *thinking about* an attractive or unattractive aspect of your emotional structure will have very little effect on altering it. For all our university wisdom, we are, by and large, no closer to self-control in these matters than Jim Carrey's character in *"Ace Ventura's When Nature Calls,"* when he mutters to himself *"bad thoughts out, good thoughts in,"* when faced with a temptation he doesn't know how to handle.

We are all the injected children of Adam and Eve's exit from paradisiacal innocence into *pride's ego*. What is instilled in us and speaks in our heads (as if it *is* us); is birthed from reaction to the trauma of parental lunacy (themselves victims of unconscious injection from their own parents) – and will not admit to a life being lived in a wrong way. Pride is in conflict with what it replaced; and wars against its prior innocence. We embrace that which corrupts us.

What we expect and don't receive makes us annoyed. When we are hurt, don't we often try to humiliate in our own turn? Don't we then try to get the *"other"* to feel pained, embarrassed and *'less-than'* when it suits us and/or when we're able to? The boss dumps on you. You dump on your mate. The mate on the kids. The kids on each other, with the weakest winding up kicking the dog. Then we can all *"feel better"* about our dis-*'ease;'* about *'our reality.'* We have disparaged the esteem, the prestige, the emotional needs of this *other's* sense of self. Consequently, he or she – now feeling pained, *'less-than,'* and *"one-upped,"* may burn in the wrath

---

[65] *It is certainly no accident that all atomic structure has – as its base elements protons, neutrons and electrons. It's ALL the same "stuff" except for the amount of little electrons circling the nucleus. So hydrogen is the same "stuff" as gold. They each just carry a different number of little moons circling their centers. Such is the magnitude of G-d that our tiny little minds cannot grasp it. You will, however, travel "behind" these atomic structures when you die.*

How can we grasp the glory of an egg coming out of a chicken? If you try to really objectify 'creation' you go 'koo-koo' (as my friend Roy Masters says). The chicken costs $2. We can make a $400,000 Mercedes Benz, but we cannot make a $2 chicken. We think we "own" a tree, but the tree "watches us" grow old and die, and be buried amongst its roots. It is not effected by what name is on your real estate deed. Its majesty lies in the single acorn's DNA. All the forest raises its limbs up to the Creator, longing for his light, which gives it life. The roots of a plant are so flimsy a child could rip them apart, yet before long they'll break through cement and destroy a granite foundation.

Take a seed of any fruit or herb. Just add dirt. Let it rain. More food grows. Human excrement is the greatest fertilizer in the world. There's a lot going on in creation.

of our judgment – and can now *"feel worse."* You are a *'god'* with a lower-case *"g."* You are a god who craps.

The "self" that's helping you run from the truth is the "self" that would be exposed by the very truth it's seeking to prevent the objective "you" from finding. The human being is always able to go one layer further in 'self' consciousness. One layer more can always be observed in understanding the 'layers of the onion.' Your thoughts become like the villains in movies seeking to thwart the progress of the good detective. It is that which was created and nurtured from the early trauma, which replaced that which was created in the image of G-d in the first place. It has been created in the pride of the lie that our father Adam embraced. Because the new "father" for Adam was the father of lies, and the father of pride, this trait gets passed down from parent to child unwittingly, unconsciously, inescapably.

We are thus "born in the sin" of our proud self's "ego." Our ego will do anything to prevent us from seeing ourselves (itself) as wrong. It's the spirit of darkness helping you not to turn on the light. It's like a dishonest guide trying to keep you from your healthy destination, for this "guide" who speaks in your head will be terminated when you find the truth in your enlightened destiny. It is in conflict with the aware 'truth.' It torments you using your hidden resentment of the gods-of-this earth – in this case your parental authority figures – and you writhe like a voodoo doll, the darts of temptation scanning your armor to make you its victim; impregnated by the waspish anxieties of parental authority and culture.

Adam was born a fully grown man. We enter the world as utterly helpless babies, and our ego needs to grow from that infantile state to adulthood. Sullivan describes a series of personality stages or "growth cycles" from infancy to late adolescence,[66] leaving the subject of "adult" conveniently missing, as in a spiritual shout of silence. Yes, we do have to learn how to grow our ego with combinations of standing up for ourselves, behavioral accomplishments, sexual adventures and the like (confidence), but at a certain stage of our growth, the soul no longer finds nourishment in these activities, and turns, as the salmon going home, to that which created it.

It's like you have a dark companion who is talking in your ear 24/7. You know your ancient ancestor left you a treasure somewhere, but whenever you seek to uncover it, your dark companion is always suggesting an alternative behavior. When you find that treasure that is your inheritance, that dark companion is going to be out of business, and

---

[66] *"Interpersonal Theory of Psychiatry"* Sullivan (Norton, New York)

in a *hell* of a lot of trouble with his boss. I found, as you will find, it's the *job* of this nagging voice to keep you busy with other things.

This was my challenge when I started meditating. It is still my challenge every day. Jesus was tempted. You will be too. This will be your challenge as well, should you choose to journey with me.

While in the Observation Exercise, simple awareness is the goal and the currency of life. Nevertheless, I began to recite this silently so often that it became a part of me. I no longer needed to devote conscious attention to remember the words, as the words rose up in me by themselves. All that was needed was for me to **not do it mechanically**, and this also brought "change" and 'light" into dark, anxious areas perceived in the meditation. Unwanted, unnecessary thoughts began to weaken in their power over me, and then disintegrate as time went by. Perhaps this is what was meant by the biblical injunction to *'pray without ceasing.*"

Our **Father**, who art in heaven
Hallowed be ***thy*** name (not `my` name)
Let ***your*** kingdom come.
Let ***your*** will (not `my will`) be done;
On this earth (`thru my life`)
As it is done in heaven.

Give us this day
Our daily bread (`of eternal life`).
Forgive us our sins
Even as we forgive those
Who sin against us.

Lead us out of temptation
And deliver us from evil;
For yours is the Kingdom, the Power and the Glory
Forever and ever, amen.

Concepts of discernment, judgment and forgiveness began to come alive for me. For example, suppose I discern someone hates me, and is cheating and betraying me. If I get angry and start insulting him, that is, trying to bring into his mind's eye feelings of shame, guilt and embarrassment for himself, I am bringing "judgment" (ie, 'you've done wrong in my "eye" and you must suffer pangs of negative emotion concerning your own "self's pride' for your act). So I am a god of sorts, one who craps, as Eve promised Adam he would be.

If I say to an individual that his actions were such that I no longer deem a relationship with him to be in my best interests, I am not judging that person, but discerning him. To "forgive" is to "forget" in a way, and not "resent." Judgment always brings resentment. Resentment spiritually is of a part of that same dark energy that entered your enemy which has you now so moved as well. Hate was in your enemy and now that same spirit is seeking to enter you. So I try to leave "judgment" to God. I am not emotional nor angry. I could have a job as an executioner, and pull the switch on a pedophile killer, and still have neither "judgment" nor "anger." The idea that as humans anger is natural and acceptable is totally false. You can stand up for yourself just as much and struggle just as hard without becoming angry. Except you'll do all these behaviors better.

Now this same determination of 'who's in charge' was becoming common in my waking everyday life and was having the most profound effect. The first decision every morning was to do the Meditation Exercise – even for just a minute – if I was pressed for time. From sexual fantasy to road rage, from rage-reaction to the headlines or from imaginatively engaging in some covert conversational scenario, my ability to be aware of my reaction (to submerge into reverie) was all that was necessary to regain my objectivity. This led to increased patience and bouts of unexpected contentment, in effect no longer becoming anxious while alone or with significant others.

More often and more telling, however, was that the fact that I often found myself about to blurt out something and interrupt another's communication to me, and instead now allowed a patience to prosper within, actually listening to this person, hearing things within these words that alerted me to what he or she was really trying to communicate. It was like sitting in the 'eye-of-the-storm.' It was also remarkable for me to see how hungry people are for a tidbit of approval, how quick they are to assign blame to others, and I realized also with no small embarrassment that I was just like "them," and only a temptation away from being so again at any moment.

I saw – with no small degree of horror – that I had been unnecessarily fleeing further communication from 'the other' as if I would be 'hurt' egotistically somehow by not interrupting. I saw the illusion, weakness and counter-productivity of reacting to this illusion as I allowed myself to become patient and receptive. I had been too quick to react to what I had imagined – or anticipated – was unfavorable reflection (disapproval) upon something being said concerning my self-esteem. By interrupting others, I was protecting something that didn't need to be protected. This 'mental B-O' (body odor) was so full of childish (and often infantile) concerns, that by engaging in these early reference processes I was demonstrating an impoverished self-system far lower than anything I was consciously aware of. By interrupting others, I actually lowered the very same self-esteem I was trying to protect. My understanding of this created a door into my new reality, and a life based on patience and lack-of-anxiety. The awareness was based on a continuing commitment to meditate. Understanding was ongoing; and if not strengthened, would diminish. I didn't go ten days a year without meditating.

By working on the Britneyzian Prophecies (www.trailopen.com/index-3.html). I could see my eagerness to speak in 'substitute processes' within my own 'self-system' in the same way my heroine was experiencing her situation with her husband. I had, of course, experienced my own similar enslaved devolution in 1968. But today, I was no longer impulsively reacting to the temptation regarding my (thin-skinned) self-esteem. I had no idea up to that point how much of myself I was showing in that unflattering light in trying to 'protect' myself from a total delusionary vulnerability. I had no miraculous video to record my surrender and disintegration. The extent to which I allowed another's power to overwhelm me was causing a birth into becoming that actual loser; helped into being so by a hypnotized commitment to **blindness** of *actual* vulnerabilities. ***In other words, within the infinite permutations that make up personality structure, if I agree with my tormentor that I'm wrong, than I'm wrong.***

I realized with a sense of newfound baby-step security that all I needed was right between my ears.

Stay calm and it's you;
You see everything…

As I've said many times above, the dream/nightmare we "snap out of" is also a metaphor for our being lost in thought and then coming out of it and into objectivity. We can see this most clearly in the example of *road-rage*. We submerge ourselves into momentary rage on the highway, only to later regard our emotionality concerning that angry event as "thought stuff." In other words, the same car who five minutes before you imagined destroying as he carelessly endangered you and your family's lives is, minutes later, seen in another lane. You are no longer emotional, and in your mind you process the new image of this same automobile combined with the thought how angry you were at this so-and-so for his indiscretion. But you no longer have the intense resentment concerning it. It might even cross your mind that you have also, on occasion, accidentally erred in driving performance. This will further diminish the feeling attached to the "so-and-so" in that car, and thus with a mental synopsis of *"I was angry"* you reference the prior event. What was then emotional fury is now relatively objective dry data.

The road-rage analogy is the same in relation to the dream state of ordinary waking fantasy as well. In such a state, we are held captive in emotional turmoil only to be liberated by the light of objective consciousness. This is discernment stemming from 'awareness.'

In another newly discovered 'track' of conscious submergence, I saw that we have all had that experience where we are the recipient of a disconcerting comment in a social setting, only to think of the perfect rejoinder long after the event has past into history. However, it is not long after your (now useless) witty rejoinder passes from the mental netherland from which it sprung, that it is replaced by imagery well-beyond the subject matter spoken of at the party. We may easily find ourselves in imaginative scenarios of social triumph, sexual satisfaction, revenge, approval and victories dressed in many different robes. One needn't be involved too deeply in one's covert operations to slip into a fantasy world making wonderful judgments, receiving approval, triumph and adoration. The mind enjoys submerging into satisfying sequences of heroic imagery, and soon finds such awareness somewhat embarrassing to acknowledge. But the flight into fancy is certainly a pleasant alternative to having to face any real-life inadequacies; however real or imagined they may be.

I was becoming aware of relationships between wish-fulfilling fantasies and jealousies I never knew I had toward people and things I never knew I envied. Within this dynamic power fueled by this Observation Exercise, this matter – once its embarrassing presence was looked at fully-in-the-face, lessened as a destructive force and soon disappeared altogether, leaving a vacuum being filled with more awareness and understanding.

In a somewhat different tack of submergence, I have often found myself imaginatively communicating in dialogue with someone, having a winning and convincing conversation/monologue that only exists in my mind. We have all seen people walking down the street with their lips moving, who could easily pass friends on the street without noticing them.

How many times have we locked the door to our dwelling (or some similar measure), and, being "deep in thought," are struck shortly afterwards by the nagging doubt that perhaps we didn't lock that door at all. So we turn around and go back, only to find we had indeed locked the door, and we suffer some covert ridicule over our unnecessary behavior from the same voice that urged us to *"go back and make sure it was locked"* in the first place. Remember *Chewey* and the *Imperial Walker*. The example of the *locked door* is multiplied in infinite variations, and while these thoughts claim us, heralding their importance, how many of us can remember what we were actually thinking yesterday? This morning? Five minutes ago? Thirty seconds ago? I am not referring to vague considerations of memory regarding the general concerns of your personal calendar, but the actual reverie itself; that matter of *thought*, to which the mind holds most tenaciously in 'the moment.' The Exercise will allow the meditator a fuller appreciation of this latter point, when thought is isolated outside of its emotional content.[67]

I will maintain that in the objective state one is encouraged to maintain, an awareness grows which will shed light on the true nature of such thought. We are often the fish swimming after the tempting bait of mental reverie. Al Pacino says in *Glengarry Glenross*, *"We're either looking forward, or we're looking back. Where's the moment?"*

This is the immediacy of reality we seek to run from, and the space in which meditation seeks to grow our soul's illumination out from. This is where I park my *Imperial Walker* for its daily refueling.

So when I speak of *'thought,'* I speak of this "tempting bait." I am not talking about the considerations necessary to determine what size carburetor to order on the Chevy you're repairing, unless your thought-stream flows out into the possibility of whom you'll impress by your choice. When I speak of thought and emotion I'm not referring to how to calculate the next lunar trajectory for your rocket launch, but if your thoughts should veer off into how satisfying it will be to show so-and-so that he's wrong and you're right, than it does become relevant. So, one can easily see that I am speaking about the conflict inherent in the stress and anxiety of self-regard, which afflicts both beggar and billionaire.

There are those who will refuse this path, but for me I know the Light of He who was raised from the dead – the Hebrew Messiah – will meet the meditator in the stillness of the Observation Exercise.

The depth of the exercise is centered in the middle of one's forehead. It is the biological Pineal Gland;[68] it is the 'Third Eye" sought by Eastern

---

[67] *Free samples at www.trailopen.com (Be Still and Know)*
[68] *"DMT–The Spirit Molecule" (A Doctor's Revolutionary Research into the Biology of Near-Death and Mystical Experiences); Park Street Press (Vermont) 2001, Rick Strassman, MD pp. 58-61*
"The pineal is unique in its solitary status within the brain. All other brain sites are paired, meaning that they have left and right counterparts; for example, there are left and right frontal lobes and left and right temporal lobes. As the only unpaired organ deep within the brain, the pineal gland remained an anatomical

curiosity for nearly two thousand years. No one in the West had any idea what its function was."

"... The human pineal gland becomes visible in the developing fetus at seven weeks, or forty-nine days, after conception. Of great interest to me was finding out that this was nearly exactly the moment in which one can clearly see the first indication of male or female gender. Before this, the sex of the fetus is indeterminate. Thus, the pineal gland and the most important differentiation of humanity, male and female gender, appear at the same time."

"The human pineal gland is not actually part of the brain. Rather, it develops from specialized tissues in the roof of the fetal mouth. From there it migrates to the center of the brain, where it seems to have the best seat in the house."

"We have already noted the Pineal's proximity to cerebrospinal fluid channels, which allows its secretions easy access to the brain's deepest recesses. Additionally, it sits in strategic closeness to the crucial emotional and sensory brain centers."

"These sensory or perceptual hubs are called visual and auditory colliculi, little mounds of specialized brain tissue. They are relay stations for the transmission of sense data to brain sites involved in their registration and interpretation. That is, electrical and chemical impulses that begin in the eyes and ears must pass through the colliculi before we experience them in our minds as sights and sounds. The pineal gland hangs directly over these colliculi, separated only by a narrow channel of cerebrospinal fluid. Anything secreted by the pineal into that fluid would settle onto the colliculi in a moment."

"In addition, the limbic, or 'emotional' brain, surrounds the tiny pineal. The limbic 'system' is a collection of brain structures intimately involved in the experience of feelings, such as joy, rage, fear, anxiety and pleasure. Therefore, the pineal also has direct access to the brain's emotional centers." (pp58-61)

The psychedelic compound DMT is one of the most potent of the mind-expanding chemicals.

"The pineal gland contains the necessary building blocks to make DMT. For example, it possesses the highest levels of serotonin anywhere in the body, and serotonin is a crucial precursor for pineal melatonin. The pineal also has the ability to convert serotonin to tryptamine, a critical step in DMT formation." Surprisingly, no one has looked for DMT in the pineal."

"**In some of us, pineal DMT mediates the pivotal experiences of deep meditation, psychosis and near-death experiences**."

"The unique enzymes that convert serotonin, melatonin, or tryptamine into psychedelic compounds are also present in extraordinarily high concentrations in the pineal. These enzymes, the methyltransferases, attach a methyl group – that is one carbon and three hydrogens – onto other molecules, thus methylating them. Simply methylate tryptamine twice, and we have di-methyl-tryptamine, or mystics. It is the angelic *"flaming sword that turns every way"* spoken of in Genesis 3:24,[69] and when Meditating with the Observation Exercise, traces of dark qualities reflecting the soulish exploration will float up out of the stillness. They tempt my awareness/consciousness to react. I have learned that if I can be aware of that "thought/dark quality/horrible emotion" even for the slightest second, it would start to disintegrate its power within, but the 'light' of this momentary experience was not unlike looking into the sun, and reflected spiritual forces outside normal life.

I began to be aware that spiritual forces were becoming more and more obvious in my life. If I get an urge to do something I know in my heart is wrong, I know I'm wandering off the path to do so. There is such a thing as fealty. There is such a thing as loyalty, to simply do what's right, that was so new to me it was being *'born again'* to live like this. If I'm broke and my someone's wallet is left on the table, I know it's wrong to slip money out of it. I will know it's wrong if it's a penny or a thousand dollars. There is such a thing as honor, that answers to an inner commander whether anybody on the outside knows about it or not.

Our tribal-society witch-doctors who went to school to learn what's right and wrong are eager to advise. Often they remain as 'agents' between the spiritual sufferer and G-d. They thwart the conscience or – while acknowledging the petitioner's need for the Almighty – have

---

DMT. Because it possesses the high levels of the necessary enzymes and precursors, the pineal gland is the most reasonable place for DMT formation to occur." (p. 69)
"Western and Eastern mystical traditions are replete with descriptions of a blinding bright white light accompanying deep spiritual realization. This "enlightenment" usually is the result of a progression of consciousness through various levels of spiritual, psychological and ethical development. All mystical traditions describe the process and stages."

"In Judaism, for example, consciousness moves through the Sefirot, or Kabalistic centers of spiritual development, the highest being Keter, or Crown. In the Eastern Ayurvedic tradition, these centers are called Chakras, and particular experiences likewise accompany the movement of energy through them. The highest chakra is also called the Crown, or the thousand-petaled Lotus. In both traditions, the location of this crown Sefira or Chakra is the center and top of the skull, anatomically corresponding to the human pineal gland."

[69] *"I will place a flame which fires in all directions at the entrance to the Garden." The ego-less awareness one is capable of attaining by 'stillness' in the meditation will always be accompanied by a 'burning' that you cannot take for more than half-a-second.*

themselves no understanding of salvation, and are today's 'blind guides.' Jesus said:

> "*Woe to the Pharisees. Like a dog dozing in a food trough for cattle, they neither eat nor do they let the cattle eat.*"[70]

We understand the happiness a mechanic feels to finally see what he failed to see before, so now he can fix what before he could not. We understand the joy of the rocket-scientist to see where the mistake is, so that now his rocket can get to its destination. **Why should we not be pleased to find out what is wrong with us**? Why can't we feel that way about ourselves? The prophet says '*be still and know.*'

Which is, or what is, the "self" that's not happy to discover its own deficiencies? It is the 'self' that will 'disintegrate.' It is that self that found a home in you when you were stung by 'parental larvae' in your own 'Garden' experience of trauma. The stress of that trauma resulted in your own post-traumatic stress; creating in you more emotional upheaval, or the next '*dis-order*' within the *Post Traumatic Stress Disorder*. The trauma that stole our butterfly innocence is fighting for its life through our resentment still. It will fight the stillness. It tempts. It brings an egoism that inflates and blames; and an esteem that appears to grow only at another's expense; by beating, shaming, taking advantage of, tricking and manipulating with guilt, embarrassment and anxiety; using approval or the threat of disapproval to finalize the domination of – or the submission to – "the other." This is our *ego legacy* from Eden. This is the stuff of "judging," which is a different animal from discernment. It is "discernment plus penalty." I – as a '*god-who-craps*' – determine that the self-system of 'the other,' built on the fallen nature of man just as mine is, may or may not be punished and shamed, degraded and made to feel "less-than" under circumstances subjectively determined to enhance my own sense of discernment, judgment and "self."

What we call 'love' may in some cases be actually much closer to hatred. This may be on display in relationships as early as the couples' wedding. This is the fascinating concept of "*embracing that which corrupts us.*" The wife being beaten by her abusive husband joins the man in attacking the police who come to rescue her from her abusive mate (cause I '*love*' him). The son who suddenly becomes a drug addict is now loving and protective of the dealer as well as the other addicts. Parents,

---

[70] "*Sayings of the Gospel of Thomas*" Davies, Skylight Paths Publishing, Vermont (2002) Saying #102 pp 125

teachers, police are all "enemies" now. Fealty changes. The dealer is now the friend. We set up relationships guaranteed to fail, and in the wrestling-for-dominance, we pretend this hatred is normal.

Soon after the wedding, you realize your new bride is a "witch," (*I never saw that in her before*) and she sees you as a "son-of-a-witch." Your relationship boils down to protecting one's own self-esteem while lashing out at that of the other. Drowning this reality in more alcohol, more powerful drugs and more lurid sex, we reproduce like jackrabbits, adding to the bill that we must pay to hell.

These relationships are often encapsulated with the notion that *"they really **do** love each other,"* when the opposite is true, regardless of how much physical and financial sacrifice is made to keep the relationship in place. One cries when the other dies, as they'll miss their life's identification with the role of master-slave.

Our pathetic slavery to the pressure of Christmas is a good indicator of our "sincerity." The atmosphere is so demanding in its insistence to be worshipped it's almost like being violated; as if one's will should be superceded by the demands of material largess. The pressure to spend unwisely is so palpable we embrace it as master and find ourselves apologizing to all how "this year" we decided not to go into debt for six-months. The eagerness with which we hope to buy another's "smile" at Christmas morning is yet another nail in the coffin of our pathetic self concept. *Maybe my wife and kids will love me;* approve of me – even for ten seconds – as they rip open what I've gone into debt for 6 months to get them. The madness of lemmings on their way over the cliff; we are tortured by betrayal and disappointment that we are not receiving the approval "paid for," but instead only earning the others' contempt. What we expect and don't receive leaves us annoyed. Our hell is punctuated with wild gasms that more and more don't even have the pretense of intimacy or affection. We are each others' sex toys, our minds totally removed from each other even while physically joined in exhilarated sex. You went for the gusto but the gusto got you.

This is where His love comes in to make us new. A sexual behavior within moderation; not slavery. Separate bedrooms might actually allow the man and woman an opportunity to become – and/or remain – friends. A man who looks to G-d, and a woman who looks and trusts this honorable man gives birth to children who see the mother honoring their father, and are able to love the heavenly "Father" that one cannot see in addition to respecting the father they *can* see. This is the ideal. To help facilitate this, it would certainly help if the woman saves herself for marriage. Imagine if you will that within their year's engagement they do not have sex, but actually learn to be each others' loyal friend! As shocking an idea as this is, it remains the most exciting concept against pre-marital sex I can think of, as you actually have something of importance to give to each other on your wedding night. It certainly makes the vow to stay faithful with each other more real.

A love that allows you to be with other people, but with enough self-regard that your esteem needn't suffer while acknowledging the achievements of others, nor is your esteem built on disparaging others to elevate your own "self." To not-hate is to love.

Living Without Disparaging Others: What has love to do with it?

I remember as a young teen noting my older cousin's graduation from Yale University. He would soon be assuming his role in his father's multimillion dollar company. My father brazenly responded to my mother, "*Marty could put him in his hip pocket.*" He went on to imply that any success this young man achieved was because of his privileged position as the son of my millionaire uncle, and I, barely able to cope with high school at the time, was alleged to have whatever qualities were necessary to put this older, admired cousin "*into my hip pocket.*" Within my father's insecurity, people who succeeded did so because of 'connections,' or through circumstances we were not fortunate enough to have.

Sullivan goes on to state that an entire snapshot of a human being may be had by the amount of weight he gives to the disparagement of others:

"*In this (juvenile) era there is the learning of disparagement, with the possibility for chronic defect in one's self esteem. This disparagement has its beginnings for the most part in influence exerted by the parental group, who teach the juvenile to notice the shortcomings of others. And this necessity of maintaining self-esteem by pulling down the standing of others, if uncorrected in subsequent developmental eras, has unfortunate later outcomes. In the juvenile era this kind of security operation literally and importantly interferes with adequate appraisal of personal worth. Since one has to protect his feeling of self esteem by noting how unworthy everyone else is, this fails to provide any convincing data as to one having any personal worth; and one is left to think: 'I'm not as bad as the other swine.'*

"These are important influences exerted by the parental group. This is a parental morbidity of security operations, such that the juvenile is taught to disparage others – a common phenomenon on the American scene. ***It may be the way, for instance, that the significant figure in the house handles "misfortune," such as being average instead of superior***. It may occur because the parental figure has always disparaged all people who made him or her uncomfortable. It may occur because one or both parents feel threatened by the revealing nature of juvenile communication and so disparage teachers and other people with whom they feel compared. This disparaging business is like the dust of the streets – it settles everywhere. It is perhaps not so disastrous in the juvenile era as it is from then on; but it is very disastrous at any time."

"…If you have to maintain self-esteem by pulling down the standing of others, you are extraordinarily unfortunate in a variety of ways. Since you have to protect your personal feeling of self worth by noting how unworthy everyone around you is, you are not provided with any data that are convincing evidence of your having personal worth; so it gradually evolves into that same *"I am not as bad as the other swine."* To be the best of swine, when it would be nice to be a person, is not a good way of furthering anything except security operations. When security is achieved that way, it strikes at the very roots of that which is essentially human – the utterly vital role of interpersonal relations."

"In other words, if another boy does well and little Willie reports it to his mother, and mother promptly knocks the spots off the other boy and his family, that tends to indicate that little Willie's impression of how the other fellow was behaving was groundless, or the rewards which the other fellow's behavior got from teachers, and so on, was undeserved. In other words, *one is encouraged to feel incapable of knowing what is good.*"

"Learning from human examples is extremely important, as I have stressed; but if every example that seems to be worth emulating, learning something from, is reduced to no importance or worth, than who are the models going to be? *I think that this is probably the most vicious of the inadequate, inappropriate, and ineffectual performances of parents with juveniles–this interference with a sound development of appreciation of personal worth, by universal derogatory and disparaging attitudes toward anybody who seems to stand out at all*. It is in this way that parents are apt to very markedly handicap the 'sane' development of standards of personal worth in their young. To that extent – barring great good fortune in subsequent eras of personality development – they literally will guarantee that their children will be barely *better than the other swine*." [71]

---

[71] *Interpersonal Theory of Psychiatry;* Sullivan, pp243

Self Respect and Human Maturity
"From all that I have suggested you may see that it is of no extraordinary use of inference to presume if you cannot respect others, you cannot respect yourself. And people who are very high in self-respect; that is, whose life experience has permitted them to uncover and demonstrate to their own satisfaction remarkable capacity for living with – and among –others- are people who find no particular expense to themselves connected with respecting any meritorious performance of anyone else. One of the feeblest props for an inadequate self-system is the attitude of disparaging others. In a good many ways, one can read the whole state of a person's self-respect by his disparagement of others.

The disparagement is built on two ingredients, that which one despises about oneself, and a great many "*not*" operations. Thus the person who greatly respects himself for his generosity, which is probably always of a very public character, finds an incredible amount of people **not**-generous, instead stingy, mean and so on.

I think it has been known since the beginning of recorded thought that a person who is very bitter towards others, very hard on his fellow man for certain faults, is usually very sensitive to these particular faults because they are secret vices of his own. Insofar as self-respect has been permitted to grow without restrictions, because of comparatively un-warped personal development or because warp of personal development has been remedied, there is no expense, no feeling of impoverishment, no hints of anxiety connected with discovering that somebody else is much better than you are in a particular field."

It has always been a reflection of the secure – and that often means accomplished – to offer praise to others. *Britney Spears* says in interviews that she wishes her voice was as good as *Christine Aguilera's. Michael Jordan* does not feel diminished when he compliments the abilities of other players. It is only those who secretly resent because they have not accomplished their own inner goals who must tear others down. As Sullivan will later write concerning the attitudes of these people: "*If I'm a molehill, then, by G-d, there will be no mountains.*"

It is lamentably true that in so highly specialized and intricate a social organization as any extant culture is, it is virtually certain that there are very few top figures in any complex organization. Most people are not as good as the very few, and many people are much worse than average. But there is such an enormous field for living, one does not have to depend on what one is not good at, and therefore one has no particular need for keeping a bookkeeping record on how many people are worse in a field in which one is bad. But some people, because of certain warps in personal development, make this an outstanding operation, in order to reduce anxiety from invidious comparison with others.[72]

Disparagement Brings Anxiety: Conjunctive and Disjunctive Energy

"My conception of anxiety is in point here. While we may be unaware, at least temporarily, of milder degrees of any one of the other tensions connected with living, **we are never unaware of anxiety at the very time that it occurs.** The awareness can be, and very often is, fleeting, especially when an appropriate security operation is called out. The awareness can be most variously characterized from person to person, or even from incident to incident, excepting that it is always unpleasant. At the moment that anxiety occurs, one becomes aware of something unpleasant; but whether this seems to be a mere realization that all is not going so well, or a noticing of some disturbance in the activity or postural tone in one of the zones of interaction – a change in one's facial expression, or in one's voice, for example – a feeling of tightening up in some group of skeletal muscles, a disturbance of the action of one's heart, a discomfort in one's belly, a realization that one has begun to sweat; as I say, whether it be one of these or yet another variety of symptoms, one is almost at least momentarily aware that one has become uncomfortable, or more acutely uncomfortable, as the case may be.

No matter what might have followed upon this awareness of diminished feeling of well-being, there was the awareness. It best serves in ordinary interpersonal relations to *"pay as little attention to it as one can,"* and to *"forget it."* But if one is intent on refining oneself as an instrument of participant observation, ***it is necessary to pay the greatest attention, at least retrospectively, to these fleeting moments of anxiety***. They are the telltales that show increased activity of the self-system in the interpersonal field of the moment concerned.

They mark the point in the course of events at which **something disjunctive**, something that tends to pull away from the other fellow, has first appeared or **has suddenly increased**. They signal a change from relatively uncomplicated movement from a presumptively common goal to a protecting of one's self esteem, with a definite complicating of the interpersonal action.

---

[72] *Interpersonal Theory of Psychiatry*; (Sullivan) pp351, 380

To the extent that one can retrospectively observe the exact situation in which one's anxiety was called out, one may be able to infer the corresponding pattern of difficulty in dealing with others. As these patterns are usually a matter of past training or its absence, detecting them is seldom an easy matter, but I repeat, **it is by no means impossible – unless there is an actual dissociation in one's personality system, in which case there will be prohibitively great difficulty in recalling anything significant in the actual situation which invoked the anxiety.**"[73]

Two things more remain to be said about this, shall I say, self-observation of disjunctive processes in interpersonal relations.

"Anxiety appears not only as awareness of itself but also in the experience of complex 'emotions' into which it has been elaborated by specific early training. I cannot say what all these are, but I can use names for a few of them which should 'open the mind' to their nature: **embarrassment, shame, humiliation, guilt or chagrin**. It is peculiarly difficult to observe retrospectively and to subject to analysis the exact circumstances under which we are moved to act as if the other person **"should be ashamed of himself,"** is **"stupid,"** or is **guilty of anything from a breach of good taste to a mortal sin**. These interpersonal movements which put the other fellow at a disadvantage on the basis of a low relative personal worth are extremely troublesome elements in living and very great handicaps to investigating strange people."

"Disparaging and derogatory thought and action that make one feel "better" than the other person concerned, that expand one's self-esteem, as it were, at his cost, are always to be suspected of arising from anxiety. These processes are far removed from a judicious inquiry into one's relative personal skill in living. They do not reflect a good use of observation and analysis but rather indicate a low self-esteem in the person who uses them. The quicker one comes to a low opinion of another, other things being equal, the poorer is one's secret view of one's own worth in the field of the disparagement; …and if one customarily entertains a low opinion of oneself, a great handicap is imposed on what I call *conjunctive motivations*. By this term I refer to those impulses which integrate situations in which needs can be satisfied and security enhanced. The great classic example of

---

[73] *This is why "Britneyzian Prophecies" are so special; and where the Meditation/Observation Exercise becomes so KEY in the treatment of heretofore untreatable delusion; precisely where this dissociation exists.*

conjunctive motivation is **love**, which however rare in itself, has its great root tendencies in the many impulses which make up our need for intimacy."[74]

One can't help but think of the saying of Jesus in Luke 6:41:

> *Why behold the splinter in your brother's eye?*
> *First get the beam out of your own eye.*
> *How can you say to your brother;*
> *brother, let me get that speck out of your eye,*
> *When you cannot even see the beam in your own eye?*
> *O false one*[75]*;*
> *You hypocrite* [76], *You fraud*[77], *you actor; pretender*[78]

---

[74] *Interpersonal Theory of Psychiatry;* (Sullivan) pp380
[75] *I wish to give various translations of this last line.*
 New Testament in Basic English
[76] *The New Testament: A Translation in the Language of the People (Williams)*
[77] *The New Testament in Modern English (Phillips)*
[78] *Amplified Bible*

Chapter 25 – The Tree of Knowledge

I would like to leave now the genius of Dr. Sullivan vis-a-vis this area we've just investigated – this concept of *'disparagement of others'* – and link it to another, higher dimension; one that hearkens back to ancestral voices within our Western civilization. Since *'disparagement of others'* is a character-trait instilled in us by parents, let us now together seek to discover the etymology of this behavior. Let us see our deepest psychological understanding merge with this concept of the earliest legend and myth concerning the human race.

In a momentary experience of the ego-death inherent in *Samadhi consciousness*, I surrender to the *not-me* and then into the *non-me*. The stillness of consciousness here is beneath grammatical experience. It is the beginning ascent into a layer of energy transformations without categories. Since grammar is necessary to communicate to the reader, I will approximate the experience as best I can. The scene of a river changes into that of a garden. The river itself became a small pool, the area around it taken up by this huge tree, which takes up 90% of my garden-like vision.

The right and left parts of the tree mirror each others' basic architecture of limbs off the main tree trunk, the number of branches, limb thickness, etc. Crackling energies go up into the outer limbs of the perimeter of the tree in consonance with the very thoughts decribed in the previous sentence. I see that the energies – like small lightning crackles of electrostatic charges, were hints of thought; the merest beginnings of a thought that would need only the slightest regard or *paying-of-my-attention* in order for it to become more conscious, more definable, and with that identification, "branch out" – just as any sprig would with its little nodes and branches – into more "logical" extensions of culturally acknowledged thought processes vis-à-vis content.

The sense that I was about to think *specifically* about something appeared as slight breezes through the branches. "Small" or "insignificant" thoughts crackled up through outer thin branches and twigs. Heavier limbs would represent more major belief systems in a tree of logic which was multidimensional, yet not difficult to comprehend. A type of 'spirit-wind' would create an emotional climate which would color the tree's instantaneous offerings.

We all experience multiple dimensionality within our thought-sets. Can't seemingly insignificant questions take up our whole world in a moment-to-moment reality? You have a general sense of well being upon driving your new car to the gas pump for the first time. Your entire mental state is replaced by the attention-to-detail as you decide to figure your mpg. Your entire universe of thought may become a mathematical concept with a finite result. So we can all easily understand that there are literally *infinite* "sets" or "combinations" of thought-associations relating to the architecture of this tree. Anything the mind of man can create, will create or does create appears through this tree, and looking at our modern world, we might add the philosopher's adage that *"anything the mind of man can create, can be done."* Neither iPods nor H-bombs grow on trees.

My eyes were closed. It was as if "I" was "seeing" a tree in my foreground, in the stage-like setting in which the inside of my forehead functioned as a viewing screen of sorts (looking at it objectively from inside my mind) while the 'no-mans-land' gave the impression of an infinite ether which floated out from my innermost being out past the 'conscious horizon' into infinity. Coming from over the horizon toward "me" was thought which could enter the 'no man's land' coming towards the tree, but it originated in, through and from the tree branches at the same time as well (hence the expression "dimensions *outside* of time and space.")

The pool of water morphed into the suggestion of a female hourglass figure. This is also part of the multidimensionality of the spirit world. In this case, it was reacting to the hourglass female figure hinted at by the morphing behavior of the pool of water that was now definitely hinting a sexually charged image. The pool of water had morphed into the kind of figure suggested by those tacky trucker's mud flaps or in the abstractions of the female form advertised in neon outside of strip joints.

"*You could use* some *relief*," indicated the tiniest whisper of thought, the word "relief" barely coming to conscious fruition from out of the breeze of spirit drifting through the vague scene. It had been below full consciousness in emotion filled with unspoken sexual innuendo as it floated out of the ozone. Now it was an entire conscious thought as I decided ***to give it*** my attention, rather than merely observing it. *Luke, I'm goin' in.*

The right side's energies sent up its own electrostatic current to counter the idea of going "on the hunt:" "*You're a spiritual being.*"

The "good cop - bad cop" routine within my own branches expanded rapidly, as the subject matter was too attractive for my egocentric hunger to ignore. The fact that I hadn't had sex in years – nor ejaculated in days – lent a sensual energy I did nothing to counter.

'*You can find a nice woman*," suggested *good cop - bad cop* below grammatical identification, its smaller twigs ready to bolster this conclusion with a supportive hinting consciousness for, on and in dating, patience, honor and chivalry. It directed my attention with the hint of an image of a pleasant, interesting discussion with someone attractive, mature, soft and female concerning a movie we had just seen, and we were walking outside on our way to a restaurant where we could discuss it further. This branch of reasoning was in-between the polarity developing between the "*I need to get laid*" branch and the second branch of reasoning maintaining my identity now should be one of complete celibacy. This latter thought represented an entire different tree structure as I good copped - bad copped:" *If I'm going to remain celibate, why would I want to go out on a date?"*

From a different s *good cop - bad cop* of the tree loyal to the promotion of immediate physical satisfaction came a different twist. "*You know if you go dating, you'll soon give in to sex. The girl is going to like you, and after sex, is soon going to expect you at her side every weekend. You should pay a prostitute rather than get some hopeful woman all emotional…*" The imagery of a mature, affable and attractive woman crying on the phone now that we had had sex and I hadn't asked her out for the second weekend in a row settled in to buffer this latest posture. I would react, driven by guilt and lust, to be either stuck in captivity or else wander the guilt-tinged wilderness pained by her tears.

'*I'm better off paying a professional.*' Says *good cop - bad cop*.

'*That's fornication!*' Responds *good cop - bad cop*, seeing my spiritual self going to hell and with a deeper set of its own convictions that *something other* than the mere physical sex transpires when you join sexually with another person, whether it's with a paid-for quickie or a piece of *I really-like-being-with-you* sex.

'*Don't you know your body is the temple of the Holy Spirit?*' states *good cop - bad cop* with an impression aghast at the thought of copulating with a prostitute.

'*King David had lots of girls,*' another *good cop - bad cop* branch midway between the 'find-a-nice-girl' branch and the 'find a friendly professional' opined.

'*King David was before redemption! You're saved. Flee fornication with prostitutes*' ordered a more serious branch of *good cop - bad cop*, with ominous threat of consequence within dark clouds of admonition.

Good cop - bad cop side countered with '*So it's ok to get some girl all mushy over you, dip into her, and then end it now that you're bored? That's what'll happen ya know. Y'think you're gonna live with this woman you take out, get to know and boink?*'

The entire neutral trunk announced through the energy of relief: *"I'm never getting involved like that again."*

'*Suppose you like a woman, but find you need deep dark fantasies to keep the wood up? Wha'choo got then?*' spoke a *good cop - bad cop* voice deep within the branches. *Drugs? Alcohol? Freak scenes*? Was this a voice of reason rustling with unconscious revelation, or a dick-wilting demon, or both? Is that the voice of fear or is that a revelation of genuine concern and insight?

These proffers of 'right and wrong,' were so tempting to grab hold of that I hadn't realized what they were until the unsounded voice made itself known to me with its own silent tsunami: *"Don't 'swallow' this fruit of Good and Evil."* Again, *"Don't eat from this **Tree of Knowledge**."*

Left side, right side, good cop, bad cop. Reasonable, unreasonable, emotional, rational, irrational, normal, natural, patient, impulsive, all clamored for my attention, all said *"pay me"* with your soul's attention! They were occurring and becoming veritable clusters of various opinion, of knowledge clusters that bore fruit like grapes, as university studies regarding what age groups have what amount of sex at what times in their lives began to blister up into little buds of fruit. They were all reassuring with promise and tempting to grab hold of. The *emotional climate* created calm breezes or roared mightily as spiritual wind amongst these ethereal boughs. Then again the unsounded voice, that voice that you have to want to hear, that you have to place above your own desires, that you bend the knee of your will in order to hear on the plain of humility and servitude speaks to the heart in a quiet unsounded light: *"My sheep know my voice."*

At a certain level, "good word-thoughts" in my head are no more valid than "bad" ones are. They are all – at their root – symptomatic of our fall. Your emotions are your undoing. These words in your head are emotionally connected. They are the smoke that comes up under the door to let the vampire in.

If you hold on to any reactive-thought, emotion will react in the dynamism of your peculiar traumatized structure, in order that you choose a reality by which to engage reaction to that initial thought. If you react again, you are in that emotion and are "lost" in a dream-world of "good-cop bad-cop" thinking on a 'deeper' commitment emotionally. This tennis match of opinion, loyalties, compensations and rationalizations will so confuse you that you are soon in a dream not all that different from the man walking down the street talking to himself, or in a *Star Trek* movie in which the crew finds themselves traveling on an 18th century schooner when they are really in space hundreds of years later. It's virtual reality.

Nevertheless, little occurs in a vacuum. To see how you, the reader, dance to this tune, let us replay the genius of Dr. Sullivan:

> *"One of the truly remarkable characteristics of man is his development of speech, which is so extraordinarily suited to his purposes. When one observes a child, he sees a person who is interested in all that goes on about him, who is curious, who asks all manner of questions, and who uses speech as a wonderful means of getting acquainted with the world which opens out before him. Then comes the experience of anxiety in relationship with others – which is not to discount the influence of anxiety in the pre-verbal years – and the child discovers that certain magical qualities of speech may somehow save him from these painful decreases in his self-esteem. He learns that certain phrases such as "excuse me, I'm sorry," and other elaborations of words may win some semblance of approval. Thus a remarkable process occurs. At the very time a child is expanding his knowledge of the universe and the people in it, and is beginning to acquire skill with the marvelous tool of speech – which, when joined onto his lively curiosity, will hasten that expansion – he undergoes a change which is marked by withdrawal and constriction. His curiosity is curbed. His interest in people is dulled, **and he may become more concerned with the protection of his self-esteem, and with the use of language for this purpose, than with much else**.*
>
> *This process apparently occurs to some extent with all people in our culture–and any other of which I have any knowledge. **Thus there appears to be almost a race between the circumstances which favor the use of language for the communication of ideas, and the circumstances favoring its use for their concealment and distortion.***
>
> *Should the experience of anxiety be so intense that the concealment value of language is of primary importance; there is a considerable reduction in the person's curiosity and in the possibilities of him experiencing anything like a marked realization of his potentialities. Such are those that the psychiatrist sees as patients – and many others who never come his way.*
>
> *It is this remarkable intermingling of the communicative and defensive aspects of speech which characterizes every interview (meeting with patient).*
>
> ***I would maintain it is also these aspects of speech that characterize the beginnings of every relationship**.*[79]

"Bravo, Harry!" Sometimes my eyes tear up understanding Dr. Sullivan's genius. However, he's missed a link here. Perhaps you've noticed it. After experiencing "anxiety" he goes on to use words reflecting his need for security. I would say it's something that has "entered him,"

---

[79] *The Psychiatric Interview*, Norton, *(1954)* Harry Stack Sullivan pp xxi

and changed that created in the image of G-d, into that Adam and Eve created. Reader, see here your "wasp." When this happened to YOU, you also ceased to be "made in the image of G-d," and you, dear reader, have never drawn a sane breath since, unless you've been changed by the Spirit. Born anew. It was the secret of life being revealed in ways impossible to intellectualize.

What Eve longed for was this promised sense of 'self/ego esteem' that was foreseen by her in 'listening' to a voice known as 'the serpent.' You can "judge" people using words that induce shame, guilt, and sorrow in them, or you can communicate with words composed to create quite the opposite effect. Don't forget, you are the lower-case "g" in the 'god-who-craps.'

It is referred to in the earliest of man's writings as The Garden of Eden, or *The Tree of Knowledge* or *Knowledge of Good and Evil*." Let us, for the sake of those readers uncomfortable with biblical terminology, use the word "**conscience**" in addition to the "***Voice of G-d***" to identify the voice Adam and Eve are responding to within the early legends of our people. The woman is challenged by conscience/Voice of G-d to explain how she became disobedient in Genesis 3:13:

> "...and the woman said,
> *The serpent beguiled me, and I did eat.* (King James Version)
> *Duped me...* (Torah_5 Books of Moses)
> *Seduced me...* (The Septuagint - Thompson)
> *Tempted me...* (The Jerusalem Bible)
> *Caused me to forget...* (Young's Literal Translation of the Holy Bible)
> *Misled me...* (An American Translation (Smith and Goodspeed)
> *Deceived me...* (The Holy Bible from Ancient Eastern Manuscripts – George Lamsa)
> *I was tricked by the deceit of the snake...* (Bible in Basic English

Check out Grandpa's response in Genesis 3:12:
"*The woman that thou gavest to be with me,
she gave me of the tree... and I did eat.*"

Everyone thinks this last statement is a bit of a knuckle-dragging "**duh**." Rabbis, priests and pastors the world over have missed what actually transpired here in the way of human personality. It is obvious from Eve's statements that she knows she not only made a mistake, but that she allowed something into her that seduced her into *"falling"* from something *better* than what she's now stuck in.

But Adam's words are the first reflection – in recorded human spiritual communication – of what actually got into Adam and has thus transformed him. While he also doesn't deny the negative result of his behavior, in Adam's communication there lies the evidence of the first ego-game in our human world. Circumstance here (Gen 3:11) demands that Adam explain himself.

> Adam is being challenged by pride to his first *'I'm going to stand up for myself;' 'it's not **my** fault;'* or my personal favorite: *'I'm not gonna take the fall for this...'*

He can forsake the challenge and ask forgiveness; admit error, that he *"missed it."* Guess what is in Adam now that was not in him before? What is the spiritual offspring of Eve's disobedience that he embraced and received now into his own soul? His lack of obedience – his missing it – has stirred something new; *his pride*. He chooses this instead of repentance, and becomes subtly aggressive in trying to disparage G-d.

Obedience is the prime topic under discussion in Genesis 3:11, when the **Conscience/Voice of G-d says:'** *"Hast thou eaten of the tree I commanded thee not to eat of?"* Instead of a *"yes"* or *"no,"* Adam goes passive-aggressive. There is no expression of sorrow or regret. What great-great-first Grandpa Adam is actually saying to the creator (in 2009 language) is this:

> 'It's *not **my*** fault. **YOU** *gave me this beeyatch*!
>
> *"The woman **that thou gavest** to be with me,
> **she** gave me of the tree... and I did eat."*
> *'You're the creator! It's obvious she's defective. Don't these things come with guarantees? They should, you know. Consequently, don't look at me; maybe check yourself out here... Couldn't you have given me an obedient one?*

Adam indicates it's not his responsibility. What is also left to consider is perhaps a willingness on Adam's part to imply,

> *"**SHE** GAVE it to me. If you have to, you can punish **her**, I guess. Do what ya gotta do... I do have more ribs, y'know."*

Genesis was written by Moses, *"the Lawgiver."* Consequently, one wouldn't be too far off to say what we have in Adam is the first *'Jewish lawyer.'*[80] What Adam is doing is to take this "disparagement" phenomenon and place it squarely on the creator. **He is disparaging G-d's behavior, his creational work (in Eve)** and there is the implication that G-d's judgment is also somewhat skewed (lacking?) vis-a-vis Adam's own responsibility for the situation. Notice how he tries to build esteem by dumping on Eve and, in the sense just described, the Creator Himself.

I'm the god here, says Adam's new 'personality.' **I SAY** *I'm not to blame. You created this female out of my rib and gave her to me, and maybe you should apologize for the poor-quality of the model.*

But G-d is Creator, King and Judge; the only infallible ego in all creation. The Lord of all responds to Adam's point:
> *"Because thou has hearkened unto the voice of thy WIFE… cursed is the ground for your sake, and in the sweat of thy face shall you eat the bread gained from it; till you go back to the dirt from which you were taken from; for you are dirt."* (Genesis 3:19)

Hmmm. Let us all never forget that
"the fear of the Lord is the beginning of wisdom."

Chills ran up my back and through my shoulders. My arms and legs tingled with Goosebumps.

I saw the flashing light spoken of in Genesis 3:24 as the meditation deepened. A man or woman "returns" to the garden through the denial of the ego's spiritual "flesh;" through the yearning to be free of Adam's disobedience. Forgiveness is the toll fare; love is the coin of the realm to throw off the sin-filled resentment. And where would someone like myself – living lower-than-a-snail's-belly – find that kind of love? Deep in the Observation Exercise, the Hebrew Messiah, raised from the dead two

---

[80] *Since the author is a son of Abraham (Abram's son), he takes leave of Political Correctness.*

thousand years ago, sent by the Father to put an end to religion, but live instead in man's heart, was being made manifest to me. Me, the madman of Gaderra, the craziest son a witch's bitch ever to be touched by His mercy, was finding Him sitting still in a room by myself.

This is the awareness of the Spirit-filled experience; the Pineal's Central Eye; the Samadhi consciousness.

The knock must have come on the fingers of heaven. Jacob entered with a smile in his soulish eyes. I looked at him with a love that almost made me lower my own. Goosebumps flourished up and down my arms. No more fear or concern. No more doubt as to abilities or inabilities, and no more doubt that the Jewish rabbi from 2000 years ago had been raised from the dead, and was my very personal savior, and I needn't give troubled care, concern or anxiety another thought the rest of my life. I was being blessed.

I blinked again, but refused the temptation to "think about" what I was experiencing, noticing Jacob's eyes were full of light.

"*You've been to the Garden,*" he said, but I'm not sure his mouth moved. I nodded, refusing the temptation to think of what to say.

"*He showed you the truth, didn't he? He showed you the tree.*"

I bowed in reverence and love, tears filling my eyes.

I determined to stay in the awareness, and as I looked up Jacob was transforming before my eyes. He grew sticky with a beautiful ugliness. His face, neck and trunk formed the body of the old poisoned caterpillar hanging in its moth-like cocoon, and it's sticky, atomic nature came apart.

The nature I inherited from Adam was disintegrating before my soul. I saw the angry devastated child lose the acidic, soul-devouring resentment; the angry, needy dynamism reflecting the emotional sexual excitement. My love and adoration of the evil power mother wielded over my father mixed immediately with my resentment of him for allowing it to happen.

I saw myself as an infant, then the child tortured out of my identification with G-d-given innocence. I saw myself nurtured by my wasp-like poison. My self-justification, the ugly ego identification soaked through with pride's dark existence almost causing my death; then the sincere crying out for His mercy, with a yearning faith that He provides for beings such as myself.

The emotional complex industriously churning out stress and failure was disintegrating under the light of awareness; decomposing under the non-response of my own observation of it.

Now aware of the resentment instead of drowning in it, I saw them, my parents, themselves lost as children much like I was, staying permanently blinded by their stresses all their lives. The darkness was no longer in charge.

I sensed what I was to do, and with a courage born of love and trust somehow observed what was no longer Jacob, but was the spirit of all that I had come to trust and love with a faith no longer needing words.

As I wondered if I should try to reach out and embrace him, I realized in an instant there was no need, for there was no longer any flesh. Through the chrysalis, the ugliness transformed into wings of revelation; merging what was left of my self into the butterfly freedom of His light.

END

www.ingramcontent.com/pod-product-compliance
Lightning Source LLC
Chambersburg PA
CBHW020633230426
43665CB00008B/150